NATURE'S ARMY

DEVELOPMENT OF WESTERN RESOURCES

The Development of Western Resources is an interdisciplinary series focusing on the use and misuse of resources in the American West. Written for a broad readership of humanists, social scientists, and resource specialists, the books in this series emphasize both historical and contemporary perspectives as they explore the interplay between resource exploitation and economic, social, and political experiences.

John G. Clark, University of Kansas, Founding Editor
Hal K. Rothman, University of Nevada, Las Vegas, Series Editor

RE'S ARMY

When Soldiers Fought for Yosemite

Harvey Meyerson

University Press of Kansas

Published by the University Press of Kansas (Lawrence, Kansas 66049), which was
organized by the Kansas Board of Regents and is operated and funded by Emporia State
University, Fort Hays State University, Kansas State University, Pittsburg State University,
the University of Kansas, and Wichita State University.

Library of Congress Cataloging-in-Publication Data

Meyerson, Harvey.
    Nature's army : when soldiers fought for Yosemite / Harvey Meyerson.
        p.cm. — (Development of western resources)
    Includes bibliographical references and index.
      ISBN 0-7006-1121-5 (cloth : alk. paper)
    1. Yosemite National Park (Calif.)—History. 2. Yosemite National
Park (Calif.)—Management—History. 3. Yosemite National Park
(Calif.)—Environmental conditions. 4. United States. Army.
Cavalry—History. 5. Environmental policy—United States—History.
6. Environmental protection—California—Yosemite National Park—History.
I. Title. II. Series.
    F868.Y6 M5 2001
    979.4'47052—dc21   2001000912

British Library Cataloguing in Publication Data is available.

Printed in the United States of America

10 9 8 7 6 5 4 3 2 1

The paper used in this publication meets the minimum requirements of the American
National Standard for Permanence of Paper for Printed Library Materials Z39.48-1984.

This book about a band of men
is dedicated to three awesome women:
Ida, Gladi, Linda

CONTENTS

Preface   ix

Acknowledgments   xv

Part I. An Army Like No Other   1

1. Bizarre Beginnings   3

2. Earthy Patriots   24

Part II. The Call   49

3. "This Wonderland"   51

4. Captain Wood Starts a Park   84

5. Running a Cavalryman's Paradise   118

6. "He Was No Ordinary Man"   156

Part III. Inside Connections   183

7. A Conquering Nature   185

8. The Military Metaphor   214

Epilogue   233

Abbreviations Used in the Notes   247

Notes   251

Index   303

If I succeed, you shall find there according to your desserts: encouragement, consolation, fear, charm—all you demand—and, perhaps, also that glimpse of truth for which you have forgotten to ask.

—*Joseph Conrad*

Blessings on Uncle Sam's soldiers! They have done their job well, and every pine tree is waving its arms for joy.

—*John Muir*

PREFACE

O, readers, list!
I've chartless voyaged!
Cast off all cables.
—*Herman Melville*, Mardi[1]

This book is about a largely forgotten episode in American history. Our national park system got its start more than a century ago under the United States Army. The first national parks—Yellowstone, Yosemite, and Sequoia—were run by blue-coated frontier cavalry troopers for twenty-five years before the National Park Service was created to replace them. With virtually no policy guidance, employing an army-fostered environmental ethic that was generations ahead of its time, cavalrymen probably saved the controversial new park system from early extinction.

The cavalry's role in Yosemite stood out from other national parks for the intriguing alliances it engendered. The army's most prominent supporter was John Muir, the prophet of modern environmental activism. Muir led the campaign for Yosemite's creation in 1890. Two years later, he founded the Sierra Club with Yosemite's protection in mind. Some of the club's most radically outspoken early members were cavalry officers serving in Yosemite.[2]

For someone carrying a mental picture of the U.S. cavalry formed by John Ford and John Wayne, a combined image of the "Indian-fighting" cavalry and John Muir's Sierra Club can be disorienting. When I first stumbled on a reference to it in 1981, the cavalry's role in Yosemite seemed to have the makings of a good story. It also seemed like a worthy topic for the doctoral dissertation in American history that personal obligations had prevented me from completing many years earlier.

But it would be another decade before sufficient time and resources could be assembled for an attempt to bring a receding aspiration to fulfillment. In 1992, the Department of History at Brandeis University reviewed and accepted my dissertation proposal. Formal reinstatement as a history graduate student followed soon afterward. My grandchildren were unimpressed.

During the next four years, I lived in archives. I began with the correspondence and reports of Yosemite's "acting superintendents," as the park's army commanders were called. The more I got to know them, the stronger the feeling that what they did in Yosemite constituted only half the story. The other half, even more intriguing it seemed, was how they got to be who they surprisingly were. I decided to broaden the inquiry.

Since I was bereft of that powerful impetus for keeping one's focus narrow—a career track—the decision to wander off from Yosemite was easy. I headed backward and eastward across time and space, beginning with the careers of park commanders. Most of them were hardened veterans who joined the army during the Civil War or shortly thereafter. Their careers followed the path of postwar settlement across the Great Plains and the Rockies to the Pacific. During Yosemite's crucial initial decade—the 1890s—park commanders came from the Fourth Cavalry regiment. This connection added a broader institutional dimension to my inquiry. Individual careers could be studied in the context of a westward-marching army regiment with a history of its own. In my willfully unmoored state, questions about the Fourth Cavalry led inevitably to questions about the army institution overall. That broader and deeper current of inquiry carried me into the early years of the Republic, when the frontier meant Kentucky and Ohio rather than Wyoming and Arizona, and when Americans had ambivalent feelings about the mere idea of establishing a regular U.S. Army.

Time passed quickly at my table at the National Archives. The records of the so-called Old Army of the nineteenth century were, for all practical purposes, bottomless. They came to me by the cartload. Fascinating. At home in the evening, my wife began asking with mounting anxiety, "Are the troops back in the park yet?"

Park? By then, I was far out to sea, exploring randomly selected islands of information at the National Archives and other repositories of American lore from coast to coast. As time passed, my perspective shifted markedly, not only on the Old Army but also on American society as a whole. Familiar aspects of (for lack of a better phrase) civilian society appeared in a new light. A major contributing factor was the offbeat question I had been asking: Where did the Old Army get its environmental ethic? The question had little to do with military history in the traditional sense, and the answers it provoked refracted onto the nonmilitary world. I was seeing the American nation through the eyes of Old Army soldiers, and what they saw caught me by surprise.

For example, many of the Old Army's western contemporaries—economic speculators, religious missionaries, political empire builders, among others—relied on values and methods that were often deplored by the soldiers who marched under civilian orders. On the other hand, Old Army soldiers and American Indian warriors had much in common in their relationships with a so-called natural world that had been devalued by Western civilization during its redemptive ascent to world power. The Old Army was, at heart, a drumbeating pagan institution.

My quest after the heart and soul of the Old Army took me through numerous historical archipelagoes before the troops finally made it back to the park, writing resumed, and the six-year doctoral dissertation odyssey concluded successfully. Much of the credit for a conclusive outcome belongs to the scholars who were so generous with time and expertise during this chartless voyage. At the top of that list is Morton Keller, chairman of my dissertation committee. At times, Professor Keller singlehandedly kept me afloat and committed to at least the concept of a home port. I am also deeply grateful to the other dissertation committee members, Professors James T. Kloppenberg and Russell F. Weigley (of Temple University, who graciously served as "outside reader"), for critiquing the entire final draft to my vast benefit; Professors Edward M. Coffman and William H. McNeill, who reviewed key segments; and James B. Snyder, nominally chief of the Yosemite National Park Library but really a library of Yosemite history unto himself. Thanks also to many others too numerous to mention here who responded with puzzled good cheer to my unorthodox inquiries. What did John Muir's margin notes in his book of Emerson's essays have to do with the Old Army's heritage? What did Colonel S. B. M. Young's views on capital punishment have to do with environmental protection? Well, I really wasn't sure—at least not at first.

Three more years of research, reflection, and composition followed before *Nature's Army* emerged from the foundation constructed by the doctoral dissertation. Most of the work during that phase was conducted during evenings, weekends, and vacations while I also worked full-time at the Congressional Research Service (CRS), a division of the Library of Congress. My colleagues at CRS have no idea how much their real-world competence and good sense kept me on an even keel while I was steering my barnacled research vessel into port. The views expressed herein are, of course, mine alone.

The book is in three parts. Part I (Chapters 1 and 2) discusses the unique institutional origins, character, and mission of the Old Army, an army unlike any other in modern history. Part II (Chapters 3 through 6) describes cavalry administration of Yosemite, focusing on the crucial initial decade of the 1890s. In Part III (Chapters 7 and 8), the lens shifts onto nineteenth-century American society from the complementary perspectives of the Old Army and its civilian environmentalist champions. Part III concludes with a plunge into the deeper meaning of the military metaphor, taking it back to ancient times and inward into obscure pathways of human nature. The Epilogue summarizes the army's last years in Yosemite before passing the torch to the newly established National Park Service.

Two preliminary caveats relating to the book's point of view are in order. The first concerns the civic dimension of the Old Army's martial virtues. Although many of the values of civilian society fare poorly by comparison in this study, I do not mean to suggest that civilian institutions should adopt military values, nor do I believe that any dedicated professional soldier would offer such a suggestion. Military and civilian institutional outlooks serve different principles and purposes. Old Army virtues are examined here on their own terms and for the historical illumination the perspective they fostered provides.

Second, I am acutely aware that American society is, as specialists like to say about their specialties, complex. I announce this acute awareness of American cultural complexity because when the primary focus of a historical reconnaissance is cultural values, as is the case here, and when those values have oppositional moralistic roots that pit good against evil and convert religious concepts of corruption and reform into a central political dynamic, as is also the case here, the resulting portrait can seem too stark and unyielding to be assigned to average people adjusting to myriad daily contingencies. Personified core values only exist outside history as archetypal figures like Melville's Ahab.

But it also can be said that Ahab is as historically real as the complex historical record that can never empirically confirm his existence. He represents an archetypal impulse against which all Americans struggle and in so doing create complex personalities—heroic, tragic, comic, the whole gamut. Old Army soldiers patrolling the boundaries of Western settlement dealt daily with whites driven to extremes of selfishness and self-righteousness that, when viewed from the army's perspective, illuminated the roots of motivations that played an important part in American history.

The above caveat deserves special emphasis with regard to the symbol-charged history of the American West. Until well into the twentieth century, perceptions of the West were dominated by stereotypes—hell-for-leather cowboys, savage Indians, and so on. The Far West was less living history than a mythic popular culture genre. Not until after World War II did perceptions undergo significant, broad-based change. Reexamination reached full flower in the 1980s when a new generation of historians introduced a New Western History that demolished one false stereotype after another. Perceptions of the American West expanded to include diverse racial and ethnic groups inhabiting a distinctive geographic entity subject to singular internal and external influences. This overdue recognition of the West's empirical reality is good.[3]

But, it isn't everything. History is *both* that and empirically unverifiable symbol; they constitute the two voices of human values. A twelve-lane expressway is both a technological reality and a value judgment.

Where do the values that give an added human dimension to empirical reality come from? Some natural scientists have placed them in inherited animal impulses or environmental influences or both, with varying levels of support from various schools of history. Political scientists talk of interest groups; sociologists, of social forces; theologists, of religious impulses. And there is the usual plenitude of combinations. My position is laid out in Part III. It is in opposition to none of the above, alone or in combination. Derived from observations of the Old Army, it assigns special significance to the relationship within each of us of primal emotions and abstract intellection—how that culturally influenced inner relationship has affected human attitudes toward nature, including attitudes toward the natural world inside our skins.

In that latter inwardly reconciling context, the reader should know that what may appear critical of the West in this study is not aimed at what has been reclaimed from stereotype. King Philip's War in New England in the seventeenth century or the expropriation of Cherokee lands in the South in the early nineteenth century match or exceed any indefensible behavior toward Indians that occurred in the West, and the same can be said about virtually any cultural criticism of the region based on imposed stereotypes.[4]

But with that respectful caveat, I must add the personal view that the settlement of the trans-Mississippi West during the second half of the nineteenth century offers a kind of access into important nationally shared motivations not available from the history of the East, the South, or anywhere else, an access traceable to sheer geographical scope, technological impetus, individualistic drive, moralistic fervor, democratically accessible wealth in the form of natural resources (e.g., gold and silver), and, dominating them all and configuring their expression, mind-boggling velocity. The rush into the trans-Mississippi West—the laying down of the infrastructure for mass settlement of half of a giant continent in less than fifty years—created a unique cultural dynamo of extraordinary power. It blew the lid off layered social and political refinements and brought rationalized motivations to the surface and into the line of vision of the western-patrolling members of a widely maligned federal institution.

The culture-straddling Old Army of the western frontier, in many ways an army of Ishmaels, often saw what the restless civilian society it served could not. Its institutionalized ties with nature, inherited from primeval times, including ties with pre-"civilized" human nature, opened up a unique perspective on western settlement. The Old Army's perspective took nothing away from the diverse character and accomplishments of western settlement; it merely added a dimension of perception.

So that, in summary, is how this book happened—how a straightforward historical inquiry on frontier administration evolved into a chartless voyage that took a long time getting back to port. The quest after the origins of the values cavalrymen invoked in defending Yosemite National Park led into overlooked aspects of an unappreciated American institution. Soldiers of the Old Army did not celebrate their environmental defense missions and were awarded no medals for them. Since then, interpreters of military and nonmilitary history have pretty much ignored those and other related civic activities performed by the Old Army. Yet over the course of a century of continental expansion, these "frontiersmen in blue" relied on a uniquely institutionalized relationship with the natural world to fashion an environmental ethic whose distinctiveness still resonates. My aim here is to shed light on how that unconventional outlook emerged and evolved toward conclusive expression at Yosemite, and what it signified.[5]

ACKNOWLEDGMENTS

Scholars who reviewed all or part of this book's early formulations are mentioned with appreciation in the Preface, but they cannot be thanked too much: Morton Keller, James T. Kloppenberg, Russell F. Weigley, Edward M. Coffman, William H. McNeill, and James B. Snyder. A reading by National Park Service historian Barry Mackintosh provided a welcome lift at a crucial juncture. I also benefited from opportunities to develop papers based on the dissertation for annual meetings of the Organization of American Historians (OAH, 1997) and the American Society for Environmental History (ASEH, 1999), and owe thanks to panel chairmen Donald Worster (OAH) and Samuel P. Hays (ASEH). A version of the OAH paper appeared in the *Journal of the West* (January 1999), thanks to Robin Higham. Preparation of the ASEH paper helped greatly during the formulation of Chapter 7, as did comments on the dissertation's Sargent section by Donald K. Pisani, although the aforementioned bear no responsibility for the final product's audacities.

Archivists were unfailingly helpful, especially Michael T. Meier and Michael P. Musick, National Archives and Records Administration; David A. Keough, Richard J. Sommers, and Mike Winey, U.S. Army Military History Institute; Jeffrey J. Clarke and Edgar F. Raines, U.S. Army Center of Military History; Alan Aimone and Sheila Biles, U.S. Military Academy Library; Bonnie Hardwick and Judy Snyder, Bancroft Library; Linda Eade and James B. Snyder, Yosemite National Park Library; Sheila Connor and Carol David, the Arnold Arboretum; William E. Cox, Smithsonian Archives; Maureen D. Heher, Beinecke Library; and the ever helpful special collections staff at the Library of Congress.

I am also grateful to William R. Roberts for allowing me to see an early draft of his article on S. B. M. Young; Stephen A. Haller, National Park Service historian, Presidio of San Francisco, for his varied assistance, including making available an early draft of Erwin Thompson's history of the Presidio prepared for the Park Service; Mr. Thompson, for additional comments from Colorado; Colonel Milton B. Halsey Jr., retired, for sharing his personal collection on the Presidio and his extensive knowledge of California military history and for a last-minute fact check; Colonel William F. Strobridge, retired, who also shared his knowledge of California military history; and so many others encountered along the way to whom I am no less grateful.

Travel and other expenses for the dissertation phase of this unconventional midcareer project were supported by (besides a hardworking spouse) the Spark M. Matsunaga Peace Foundation and its successor, the Spark M. Matsunaga Charitable Foundation. I am grateful to Cherry Matano of the former and Matthew M. Matsunaga of both for taking a personal interest in this undertaking, which was initially conceived while working for the late Senator Spark M. Matsunaga, a rare person whom I will always remember with deep respect and affection.

Readers may note an inordinate number of references to Herman Melville for a work of this nature. We go back thirty years, Herman and I, to a biography (never completed) that was really a pretext for a relationship. His perspective has been helpful ever since in reminding me about things I might otherwise leave out. Ditto for Moby, a feline associate who closely monitored my compositional activities from a fluffy perch alongside my computer while pretending to be asleep.

The anonymous reviewers for the University Press of Kansas were enormously helpful during the lengthy recasting process. Copyeditor Leslee Anderson was a saving force; I shudder when imagining an outcome without her. Michael Briggs and Nancy Jackson captained that crew and spurred me on with unfailing competence and good cheer. Then there are the three women to whom this book is dedicated—wife, mother, late beloved sister. What I owe to them, and especially, as the others would at once agree and insist, to Gladi, goes deeper than words.

PART I: AN ARMY LIKE NO OTHER

[America posed] a menacing challenge to the European military system.
—*Alfred Vagts*, The History of Militarism[1]

On May 19, 1890, Captain Abram Epperson "Jug" Wood received what must have seemed like a summons to Shangri-la. At the time, Wood commanded I Troop, Fourth U.S. Cavalry, based at Fort Huachuca in the barren Arizona mountains fifteen miles north of the Mexican border. Temperatures in the area hit 120 degrees in summer and below freezing in winter. Scorpions, tarantulas, and rattlesnakes thrived; so did silver miners. The closest town, sixteen miles to the east, was a hastily constructed collection of rococo storefronts, saloons, banks, brothels, and homes with white picket fences, a frontier hub of cheerfully insane aspirations called Tombstone. But for Jug Wood, all that would soon change. His troop had received orders to proceed to the fabulous metropolis of San Francisco, the largest city west of the Rockies, with its grand boulevards, trolley cars, glittering department stores, and marble bathrooms. Wood's troop would be based at the Presidio, the oldest continuously occupied fort in North America. The Presidio stood at the entrance to San Francisco Bay on a site so breathtakingly beautiful that an early U.S. Army explorer had named it the Golden Gate.[2]

And yet, despite the dramatic leap in comfort, glamour, and sophistication that the new posting promised, forty-six-year-old Jug Wood could not have accepted his transfer without mixed feelings. He had spent most of his adult life traversing the trans-Mississippi frontier on horseback, camping out in every kind of weather, from the scorching Texas Panhandle to the freezing Rockies, from the Great Plains to Arizona's rugged southern border. That hard, hierarchical, regimented, nomadic outdoor life shaped the character of the man who would become the first superintendent of a new national park called Yosemite, as it had shaped his predecessors in a U.S. Army unlike any other military force in modern history.

Military historians call the distinctive institution to which Jug Wood belonged the Old Army. The term is used to distinguish its blue-coated

1

members from the khaki-clad New Army of the twentieth century. The Old Army served westward continental expansion. The New Army replaced it during the Spanish-American War of 1898 when America's engagements turned global and World War I loomed on the horizon.

The Old Army exists in American memory mainly in popular myths, such as the Indian-fighting cavalry films of John Ford. Its historical reality is far more complex, remarkable, and instructive about American culture—instructive not only on its own terms but also for the perspective it offers on the civilian society it served. Jug Wood's Yosemite story begins with the origins of the Old Army during the turbulent early years of the American Republic.

CHAPTER ONE
Bizarre Beginnings

> They have kept among us . . . standing armies.
> —*Declaration of Independence*

The successful War for Independence left Americans with a dilemma: what to do with their victorious army. The prospect of a professional military force in peacetime was unacceptable in the wake of recent experience. "They [the British] have kept among us in times of peace standing armies," wrote Thomas Jefferson in the Declaration of Independence in 1776. Seven years later, with the British "standing army" defeated and heading home, Congressman Stephen Higginson worried that "there are those also among us who wish to keep up a large force, to have large Garrisons. . . . [I]t is easy to see where all this will lead us, and Congress I think is not yet prepared for such Systems." So the Continental Congress voted to abolish the army that had defeated the expeditionary forces of the world's greatest empire.[1]

The "such Systems" that members of Congress sought to avoid by disbanding their triumphant army were the despotic systems of government prevailing in Europe. Under those systems, professional armies served as domestic enforcers for kings, nobles, and established churches. Many Americans worried that their army would be used to support a new class of moneyed aristocrats—an American version of European nobility—seeking to bend the nation's newly forged democratic institutions to their own selfish purposes.[2]

THE PRINCIPLE OF CIVILIAN AUTHORITY

> The idea of a redress by force is too chimerical to have had a place in the
> imagination of any serious mind in this Army.
> —*George Washington*[3]

As it turned out, there was some initial basis for the compulsive fear of many Americans of an American standing army. During the years immediately following independence, the new nation's leaders debated heatedly over the extent to which the rights of individuals and states should be surrendered to create a viable national government. Spokesmen for both sides feared the worst: nationalists predicted anarchy under the "weak" Articles of Confederation, while antinationalists feared despotism

3

from the proposed alternative of a "strong" central government. Alexander Hamilton and Alexander Morris were two of the most prominent nationalists. The financier Morris believed that a weak and insolvent national administration would never repay the money it owed to him and other businessmen who had helped bankroll the revolution. Hamilton had grander objectives. He wanted a modern, efficient nation-state that could inherit the mantle of England and France on the world stage. Frustrated by a fractious and parochial Continental Congress, Hamilton and Morris and a few other nationalist ultras sought a pretext and a weapon to realize their centralizing aims. They found both, they thought, in George Washington's victorious Continental Army.

It seemed like an ideal convergence of interests. The army seethed with discontent over the failure of Congress to provide back pay or promised pensions. A group of officers led by Major Generals Horatio Gates and Alexander McDougall began discussing mutiny. Morris and Hamilton heard of the cabal and hatched a scheme of their own to encourage the mutiny and ride it to power before snuffing it out in exchange for money for the army and more authority for the central government. To succeed, the plotters needed the support of two key army officers: the chief of artillery, Major General Henry Knox, and Commanding General George Washington.

McDougall and Morris first targeted Knox, commander of the arsenal at West Point and a close confidant of Washington. Knox had been one of the leaders in the public campaign for army compensation ("We have borne all that men can bear," he wrote to Congress), and the plotters assumed he would welcome their overtures. But Knox balked. He was not prepared to cross what he considered a sacred boundary between military and civilian authority. In rejecting the nationalist scheme, Knox wrote to McDougall: "I consider the reputation of the American Army as one of the most immaculate things on earth." He added that he was prepared to submit to virtually any injustice "rather than sully [the Army] in the least degree."[4]

Meanwhile, Hamilton was sounding out Washington. Hamilton had served as Washington's military aide during the war, and they remained close as mentor and protégé. Hamilton knew that Washington sympathized with the army's plight and also feared that the new nation could not survive without a stronger central government. In a letter to Washington written early in 1783, Hamilton outlined his plan to exploit army discontent. Washington's role, which he alone could fulfill, would be to rein in the army once it had been unleashed, "to take direction of" its anger, to "guide the torrent."[5]

One can only wonder what emotions Washington experienced as he perused the secret communication from a protégé who misunderstood him so completely. He received Hamilton's letter at the army's principal cantonment in Newburgh, Pennsylvania, where most of the army conspirators were also encamped. Even then, rumors circulated at the Continental Congress in nearby Philadelphia that a peace treaty was about to be signed in London. This could mean the demise of the American army, the civilian plotters' blunt instrument. While Washington pondered, they dispatched an emissary to Newburgh to urge the malcontents there to bring their views into the open by refusing to disband unless financial demands were met. The army conspirators quickly circulated two letters, calling upon their fellow officers to abandon their "milk-and-water style" of protest and announcing a meeting on March 11 to plan a more activist course of action.

Washington reacted at once. Alerted to the full scope of the scheme by Hamilton's attempt to enlist him in it, the commander in chief published general orders pronouncing the mutinous communications "disorderly" and "irregular." He forbade the March 11 meeting and fixed another meeting for March 15 to discuss the incendiary issue. Newburgh commandant (and leading conspirator) General Gates would preside, and Washington would say a few words. The meeting was convened on the newly appointed date. It had scarcely begun when Washington entered the room and requested the presiding officer's permission to speak. Could the army, he asked the assembled officers, undertake "something so shocking" as open rebellion against Congress, "plotting the ruin of both, by sowing the seeds of discord and separation between the Civil and Military powers of the Continent? . . . My God!" By the time Washington left the packed hall, the incipient rebellion was history. In the aftermath he wrote to Hamilton, as a father to an impetuous son, warning him that in the affairs of government "the army is a dangerous instrument to play with."[6]

The Newburgh conspiracy (as this sequence of events came to be called) was a defining moment in American history. Thomas Jefferson wrote of its outcome that "the moderation and virtue of a single character has probably prevented this revolution from being closed as most others have been by a subversion of that liberty it was intended to establish." Jefferson exaggerated the danger (as did Hamilton at the other extreme). It was unlikely the conspirators could have pulled off a monarchistic coup, or would have done so if they could. But Newburgh's real significance was of a different order. The conspiracy had unfolded while Americans were organizing the institutions of a government that would shape their identity as a nation. The unequivocal positions taken by Washington and Knox, besides suppressing the army rebellion, had a crucial long-term effect in assuring that civilian control over the military would be a founding principle of American democracy. "Once civilian control is violated, even by the most halting attempt, a certain purity is irretrievably lost," writes the Newburgh conspiracy's most insightful historian. Washington invoked it and kept it pure from the start.[7]

Yet who remembers Newburgh? Who studies it for instruction? In most American histories, it is largely overlooked, as if it hardly mattered. The significant exceptions are military histories, where it serves as a celebrated reminder that in America the principle of civilian control of the military is based on a deliberate choice made by the army's first and most revered commanding general. Besides determining the institutional status of the army in American society, Washington's decisive actions in the heat of a political crisis dramatized for future generations of army officers something about which a great deal more will be said in this study of the U.S. Army's formative years—personal character.[8]

After Newburgh, Hamilton did not slacken his efforts to strengthen the military institution, although his methods showed more prudence. In retrospect, it is clear that he had good cause. The new nation already suffered from an abundance of self-styled armies, namely the chaotically managed state militias inherited from the colonial era who often found it easier to squabble among themselves than unite against a common foe. They were the bane of Washington's existence during the Revolutionary War. "*No militia*," he wrote (his emphasis), "will ever acquire the habits necessary to resist a regular force." Moreover, England's retreat from the colonies did not liberate the continent from potentially threatening European armies. England remained in Canada and elsewhere nearby, along with Spain, France, and (in Alaska) Russia. The Continental Congress grudgingly recognized the problem even as it resisted a solution. In the spring of 1783, Congress appointed a committee under Hamilton to explore the idea of a peacetime army.

Hamilton solicited Washington's views, prompting the commanding general's "Sentiments on a Peace Establishment" (again, famous mainly in military history circles), dated May 2, 1783, barely two months after he had snuffed out Newburgh. The former commanding general and future president endorsed a small regular army, a system of uniformly trained state militia, well-placed arsenals, and a military academy to be used primarily for training artillery and engineer officers. The crux of Washington's proposal was the proviso for uniform training of the militia under the supervision of a small cadre of professional soldiers, so that a full-scale army could be mobilized quickly and efficiently in wartime. This, he said, was the best alternative to a permanent standing army on the European model, which he neither favored personally nor gave the slightest chance of public acceptance: "Altho' a *large* standing Army in time of

Peace hath ever been considered dangerous to the liberties of a Country, yet a few Troops, under certain circumstances, are not only safe, but indispensably necessary." The number Washington mentioned, after calculating various strategic requirements (coastal defenses, forts astride frontier trade routes, and so on), was 2,631 men.[9]

Hamilton retained Washington's troop number in his report to Congress (four regiments of infantry, one of artillery), although he could not resist embellishing the rationale. He included his own proposals for more rigorous training of state militia under regular army supervision and placed them in the context of his well-known arguments for stronger national authority at the expense of the states. This approach was guaranteed to link suspicions of Hamilton's centralistic and globalistic worldview with his desire for a strong national army, which was no way to launch an army in America in the 1780s. Hamilton's proposals added impetus to a tide that by then, with peace at hand, was running so strongly against the army that it ultimately swamped even Washington's modest proposals. On June 2, 1784, Congress dismissed the entire revolutionary army—eighty-six regiments—and replaced it with a force of eighty men to guard the military stores at Fort Pitt and West Point.[10]

THE OFFBEAT MISSION

> We cannot in the U.S. find a person who to courage, prudence, habits and health adapted to the woods, and some familiarity with the Indian character, joins a perfect knowledge of botany, natural history, mineralogy, and astonomy, all of which would be desirable.
>
> —*Thomas Jefferson*[11]

At this point, the nascent history of the United States Army, already distinctive for the unequivocal commitment to civilian control by its first commander, took an even more unorthodox turn. After eliminating the revolutionary army and rejecting Hamilton's vision that assigned the army a mission comparable to the armies of European nation-states, Congress embraced a vision of an army with a mission dedicated to a different complex of ideas. On June 3, 1784, the day after rejecting Hamilton's elaborate philosophical and institutional package and substituting a janitorial force of eighty men to guard munitions stores, Congress authorized a "peacetime establishment" of seven hundred men for one year only.

This force would consist of units donated voluntarily by individual states. Its primary mission was not to help construct a modern nation-state, as Hamilton aspired, or even to protect settlers from Indians, which colonial (now state) militia had been doing quite aggressively for nearly two hundred years. Rather, this novel "peacetime establishment" was assigned the primary mission of protecting something wholly new: a *national* public domain created from land donated to the new nation by state governments, notably Virginia, Massachusetts, and Connecticut. When the act creating a peacetime establishment expired in 1784, it was renewed for three more years, then renewed again on the same ad hoc basis. The regular U.S. Army evolved uninterruptedly out of those initiating acts of Congress aimed at establishing federal authority on national frontier lands and supporting their westward development.[12]

Thus, the U.S. Army began as a kind of domestic constabulary, and it refined that unorthodox mission during more than a century of continental exploration, settlement, and conquest. This curious military mission was equally curious politically: it derived from a seemingly out-of-character decision by former colonies economically obsessed with land, often fighting over it among themselves, to suddenly donate a batch of it to a national government whose mere existence many of them viewed as a threat. Why did the most outspoken opponents of a strong national government donate vast tracts of valuable land to an institution whose powers they sought to limit?

These seemingly paradoxical actions by opponents of big government were nonetheless consistent with their aims. Power traditionally accrued to central governments through taxation, and a prime cause of the war for national independence was abusive British taxation. Now, with independence achieved, those who favored a stronger central government sought increased federal taxing powers in order, they said, to pay off the Revolutionary War debt. Their opponents saw this as a pretext for dreaded centralism. To get rid of the pretext—to cut off the serpent's head—they donated frontier land with the proviso that it be sold to pay off the national debt. Hence the need for a national army: to protect land donated by states until it could be sold to raise money that would block the development of big government and big business. This rationale for a national army stood the ideas of Morris and Hamilton on their head.

That primarily anti–big government motivation for supporting a national army, so different from traditional ideas about the role of national armies, had an even more curious dimension in the nature of the "enemies" against whom the national domain had to be protected until it could be sold. They consisted largely of white squatters pouring onto the frontier. "The grand object of the public is to prevent lawless men from settling on their land," said the first commander of America's postrevolutionary regular army, Lieutenant Colonial Josiah Harmar. Not long before, Harmar's troops had arrived on the frontier to discover that the gates, nails, and boards from their fort on the Ohio River had been stolen by fellow white citizens. That was only a hint of things to come. The army found itself constantly battling hordes of white invaders whom one officer called "banditti whose actions are a disgrace to human nature." The army campaigned on the frontier for three years before a soldier was killed by Indians.[13]

Indian-fighting would soon become more prominent in the army's mission, but the other originating mission—to restrain land-hungry whites—did not diminish throughout a century of continental expansion. This continuous conflict with white settlers and the values they represented created a persistent ambivalence within the army about the march of "progress" across the American continent even as soldiers participated in it under civilian orders. As the new Republic's first great waves of white settlers spilled northward from Kentucky across the Ohio River, a conflict developed that would continue throughout nineteenth-century westward expansion. A prominent historian of the Ohio frontier described it thusly:

> The soldiers who had crossed into Ohio came in peace, but they had orders to exercise force. The Indians, however, were not the enemy for the moment, but [the U.S. Army's] target was just as fearless, tenacious, and obstinate as the Native Americans who made the Ohio country their home. It was the squatters who had crossed the Ohio River by the hundreds and illegally settled government and sometimes Indian lands. The army would soon learn that it could repel Indians far more successfully than it could drive the squatters from the Ohio frontier.[14]

Besides protecting the national domain from illegal white invasion, the army's culturally distinctive originating mission also included preventing settlers from invading lands recognized by the national government as belonging to Indian nations. This assignment was codified into law with the passage by Congress in the 1790s of three bills known as the Trade and Intercourse Acts, proposed by President Washington and Secretary of War Henry Knox (the ex-general and steadfast opponent of the Newburgh conspiracy). Although the bills' ostensible purpose was to regulate the Indian fur trade, their effect was to restrict the activity of whites on Indian lands, including squatters, whiskey dealers, hunters, traders, and timber cutters. Primary responsibility for enforcing the Trade and Intercourse Acts belonged to the army.[15]

The Trade and Intercourse Acts reflected a desire by moderate nationalists like Washington and Knox to negotiate with Indian tribes as sovereign nations rather than to seize their lands by force and provoke bloodshed. In 1792, Knox included these words, which he marked for emphasis, in his instructions to a government emissary sent to negotiate with Indians inhabiting frontier lands: "You will make it clearly understood that we want not a foot of their land, and that it is theirs, and theirs only; that they have a right to sell, and . . . to refuse to sell, and that the United States will guaranty to them their said just right." Knox's desire to make the United States' conciliatory position emphatically clear to Native Americans grew out of frustrations with settler incursions and provocations that he had complained about to Congress as early as 1787 in explaining why a peacetime army remained a necessity. Unless a national military force was authorized, Knox told Congress that year, "the whole western territory is liable to be wrested out of the hands of the Union, by lawless [white] adventurers, or by the savages whose imperfect perceptions render them unable to distinguish between the aforesaid description of persons, and the regular authority of the United States."[16]

Some historians have argued, correctly I think, that Washington, Knox, and other national leaders were as desirous of Indian land as everyone else and differed from extremists only in pursuing a more measured policy of national expansion. But that distinction does not negate the effect of this essentially hypocritical policy on the army assigned to implement it. The army did not formulate long-term national policy goals; that was the responsibility of higher civilian authority. The army's simpler, more modest task was to perform its assigned duties honorably. Again and again, as we'll see, when settlers sought to exploit the law, soldiers reacted against them even when those settlers correctly presumed that the laws were meant to be exploited. Hypocritical policies toward Indians stood out glaringly for soldiers responsible merely for implementing the law as written rather than pursuing its subtle contrary aims formulated by higher authorities often unwilling or psychologically incapable of recognizing their duplicitous objectives.[17]

As time progressed, the army's mission to defend both the public domain and Indian lands blended more and more. An example was the struggle to protect Native Americans from unscrupulous whiskey traders. Even congressional legislation in 1832 specifically banning the sale of whiskey to Indians had minimal effect on the frontier. Profits from sales aside, the knowledge that whiskey provoked Indian excesses that could be used to justify white retaliation, including land-grabbing, provided incentive enough to many frontiersmen who eyed Indian lands. In 1833, Captain John Stuart, commander of Fort Smith on the Arkansas River, wrote the secretary of war that although he might interrupt whiskey trade on the river, he could not "put a final Stop to its Introduction [because] . . . the Inhabitants of the Territory of Arkansas, Particularly Such of them as border on the Indian Country, are . . . adventurers from different Parts of the world, whose Purpose it is to make money in any way they can . . . who have for their Governing Principles Self Interest alone, Without regard to Law or honesty."[18]

Today, we would call this aspect of the U.S. Army's formative mission "peacekeeping." It was as thankless then as it is now. Soldiers who sought to enforce the law on white frontiersmen encroaching on federal lands frequently found themselves placed under local arrest or sued in local courts. In 1829, a force was dispatched from Fort Winnebago in Wisconsin with orders to remove whites who had invaded Indian lands. The commanding officer of that U.S. Army unit was arrested by the local county sheriff on a complaint filed by the white lawbreakers. The army had to post bail in a Wisconsin court to get the officer back. Legal proceedings in that case dragged on for two years, with army officers from throughout the region called to the county seat to answer various court orders. The commander at Fort Armstrong, Wisconsin, complained in 1833 that it was "impossible" to move against land thieves or other Indian provocateurs "even upon an order from the highest authority, without having a law suit upon our hands." Should the case come before a local jury, he warned, the army could forget about fair treatment.[19]

Ultimately, of course, whether Indian lands were obtained by negotiation or by force made little difference in the outcome from a Native American perspective: western "progress" was a master of moral disguise, and its economic and spiritual missionaries were bent on conquering Indian lands (and souls) under any circumstances. But again, the assigned character and role of the U.S. Army in the cultural conquest of a continent and its indigenous inhabitants (along with inherited army values to be discussed later) profoundly affected American soldiers' perceptions of the values guiding the nation they served. Army officers believed in western "progress," but that sympathetic faith did not always extend to its raucous apostles on the western frontier. The greedy manipulation of federal law that soldiers witnessed, and the widespread opposition to soldiers who tried to enforce the law, was bound to influence their values. Their peacekeeping mission promoted uncommon introspection on the character and motivations of many of their fellow citizens during a century of continental expansion.

Similarly, the army's public domain responsibilities shaped soldiers' concepts of American patriotism. American patriots of that era generally equated their nation with abstract ideas like freedom, liberty, or justice, for which America served as a beacon for the world. But when frontier officers spoke of defending America's land of the free, physical geography more than moral and political philosophy shaped their patriotic feelings. That earthy patriotism was reinforced by another core aspect of the army's mission dating back to the legislation that first created a national public domain and an army to protect it. Before the donated domain could be sold to pay off the national debt, it had to be mapped and surveyed, its boundaries marked; or, as the congressional resolution renewing the army's existence in 1787 stated, the army must "facilitate the surveying and selling of the said lands in Order to reduce the public debt and to prevent all unwarrantable intrusions thereon." And as the national domain expanded, and the government's role shifted from selling it to making it more accessible and easier to dole out for free, the army's surveying and exploring mission acquired additional layers of responsibility.[20]

In the twentieth century, the responsibilities growing out of the surveying and exploring component of the U.S. Army's originating mission would be called "nation-building." This activity came into its own after the Louisiana Purchase of 1803, when the American government suddenly needed to secure dominion over a tract of land reaching across the entire North American continent. From the beginning of the nineteenth century until the Civil War, the army played a central role in the exploration of the American continent, in the development of a national transportation and communications infrastructure, primarily east of the Mississippi, and in what might be called extending the laws of government and other benefits of civilized community to isolated white settlers on the trans-Appalachian frontier. After the Civil War, the army carried its civic mission further westward, in a single generation riding a tide of settlement across the Mississippi, through the Great Plains, over the Rockies to the Pacific coast, and ultimately into our national parks. This was the era, enshrined in popular myth, of cowboys, cattle drives, gold miners, gunslingers, and Custer's last stand. It was also a time, less remarked upon by popular mythmakers, when the clash between the values of the U.S. Army and the westward-marching society it served intensified in culturally revealing ways.

EARLY ACHIEVEMENTS

> The ax, pick, saw and trowel, has become more the implement of the
> American soldier, than the cannon, musket or sword.
> —*President (and former general) Zachary Taylor*[21]

Trappers, hunters, and missionaries were in the vanguard of white exploration of the American West, but it was disciplined expeditions led by soldiers producing detailed maps and systematic accounts of their continent-spanning activities that created a national "continental consciousness" and large-scale settlement. In 1800, nearly two-thirds of the nation's population still lived within fifty miles of tidewater and looked eastward across the Atlantic for the "wants of civilized life." To many Americans of that era, as to Columbus when he bumped into America while looking for

Asia, the Far West was merely an obstacle to overcome en route to the lands of Marco Polo. Thomas Jefferson, more than anyone, changed those perceptions, beginning with his purchase of the Louisiana Territory in 1803 and his organization of an expedition led by two army officers, Meriwether Lewis and William Clark. Jefferson instructed Captains Lewis and Clark to combine their search for a route to the Pacific with the systematic collection of data useful for trade and settlement within the interior of the continent, which resulted in a series of army-led expeditions that continued throughout much of the century.[22]

They produced what their most prominent historian calls "a new type of explorer": an army officer heading an expedition that included geologists, botanists, zoologists, artists, surveyors, astronomers, meteorologists, and other information gatherers, both civilian and military. These expeditions blended science and art in their poetic yet scrupulously documented reports, their maps and drawings, their carefully cataloged specimens. Captain Stephen D. Long's report and map of the Great Plains to the front range of the Rockies became the standard for information on that region into the 1830s. The army-led Pacific Railroad Surveys during the 1850s, covering three potential transcontinental routes and one north-south connecting route, provided unprecedented scientific data on western climate and natural resources. The Pacific Surveys' thirteen volumes, 147 lithographs, uncounted specimens, and more than twenty separate papers delivered to learned societies constituted "an encyclopedia of western experience." Under such systematic scrutiny, the West sprang up before Americans as a concrete, workable reality. The effect on public consciousness was profound:

> These early military-scientific expeditions into the West, chiefly Jeffersonian in inspiration . . . turned the country's focus from the far Pacific to the West itself, and by the very Enlightenment-naturalist range of their inquiry they set the pattern for flexibility in American exploration. Their labors were meant to be the vanguard of the central adventure of nineteenth-century America: the settlement of the West.[23]

As army explorers mapped and classified the remote trans-Mississippi West, other army units worked to integrate the still widely scattered population east of the Mississippi. Settlements from New Orleans to St. Paul were linked by networks of strategic outposts and military roads built under the direction of army officers, often with army labor. Secretary of War John C. Calhoun saw no difference between a strategic and a commercial road on the frontier. He made his troops liberally available for road construction and related nation-building activities to improve their "usefulness and health." Local officials competed furiously for military roads and the outposts that guarded them. By 1830, the army had constructed 1,900 miles of military roads used mainly for nonmilitary purposes.[24]

Perhaps even more important than army road-building was the work of army engineers in providing technical services to states, counties, and private developers at a time when such expertise was desperately needed. A French observer wrote in 1830 that "the greatest difficulty which the Americans encountered in the execution of their public works, was not to procure the necessary capital, but to find men capable of directing operations." He then went on to describe how army civil engineers had filled the gap.

The use of the army for these nation-building activities reflected a consistent national policy pursued at the highest level. Presidents Jefferson, Madison, Monroe, John Quincy Adams, Jackson, Van Buren, Polk, Harrison, Taylor, and their War Department heads actively promoted nation-building assignments for the army. Populist President Andrew Jackson (1829–1837) professed to despise the "elitist" regular army, but he loved military roads. Jackson's Military Road, named in honor of its chief sponsor, was three hundred miles long, with thirty-five bridges and 392 causeways. Designed by army engineers and built with army labor, it cut the travel distance from Nashville to New Orleans nearly in half.[25]

In addition to exploration and infrastructure development, the army had an even broader nation-building mission assigned to it virtually by default: to serve as the primary representative of a national government of laws, often as the only visible incarnation of a national community, on an anarchic frontier. This was especially true after Jefferson's Louisiana Purchase. American sovereignty on paper would be useless in fact without some institutional presence in the Louisiana Territory that could develop American substitutes for the network of treaties and trade agreements, of forts and trading posts, put in place by previous European occupiers in their relations with Indian tribes who occupied over 99 percent of the region. Who could provide that essential continentwide presence but the United States Army, which by 1803 numbered a grand total of 2,486 men?

The first governor of the Louisiana Territory was an army general, and the introduction of American political authority over that sprawling domain was pretty much an army task. Army Captain Meriwether Lewis described the challenge as twofold: First, British traders who dominated the interior of the continent had to be brought to heel by establishing forts under the American flag. Second, the complex Indian cultures of the West, with their colorful stylized ceremonies and proud warrior leaders, deserved a statecraft apparatus that lone-wolf American frontiersmen or political emissaries in homespun garb could not possibly provide. Colorful army troops, bands, banners, all moving to the rhythm of drums in stylized formations, became a requisite part of major parlays between Indians and representatives of the American government.[26]

The army exerted many other subtle, pervasive, and now largely forgotten influences over frontier (and national) development. The topographical maps that the War Department required of its post commanders for their respective regions were prized by everyone. In some areas, army units provided the only regular mail delivery. Army posts were often the only source of medical care, sometimes of food, shelter, and even clothing, for struggling settlers. Frontier forts also served as the only relief centers in the aftermath of floods, earthquakes, and other natural disasters. They introduced new methods of farming and irrigation as part of a nationwide effort to create accessible supplies of scurvy-preventing fruits and vegetables for frontier soldiers. They also served as centers for scientific data collection and investigation.

The first national system of meteorological observations was organized by the army's surgeon general in 1818. Initially, it was intended for research on the influence of weather conditions on illness, but it soon acquired numerous other functions. Frontier outpost duties included "four daily readings of the barometer, thermometer, clearness of the sky, direction and force of the wind, and direction and velocity of the clouds, and two daily observations of the wet-bulb thermometer and amount of precipitation," prepared uniformly nationwide according to detailed instructions from the surgeon general in Washington. Those and other similar scientific assignments made the army into the most precise and well-organized body of observers of natural phenomena on the early frontier.[27]

Army frontier forts also served as outposts of cultural refinement. Theater made its debut in the Northwest wilderness at army posts, with directors, performers, and stagehands drawn from garrison personnel. Regimental bands offered public concerts featuring works by Bellini, Rossini, and other composers of what one local critic called "highly artificial compositions." A class apart from local fiddlers, they played a role that would be assumed much later by urban symphony orchestras. Military balls were pinnacle social events on the frontier, with officers in dashing full-dress uniforms guiding their local partners through elegant minuets and waltzes. (All West Point cadets learned ballroom dancing.) Garrison libraries, stocking up-to-date national periodicals as well as books, were often the only regional reading centers.[28]

Finally, despite its comparatively miniscule size, the early nineteenth-century army introduced unheard-of scales of grandeur to frontier life by drawing on its unmatched access to organized manpower. Within three years of the construction of Fort Snelling in Minnesota Territory in 1819, its soldiers were cultivating the largest farm in the area—210 acres planted in corn, potatoes, oats, and garden vegetables. Soldiers were also grinding flour at a mill they had built when they weren't constructing roads and performing other nation-building duties. The soldier-constructed fort itself not only "awed the Indians," as originally intended, but also everyone else around. Built on a bluff at the mouth of the Minnesota River, the looming stone and wood garrison rose up out of the northwest wilderness like some medieval castle, formations of blue-coated soldiers parading in and out, bugles echoing from within the walls from dawn into the night, presenting frontier whites as well as Indians with tangible local evidence of the existence of a national government that otherwise seemed like a rumor.[29]

The work never seemed to end. From an outpost on the frontier, a young enlisted man complained to a military journal in 1838:

> I am deceived. . . . I enlisted because I preferred military duty to hard work; I never was given to understand that the *implements of agriculture and the mechanic's tools* were to be placed in my hands *before I had received a musket or drawn a uniform coat.* I never was told that I would be called on to *make roads, build bridges, quarry stone, burn brick and lime, carry the hod, cut wood, hew timber, construct it into rafts and float it to the garrisons, make shingles, saw plank, build mills, maul rails, drive teams, make hay, herd cattle, build stables, constructs barracks, hospitals, etc. etc. etc.*[30]

THAT "MARVEL OF INNOVATION"

George Washington's early recommendations for a "peacetime establishment" included "an Institution calculated to keep alive and diffuse the knowledge of the Military Art," with an emphasis on artillery skills and military engineering (e.g., frontier forts, coastal defenses), but he gave the proposed institution a low priority for budgetary reasons. As a working alternative, he suggested training courses at army posts. Hamilton's 1783 report to Congress based on Washington's recommendations addressed the issue briefly in a section on "Artillery and Engineers," noting that these specialists required "particular institutions for the instruction and formation of officers." Congress would have none of it. An institution of any kind dedicated to creating what the public perceived as a European-style "aristocratical" caste of military officers was out of the question.[31]

Meanwhile, on another track entirely, Thomas Jefferson was formulating views on the role of education in America that would have a decisive influence on the character of the U.S. Army. For Jefferson, universal political freedom was inextricably linked to universal education. The chief project of his "retirement" years after 1808, following two terms as president, was the conceptual design and construction of the University of Virginia, a personal achievement that he ranked higher than the Declaration of Independence or the Louisiana Purchase.[32]

Jefferson's linkage of the future of American democracy to education was not new, nor were his schemes for a nationwide grassroots educational system. The Puritans in New England had set the standard in that domain, both with institutions of higher learning (Harvard and Yale) and community schools, and of course frontier missionaries would rely heavily on schools for bringing what European Americans called "Christian civilization" to the continent's indigenous peoples. But Jefferson added a new dimension to the growing nation's religion-based educational pursuits. Harvard and Yale, as well as Princeton and Columbia, had been founded by Protestant churches and offered classical curricula, including heavy doses of theology. Jefferson, on the other hand, spoke for the alternative worldview of the Enlightenment, with its reliance on empirical scientific observation of the natural world. This included the study of practical arts such as engineering and mapping, virtually ignored in American higher education at the time, that Jefferson correctly believed were crucial for the settlement of the North American continent.

In his sixth annual message as president, Jefferson proposed "a national establishment for education" that would serve, according to one biographer, as "both a scientific academy and an educational institution, combining teaching and research in a fashion unknown to American universities." Only an institution of this kind could answer a growing national need for expertise in designing canals, roads, and other "internal improvements" necessary for successful settlement of the continent. Jefferson converted his visionary proposal into legislation, but it was too much for Congress to handle. Nonetheless, almost surreptitiously, he moved forward on converting his dream of a national university for science and engineering into reality. His mechanism was the United States Military Academy at West Point established by Jefferson in 1802 during his first term as president.[33]

When Jefferson's role as founder of West Point is mentioned by presidential historians, it is usually in passing and with ironic reference to his antimilitary attitudes. Yet Jefferson's West Point constituted a truly original educational achievement whose contributions to national development as well as the character of the U.S. Army in the nineteenth century were extensive and profound. The Academy grew out of an idea that had been in circulation for nearly two decades, mainly among Jefferson's Federalist adversaries. The history of the idea is important because it explains the significance of Jefferson's refinements to it in principle and in practice.[34]

It began with George Washington's solicited suggestions to Hamilton in 1783 on a peacetime establishment that included a military school emphasizing science and engineering. As mentioned, Washington doubted that Congress would fund such a school, and Hamilton merely proposed a few courses of instruction in his subsequent report on a peacetime army that Congress rejected in toto. The idea resurfaced in 1793 during a discussion on coastal defenses among the members of President Washington's cabinet. When Treasury Secretary Hamilton proposed that the federal government build coastal defenses and Secretary of State Jefferson countered that the states should do the job instead, Secretary of War Knox said it didn't matter because no one in the United States knew how to build coastal defenses anyway, and he came out for a military academy specializing in military science and engineering similar to what Washington had originally proposed. Hamilton favored it and Jefferson opposed it. Washington, fearing that a public debate on it "might generate heat and ill humor," ordered the issue dropped.

Not long afterward, Congress reactivated the idea in a more general form and set it in motion by providing for courses of instruction for the engineers and artillerists stationed at West Point, the U.S. Army's largest post. But the soldiers there did not follow up, being less interested in military education than their civilian benefactors. The idea bubbled up again in the late 1790s, during the "quasi-war" with France, when Congress gave President John Adams authority to hire four instructors for the Corps of Artillerists and Engineers at West Point; none could be found, however, and the initiative foundered.

Now it was Hamilton's turn again, this time on a much grander scale than before, with his proposal near the end of the decade for a comprehensive military education system. Under this system, the school for engineers and artillerists became one of several military schools subordinated to a "fundamental school" at West Point focusing on the strategy and tactics of war. Hamilton got the attention of Secretary of War James McHenry, who forwarded a revised version of Hamilton's proposal to Congress in January 1800. There it encountered the exaggerated response Hamilton's actions (in contrast to his more prudent writings) continually provoked, being viewed in this case as part of an imperious scheme to create a Napoleonic Republic. It did not help that at the time Hamilton was actually in the midst of an abortive scheme to lead an army southward to conquer New Orleans and the Floridas and join England in taking South America from Spain, then divvying it up, in grand Napoleonic tradition. Jefferson, in a private letter on science education in America, referred to "almost the whole of the institution" proposed by Hamilton "as an example" of an approach that would be "useless to us for ages to come."[35]

The operative word in Jefferson's rejection of Hamilton's ballooning version of Washington's original proposal was the "almost" that preceded his reference to "the whole of the institution." Jefferson was not against all of it. He had objected to Hamilton's military academy proposal because he saw it in the context of the military's potential role in Hamilton's global vision for America. With regard to the latter, Hamilton adopted the traditional view of armies as agents of war between nations and military education as training for such warfare, with science and engineering subordinate to strategic and tactical studies. Jefferson, on the other hand, had a different vision of decentralized continental development, in which the army appeared in a nontraditional light. In the Jeffersonian vision, soldiers under civilian orders would have a primary mission of supporting continental exploration and development.

Consequently, Jefferson saw "almost" nothing of value in the Federalist proposals for a military academy, *except* their interesting potential for establishing a center of national instruction for science and engineering that could institutionalize the unconventional nation-building mission he had in mind for the army. That was the context for the establishment by Jefferson in March 1802 of the U.S. Military Academy at West Point. Although it compared to (and in its early years drew heavily upon) the French army's famous Ecole Polytechnique, it was far more committed to elevating science and engineering to almost sacred status throughout the army. For the period through the Civil War, the army's chief engineer was inspector of the academy, only an engineering officer could serve as its superintendent, and the top two or three members of each graduating class were automatically assigned to the Corps of Engineers as an indication of the superior status of that branch of military service. (This favoritism was not wholly broken until late in the nineteenth century.) Another major difference with the Ecole Polytechnique model was the extent to which West Point graduates pursued a nation-building mission. That is, the "military" science and engineering taught at West Point was, to a unique extent, employed less for war-related pursuits than for the design and construction of a new nation.[36]

Two of Jefferson's initiatives immediately following the establishment of the Military Academy in March 1802 hinted at the motivating direction of the new president's military education interests. In April, he sharply reduced the size of the U.S. Army to a little more than 3,000 men. In May, he named Jonathan Williams the Military Academy's first superintendent. Williams, a personal friend of Jefferson, was a favorite grandnephew and former personal secretary of Benjamin Franklin. Williams shared his great-uncle's keen interest in science. He inherited the bulk of Franklin's scientific library and became an officer of the American Philosophical Society that Franklin founded for "the promotion of useful knowledge . . . Mathematicks . . . Chemistry . . . New Mechanical Inventions for Saving Labour . . . Surveys, Maps and Charts." In 1797, Williams was one of four signatories of a letter advising Jefferson of his election as the society's president.

During that era, the cultures of military and civilian engineering were much less separate than today, and Franklin, Williams, and Jefferson shared common interests in the construction of military outposts, bridges, and other facilities, which required knowledge and skills that also had immediately needed civilian applications. In February 1801, the fifty-year-old Williams prevailed on lame-duck President John Adams, another old friend, to grant him an army commission to pursue his engineering interests. This occurred just in time for the arrival in the White House of that other friend with whom Williams had a great deal in common, incoming President Thomas Jefferson.[37]

President Jefferson spent an unusual proportion of his time reviewing the initial drafts of the science and engineering curriculum for his new military academy. Superintendent Williams, no doubt guided by the same integrative motives, poured his energy into making West Point the home of a new Military Philosophical Society modeled after the American Philosophical Society to which he and Jefferson belonged. The entire West Point faculty joined the Military Philosophical Society, along with other military officers and many prominent civilians interested in science, including President Jefferson and former President Adams. This West Point satellite of the American Philosophical Society was similarly dedicated to the public dissemination of "useful knowledge." A typical outcome was the presentation of a paper at a society meeting in 1807 by West Point professor Ferdinand Hassler, on the need for extensive inland and coastal surveys in the young nation, that eventually resulted in Hassler's appointment as governmental surveyer and later as head of the United States Coast Survey. At another meeting at West Point, in 1809, Williams reported that an army major "has notified his intention to publish a history and description of Louisiana, including its various soils and climates . . . [and] mineral riches." The Military Philosophical Society would pass from the scene not long after Williams left the Academy in 1812, but its character and interests left an indelible imprint on the personality of West Point and the U.S. Army throughout a century of continental expansion.[38]

Thus, the visionary "national" university for science and engineering that Jefferson unsuccessfully solicited in his sixth inaugural came into being anyhow, incrementally, through his less visible efforts in creating and shaping the U.S. Military Academy at West Point. For the first half of the nineteenth century, West Point was unique among American universities in granting a four-year degree in engineering. In 1825, President John

Quincy Adams told Congress that the graduates of West Point were providing "the means of multiplying the undertaking of public improvements, to which the acquirements of that institution are peculiarly
adapted." Adams's Secretary of War, Peter B. Porter, described West Point
as a national university for engineers that was "scattering the fruits of its
science" in a commitment to support the training and field work of "a
new generation of engineers." The first dean of Harvard's Lawrence
School of Engineering (1846) was a West Point graduate, as was the first
civil engineering professor at Yale's new science and engineering school
(1847) and the first professor of physics and engineering at Michigan
(1852); and many of the textbooks they used were authored by West Point
graduates. Virtually all the other degree-granting engineering programs
established in the nineteenth century drew their inspiration, and often
their faculty, from West Point. To a leading historian of American education, nineteenth-century West Point was a "marvel of innovation."[39]

West Point's curriculum assigned a central role to mathematics, both
for the grounding for engineering it provided and the disciplined thinking it cultivated. (Analytical trigonometry entered American higher education by way of West Point.) At the next level of importance stood the
physical sciences—astronomy, magnetism, geology, and so on—and engineering. Other early core areas included drawing, tactics, conduct, history, geography, and French. As the years passed, courses were added in
chemistry, ethics, rhetoric, law, logic, grammar, ordnance, gunnery, Spanish, practical engineering, military efficiency, and military deportment.
But the main emphasis remained math, science, and practically applied
engineering. The influence of this curriculum, so unusual for its time, on
the Old Army's character, including army attitudes toward the natural
environment, was felt on many levels.[40]

First, it made army officers skilled and knowledgeable scientific observers of nature. Young West Pointers reporting for duty in frontier outposts had already studied their country's geography, meteorology, and
geological composition. They could prepare detailed topographical maps
of its mountains and valleys. They had learned to identify and sketch its
flora and fauna. And they had been trained to write about the natural environment with scientific clarity and precision.

Second, a West Point education stood out for merging scientific and
aesthetic perspectives on nature. "A rare combination of the practical and
the visionary, the empirical and the poetic," was how a twentieth-century
professor of English literature described nineteenth-century army reports
on the Yellowstone region. His introduction to an anthology of such reports included this account by Captain William Ludlow, which "began by
citing exact measurements and gradually built to a dramatic climax of
Shelleyan prose":

Again and again the geyser renewed its strength, sending out vast volumes of steam with a deafening roar that shook the whole valley, and occasionally snatching hold of a new reservoir of water and instantly ejecting it; each fresh access of wrath or travail being heralded by deep mighty thuds, as though some vast machinery were at work beneath. The exhibition of enormous power wasted in these prolonged spasms of blind rage was both fascinating and terrible, and the imagination, powerfully stimulated in the presence of such strength and fury, could not avoid imputing to the scene the attributes of gigantic passion and suffering. It seemed as though the geyser, maddened by some inexpressible and mysterious torment, were imprisoned beneath and gradually exhausting herself in unavailing struggles to escape it by bursting the bonds that held her, the paroxysms of efforts being alternated with intervals of stupor, again and again overcome by her still unabated rage.[41]

Captain Ludlow's integration of the literal and the symbolic invites comparison with John Muir's lyrical scientific descriptions of nature, his "intuitive ecology" that has been called a forerunner of the modern ecological outlook. Like Muir, scientifically trained Ludlow used his poet's sensitivity to natural harmonies to find suggestions of interconnectivity in nature that would be proven correct. Although Ludlow's prose stood out among his professional peers (as did Muir's among his), the disciplined aesthetic values it expressed derived from a curriculum shared equally in the nineteenth century by all young men who attended West Point before being dispersed over the American landscape.[42]

The scientific-aesthetic outlook of West Point–trained officers had a socioeconomic dimension as well. Almost from the Academy's beginning, its administrators went out of their way to democratize the cadet selection process to meet public concerns that the institution would become a breeding ground for an antidemocratic officer corps, like military academies in monarchical Europe. West Point was required by law to be different. The nomination of cadets by congressional district had the specific purpose of democratically decentralizing student selection, as did the publication through most of the century of the social and economic backgrounds of West Point cadets. Those publicly available records provided information on parental profession, income, even local demography (town, city, county) for each cadet. One by-product of that effort to avoid an "aristocratical" selection process was to make the West Point student body into the closest approximation of a national socioeconomic and geographic microcosm as could be found in any institution of higher learning in nineteenth-century America.[43]

Another singular by-product was a unified, public service–oriented sense of nationhood. Today, when the concept of national public service is institutionalized in a thousand ways throughout society, it is hard to imagine the unusual character of the proclamation by the army's chief of engineers in 1846 that each West Point cadet was taught "that he belongs no longer to section or party, but, in his life and all his faculties, to his country." Additionally, compared to ideas of nationhood prevailing at the time, with their zealous commitment to abstract ideals, the army's nationalism was remarkably grounded: the terrain that West Point instructors had taught cadets to map, draw, and analyze for its physical properties, appreciate for its aesthetic harmonies, and experience as a democratically decentralized socioeconomic entity also happened to be a nationally institutionalized political construction that they had taken an oath to serve. For these "frontiersmen in blue," the American polity was a physically integrated, aesthetically inspiring national land. Before taking up duty on the frontier, West Point cadets studied the Constitution and committed themselves in solemn ceremonies to serve unitedly under its national banner. Their adversaries within American culture rode solo, disdained national democratic institutions, and sang, "It's your misfortune and none of my own."[44]

Civilian authority, nation-building, peacekeeping, distinctive earthy patriotism, environmentalism—America was creating a military institution as different from those serving the great land armies of Europe as were America's political institutions from their Old World counterparts. Other armies had provided their nations with explorers, builders, public administrators, scientists, lawgivers, ambassadors of national unity, but not in the same context of messianic, entrepreneurial, continental conquest by millions of settlers gobbling up land and planting institutions with unprecedented rapidity, or with the same public service mission conceived as much to restrain American citizens as to defend them. During a century of explosive continental expansion, the U.S. Army came to be the visible embodiment of ideas of national community that ranked a distant second alongside the unfettered freedom to grab as much as one could get. More and more, Old Army officers questioned dominant self-seeking values, not as social rebels but as patriotic defenders of another equally American civic value system that got swamped in the rush.

CHAPTER TWO

Earthy Patriots

The previous chapter outlined the inherited institutional history that Old Army captain Jug Wood and his contemporaries carried with them into Yosemite National Park. Wood's generation also added to the Old Army's inheritance through personal experiences during the Civil War and the subsequent surge of settlement westward across the Mississippi into the Far West. This was their own special contribution to the history of the Old Army, to which we now turn.

AT WAR AND THE POINT

When the Civil War began in April 1861, Abram Epperson Wood was sixteen years old, living and working on his family's farm in eastern Iowa close by the Mississippi. He immediately enlisted in the Thirteenth Iowa Infantry Regiment formed in nearby Davenport. Within a few weeks he was promoted to corporal, which meant giving orders to some of the young friends who had enlisted with him. The following spring, after rudimentary winter training at Benton Barracks, Missouri, the teenage corporal was rushed into battle at Shiloh. He withstood that terrible test, wounded but at least alive, and joined the Union march southward under Grant, into Alabama and Mississippi, where the Thirteenth Iowa fought continuously for two years—Corinth, Vicksburg, the Meridian campaign. From there he headed north to Tennessee to join Sherman's Army of the West, eventually nearly 90,000 strong; then south again for the decisive campaign climaxed by the siege of Atlanta, the devastating "march to the sea," the capture of Savannah and of Columbia (where members of the Thirteenth Iowa planted the Union flag atop the state capitol); then north once more to Raleigh and Richmond and final victory in 1865.[1]

During four years of nonstop campaigning, Jug Wood's regiment covered 8,900 miles in crisscross patterns through the South—4,200 miles on foot, 4,700 by rail. The ordeal concluded on a warm, sunny day in May 1865, when Sherman led his army in a victory march down Pennsylvania Avenue in the nation's capital. From there, the Thirteenth Iowa traveled by rail and steamer back to Davenport, where, on July 29, 1865, the regiment disbanded "and the survivors returned to their homes."

Altogether, 1,788 Iowans served in Wood's regiment during the war. Jug was one of the few who fought in every battle and marched nearly every weary mile. On the eve of his discharge, in recognition of his stead-fast valor, he received the bars of a second lieutenant. He was twenty-one years old, but those were only calendar years.

Although records of the next four years of Jug Wood's life are skimpy, it is clear that he set a goal and attained it. On July 1, 1868, after a period at the University of Iowa, he gained admittance to the United States Military Academy at West Point. (Often in those days a West Point aspirant cut his teeth at another university before seeking an appointment.) There he added a dimension to the disciplined education he had acquired in combat.[2]

Wood graduated fourteenth in a class of fifty-seven at West Point. His strong performance probably owed much to the bulldog perseverance that carried him through the war and would characterize his career as an army officer. His graduation photo shows a slim, dark-haired, sturdily handsome young man with a direct and determined expression. He holds his thin lips compressed, and his clear eyes, gazing off-camera as required, seem to be locked onto an object in the near distance.[3]

Jug Wood had set his sights, not on distant peaks of fame and glory but on a short-range vision that was clear and sharp. He had been at Shiloh, Corinth, and Vicksburg. He knew what to do. He was brave and bedrock honest. In an application for a promotion nearly twenty years later he would write: "I did not miss a fight or skirmish in which my Regiment was engaged during the entire [Civil] war. I was absent sick when it made a march of twelve miles, but with that exception, I was on every march made by the Regiment during the war." Although no one else cared or remembered, Jug Wood felt honor-bound to admit missing those twelve miles out of 4,200. Here was a man you could count on. He would do his duty without flinching. And as Yosemite intruders would learn, it would not be wise to cross him when he was under orders.[4]

AMERICAN NATURE AS A FIELD OF OPERATIONS

After graduating from West Point in 1872, Jug Wood was assigned to the Fourth U.S. Cavalry in Fort Richardson, Texas. He would serve with that regiment continuously until his untimely death twenty-two years later at the Presidio in San Francisco. To a twenty-first-century observer, perhaps the most striking aspect of Jug's extensive military career was its geography.

Anson Mills captured that aspect in a single page of his memoirs. Mills's career paralleled Jug's after the Civil War. He commanded Wood's

Abram E. Wood, Yosemite's first commander, West Point graduation photo. U.S. Military Academy Library.

squadron when it served in Yosemite and Sequoia in the early 1890s and retired soon afterward as a brigadier general. On the opening page of his memoirs was a map of the United States crosshatched with lines, arrows, and circles. The markings traced the route he followed as he moved from one post to another—thirty-five years, twenty-six posts. With the exception of a tour as a military attaché in Paris, they were all located in the continental United States. During Anson Mills's entire career, the U.S.

Army's field of operations was confined to the American continent. His last army posting, as regimental commander, was in Washington State, where the Fourth Cavalry concluded an uninterrupted campaign that had begun in Texas a generation earlier.[5]

How different the army was in those days. Mills, Wood, and their Old Army contemporaries spent their adult lives crisscrossing the American landscape, camping out in its forests, mountains, plains, and deserts; mapping it; observing and recording its natural phenomena. They followed the advancing frontier, occasionally doubling back for staff duty at regional headquarters in urban centers such as Omaha, St. Louis, Chicago, Atlanta, New Orleans, New York, and Washington, D.C., but always returning to duty on the frontier. No other American public or private institution in the nineteenth century offered its members a more comprehensive exposure to the American nation as a *physical* entity. Old Army officers related to American political, social, and economic issues mainly as outsiders under civilian orders, but the American land was another matter. On that level, the connection was intimate and profound.[6]

At army headquarters in Washington, D.C., instead of the global wall maps that dominate the scene today, there were maps showing the boundaries of the various army commands between the Atlantic and Pacific coasts. Those boundaries shifted constantly throughout the century to meet the changing needs of a nation in the process of creating itself. At one time or another between 1866 and 1880, the army's continental maps showed a national field of operations divided into five divisions, thirty departments, and six districts. The most senior of those regional commands took their names from their natural surroundings—Pacific, Platte, Missouri, Cumberland, Gulf, Atlantic. Political boundaries (states, cities, and towns) were secondary to natural contours in shaping Old Army perceptions of the American nation.[7]

The Old Army's physically grounded perception of the nation it served was unique not only among American social groups but also among the armies of its time. In Europe, armies continually roamed across national frontiers, continents, seas, and oceans and developed strategies and infrastructures that met those extranational requirements. But America's army remained focused on a national field of operations joined together by a transportation and communications infrastructure that also served as a primary tool for integrating the nation as a whole.[8]

Old Army communications were the responsibility of the Signal Corps, established during the Civil War to handle the Union Army's field communications. During the post–Civil War period, when trans-Mississippi expansion coincided with a new era in telegraph communications, the Signal Corps played a central role in wiring the American nation, much as the Old Army had done with the construction of military roads on the pre–Civil War frontier. Telegraph lines in the trans-Mississippi West, constructed by soldiers to maintain military communications, also were used for civilian purposes and eventually transferred to civilian administration. That fruitful civil-military interaction continued into the twentieth century in places like Yosemite National Park, where Signal Corps personnel strung telephone and telegraph wires and installed and manned switchboards under the direction of army park superintendents who had learned about field communications while commanding troops on the Western frontier.[9]

Among the Army Signal Corps's more prominent forgotten legacies was the National Weather Bureau. In 1878, at the request of Congress, the secretary of war ordered the Signal Corps to take over the program dating from the beginning of the century in which army field units logged meteorological observations. This was the only systematic effort of its kind, and frontier settlers relied heavily on the army's weather data. Information was also forwarded to army headquarters in Washington, where the high command constructed the first national weather maps. Henceforth, said Congress in 1878, that "strategic" military data was also to be published nationally "for the benefit of agriculture and commerce." The result was the establishment of an army-run national weather forecasting service that, thirteen years later, was transferred to the Department of Agriculture and renamed the National Weather Bureau. Subsequently, army posts and encampments, including those in the national parks, continued to measure the weather and send their findings to the new civilian agency the army had brought into being.[10]

The Old Army's continental mission also shaped the basic character of the army in ways at once self-evident and easily overlooked. For instance, the army supply network serviced what amounted to a parallel national economy that further contributed to the army's distinctive national consciousness. The army produced and distributed tents, pickaxes, bedsheets, camp kettles, pants, boots, shirts, suspenders, buttons, tassels, bugles, horses, brooms, pens, stationery, bread, coffee, beans, bacon, and so on and on. Alongside the civilian economy, the Old Army's economy stood out for being nationally integrated rather than regionally fragmented, more communal than competitive, dedicated to national public service rather than individual gain. Although never discussed as such, *experientially* it was different.[11]

The Old Army's national communications and supply system assured that no matter how isolated frontier soldiers appeared to be, they were always plugged into a pulsating national network shaped by physical geography. Old Army officers sent requisitions, accepted deliveries, and received orders through bureaucratic "channels" covering the continent like a vast seamless web. Even when posted in the most isolated corner of the continent, soldiers could not help but think in integrative national terms. Their supply network led from giant depots in Philadelphia and New York to remote outposts in Montana and Arizona by train, steamer, wagon, pack mule, and any other conveyance that lent itself to the task. Army officers had to know the lay of the land from coast to coast, with its "vast distances and climatic extremes," if they were to keep their troops fed and sheltered while in continuous movement over the American landscape. With that knowledge came deep respect. For the Old Army, geography was "a more formidable foe than the Indian."[12]

In this roaming continental army, the study of natural topography received the highest priority. Its methodical daily pursuit by all units in the field drew soldiers into an unusual sensually intimate yet also scientifically detached relationship with the American land. Along with the well-documented contributions of the Army Corps of Topographical Engineers and other army "scientific explorers," less spectacular but no less vital contributions came from thousands of army units in the field—scouts, patrols, units of every size in continual movement. Their duties included filing written reports and maps detailing the terrain covered during each day's march. When time permitted, those reports appeared as elaborate bound volumes. The volume produced during a six-week "728.96"-mile march by a Seventh Cavalry battalion in 1887 (July 25–September 8) from Fort Meade, Dakota, to Fort Riley, Kansas, contained maps of each day's itinerary, a daily diary of activities, and daily descriptions of the line of march. Here is the account of the first day's "9.75"-mile itinerary:

> The road immediately after leaving Fort Meade, D.T., ascends hill very bad in wet weather, crossing a dry run on bridge about 1 mile from Post, it then descends a very steep hill and 1 mile is in a soft flat and then passes through gap in foot hills and crosses Alkali Creek; crossings of both forks good, bottom stony, banks low, scattered timber, water in pools, both above and below crossings, road from there to Bull Dog Ranch rough and very bad in wet weather, road thence to Morse's Ranch over rolling ground and generally good but stony with the exception of short distances over both sides of Pleasant Valley Creek, which is crossed on bridge, water 2"x2" heavy timber in places, banks deep and miry. Camped at Morse's Ranch, good water in fine spring.

The description of the day's itinerary was followed by an account of activities (meals, bivouac, availability of wood and forage, and so on), then environmental observations such as the weather and the availability and quality of water, then a topographical map of the day's route. Each day's march produced another chapter in what grew in six weeks into an illustrated book on the topography of the region between Fort Meade and Fort Riley. This artful piece of work went up the chain of command to army mapping bureaus where it contributed to the continuously updated composite portrait of the American land maintained by the Old Army.[13]

First Lieutenant Joseph Dorst, a Fourth Cavalry adjutant and future commander at Sequoia National Park, applied those finely honed observational skills during a leave spent exploring Mexico on horseback in 1883. Upon his return, on his own time, Dorst prepared a report that he submitted to the army's adjutant general that described five itineraries and included maps of each. Half of his text consisted of physical description, including terrain and plant life. The other half offered observations on social, political, and economic conditions, transportation infrastructure, and the military establishment. His report began with this disclaimer: "In what follows it must be borne in mind that all general statements descriptive of the Country or people are applicable to only just so much as I saw myself, and no more. Where the matter is one of opinion, the opinion expressed is mine, educated by my own observations and submitted for whatever it is worth. Where a statement is made not based on my personal knowledge it is generally so qualified as to show it." Applying what he had learned at West Point and in the field, Dorst was deliberately distancing himself from the florid word inflation that characterized travel writing among civilians during that era.[14]

Documents such as Joseph Dorst's report on Mexico, combining disciplined composition and an aesthetically sensitive eye for detail, crop up continually in the personal papers and official reports of Old Army officers. They show the trademark Old Army style cited earlier in reference to the prophetic "intuitive ecology" of army captain William Ludlow and the naturalist John Muir, in which emotive responses suggest connections ultimately verified by scientific observation. A book by Old Army officer John G. Bourke, about the Southwest when the Fourth Cavalry was stationed there, included this typical description of a descent through "immense pine forests" in the mountains of northern Arizona into "civilization":

> At one point . . . has . . . been established the great Ayers-Riordan saw and planing mill, equipped with every modern appliance for the destruction of the old giants whose heads had nodded in the breezes for centuries. . . . Trees are nearly human; they used to console man with their oracles, and I must confess my regret that the Christian dispensation has so changed the opinions of the world that the sighing of the evening wind through their branches is no longer a message of hope or a solace of sorrow.[15]

Bourke interspersed such musings with scientific descriptions of natural phenomena and precise admiring accounts of Apache customs in a study that gained recognition as a major contribution to history, literature, anthropology, and natural science from a singular man. In 1895, a year before his retirement after thirty-four years of army service, this Civil War Medal of Honor winner was named an officer of the American Association for the Advancement of Science and president of the American Folk Lore Society.[16]

Even General William T. Sherman—so terrible in battle, so triumphant and so tortured by the contradictory emotions he activated in himself—even that hard-hearted, manic-depressive old warhorse softened, grew respectful, and opened himself to poetic inspiration when describing the American landscape, as in this Conradesque recollection of his arrival in California in 1848, soon after graduating from West Point:

> Slowly the land came out of the water, the high mountains about Santa Cruz, the low beach of the Salinas, and the strongly-marked ridge terminating in the sea in a point of dark pine-trees. Then the line of whitewashed houses of adobe, backed by the groves of dark oaks, resembling old apple-trees; and then we saw two vessels anchored close to the town. One was a small merchant-brig and another a large ship apparently dismasted. At last we saw a boat coming out to meet us, and when it came alongside, we were surprised to find Lieutenant Henry Wise, master of the Independence frigate, that we had left at Valparaiso.[17]

Down-home Jug Wood wasn't the memoir-writing type. But he left a logbook that in its way was just as powerful and graphic in capturing the ties that bound him to the American land, beginning with his arrival on the frontier in late 1872:

1873

Changed station [from Fort Concho, Texas] to Ft. Clark, Texas, May and June 1873, marched 215 miles. From Ft. Clark in pursuit of hostile Indians June 30th to July 17th, 135 miles.

From Ft. Clark in pursuit of hostile Indians July 22nd to August 14th, distance marched 410 miles.

Changed station to Kerrville, Tex., distance marched 198 miles. From Kerrville, Tex., in pursuit of hostile Indians Oct., distance marched 130 miles. From Kerrville, Tex., in pursuit of hostile Indians Dec. 14th–23th [sic], distance marched 217 miles. Total number of miles marched in 1873—1,305.

1874

Changed station to Ft. Clark, Tex., March 16th to 22nd, distance marched 198 miles. From Ft. Clark, Tex., in pursuit of hostile Indians, April, distance marched 170 miles.

From Ft. Clark in pursuit of Lone Wolf a Kiowa Chief May 17th to June 16th, distance marched 548 miles.

Put in command of Troop "F" 4th Cav., June 9th. Engaged in the Kiowa and Comanche war in Texas, Pan-Handle and Indian Territory from August 6th to December 24th, distance marched 1,484 miles.

Total number of miles marched in 1874—2,400.

So Jug Wood's career memoir went, mile by mile, year by year, across the American land. By 1888, the number of miles in the saddle recorded in his personal logbook totaled 15,183—the equivalent of five trips across the North American continent, rarely using roads, picking his way over the rugged land on horseback. If Jug Wood had been asked to describe his career in the frontier army in a phrase, he might have replied: "I rode!"[18]

That was how Wood's hard-riding contemporaries remembered him in the few recorded comments on his frontier career. A West Point lecturer on the frontier army recounted Jug's storied ride in successful pursuit of deserters in Indian Territory that covered 140 miles in thirty-one sleepless hours. He appeared and disappeared like an apparition in a published account of the 1885–1886 Geronimo campaign by a fellow officer (also a future Yosemite commander), Lieutenant John Bigelow Jr.: "About ten o-clock the dust of [Wood's troop] emerging from the range of hills, on the horizon, was seen sluggishly rolling and reeling over the foot-slopes toward the station." Or: "Lawton is behind the Indians and expects to have Wood with a strong force south and west of the Indians before daylight tomorrow." Again: "General [Nelson A.] Miles went through here last night on his way to Nogales. On the same train with him [was] Captain Wood . . . referred to in the general's despatch of yesterday."[19]

General Miles, who oversaw the Geronimo campaign and was later named commanding general of the army, published a book of reminiscences in 1896 in which he used a pursuit by a patrol led by Wood as a model example of its kind. Wood even gained immortality of sorts by appearing in the first published series of sketches by Frederic Remington, illustrating Bigelow's narrative of the Geronimo campaign. That description of troopers "rolling and reeling over the foot-slopes" was followed by a Remington sketch of galloping cavalrymen entitled "Captain Wood's Troop."[20]

Remington's portraits contributed to the dashing frontier cavalry image enshrined by the Hollywood film industry. It related only incidentally to reality. The daily rides on horseback of Jug Wood and his comrades, often in fruitless pursuit across fiery deserts and in subzero snowstorms, day after day, year after year, covering thousands of miles, took a terrible toll on the constitutions of the most vigorous men, even tough-as-nails Jug Wood. In 1888, shortly after the Geronimo campaign, Wood finally gave in to pleas from army doctors and applied for sick leave to be spent at the Army and Navy Hospital in Hot Springs, Arkansas. The post surgeon at Fort Huachuca who signed the necessary papers reported that Wood suffered from "chronic diarrhera, dyspepsia and chronic rheumatism, contracted in the line of duty by exposure and hardships incident to long and arduous service." Wood's required leave application began with a long apology. "I preferred doing duty as long as I could," he wrote in reference to the surgeon's account of previously unsuccessful efforts to put him on sick report. But he had to admit the facts: "I am now completely rundown. . . . I weigh 30 lbs less than my normal weight and 12 lbs less than I have weighed since I have been sixteen years old. I was operated upon for the piles April 17, 1886, and was in the saddle May 21 following, long before I was well." Wood was hospitalized at Hot Springs for four months.[21]

Soon after his release from the hospital, Wood wrote the memorandum summarizing his career activities that is cited above. It accompanied an application for promotion out of the cavalry into a staff position with the Inspector General's Department. For a loyal cavalryman, that was a dramatic step, and Wood took it only because he was utterly worn out. The army turned down his application. Resignation for health reasons was out of the question for Jug, so 1889 opened with him back in the saddle, leading scouting parties through the beautiful, brutal Huachuca Mountains.[22]

Wood's case was not unusual. In 1891, after the Fourth Cavalry troops under Wood and Joe Dorst had been transferred from Fort Huachuca to the Presidio in San Francisco en route to their assignments in Yosemite and Sequoia national parks, Dorst recalled past experiences and wondered how he survived:

> I have had chills & fever in Indian Territory, have been near death's door with mountain fever in the field in Colorado & have had two doctors in consultation over me when I had dysentery, in the field, in Arizona, and have had rheumatism more or less since the Powder River expedition in 1876. . . . In Arizona in '85–'86 I was in the field ten months without seeing a military post, and for five months of that winter was in the heart of the Sierra Madres, with the temperature sometimes 6 degrees below zero. . . . During this time, except for about three weeks in January, and a week in February, I had not even a piece of canvas over me. [In 1887, while enjoying some respite at

West Point,] I went to a physician & found that I had an enlarged liver and spleen, and that a system full of malaria for years, with poor diet, much exposure & hard work had made me nervous & dyspeptic as well as rheumatic, & it was only with great care that I recovered.[23]

Dorst was among the lucky ones. He also described what happened to twenty other soldiers who provided the officer complement for six Fourth Cavalry troops sent north in 1876 after a two-year campaign on the southern plains pursued through steaming summers and subzero winters without interruption. The northern destination was Fort Robinson, Nebraska, for the campaign following Custer's destruction—a winter campaign in the Rockies that saw "the mercury freezing in the thermometer." Even before taking to the field again from Fort Robinson, Dorst wrote, two of the twenty officers were "mere skeletons" from malaria and had to be put on sick leave. Another was hauled in an ambulance for 180 miles before he was judged beyond recovery and sent back. The ages of those three disabled officers were twenty-five, thirty-five, and thirty-six. During the years of continuous compaigning that followed, Dorst watched his comrades drop off one by one until, less than fifteen years later, only six of the twenty officers with him at Fort Robinson remained with the regiment. Only one of them had been killed in action. The rest (most in their thirties and forties, none over fifty) had been lost from "premature death," disability, transfer (for three) to office jobs, or resignation out of sheer exhaustion. "It was not one campaign that killed & disabled them," Dorst wrote, "but the wearing strain, mental & physical, of continuous work year after year till they were exhausted."[24]

"Year after year," as Dorst painfully recounted, those officers experienced the humbling power of the American land in ways denied even to mountain explorers, who were not subjected to forced marches and could at least take refuge in foul weather or interrupt their wanderings from time to time, or Indian warriors who holed up during the cruel winters on the Rockies and the Plains. As for civilian nature lovers who took to the wilds for invigoration, they could not know the same deep intimacy of pain, the sheer "wearing strain" that Wood, Dorst, and their comrades experienced through continuous years of forced all-weather marches on the trail. The fabled commander of the Fourth Cavalry, Ranald Mackenzie, "attributed the permanent breaking down of his health" (he died at forty-nine) to his brutal winter campaigns.[25]

Here, then, was another contributor to the sudden bursts of poetic emotion erupting from routine Old Army reports: Truth illuminated by deep-reaching pain, a poet's truth, occupied the core of this sensual, scientifically observant relationship with the American land. "If thou didst ever hold me in thy heart, absent thee from felicity awhile . . . [and] draw thy breath in pain, to tell my story." Like Shakespeare's Hamlet, a Fourth Cavalry officer lived an inspired life of pain. It drew him deep into himself and taught him much about his and his nation's nature.[26]

THE MACKENZIE SCHOOL OF LEADERSHIP

When Jug Wood moved from the U.S. Military Academy at West Point to the Fourth Cavalry Regiment at Fort Richardson, Texas, in 1872, a new phase in his military education began. His Texas on-the-job curriculum focused on tactics, strategy, and above all conduct. The martial virtues he had been taught in school acquired an important civic dimension during his service on the frontier, where Old Army warriors rarely engaged in combat but were constantly involved in adjudication. The values these officers applied in performing their civic duties derived from a category of training assigned the highest priority in the military, called leadership.[27]

There is no parallel in civilian society for military leadership training in either content or institutional emphasis. A poorly led business goes bankrupt and the owner moves on; a poorly led military unit is overrun, and the commander is buried or lives with the most horrid memories imaginable. The character of Old Army leadership, its unique strengths and limitations, is analyzed later. Here, preliminarily, we meet its embodiment in Jug Wood's first commanding officer, the commander of the Fourth Cavalry when Wood arrived in 1872 and for a decade afterward, Ranald Slidell Mackenzie.

Mackenzie was a legend in the Old Army for his heroic exploits and his strength of character. After he died while still in his forties in 1889, his former adjutant and personal aide, Joseph Dorst, memorialized him in an article for the West Point alumni journal. Dorst had served under Mackenzie for a dozen years. His summary of what he admired most about his hero—what he sought to emulate in his own professional behavior—has special relevance for this book because it was composed less than two years before Dorst was named the first commander of a new Sequoia National Park in California, just south of Yosemite. Dorst's lengthy homage to the man who inspired his conduct at Sequoia traced a career filled with daring exploits. It concluded with a peroration listing Mackenzie's numerous leadership virtues. The list built toward a final transcendent judgment: This great army leader embodied—and these were the last words of Dorst's tribute—"an exalted type of that noblest work of GOD, an honest man."[28]

An "honest man"; Dorst chose an interesting priority for leadership at the height of the so-called Gilded Age of rampant political and economic corruption. On the battlefield, of course, honesty, one of the most revered martial virtues, meant more than it ever could in politics. But its committed application during the Gilded Age by a military institution assigned a wide range of public duties also constituted an invaluable civic resource. The commanders of the first national parks in California received their training in honesty from Ranald Mackenzie.

Mackenzie graduated second in his West Point class in 1862, which in those days meant automatic assignment to the elite Corps of Engineers to work on fortifications and other technical support activities. But the young Academy graduate sought out frontline action, constantly placed himself at risk, was twice wounded, and soon won a combat command. He received seven battlefield brevet promotions in less than three years. The units picked by Ulysses S. Grant for the final assault leading to Lee's surrender included a division commanded by Major General Ranald Mackenzie, age twenty-five. Grant called Mackenzie "the most promising young officer in the army."[29]

During the Union Army's abrupt postwar demobilization from about 1 million men to 54,000 soldiers in twelve months, resulting in the elimination of entire divisions and corps, Brevet Major General Mackenzie reverted to his regular army rank of captain. But again he rose faster than his peers. A year after dropping to captain without a command, while the regular army's strength was being cut in half again to about 28,000, Mackenzie vaulted to the rank of colonel with command of an infantry regiment. When conflicts between frontier settlers and Indians intensified in 1870, he went west on President Grant's direct orders to take command of the Fourth Cavalry, and, according to the leading historian of the frontier army, "he whipped [it] . . . into the best cavalry regiment in the army." Many years later, during the Spanish-American War, General Henry Lawton, who had served under Mackenzie as a lieutenant, told another officer, "Whenever I am in a tight place, whenever I am uncertain what to do, I say to myself, 'What would Mackenzie do?'"[30]

Mackenzie was a frontier contemporary of George Armstrong Custer. His Fourth Cavalry was widely recognized within the army as far superior to Custer's ill-fated Seventh. The Fourth's commander "was looked upon by the whole army as the embodiment of courage, skill and dash to an eminent degree," wrote a fellow officer. But it was more than a reputation for courage that won Mackenzie the peer respect never accorded Custer. What Mackenzie had that Custer lacked was leadership character.[31]

It showed up in his first choice of command after the Civil War, which Custer and others had turned down as a dead end. Mackenzie gave up a cushy position with the Corps of Engineers, in Portsmouth,

New Hampshire, on a track leading toward command of the entire Corps, to take over a new infantry regiment slated for duty on the frontier. The new regiment, the Forty-first Infantry, consisted entirely of Negroes. White officers feared that association with it would stunt their careers. A twenty-six-year-old war hero whose patrons included Ulysses Grant and Philip Sheridan could have easily held out for something else; but that wasn't in Mackenzie's character. He had asked for a frontier command; this was the first opening; he took it and went to work.

The new regiment started out at the bottom of the army's totem pole. Its headquarters was an abandoned post, Fort McKavett, in southwestern Texas. Mackenzie ordered his men to completely rebuild the post into a model facility. When they weren't cutting and shaping timber, digging wells, raising buildings, and performing other heavy construction tasks, the soldiers of the Forty-first were drilling, day and night, always under their commander's personal direction. According to all accounts, Mackenzie's overworked, perennially exhausted troopers were devoted to him.[32]

It was the character of his leadership. Although Mackenzie undoubtedly shared prevailing white prejudices at least to some extent, they went out the window when he took command of the Forty-first. On one occasion, a subordinate shocked the local civilian community by writing a letter of affection to a white lady. Her father was so incensed that he shot and killed the first black soldier he saw. The civilian community cheered. In those days, regimental commanders belonged to the social elite in remote frontier communities. Mackenzie showed his contempt for the behavior of his social peers by posting a reward for the racist murderer and keeping his troops in the field pursuing him without letup for the remainder of their days at Fort McKavett. Only after Mackenzie and his regiment were transferred did the culprit come out of hiding and accept a trial and a foreordained acquittal from his sympathetic friends and neighbors. That, however, was a problem for higherminded civil authority. Mackenzie's troops knew where their commander stood. Racism had not ended in America during the Civil War, and in many respects it would get worse before it got better. But the black troops of the Forty-first Infantry knew that their commander was loyal to them first and foremost, that he would back them up no matter what. The results spoke for themselves. The army's biggest internal problem immediately after the Civil War was desertion, which in hard postings like Fort McKavett reached as high as 50 percent. Not so in Mackenzie's Forty-first Infantry, where its members rewarded their loyal taskmaster with one of the lowest desertion rates in the army.[33]

It was the same for Mackenzie's next assignment, the Fourth Cavalry. The Fourth already enjoyed an illustrious reputation. Created in 1855 as the First Cavalry, it was the army's first mounted unit to be called cavalry (they had previously been called dragoons). Among its first members were future commanders of the Union and Confederate armies, George McClellan and Robert E. Lee, as well as Lee's famous cavalry commander, James E. B. "Jeb" Stuart. The regiment fought in the Union army during the Civil War, minus most of its southern members, and was renamed the Fourth during a wartime reorganization. Mackenzie took over in February 1871. The Fourth was then headquartered in Fort Concho, Texas, where its duties included supporting the post–Civil War Reconstruction work of the Freedmen's Bureau.[34]

As Mackenzie had quickly learned while commanding the Forty-first Infantry, the polarized moral passions of the Civil War continued to govern attitudes during the reconstructive "peace" that followed. The army, in keeping with its pre–Civil War tradition, had taken on a thankless peacekeeping mission adjudicating disputes between whites and blacks and between white southerners and northern white carpetbaggers. Mackenzie's former cavalry commander, Phil Sheridan, was sent west to fight Indians after southern-sympathizing President Andrew Johnson found Sheridan too forceful in his dealings with white supremacists in Texas and Louisiana. Custer's Seventh Cavalry went west after postwar Reconstruction duty that included suppressing the Ku Klux Klan in Indiana. The Fourth Cavalry went directly from Civil War combat to Texas, where it supported both Reconstruction and frontier settlement policies. Its officers performed those duties faithfully but without illusion. Many of them expressed disgust with greedy federal officials raiding the Reconstruction till and with locals who flouted the law. Meanwhile, civilians on all disputing sides berated them. In short, it was business as usual for the Old Army in "peacetime" nineteenth-century America.[35]

From Texas, the Fourth Cavalry moved further west to Fort Sill in Indian Territory (now Oklahoma) to police the peace following a series of provocations and counterprovocations between white settlers and Indians. The disputes were triggered by the usual desire of frontier settlers for Indian land. In this case, it was land previously granted by treaty to Indians in exchange for their removal from other Indian lands east of the Mississippi coveted by whites in that region. Mackenzie's adjutant, Joseph Dorst, described the situation upon their arrival at Fort Sill in 1875: "The Indians had returned to their reservations, but owing to the depredations of white horse thieves on the Indians' herds, it was a difficult matter to hold them there. It was not an unusual thing for a hundred head of ponies to be stolen from an Indian camp in one night, and horses belonging to [Old Army] officers and picketed near their quarters, were stolen at midday."[36]

Shortly after the Fourth Cavalry arrived, one of its officers was arrested by local lawmen while tracking fleeing horse thieves outside the reservation. Mackenzie responded with a relentless campaign that within six months eliminated the white horse thieves problem. He went after white squatters in the same way and with similar success. At the same time, he encouraged Indians to raise cattle on the sound principle that it was closer to the lifestyles of former buffalo-hunters than farming, which Eastern reformers preferred for the more elevating moral values farming allegedly promoted. But although Indians preferred Mackenzie's alternative, it didn't work because their cattle herds fell prey to white thieves and Indian Bureau inefficiency. Those not stolen starved for want of promised supplies and had to be slaughtered while Mackenzie pleaded fruitlessly with civilian government agents. In 1876, in the midst of Mackenzie's struggles with the corruption, inefficiency, and misguided ideals of higher civilian authorities, the *New York Times* published an article containing excerpts of a report "of an agent of the Board of Indian Commissioners" attacking the army for failing to protect Indians and calling Mackenzie's Fort Sill "a sort of young Sodom." An outraged Mackenzie had to be restrained by his superiors from replying directly to the *Times*.[37]

Mackenzie's duties in Indian Territory were cut short in 1876, when he was ordered north for the campaign following Custer's annihilation. He took command of the 600-man cavalry contingent in a 2,000-man force. It was an unsuccessful campaign, the sole highlight being a raid led by Mackenzie on a Cheyenne camp in the Bighorn Mountains.[38]

That so-called Powder River raid was carried out under conditions that Mackenzie called the worst he had ever experienced. For him, that was a pretty strong statement. Although only thirty-six years old, he had been in the field almost continuously for fifteen years. Not long before the Powder River expedition, a subordinate who came upon him bathing in a river was appalled by the scars covering his body, many of them from Civil War bullet wounds. By all accounts, he lived in constant physical pain from old wounds, chronic rheumatism, migraines, and other illnesses induced by continuous exposure to battle and the elements. But he never let up. For the Powder River mission, he left his supply wagons behind and used pack mules for greater mobility and stealth. Although temperatures registered below zero when he set out (and would reach thirty below before the ordeal was over), he permitted each trooper to carry only one blanket, an overcoat, and a shelter half. Campfires were forbidden. At night, having picked their way through the ridges and valleys of the Bighorn Mountains since dawn, Mackenzie's raiders dined on cold rations and collapsed on the frozen ground. As usual, Mackenzie was reconnoitering at the head of his exhausted troops right up to the final charge that destroyed the village of the famous Northern Cheyenne warrior chief Dull Knife, the first major defeat for those important allies of the Sioux under Sitting Bull. Mackenzie and his raiders, looking like anything but victors, staggered back through the freezing mountains to their base.

"They put out a strong gard that night and I went to bed more dead than alive," wrote Mackenzie's young orderly, Private Earl Smith, in his diary. Mackenzie couldn't sleep. Although he had achieved the first and only victory of that entire massive campaign, he was depressed. His victory should have been more complete. A favorite young lieutenant should not have died. It was all his fault (as he later confided to a fellow officer). His orderly wrote: "Every time I woke I could see the Genrall walking up and down. I don't believe he slept a bit that nite. His mind must have been troubled about some thing. I don't [k]now what, for he is the bravest man I ever saw."[39]

In April, Dull Knife led 524 survivors of Mackenzie's raid into the Red Cloud Agency for a final surrender. The Indian chief sought out his adversary. "You are the one I was afraid of when you came here last summer," he said to Mackenzie. Mackenzie was his usual stern public self, but he probably found a way to communicate to his fellow warrior leader what he would later put in writing: "I regard the Cheyenne tribe of Indians as the finest body of that race which I have ever met."[40]

They were two warrior chiefs who had met in battle. One had defeated the other, but nature had defeated both. There could be dignity in that encounter as well as mutual respect. Mackenzie had no higher objective (not Indian land, not reform of "savage" souls). His primary expressed desire was that the Cheyenne receive fair treatment from the people who had ordered him into battle, which he considered a point of honor. But the war was shifting into moral and political realms beyond Mackenzie's authority. Promised food for the defeated Indian warriors did not arrive. Mackenzie was furious. He wrote to Washington, "I am expected to see that Indians behave properly whom the government is starving." He fed the Cheyenne from his own stores. Suddenly an order came down for the Fourth Cavalry to move the Cheyenne southward into Indian Territory in order to open up their lands to white settlers. Mackenzie protested. He was concerned about the effects of an abrupt shift in a way of life keyed to regional climatic conditions. He knew the land where the Northern Cheyenne lived and where they were being sent, and he saw and understood how the sharp environmental differences would affect Cheyenne culture. He wrote to the commander of Fort Reno where they were headed, who would take over the Fourth Cavalry's responsibilities, that "if the Indians from hunger [arising from failure to adjust to the foreign farm life awaiting them] run off contrary to the wishes of the agent to get buffalo, do not attempt to cause their return, or the troops will be placed in the position of assisting in a great wrong."

Most of Mackenzie's pleas fell on deaf ears. The Cheyenne sent delegations to Washington to plead their case but received only condescending words of concern from white men in offices who had never camped on the frozen ground of the Bighorn Mountains in winter, had never seen and respected Dull Knife's courage in battle. They had no bonds of shared experience with their white "fathers" in Washington. When the Cheyenne couldn't stand it anymore, they would rebel again, the army would be called in and would defeat them, white moralists would condemn the army and resume control, further "educating" the conquered Indians out of their land and values and again provoking them to strike out, and the cycle would be renewed.

The army's thankless role in that transcontinental drama was by then moving toward its conclusion in the southern Rockies and the southwestern territories. Mackenzie and his regiment marched into Texas under new orders, then into southern Colorado. In 1882, he was promoted to brigadier general, a long-sought mixed blessing, since it also meant giving up command of the Fourth Cavalry (only colonels commanded regiments). He became commander of the sprawling Department of Texas. And, as can occur with sudden relief from consuming responsibilities, intensified in Mackenzie's case by more than two decades of continuous hard riding, he began to give out. In December 1883, he suffered a breakdown. After a few months in an institution in New York, he was released into his sister's custody. His motor abilities deteriorated, and in 1887, at the age of forty-nine, he died. His death certificate identified the cause as "progressive paresis" (paralysis). He was buried with full honors at West Point.[41]

Mackenzie was gone, but the Fourth Cavalry remained his regiment. The officers who had served under him and still idolized him had internalized his credo and sought to live up to his expectations as if he were still among them. Graduates of the Mackenzie school of leadership carried his example into California's national parks during the 1890s and early 1900s, after the Indians had been defeated and the only human problems the men of the Fourth Cavalry had to face were familiar white greed, arrogance, and compulsive exploitiveness, now directed at park reservations rather than Indian reservations. One of the two officers assigned by Mackenzie to promote livestock raising among the displaced Northern Cheyenne because it would help preserve their culture was Jug Wood, future first commander of Yosemite. Alex Rodgers, who would follow Wood at Yosemite, learned about the eviction of white squatters from Indian Territory in a personal letter from Mackenzie that condemned exploitive white greed.

The regimental adjutant who wrote about Mackenzie's problems with white horse thieves, Joseph Dorst, went on to become the first commander at Sequoia National Park. The young officer arrested in Texas for trying to rescue stolen Indian horses was James Parker, who succeeded Dorst at Sequoia. The most imposing and influential national park commander, S. B. M. Young, who went on to become army chief of staff, did not belong to the Fourth Cavalry during this period, but he served under Mackenzie in several combined operations and named a son after him. In the heat of battle in the Philippines twenty years later, this same S. B. M. Young impulsively called his immediate superior "Mackenzie." One can safely assume that on more than one occasion during their national park assignments, these and other graduates of the Mackenzie school of leadership (so fundamentally different from the Custer example that dominates popular mythology) asked themselves, as would General Henry Lawton in wartime, "What would Mackenzie do?"[42]

RHYTHMIC RULES AND REGULATIONS

In 1886, the Fourth Cavalry took another big step westward in the trans-Mississippi journey that would lead into Yosemite National Park four years later. The regiment's headquarters moved from Colorado to Fort Huachuca in the barren Huachuca Mountains near Arizona's border with Mexico. The post housed four troops of cavalry, the regiment's commanding officer and his staff, and the regimental band—about three hundred soldiers in all and perhaps two dozen wives and children—plus a twelve-pound Napoleon gun that announced each new day with a blast at precisely 5:20 A.M. The regiment's seven other cavalry troops were scattered among other smaller posts in Arizona and New Mexico.[43]

Fort Huachuca was established in 1877 to protect the region's silver-hunting settlers from Apache raiding parties. Built with army labor, it had evolved into a comparatively luxurious station. Each of the eleven adobe officers' houses along the parade ground had stove heat, large fireplaces, and between 3,000 and 4,000 square feet of commodious rooms under a shingled roof. Across a broad parade ground, the enlisted men occupied four frame barracks buildings, each two stories high, with offices and sleeping quarters for noncommissioned officers on the ground floor, a cavernous bunkhouse for enlisted men on the second floor, zinc bathtubs for shared use, and individual washbasins. The upstairs bunkhouse had coal stoves at either end, bunks lining the walls, a locker at the foot of each bed, and personal gear hanging from a rack at the head, neat and ready for daily inspection. The privies were outside in the rear, a muddy walk during the torrential late summer rains.

Other buildings bordering the rectangular parade ground included a post headquarters, bakery, guardhouse, commissary office and warehouse, and a twenty-four-bed hospital. Near the sawmill south of the post were two other fixtures of post life—the sutler's store and the "soapsuds row" of huts occupied by the regimental laundresses. The ladies (four per troop) lived a hard life and were usually more than a match for the rowdy troopers. Many stormy yet enduring marriages were consummated on soapsuds row. To the northwest, over a low hill, the post cemetery was laid out. Most of its initial inhabitants were infant children of wives of young officers, victims of the harsh conditions before the fort took shape.[44]

Daily life at Fort Huachuca unfolded with a punctual regularity common to virtually every frontier outpost. Once the routine began, there were no pauses. Barely ten minutes after the 5:20 A.M. reveille, the troops were dressed and lined up for first assembly and roll call. Ten minutes later, they formed another line at the mess for breakfast followed by

6:45 A.M.	Drill call and boots and saddles (mounting up)
7:00	Assembly and cavalry drill
8:30	Recall from drill
8:45	Sick call and stable call
9:00	Assembly and fatigue call
9:30	Guard mount
11:45	Recall from fatigue and first sergeants' reports
12:00 noon	Dinner
1:00 P.M.	Fatigue call
4:30	Recall from fatigue and stable call
5:15	Assembly and retreat parade
6:00	Supper
9:00	Last roll call
9:30	"Taps" and extinguish lights

Then to sleep until a new daily round began with a blast from the regiment's Napoleon gun.[45]

The activities within Fort Huachuca's rhythmic cycle of daily routine had their own internal rhythms. Nowhere was that more evident than in the hours spent in daily drill. For the cavalry troops at Huachuca, that meant drilling with horses. In the early 1890s, the perennially revised *Drill Regulations for Cavalry of the United States Army* covered 529 dense pages of instruction. Reading through it was like entering another world. This was choreography as both science and art. Each movement responded to the call of a trumpet, and each call was different. There was a trumpet call for forming ranks, forward, turn right, turn left, halt, to the rear, and so on, with variations for movements by individuals, squads, troops, squadrons, regiments, and brigades. Each movement, each pause, each space between movements and pauses was measured with scientific precision, down to six inches for the interval between the knees of troopers in mounted formation and six inches between their elbows when dismounted.[46]

Under the cavalry drill regime, perfection was precisely known and humanly unattainable. A formation on a parade ground was like a ballet troupe pursuing an elusive ideal. Those who knew the "music" appreciated the nuances and the triumphs. Those who did not applauded the disciplined gracefulness of the performance.

At the end of each day, the entire command turned out for "retreat." They wore full-dress blue uniforms decorated with blue and yellow braid, bold stripes and bars on chests and shoulders, their heads topped by Prussian-style hats with striking yellow spikes and horsehair plumes. Bugles sounded, the troops formed ranks, and officers took up their positions. When all were still and ready, the band struck up a march, and the command passed in review before the post commander—horses prancing, troops erect in the saddle, colorful guidons and campaign flags flying, an incongruous sight in the foothills of the godforsaken Huachuca Mountains.[47]

The punctuated bugle calls and daily cavalry ballets were only highlights of a far more encompassing process regulating every aspect of daily Old Army life. It was codified in numerous books of instructions, the most important being the *Regulations of the Army of the United States,* the Old Army's Bible. Precisely detailed rules and regulations gave each activity on each day of Old Army life a time, a place, a purpose, and a function that was uniform throughout the entire service, always applied according to uniform, hierarchically organized procedures.[48]

During the intervals between drill, troopers pursued a seemingly endless variety of fatigue duties drawn up by first sergeants according to regulations and announced at troop formations or posted on evening bulletin boards. They planted trees, tended gardens, repaired buildings, prepared meals, and cleaned and cleaned and cleaned; every inch of habitable space was scoured day after day. For cavalrymen the most important daily fatigue duty was stable call for the care and feeding of horses. It was conducted on post and on the march with a strictness in routine that made it a minutely delineated category unto itself.[49]

Then there were the reports. Officers wrote reports on every conceivable aspect of the regular business of the troops under their command and the posts they administered. Among the major generators of reports were the so-called "bureaus" in Washington, D.C., that regulated army supply and management. The Subsistence Department issued sixty-nine different blank forms that Jug Wood and his fellow troop commanders filled out at one time or another: vouchers for rations, contracts for fresh beef and mutton, abstracts of sales, receipts of property, statements of property, and the like. From the quartermaster general's bureau came another seventy blank forms, vouchers and bills of lading especially, for everything from rifles and bullets to shirts, pants, buckets, and candles.[50]

Detailed regulation of daily life extended even into the digestive systems of the men at Fort Huachuca. According to regulations in effect during the late 1880s, each trooper received twelve ounces of pork or bacon or canned beef (fresh or corned), or one pound and four ounces of fresh beef, or twenty ounces of salt beef; eighteen ounces of soft bread or flour, or sixteen ounces of hard bread, or one pound and four ounces of corn meal; "and to every one hundred rations, fifteen pounds of beans or peas, or ten pounds of rice or hominy; ten pounds of green coffee or eight of roasted (or roasted and ground) coffee, or two pounds of tea; fifteen pounds of sugar; four quarts of vinegar; four pounds of soap; four pounds of salt; four ounces of pepper; one pound and eight ounces of adamantine or star candles; and to troops in the field, when necessary, four pounds of yeast powder to one hundred rations of flour" for troopers to use to bake bread over their campfires.[51]

When Jug Wood and his I Troop marched out from Fort Huachuca on a scouting expedition, they took their rules and regulations and blank forms with them. The book on cavalry drill regulations included chapters on scouting and bivouacking that assured uniformity in the field as well as on post.[52] Their overnight camps looked like army posts in miniature. When only one troop was in camp, the enlisted men's tents usually formed a single line, with horses picketed in front and officers' tents in the rear. For larger formations, enlisted men's tents faced one another to form a broad "company street" or several streets, with the officers' tents at one end of each street, wagons at the other, and horses picketed in the middle.

Immediately upon halting, saddles and bridles were removed and the horses checked for skin irritations and walked for ten minutes to cool down. After the horses had been groomed, watered, and fed, an officer walked down the line, inspecting the ears, eyes, noses, and hooves of each animal. Then the men turned to themselves. Under orders from the first sergeant, they unloaded gear, gathered wood chips, built fires, prepared dinner, and attended to other housekeeping duties before being put to sleep by the trumpeter, who woke them a few hours later with the reveille call, followed by roll call and fatigue duties just as on post, before resuming the march. (One reason cavalrymen would make good national park managers was that they had spent a good part of their professional careers "policing" campgrounds; it was second nature to them.)[53]

At night on the trail, after the men had turned in, a guard marched smartly up and down in front of the tents. Often a candle would be burning inside a troop commander's tent or at a makeshift table outside it under the starry sky. There the poor man would sit, filling out reports, forms, and requisitions. Jug Wood, hard-riding bureaucrat, rode by day and wrote by night across the southern plains, down along the Rio Grande, through the Rockies, into New Mexico and Arizona, up the California coast, over deserts and glaciers, in snowstorms, rainstorms, dust storms, and whatever else came his way. "My services have not been particularly conspicuous," he wrote in his 1888 application for a promotion, "but they have been faithful and arduous." He did not mention the paperwork.[54]

The adjutant general's department had a special role in the Old Army's nationwide bureaucratic ballet. Army units needed to be available for transfer anywhere at any time. For the system to work, its procedures had to be standardized, and those in command had to know what each soldier was doing, where, and how, at all times. That was the key responsibility of this department. No soldier or group of soldiers could move in any direction, even when on leave, without the adjutant general's knowledge. No individual could leave his post, nor could any unit, without having first received an order to do so issued through the adjutant general's office, and every subsequent movement under that order had to be reported to him.

Accordingly, the path followed during the spring of 1886 by Captain Jug Wood's I Troop, Fourth U.S. Cavalry, was recorded on his troop muster rolls submitted through channels to the adjutant general. "Since date of last Muster [Wood's neatly penned summary for May–June 1886 began] Troop continued on scout after hostile Indians marching the following distances—viz May 1, to Palonia 20 miles. May 2, 3 & 4, lay in camp at Palonia. May 5 to Azas Creek 18 miles. May 6 up Azas Creek and back on Sonora River Mexico, 22 miles." And so on, day by day. That muster roll also listed the name, rank, date and location of enlistment, recruiting officer, and period of service of every member of Wood's troop, and if any personnel were on leave or temporarily assigned to another unit, exactly where they were and what they were doing was specified. Charts with breakdowns by rank of the members of I Troop who were sick, under arrest, on leave, or absent without leave plus an evaluation of the troop's conditions in terms of discipline, instruction, appearance, arms, accoutrements, and clothing on a scale from poor to excellent were included as well. All this information from all cavalry troops and companies, posts, regiments, departments, divisions, and other commands flowed through appropriate channels to the office of the adjutant general in Washington.[55]

To manage the intersections in that nationwide system of charts and reports, the adjutant general placed adjutant officers at every level in the chain of command, such as the Fourth Cavalry's Joe Dorst. They kept meticulous records of all communications. An inspector could arrive at a post, scan the ledgers for dates and summaries of all communications, then, if he wished, peruse the full texts.[56]

If the *Regulations* were the Old Army's scriptures, then orders, supplemented by bulletins and circulars, were its sacred commentaries. General Orders read like chapters from *Regulations* and often were so incorporated when the *Regulations* were periodically revised. Special Orders and orders issued by post and unit commanders covered daily minutiae. They often appeared as interpretations of regal General Orders and *Regulations*—for example, how to alter the dress code during a flood or what prices to pay for foodstuffs during a drought. Orders generally fell into two categories: what to do (from how to wear an overcoat to how to fold a letter), and when and how to move. When Jug Wood filled out his first troop muster roll after arriving at the Presido in San Francisco from Fort Huachuca in 1890, he began: "Under the Provision of G.O. [General Orders] #22 of the Army C.G. [Commanding General] and G.O. #5 Hdqrs. Div of Pacific, May 19, 90." Those were his passports. New ones would be issued for him every time he took his troop anywhere. They were an integral part of the business of knowing where everyone was at all times. The entire Old Army lived, literally, "under orders." And when an old soldier died, he was buried under Special Orders, implemented with measured cadence.[57]

Rules, regulations, orders, reports, requisitions—they all flowed through channels. The phrases "through channels" or "through regular channels" or "through official channels" appeared regularly at the top of communications. Channels proceeded upward through the chain of command from the troop to its regiment (sometimes by way of a fort or post commander), then to the regional department or division, then to army headquarters in Washington, to the adjutant general, the commanding general, the secretary of war, and ultimately, in some instances, to the army's commander in chief under the Constitution, the president of the United States. (There were parallel channels for the different bureaus, as when a post quartermaster submitted a requisition for a new soup kettle that moved through quartermaster channels.) At each communication intersection, an officer would examine the wandering document, write an "endorsement" on it indicating approval, disapproval, or modification, and reinsert it back into the channel. The endorsement could send the document into reverse, or it could send it further up the chain of command. Some requests could go through a dozen or more endorsements before completing the circuit back to their origins with a definitive "for action" judgment, which could be no action. The main idea was to stay in channels: attempts to go around or over anyone did not work because at some point the communication usually would be sucked into channels and the freelancer would be exposed, in writing, for everyone at every level to see.

There was nothing comparable in civilian society to these channeled units and subunits guided by minutely coded, rhythmically implemented rules and regulations—least of all on the wild and woolly frontier, where rules and regulations were viewed as a threat to treasured individualistic liberty. The army's coded rhythms seemed to come from another world— a rhythmically regulated world somewhere deep in their nature.

PART II: THE CALL

The force will be soon on hand.
—*Interior Secretary John Noble to Robert Underwood Johnson, 1890*[1]

CHAPTER THREE

"This Wonderland"

NORTH TO SAN FRANCISCO

The twenty-four-year march of the Fourth U.S. Cavalry across America's trans-Mississippi west finally ended in the spring of 1890. Men like Jug Wood and Joe Dorst had spent their entire adult lives on that ride, through mountain blizzards, dust storms, parched deserts, whatever came their way. They had served their nation as warriors, explorers, administrators, naturalists, builders of roads and bridges, guides, protectors, telegraphists, weathermen, local handymen, lawmen, country doctors, engineers, surveyors, and above all mediators in an era of economic and spiritual conquest of the American land and its native inhabitants. They knew their nation in every sense of the term. Now, from their base in the Arizona mountains near the Mexican border, there was nowhere for them to go but north, up the Pacific coastline.[1]

The Fourth Cavalry would establish its new headquarters at Fort Walla Walla, Washington, but not all the regiment's personnel would be based there. The sixty-man troops commanded by Jug Wood and Joe Dorst drew the most coveted assignment: the Presidio in San Francisco. The Presidio occupied a stunning site on a bay at the Pacific Ocean entrance to the largest and gaudiest city west of the Rockies. It was a well-earned reward for two veteran warriors, worn down by their long ordeal yet still relatively young. Between them, the Iowan Wood, forty-six, and the Indianan Dorst, thirty-seven, had put in thirty-five years on the trail and manning outposts on the western frontier.[2]

Times were changing for the Old Army of Wood and Dorst. The trans-Mississippi land rush and its Indian wars were virtually over, and a sophisticated regional and national railroad network permitted rapid troop dispersal from a few central points for the few incidents that occurred. Those and related changes boosted the cause of army reformers arguing for concentrating troops in fewer posts to improve organization and training. Meanwhile, as America's interests expanded overseas, the regular army's mission was being revised to make it more an army in the traditional sense and less the nation-building/peacekeeping instrument that had set it apart from other armies since its establishment in 1784. By mid-1891, Secretary of War Redfield Proctor reported proudly that twenty-five frontier posts had been shut down in just two years, bringing the remain-

Fourth cavalry camp at Yosemite, 1890s. Yosemite National Park Library.

ing number on the continent to ninety-seven from a post–Civil War high of 250. Proctor foresaw closing "10 or 12 more" as soon as new barracks were built at larger posts.[3]

Joe Dorst's K Troop transferred to the Presidio from one of the posts on Secretary Proctor's hit list for that spring: Fort Verde, located in central Arizona's mining and farming country near Prescott. The troop abandoned Fort Verde on April 23 and rode east through the barren Arizona mountains for two days before boarding railroad cars at Prescott for the ride north to the Presidio. That "march" to their new post in San Francisco covered a total of 889 miles—44 miles on horseback, 841 miles on three connecting railroad lines to Oakland, and 4 miles by boat across San Francisco Bay to the Presidio—all meticulously recorded in the troop's muster roll as if it were a pursuit of Apache warriors.[4]

Jug Wood's I Troop left Fort Huachuca a day after Troop K's departure from Fort Verde but arrived at the Presidio a day earlier, on May 26, due to Fort Huachuca's convenient location on a railhead. I Troop's march into California was almost entirely by train.[5]

The orders that sent Wood, Dorst, and their Fourth Cavalry comrades north to California and Washington State came from army headquarters in Washington, D.C. They were transmitted through the Division of the Pacific, headquartered in San Francisco, encompassing the states and territories of Arizona, New Mexico, California, Nevada, Idaho, Oregon, and Washington. Viewed from the bottom up, the chain of command extended from the Department of California (also headquartered in San Francisco) to the Pacific Division, thence eastward across the continent to army headquarters in Washington. San Francisco might open onto the Pacific, but an eastward-facing continental perspective still governed Old Army operational management.[6]

Even so, San Francisco exerted a centripetal pull all its own. Since the gold rush of 1849, it had mushroomed from a small port and trading post into the largest metropolis west of St. Louis, with a population of 299,000. Among other western cities, Denver ranked a distant second with 107,000 inhabitants. San Francisco's harbor teemed with ships from throughout the world, manned by crews of every nationality. New crewmen were recruited from the city's notorious Barbary Coast of saloons and brothels strung along the waterfront or perhaps from one of the twenty-six commercial opium dens publicized in an 1885 survey of city attractions. Some recruiters would not take no for an answer. The phrase "shanghaied" originated in San Francisco at about this time.[7]

The city's bustling seamy side was complemented by an equally hyperactive virtuous side. San Francisco served as the Far West's chief merchandising and financial center and its cultural hub. Local boosters called their metropolis the "Paris of America." Their pride and joy was the Palace Hotel on crowded Market Street. Meant to suggest an old-world palace, it had a central courtyard and carriage turnaround paved in marble under a glass-domed ceiling; an interior gallery and promenade on each of its seven floors; and rooms furnished in mahogany, teak, ebony, and rosewood, purified with filtered air, and linked to the front desk for messages by a system of pneumatic tubes. The lobby was packed with guests ranging from President Benjamin Harrison and playwright Oscar Wilde to scruffy miners and sharecroppers. Rudyard Kipling arrived from Britain via Asia and recorded his appalled impression: "In a vast marble-paved hall under the glare of an electric sat forty or fifty men; and for their use and amusement were provided spittoons of infinite capacity and general gape. Most of the men wore frock-coats and top-hats . . . and they all spat. They spat on principle." It was that jolting combination of

ostentation and crudeness that struck Kipling again and again in his encounter with a city where "money was everything." A recent history of
the American West called San Francisco "the brightest sun in the nineteenth century western universe." To an army wife visiting from Nevada
during that time, it was a "fairyland."[8]

Experienced Fourth Cavalry officers seemed less startled by what
they saw. Captain James Parker, whose Fourth Cavalry Troop B would
join those of Wood and Dorst at the Presidio in 1891, thought that San
Francisco was "like an overgrown mining camp or Deadwood City." But
he was pleased with "beguiling" entertainments not available in Deadwood, including the city's "excellent opera company." Lieutenant
Colonel Anson Mills arrived with his family to assume command of the
Presidio's new cavalry squadron near the conclusion of a career dating
back to the Civil War. He later recalled that "this large post, adjacent to a
very large and interesting city [with its] numerous balls, dances and other
amusements" was "the most enjoyable station we ever had." Taciturn Jug
Wood left no record of his personal impressions of San Francisco, or anywhere else, but we can assume he responded to it with a characteristic reserve that could only have been strengthened by his marriage four years
earlier to the daughter of a Protestant minister who apparently tried and
failed to be named Presidio post chaplain. Dorst, who arrived in the fall
of 1890, had a mixed reaction. He enjoyed the luxuries and entertainments, but he shared Parker's discomfort with disordered excesses
brought on by so much sudden wealth and the self-centered values that
sustained it.[9]

The contrast between fort and city could not have been greater. The
city's crowded streets throbbed with the grating noises of constant construction and the hurrying to and fro of tens of thousands of Americans
on the make. In early 1890, scarcely four hundred soldiers and a few dependents inhabited the 1,500-acre wooded, hilly, parklike fort fronting
the bay. The mounted troops of Wood and Dorst increased that number
to a little over five hundred in 1890, but they were quickly swallowed up
in the post's peaceful vastness. A colonel stationed at the Presidio in the
early 1880s wrote of long evening walks along a road "wholly in the
Reservation," up and down moonlit hills, "one moment commanding a
view of the bay, and the next looking off on the Grand Pacific." The San
Francisco–based commander of the Division of the Pacific at the height of
the California gold rush, Brigadier General Ethan Allen Hitchcock, wrote
in his diary: "Have driven out to the Presidio, and listened with delight
to the surf breaking on the rocks below—relief from the everlasting talk
about 'property,' 'water lots,' etc. Great God!"[10]

The beautiful post along the bay predated the adjacent city by many
years. It began as an adobe fort constructed by the Spanish army in 1776

to protect a nearby mission. It was taken over by Mexico when that nation achieved independence in 1821, then by the United States from Mexico in 1846, making it the oldest continually occupied military post in the United States. During the first century of its existence, its grounds were mostly sand dunes and grassland where cattle grazed.[11]

After the Civil War, the Presidio's army commanders launched an extensive landscaping program. Ornamental trees and flower beds sprouted along officers' row, lacquered cannon balls lined the post's myriad winding roads and paths, and forests of new trees blossomed everywhere. Beginning in 1874, the post was opened to regular public visitation and acquired a second identity as an army-run municipal park. In 1878, the Corps of Engineers developed a systematic landscaping plan. Remarks by the plan's chief author, Major William A. Jones, capture the urban side of the frontier army's mingling of aestheticism and scientism in its relationship with nature. For the Presidio's First Avenue entrance, Major Jones proposed:

> Clear away an opening with curved borders inside the gate, displaying grass and flowers. Thin out the trees along the border and fill in with a good many flowering peach trees and first in front of them a fringe of snowballs and lilacs. . . . Fill in the space on the right hand side of the road after entering with a dense growth of eucalyptus, so as to make the first part of the drive entering the reservation dark and somber. This will conduce a feeling of awe which will suddenly be contrasted strongly with a magnificent view of the Presidio, with the Bay and Mountains beyond. [Near the Central Avenue entrance, plant] Lilacs, Forsythia, fortuneie, Snowballs, Weigeia rosea, Sirea, California privet (for filling out clumps), Japan maples, Pink Hydranges pamculata, if they will grow. Get every variety of lipine in color that will be found and plant single colors in great masses on the ridges of the grassy slopes.[12]

In this manner, the post's sand dunes and grasslands developed into a civic arboretum. A special army request to Congress produced funds to build a nursery and plant trees. San Francisco residents soon caught the tree-planting spirit. For the inaugural local observation of Arbor Day in 1886, 4,000 schoolchildren and their mothers marched into the Presidio and dug 5,000 holes for tree slips while an army band played on the parade ground. During the first two years that Fourth Cavalry units spent on the post (1890–1891), more than 150,000 trees were planted—eucalyptus, acacia, cypress, pine, bamboo, and so on. By 1892 the Presidio commander, remarking that nearly a third of the formerly barren reservation was now covered with trees, expressed concern that if the Presidio forest kept growing at the same rate, there would be no place to drill. But the planting continued under orders from the chief of engineers and the Quartermaster Corps. Everyone was proud of the nature park that the army had created at the Presidio.[13]

The post's physical plant hardly approached the grandeur of its natural surroundings, but it was still mighty pleasant for cavalrymen coming from Huachuca and Verde. It centered around a grass-covered parade ground 550 yards long and 150 yards wide, surrounded on three sides by buildings and facing the sparkling bay. Additional facilities were scattered nearby (a quartermaster report in 1884 recorded a total of ninety-four buildings), leaving most of the 1,500-acre post in parkland. To a visiting soldier, everything was familiar but made more pleasant by the natural setting and a few distinctive touches, such as the terminus of the Presidio and Ferries Railroad providing transportation directly into the city, or the stately headquarters building inherited from the original Mexican army occupants whose assembly room with its white adobe walls and beamed ceiling doubled as a ballroom, or the library whose collection included twenty-one different newspapers and periodicals from across the nation.[14]

The presence of a regimental band and the largest complement of army officers of any U.S. metropolitan area—about forty-five on the post and another thirty at nearby installations—guaranteed a lively social life for officers as committed to ballroom dancing as they were to parade ground drilling. The post band played for outdoor marches and indoor balls and also gave classical concerts with equal facility. "The officers and ladies of the Presidio gave a delightful hop last Tuesday evening, in the hop room at the Post, which was handsomely decorated in honor of the occasion," a San Francisco newspaper reported in 1887. "Dancing was enjoyed until midnight . . . and light refreshments were served during the evening." Future Army Chief of Staff Leonard Wood kept a diary while serving as post surgeon in the early 1890s; it was filled with references to "hops" attended by him and his bride, the daughter of a U.S. Supreme Court justice.[15]

The only notable discomfort experienced by the Presidio's cavalry contingent during its tenure by the bay had to do with the post being under artillery command. Six companies of the Fifth Artillery Regiment (or batteries as they were called by artillerists), the regimental headquarters staff, and the regimental band lived on post, and the post commander was an artillery officer. Within the Old Army, there was continuous rivalry between artillerists and engineers, on the one hand, and cavalry and infantry on the other. The technically oriented engineer and artillery corps were considered "elite" services. West Point's top two or three graduates went into the engineers, the next few into the artillery, and the cavalry and infantry got most of the rest. But "line" officers of the cavalry and infantry stationed on the frontier looked down on artillerymen assigned to coastal defense stations in urban centers. It was cushy duty, "preferred by a certain element," politely wrote the Fourth Cav's hard-riding Captain James Parker. The cavalry's Presidio experience was exacerbated by the personality of the post commander, Lieutenant Colonel William Montrose Graham.[16]

When the troops of Wood, Dorst, and Parker arrived at the Presidio, Graham had been in the army for thirty-five years. A Civil War hero, he had since held numerous administrative positions and acquired an awesome rote knowledge of military regulations and a compulsive desire to apply them in every conceivable instance. "Possessing a strong personality, resentful of real and imagined military discourtesies," as a Presidio historian described him, he constantly provoked the equally strong-willed cavalry officers assigned to his post. The two sides fought many intense battles over army rules and regulations that, when considered as a whole in retrospect, revealed an intriguing side of Old Army life.[17]

"'Full' dress does not mean full dress in every particular save one or two," Graham wrote in one of his innumerable Post Orders, reprimanding the cavalry for overlooking a slight change he had made in the dress code for that day. Jug Wood's first personal run-in with Graham was over a reprimand Wood received for not wearing white gloves as required one fall day in 1890 under newly issued "Para. 2, Orders No. 161, Presidio of S.F. Cal." But Graham went too far when he tried to assign frontier campaigner Lieutenant Colonel Anson Mills responsibility for managing the post garden. Mills protested to the departmental commander, Brigadier General Thomas A. Ruger, an old friend from the front lines. On Ruger's orders, the garden was reassigned to an artillery captain. But Graham didn't back down. Soon afterward, he reprimanded Mills for not being at inspection at the proper time. Gradually, a grudging mutual respect developed between Graham and his cavalry adversaries. Graham was a martinet in some ways, but he also was an efficient post commander. And Fourth Cavalry officers were also strict taskmasters when their own troops stepped out of line.[18]

Reading through the scores of heated exchanges over seemingly trivial matters between the Presidio commander and his officer underlings, and among those officers themselves, a retrospective observer is struck less by the confrontations per se than by their ritual effect. They served to restrain and channel anger in a small community living in close quarters, thus avoiding the violent face-offs all too common in frontier communities. This was a wide open era, and these uniformed frontiersmen were all armed; yet they always went through channels and bowed to a moderating superior authority. When, during a typical exchange in late 1891, Graham blasted Jug Wood for repeatedly going over his head to a departmental headquarters more sympathetic to cavalry complaints, Wood delightedly forwarded Graham's comments up the chain of command, knowing he had caught Graham implying that the departmental commander was less than neutral. Graham took it on the chin from Brigadier General Ruger for that. But after apologizing obsequiously to Ruger, Graham nailed Wood again, for allowing the ground in front of his troop's stables to be littered with horse manure. Wood accepted the rebuke and chewed out his men, they cleaned up the mess, and the ritual-loving Presidio recovered the neat and peaceful parklike appearance that was the envy (and also a source of growing pride) of San Francisco.[19]

THE CAMPAIGN FOR YOSEMITE

Meanwhile, unbeknownst to the cavalrymen at the Presidio, a political drama was unfolding that would soon catapult them onto a national stage. Throughout 1890, complementary campaigns were pursued in Congress to establish two national parks in the Sierra Nevada about 150 miles east of San Francisco. One called for a park to protect California's most famous grove of giant sequoia trees. It was led by George W. Stewart, editor of the *Delta* newspaper in Visalia, a town near the proposed park site. Stewart shared the concern of other local citizens that sheep, cattle, and lumber interests would denude a potential income-generating tourist attraction and deprive farmers in the San Joaquin Valley of a vital irrigation watershed. Stewart's campaign won support from the nation's scientific community, including the California Academy of Sciences and the American Association for the Advancement of Science. The other campaign championed the protection of Yosemite Valley and its mountainous environs. Managed by Robert Underwood Johnson, associate editor of *Century*, the nation's most prestigious general interest magazine, this initiative occupied a higher public profile. Its most prominent public advocate, who also strongly supported the Sequoia cause, was the California naturalist John Muir.[20]

Muir was then fifty-two years old and already a legend. Botanist, geologist, farmer, carpenter, sawyer, mechanic, inventor, poet, publicist, budding political activist, he had settled in California in 1869 at the conclusion of a two-year botanizing expedition from Indiana through the southern states to Havana and westward by boat to San Francisco. Muir spent his first three years in California living a hermitlike existence in and around Yosemite Valley, "that most holy mansion of the mountains." He collected flowers and plants and corresponded with Asa Gray of Harvard and other prominent botanists, but turned down a professorship at Harvard. He collected geological data proving that Yosemite Valley had been carved by a glacier (contrary to prevailing scientific theory that it was created by a cataclysm) but turned down a professorship at the Massachusetts Institute of Technology. Ralph Waldo Emerson met him on a visit to Yosemite and tried to lure him out of his self-imposed isolation to Concord to meet "better people," but Muir declined.

Despite his recognized competence as a scientific researcher and his ties with intellectual leaders like Gray and Emerson, Muir seemed more interested in communicating his discoveries to the general public than to specialists. He began writing for popular journals headquartered in the East, recording his impressions with an unmatched blend of scientific precision, aesthetic sensuality, and spiritual veneration that immediately brought him national recognition. This description of a moment on Mount Shasta in *Harper's Weekly* in 1877 was a long way, in more ways than one, from Thoreau's placid Walden Pond or Emerson's musings on nature from suburban Concord, although it was very close to the thundering geysers of Captain William Ludlow's Yellowstone:

> Presently a vigorous thunder-bolt crashes through the crisp sunny air, ringing like steel on steel, its startling detonation breaking into a spray of echoes among the rocky canyons below. Then down comes a cataract of rain to the wild gardens and groves. The big crystal drops tingle the pine needles, splash and spatter on granite pavements, and pour down the sides of ridges and domes in a net-work of gray bubbling rills. In a few minutes the firm storm cloud withers to a mesh of dim filaments and disappears, leaving the sky more sunful than before.[21]

This was the worshipper of "wildness" (one of his favorite words) who, in San Francisco in the summer of 1889, held a fateful first meeting with associate editor Johnson of the *Century* at the Palace Hotel. Muir proposed that they abandon the hotel's "confounded artificial canyons" for Yosemite, Johnson immediately agreed, and in a few days they were camping out in Yosemite and laying plans for a national park.[22]

Yosemite Valley was already well protected in law but not in fact. On June 30, 1864, President Abraham Lincoln signed into law legislation that ceded federal lands encompassing Yosemite Valley and the adjacent Mariposa Grove of giant sequoias to the State of California to be managed as a state park. The legislation was drafted by Senator John Conness of California in response to requests from a few civic-minded constituents.

The new park would be run by a board of commissioners appointed by the governor of California. Although established as a state facility, Yosemite was the first federally *mandated* park. It set the stage for Yellowstone, the nation's first federally *managed* park and the first to be explicitly named a national park, which would be established in 1872.[23]

Yosemite's inaugural board of state commissioners included Frederick Law Olmsted, the great landscape designer who laid out New York's Central Park in the 1850s. Coincidentally, a year before Yosemite was created, Olmsted had moved from New York to California to manage the seventy-square-mile estate of retired army general and former U.S. senator John C. Frémont, whose estate was in Mariposa County, close by Yosemite Valley. Olmsted presented his fellow commissioners with a plan for the preservation of Yosemite Valley as a living "museum of natural science." He submitted it shortly before returning to New York in 1865. Olmsted's plan would have assured the park's maintenance in its natural state, but it was suppressed by other commissioners who felt it might hinder the park's development as a tourist attraction. From then on, it was all downhill for Yosemite Valley. The park commissioners and managers meant well, but they had no guiding concept for preservation, no coherent plan for development in any context, and no money. Ramshackle structures, refuse, and disruptive fences proliferated; trees were cut haphazardly; domestic animals destroyed grasses, shrubs, and wildflowers. Muir and a few fellow Californians campaigned for reform with minimal effect. Some favored turning the valley back to the federal government for administration. But Muir correctly perceived that state pride stood in the way of rescission to the federal government, at least for the time being. Yet something had to be done. Trekking through the valley during his backpacking trip with Robert Underwood Johnson, Muir lamented that it looked "like a frowsy, backwoods pasture."[24]

One night during that historic ramble, Johnson and Muir were sitting at a campfire in the Tuolumne Meadows in the mountains just beyond the valley, pondering Yosemite's gloomy future, when Johnson came up with an idea that quickly won Muir's support: Why not create a national park in the breathtaking lands surrounding Yosemite Valley that were also increasingly endangered by grazing, mining, and logging? It would be an important victory for preservation in its own right, and it would set the stage for eventual incorporation of the valley into the new national park. Johnson commissioned Muir to help lead the campaign with a series of articles for *Century*. Johnson would write complementary editorials and employ his considerable personal influence with movers and shakers in Washington.[25]

Johnson launched the campaign shortly after his return to New York from California. In January 1890, *Century* published his editorial calling for a Yosemite National Park in the mountainous region surrounding Yosemite Valley. The editorial was accompanied by solicited letters of support for the idea that would henceforth appear in *Century* on a regular basis, beginning with an eloquent open letter from Olmsted. But Muir procrastinated, despite repeated pleas from Johnson for his promised articles. Then, in March, Congressman William Vandever of Los Angeles introduced a bill to establish a Yosemite National Park based on the Johnson-Muir proposal. Vandever's park covered about 230 square miles, much less than Muir and Johnson wanted. That proposal, probably more than anything, mobilized Muir. He provided Johnson with written testimony for a congressional hearing on the Vandever bill in June, where Johnson appeared as a witness; and he finally wrote the promised articles, which appeared in the August and September issues of *Century*. Other national publications, including the influential *Nation*, had by then picked up the cause.

Finally, in late September, came one of those abrupt congressional actions that hinted at backroom maneuvering. The Vandever bill, which had seemed dead for that session, was suddenly resurrected. In the new version the park grew to 1,512 square miles, precisely as Muir had publicly proposed. The bill passed Congress virtually unnoticed (aided by a shrewd decision by Interior Secretary John Noble to identify the new park as a "forest reservation," which disarmed opponents of the national park concept), and President Benjamin Harrison signed it into law on October 1, a week after he signed another Vandever bill creating Sequoia National Park (also initially identified by Noble as a forest reservation). The Yosemite legislation included clauses that tripled the size of Sequoia to 250 square miles and created General Grant National Park for the four-square-mile grove of big trees near Sequoia's northwestern boundary. (The General Grant grove was subsequently incorporated into Sequoia and will henceforth, for convenience, not be cited separately.) It was a stunning triumph for public-spirited idealism.[26]

But commercial interests had made it happen. The boys in the back room who crafted the park bills in their final form and pushed them through were agents of the Southern Pacific Railroad. To California civic reformers, the Southern Pacific was the hated monopoly that manipulated state politics for the sake of a greedy few. The monopolists used John Muir's configurations to determine the size of Yosemite because the popular support he had mustered was useful to them in realizing their primary objective: to establish a Yosemite Park as a destination point for tourists using Southern Pacific passenger lines feeding into the area. For Sequoia, they had additional incentives. Protection of the Sequoia watershed would benefit irrigation farming in the San Joaquin Valley where the Southern Pacific had major agricultural investments, and the resulting expansion in farming would also mean expanded business for the railroad's freight lines. The railroad could even hire civic-minded citizens to pursue those objectives full-time within the company's larger profit-oriented framework, where strategically applied idealism meant big bucks.[27]

NOW WHAT?

It was one thing to create three giant federal parks and something else to run them. Federal laws crafted in Washington that limited exploitation of public lands commanded limited respect on the frontier. The new parks stirred a lot of hackles in a frontier state that owed so much, including San Francisco's glitzy veneer of urban sophistication, to a recent frantic clawing after gold that had chewed up and spit out huge chunks of the Sierra Nevada's breathtaking terrain.[28]

For many land-lusting Californians, the mere idea of taking 1,800 square miles of the Sierra Nevada out of fee-simple circulation seemed inconceivable. The indignation grew stronger the closer one got to Yosemite. Homesteading farmers, cattlemen, miners, and timber speculators claimed nearly 60,000 acres within the newly designated national park, and land promoters were active throughout the area. In Mariposa County, where Yosemite was situated, the *Mariposa Gazette* headlined "Repeal the Act" and condemned the park legislation as coming from "men who have no practical knowledge of this country or its resources." The *Tulare Valley Citizen,* in Tulare County near Sequoia, under the headline "No Park Wanted," berated the mysterious "few" who would rob the "many" of their "just rights" to tear up the mountains as much as they wished. (For the Sequoia region, local opposition was more than balanced by pro-park sentiment orchestrated by George Stewart's *Delta* in Visalia with strong support from irrigation farmers; but opponents were vocal.)

The *Delano Courier* in Kern County proclaimed: "We can ill afford to sacrifice the stock, lumber, and wood interests that some fine-spun theory had experimented on and proven of little value." "Anti-park" associations sprang up throughout the area. "The Anti-Park Association of Kern and Tulare counties, Delano branch, is the name of the organization formed at this point on Saturday last," read one announcement. Reported another: "The Porterville branch of the anti-park association is doing some active work and making commendable efforts to arrest the action of the government in withdrawing the timber lands from the market." Robert Underwood Johnson and his New York–based *Century Magazine* had little influence in this part of the woods.[29]

The mood in cosmopolitan San Francisco was not much better. "The United States has recently become imbued with a remarkable zeal for the preservation of California forests," began a sarcastic editorial in the *San Francisco Chronicle*. The *Chronicle* opposed park legislation "based on sentiment"—that is, love of nature. To simply "set aside great bodies of land" without "some element of sense and business about it" was, the *Chronicle* concluded, "unacceptable."[30]

But there was also momentum the other way. Early in 1889, a year before the Johnson-Muir campaign got going, the California state legislature had held hearings on a well-publicized twenty-two-count indictment delivered against the commission appointed by the governor to oversee the state park in Yosemite Valley. The indictment was principally the work of Charles D. Robinson, an artist whose lease granted by the commission to operate a studio in the valley had been revoked and (he claimed) his studio broken into and vandalized by park guardians under commission orders. Robinson's indictment charged the commission with "squandering and misapplying public moneys," "connivance" with some leaseholders against others, illegal contracts, illegal evictions, and blighting public lands. The state legislature heard testimony from Robinson and his allies. Most of them were disgruntled residents from the region in revolt against the local powers that be—the Yosemite "ring," Robinson called them. The Robinson camp charged that the "ring" was acting in collusion with the state commission. Although the legislative report exonerated the commission, the hearing testimony and other published reports made clear that the state park was loosely run and that, from nature's perspective, the valley had seen better days.[31]

The commissioners were still reeling from those charges when Johnson and Muir launched their public offensive in the *Century*. Johnson drew much of his information, often too much, from the abovementioned Charles Robinson, who saw the Yosemite ring everywhere. Even Muir grew concerned about his feverish ally. In a letter to Johnson, he reported an encounter in which Robinson "held me with his glittering eye . . . and held forth on the wickedness and woe of the Yo. and its affairs in grand devil-may-care right or wrong style and denounced my poor peeping letter on the valley with great vigor. . . . I quoted your favorite saying on the power of understatement in contentions of this sort." Robinson promised that the strident communications on Yosemite he was sending out in all directions would henceforth be submitted first to Muir for review—a promise that, Muir later reported, he ignored. Still, Muir added, he showed "diabolical industry" on Yosemite's good behalf.[32]

Another outspoken general in the *Century*'s army of verbal artillerists was George G. Mackenzie, a valley dweller whom the park compaigners viewed initially with suspicion. Mackenzie worked for the Washburn family, owners of the Yosemite Stage and Turnpike Company. The Washburns had a monopoly on stage and wagon services in the valley. In

Robinson's boiling and bubbling mental world, Mackenzie had to be part of the conspiracy run by the evil ring. Muir's scientific intellect and tolerant disposition kept him open to contrary evidence. Despite Robinson's remonstrations, he eventually came around to Mackenzie after receiving assurances from Johnson and reading Mackenzie's consistently reformist reports. But, as with so many other public disputes in those hurly-burly times, the Yosemite reformers continued to oscillate between clear-minded criticism and delusion.[33]

By the fall of 1890, one thing was certain: whoever got the park management assignment would, to put it mildly, have his hands full, between the park supporters Muir and Johnson had activated and then struggled to keep from going off the deep end; the embittered state commission; the various "rings" of political and business interests; the angry land claimants mobilizing in and around the new parks against the mysterious "few" who were pushing the "insane" park idea; and a generalized statewide suspicion of federal involvement in anything occurring within state boundaries, which notched up toward hostility and open resistance when it involved attempts at federal enforcement.

The murky plot thickened, if that was possible, with the arrival in San Francisco in early November of an unknown outsider who would have a major say in deciding who would run the park. He was Thomas J. Newsham, general land inspector of the Department of the Interior. Newsham had been sent to California by Secretary of the Interior John W. Noble on a dual mission. First, he was to recommend how best to govern the new national parks mandated by Congress. (Noble had renamed them parks from forest reservations after the enabling act passed.) Second, Newsham was ordered to respond to less publicized congressional legislation engineered by Robert Underwood Johnson. This bill directed the interior secretary to investigate and report to Congress on whether the Yosemite Valley granted to the State of California as a public trust in 1864 had been "diverted" from its civic purpose, "and if so," to recommend what steps should be taken to protect the public interest. That legislation implemented the other half of the Johnson-Muir strategy—to keep the pressure on the state administrators of Yosemite Valley in order to pave the way for its eventual incorporation into the new national park. Clearly, how the national park was managed would be crucial to the success of that campaign: If the yet-to-be-named federal administrators of the national park stood out in favorable contrast to state administrators of the valley, support would grow for incorporating the valley into a unified Yosemite National Park under federal administration.[34]

Newsham had been sent to California after a bombardment of communications on Yosemite from Johnson to his friend Noble. Johnson seemed to know everything that was wrong and everything needed to make it right. The interior secretary finally asked the *Century* editor to assemble a dossier for investigator Newsham. Johnson quickly forwarded a thick packet containing photographs documenting park abuse, with comments on the back of each by Robinson, newspaper articles critical of park administration, and a personal note with several "insider" tips on who could be trusted. Johnson recommended that Newsham not identify himself but instead gather his information on the sly because everyone in the valley (except, of course, Johnson's allies) had an axe to grind or a selfish interest to defend.[35]

On November 16, investigator Newsham entered the sanctuary of natural beauty and human intrigue that was Yosemite Valley in 1890 and was struck at once by both aspects. "I will not try to describe it, for nothing short of a hand and pen inspired by the Supreme Architect of the Universe could begin to depict the superb grandeur and wonderful beauty of this Valley and the surrounding country," Newsham wrote to his superior. That reverent opening was followed by a depressing catalog of manmade ills in the state-run valley. A companion letter dispatched the following day on the new national park surrounding the valley was equally depressing in its descriptions and outlook.

For the valley, Newsham wrote, "There is, as near as I can judge, fully one third of the floor of the Valley under fence, most under cultivation; some of the land is fenced with pickets, some with plank, some with old fashioned rails and some I regret to say, with barbed wire." Some of the fenced land was planted in barley or wheat, some in pasture. Newsham found large clumps of tree stumps on the valley floor from indiscriminate cutting for bridges, fences, and hotels, including their stables and other support structures. Newsham found "rude huts and hovels" occupied by hotel employees that were an "eyesore." Fences that the commission claimed had been removed were still standing. Those that were cut down were left stacked in "unsightly heaps." The state park was a mess.[36]

It could not be otherwise as long as the commission granted leases for tourism facilities without a development plan. Hotels and stagecoach lines in remote locations like Yosemite required pastures for cows, henhouses, stables, and other facilities for guests and personnel. When built on an independent ad hoc basis by competing individuals, lovers of nature though they all might be, the result was bound to be catastophic for nature's harmonies.

No one knew that better than James Mason Hutchings, the dean of Yosemite Valley publicists, whose association with the valley predated

Muir's first visit by fifteen years. Hutchings had been lured to California from England to hunt for gold. He failed as a gold digger but found his true calling as a journalist, initially editing a newsletter for miners. In 1855, he led the first party of tourists into the valley. In 1863, he settled there, ran various enterprises (from a sawmill to hotels) in the valley, and touted its wonders in scores of articles and a book before his death in a riding accident in the valley in 1902. Hutchings loved the valley as much as anyone. He opposed the commission's cronyism in granting leases and the more garish exploitations of valley dwellers, but he was enmeshed in a profit-oriented value system that limited his capacity to support the concept of preservation as it had evolved under Muir's aegis. Hutchings was, in effect, a prophet of another kind—a nature-loving homesteader, a precursor of the public-spirited pioneers on the suburban frontier who tried (still try) to limit development in the neighborhood.

At one point, Hutchings filed a lawsuit and pursued it all the way to the U.S. Supreme Court in an effort to uphold his claim to own land outright in the valley rather than merely lease it, without any apparent sense of where that effort to enshrine private landholding in the park (which fortunately did not succeed) might have led. The uncompromising valley moralist Robinson loved Hutchings for reasons having little to do with nature and everything to do with Hutchings's opposition to the monopolistic ring. Robinson wanted to give Hutchings administrative authority over the new national park in a ruling triumvirate that would also include Muir and Robinson. Since Muir lived elsewhere, that meant the complex transition to a 1,500-square-mile park would be managed by a paranoid artist and an entrepreneurial evangelist.[37]

They would have faced an immense and appalling task. "You cannot imagine the utter desolation and the untold injury done by sheep to the grass, flowers and undergrowth of the mountains and valleys, roads and trails of this country," Newsham wrote in his assessment of conditions in the new national park. In addition, hunters were killing at will, "taking nothing but the hides," to the extent that in a few years many species would be "extinct." Also, the park had no marked boundaries and only a few trails traversing it, with none serving to knit the park together as an independent entity. For practical purposes, outside of the lines on a map Yosemite National Park hardly existed. [38]

Newsham stayed on in San Francisco through much of December, gathering additional information for his reports on the valley and its environs. By the time he left, he was completely enmeshed in the self-enclosing world of Yosemite intrigue. Robinson was "radical," he reported, but "better posted" than anyone. Hutchings was "conservative" but a reliable source of the "truth." Stegman (the postmaster) was a "square man" who collected sequoia seeds. Archie Leonard was a good guide whose "only fault is drink." Mackenzie knew more about the Big Tree Grove than anyone, but he also was "too fond" of drink. And hovering over them all was a "monopoly" so powerful that, according to an Interior Department summary of one of his reports, "the Government will have to take charge of Yosemite to break [it] up." There were kernels of truth in Newsham's judgments, although they were traceable less to calculated conspiracy than to competing excesses of self-interest and self-righteousness without compensating self-insight. In these Yosemite wars, nature often seemed to serve merely as an outlet, a pretext, for compulsive conflict.[39]

After Newsham went home for Christmas, at the conclusion of a year of unremitting vituperation among all parties involved in Yosemite affairs, the state commission fired a final blast in its biennial report for 1889–1890. The report denounced the "despicable deception" of Robert Underwood Johnson and *Century*, and it fingered John Muir as Yosemite's chief despoiler. "The only organized destruction of the valley's forest was attempted many years ago," the commission announced, when Muir "logged and sawed trees for commercial purposes" for James Hutchings until Hutchings's sawmill was "finally suppressed by the state." (The reference was to Muir's brief stint as a sawmill employee during his 1869–1872 Yosemite sojourn.) Muir angrily denounced the report. It also brought cries of outrage from a group of faculty at Berkeley and Stanford who had rallied to the preservationist cause.[40]

And so the year of the campaign to create national parks in California ended in a final burst of bitter charges and countercharges, of visions of plots and counterplots, of honest "citizens" battling conniving "rings." It was ironic. Yellowstone, the nation's only national park until then, had been joined by two more beauties—Yosemite and Sequoia. Together, the new parks encompassed nearly 2,000 square miles extending through the heart of the Sierra Nevada, described by John Muir as "the most beautiful . . . landscape . . . I have ever beheld." Furthermore, run-down Yosemite Valley was now encircled by national parkland that made the valley ripe for federal administration if the Johnson-Muir plan worked out. But instead of discussion turning to the practical business of managing this magnificent prize, the moralistic conflict of personalities intensified. They could not stop themselves.[41]

Robinson, Mackenzie, Hutchings, Muir, and Johnson were fine crusaders, and their adversaries made fine villains for a prototypical American morality play. But if the Yosemite park idea was to acquire the broad-based community respect necessary for its long-term institutional survival, if the park's boundaries were to be marked out, its rugged terrain equipped with a network of trails and bridges contoured to their natural surroundings that would give it a bounded and integrated identity in fact as well as in name, a special class of administrators was needed. They would have to be aloof from bluster and intrigue, committed to converting the idealistic park concept into a workable reality, tough but fair, hardy, mobile, disciplined, accustomed to life on the trail, trained in mapmaking, surveying, and rural infrastructure development, capable of winning respect at the local level for an idea that challenged local interests and even local ideals. In sum, Yosemite administration required the rarest of combinations in that era of rampant individualism, social fragmentation, and hysterical paranoia—a disciplined team of technically skilled, trail-savvy, public-spirited, straight-talking mediators.[42]

Muir sensed it, but he lacked practical experience. Early in that tempestuous year of 1890, he took up the issue of Yosemite governance in a letter to Robert Underwood Johnson. Muir suggested that the new park surrounding the valley be governed by "a commission consisting of the President of the University, the President of the State Board of Agriculture, and the President of the Mechanics Institute," which would be a "vast improvement on the present [state] commission." At that point, the proverbial lightbulb probably switched on in Muir's head. Blue-ribbon boards were fine for running public associations and campaigns, but Yosemite had practical needs that could not be met by university presidents or an understaffed Interior Department, so Muir added this afterthought in his letter to Johnson: "Perhaps one of the Commissioners should be an Army officer." Johnson already had begun thinking along those lines. In his January editorial launching the Yosemite campaign, he suggested that park legislation include "an assurance of as capable administration in government as now characterizes the Yellowstone Park." The "capable administration" that Johnson sought to emulate consisted of two sixty-man troops of U.S. Cavalry.[43]

YELLOWSTONE'S EXAMPLE

When Yosemite National Park was established in 1890, the army already enjoyed a long, intimate relationship with the only other national park at the time, the Yellowstone "wonderland," as it was popularly known. The relationship predated by many years Yellowstone's establishment in 1872 as the first national park. Now also largely forgotten, the history and character of the Old Army's ties with Yellowstone add perspective to its Yosemite experience.[44]

The story begins in 1805 when the "Yellow Stone" was identified as the principal tributary of the Missouri River in a progress map sent to

Thomas Jefferson by army officers Meriwether Lewis and William Clark during their epic expedition across the continent. But Lewis and Clark skirted the river valley, leaving it to be "discovered," in a manner of speaking, in 1807 by John Colter, a member of the expedition who stayed behind to hunt beaver. (Human habitation of the Yellowstone first occurred about 12,000 years before Colter showed up, and as with most of the continent at the time of its discovery by Europeans, in 1807 the Yellowstone region was home to Indian communities whose complex cultures were in the eyes of most European intruders either invisible, simplistic, or depraved.) Colter's report of a fabulous land of bubbling springs and smoky geysers was dismissed as a trapper's tall tale. Even those who gave it credence called "Colter's Hell" a place to be avoided.

In 1819, the region was further undiscovered during a two-pronged expedition from St. Louis. The main body, under Colonel Henry A. Atkinson, set out to establish an army garrison at the mouth of the Yellowstone River. The other group, a "scientific corps of geologists, naturalists, artists and topographers" under Major Stephen A. Long, was ordered to explore the entire region. The Atkinson-led brigade of several hundred men in this oversized and undersupplied initiative (which included a custom-built fleet of five steamboats) had barely entered the Missouri River when it was forced to establish what is now Fort Leavenworth in order to ride out a bitter winter that cost more than one hundred lives.

Major Long's scientific corps of seventeen men continued on, however, and wrote a detailed report that buttressed Captain Zebulon M. Pike's earlier "Great American Desert" thesis—namely, that the headwaters region of the Missouri River offered little prospect for settlement and served best as a barrier to hostile intrusion from the west. This false impression may have saved Yellowstone for preservation by a later generation better prepared for that responsibility. White habitation for the next few decades was pretty much limited to itinerant trappers like Jim Bridger, whose confirming reports of a wondrous world of lakes, canyons, and geysers got the same unbelieving reception as Colter's.[45]

Then came the discovery of gold and silver in the 1840s. Continental visionaries took another look at the Great American Desert and saw Eldorado. Again the army was called upon to provide scientific information on natural topography. During 1859–1860, Captain William F. Raynolds led a military/civilian expedition on what a Yellowstone historian calls "the first organized exploration of what is now Yellowstone National Park." But despite having Jim Bridger as his knowledgeable guide, the weather and other circumstances prevented Raynolds from attaining his goal of eyeballing the rumored natural wonders. Moreover, the Civil War forestalled delivery of the expedition's report, with its enticing information on the lay of the land, until 1870. By then the vanguard of western "civilization" had transformed the area of southern Montana adjacent to the future park into a center of mining culture, inhabited by restless diggers, merchants, saloon keepers, missionaries, lawyers, dealmakers, and other frontier standbys.

This sudden growth in population, plus sheer curiosity about Yellowstone's rumored but still unsubstantiated wonders, plus railroad companies looking for exotic destinations for Eastern tourists, plus Montana entrepreneurs hoping to mine tourist gold—"a few years more and the U.P. Railroad will bring thousands of . . . sightseers and invalids from every part of the globe," wrote a Helena, Montana, newspaper in 1867—all this interest led inevitably to a sequence of expeditions that finally solved the Yellowstone mystery once and for all. In 1869, David E. Folsom and a couple of surveyor colleagues from Helena penetrated the valley and confirmed the reports of Colter and Bridger, but Folsom lacked influence or flair, and his dull reports got little circulation. The necessary ingredients came together in 1870 under the leadership of Montana's newly arrived surveyor general, a former Indiana congressman and commander of a volunteer regiment during the Civil War named Henry Dana Washburn. Washburn's expeditionary cohort included Nathaniel P. Langford, a former internal revenue collector of Montana who had resigned that post on the mistaken belief he would be named territorial governor. Langford cut a deal to publicize the expedition's discoveries through a series of lectures in the East under the sponsorship of Jay Cooke, a New York financier and owner of the Northern Pacific Railroad who envisioned steam-powered safaris into the Yellowstone wilderness. The other expedition member who would play a key role in creating the park was a young army lieutenant named Gustavus C. Doane, commander of the expedition's military escort provided at no charge by the War Department, along with army-issue tents and other equipment for the civilian participants.[46]

The fifteen-member Washburn party—nine prominent citizens of Montana and six soldiers—departed from Fort Ellis, Montana, on August 22, 1870, and returned a month later. It was by all accounts an extremely difficult journey. One member of the party was cut off and believed lost until he found his way back, nearly done in, thirty-seven days after he disappeared. But the explorers accomplished what they had set out to do. Rumors of a "wonderland" in the valley of the Yellowstone finally gained respectable confirmation and attention all the way to the nation's capital. Langford laid the groundwork by quickly heading east to deliver his previously contracted lectures, reaching Washington, D.C., in January 1871. The broadest and deepest impact was made by the expedition's official report prepared by Lieutenant Doane and submitted to Congress by the secretary of war in February 1871.

Called "remarkably thorough" by one historian, "masterly" by another, Doane's report provided the first "official information" on the region in a style that demonstrated great observational skill and literary flair. Many others would claim authorship of the Yellowstone National Park idea, but ultimately it would be an Old Army lieutenant whose graphic and poetic report brought Yellowstone's wonders to life who would become widely known and remembered as "the man who invented Wonderland." As for expedition leader Washburn, he literally gave his life for Yellowstone. He died shortly after his return from overexposure and exhaustion, with no idea that the influence of the "Washburn expedition" would be enshrined in history as opening the way for the establishment of the first national park.[47]

The back-to-back Langford lectures and Doane report created a sensation in Washington that was exploited to good purpose by Ferdinand V. Hayden, a government geologist based there who had accompanied Captain Raynolds in 1859. Hayden seized the moment to obtain a special congressional appropriation for a follow-up expedition in 1871. Meanwhile, the commander of the army's Chicago-headquartered Division of the Missouri, General Philip Sheridan, was so impressed by Doane's report that he ordered a follow-up military reconnaissance under Captains John W. Barlow and David P. Heap of the Army Corps of Engineers, marking the beginning of an extraordinary commitment by Sheridan that continued for fifteen years.

The Hayden and Barlow/Heap parties left Fort Ellis a day apart in July 1871. Both had army supplies and escorts, and they followed similar tracks. Most of the Barlow/Heap findings, including an invaluable collection of two hundred photographs, were lost in the great Chicago fire that occurred shortly after their return. Fortunately, Captain Heap had continued on to his home base in St. Paul with topographic and astronomical information that he used to make the first reliable map of the Yellowstone region, with sites marked according to their proper latitude and longitude. It was a perfect complement to Hayden's comprehensive report. The final push came from the Northern Pacific Railroad in concert with Hayden. At their urging, a bill modeled on the Yosemite legislation of 1864 was introduced in Congress in 1872 and passed with little opposition.[48]

Only one issue remained: who would manage this two million acres of forested mountains and canyons? The enabling act placed the park "under the exclusive control of the Secretary of the Interior," a seemingly reasonable choice considering Interior's responsibility for public lands— except that the agency had no experience managing a park, no personnel for it, no idea how to go about it, and no money. The authors of the park legislation had made their proposal palatable to congressional opponents of the mere idea of using land for anything but economic exploitation by presenting the park as a self-paying operation that would rely on income from leases granted to concessionaires. The concessionaires would, for their part, cash in on tourists ferried into the park by Jay Cooke's Northern Pacific Railroad, which was then rapidly building track westward toward his wonderland cash cow. That fantasy of geysers and dollars exploded a year later when the Northern Pacific went bankrupt during the panic of 1873, having progressed no farther than Bismarck in Dakota Territory. The Northern Pacific would resume its westward journey a few years later, with interesting results for Yellowstone, as we'll see.

During the interim, the usual motley crew of frontier entrepreneurs battled for a foothold in the park in advance of the Yellowstone "rush." The only official on-site restraint on their behavior came from that well-intentioned promoter of good paying causes, Nathaniel P. Langford, who had wrangled an appointment as park superintendent without salary. Langford was counting on his patron Jay Cooke bringing the Northern Pacific into the park, and with it tourists and leasors—in other words, money. After Cooke and his railroad went broke, Langford kept the superintendent's title but pretty much stayed away, while fruitlessly pleading a chicken-and-egg case with the Interior Department in Washington. In order to entice hotel operators who would also serve as protective "custodians" at the park's main points of interest, Langford wrote, Interior must first provide "such road improvement as will induce responsible persons to take leases," which, as he knew, the department lacked the means to do. There were indications that Langford was also working the other side of the street by questioning the "reliability" of those concessionaires willing to take a chance, in order to limit park activity until Jay Cooke could resume operations and make the park into his fiefdom as originally planned.[49]

So there it was—a park in name but hardly in fact, in many respects worse off than before. The publicity had brought tourists who tore up natural formations for souvenirs, entrepreneurs who required lumber, game, pastureland, chicken coops, hog sheds, and so on, in order to sustain the enterprises serving the thieving tourists, and poachers who sought game for the expanding adjacent populations of Montana and Wyoming. The national park and the nascent preservationist concept it embodied were going nowhere fast.

The U.S. Army sounded the alarm in 1875 from two complementary quarters. First came the Ludlow reconnaissance in the summer of 1875, under Captain William Ludlow of the Corps of Engineers. Ludlow led a small army detachment into the park on a mapping and surveying expedition. Two young graduate students from Yale's Sheffield School of Engineering, George Bird Grinnell and Edward S. Dana, came along to report on the park's zoology, paleontology, and geology. Grinnell, future editor of *Forest and Stream* and cofounder of the conservationist Boone and Crockett Club, would one day play a major role in defending the park. But the moment belonged to Ludlow, an intelligent and sensitive West Point graduate. As chief engineer for Dakota Territory, Ludlow had acquired a reputation for outspokennness the year before when he accompanied George Armstrong Custer on an expedition into the Black Hills and filed a separate report that, contrary to Custer's, downplayed rumors of gold in the area and urged that white prospectors be kept out and the region be reserved for the Sioux. Ludlow's Yellowstone report displayed a similar dissenting outlook in opposing unrestrained economic development. Although it revealed little that was new scientifically, its assessment of the purpose and status of the new park earned it a place as a pioneer conservationist work.[50]

Much of the report's descriptive power, and ultimately its political influence, derived from Ludlow's vivid contrasts between the natural environment and its human despoilers. In one instance he painted a reverent portrait of Old Faithful with its "little terraced pools, tinted with the most delicate shades of white, cream, brown, and gray, so soft and velvety it seemed as though a touch would soil them." This was followed by: "The visitors prowled about with shovel and ax, chopping and hacking and prying up great pieces of the most ornamental work they could find; women and men alike joining in the barbarous pastime." Descrying the "utter ruthlessness of these sacreligious invaders of nature's sanctuary," who were destroying or carrying away priceless "treasures of art and beauty," and also condemning the "wholesale and wasteful butchery" of the park's wildlife "for skins only," Ludlow saw only one way to ward off disaster. He recommended "the transfer of the park to the control of the War Department" until an effective civilian park service could be established.[51]

The Belknap expedition reached Yellowstone soon after Ludlow's. Although complementary in purpose, it had an entirely different character. William W. Belknap, secretary of war, led a group of military VIPs from Washington, D.C., to Yellowstone, most of the way in luxurious private railroad cars. They stopped briefly in Chicago to pick up a few members of Phil Sheridan's staff plus William E. Strong, an ex–Civil War general and the only noncareer officer in the group other than Belknap. Strong later published a lively account of this trip into the wilds where champagne and claret were served at dinner under the stars, and the explorers emerged from their tents in the morning to find their boots polished overnight by orderlies who also pitched their tents, cooked their meals, and cared for their horses. But this was luxury with a purpose. The army had supported the park's establishment, and Secretary of War Belknap wanted to personally investigate conditions in wonderland. The annual report of the War Department for 1875 included the text of Ludlow's report and a separate account by Belknap in which he described wanton destruction in the park and offered the services of the Corps of Engineers and the cavalry for its protection and administration.[52]

Interior declined the War Department's offer while doing nothing to correct the abuses that inspired it. During the five years from the park's establishment to Langford's removal by a new interior secretary in 1877, the park superintendent paid only two brief visits to the park he was charged with administering. The new interior secretary, the reformer Carl Schurz, fired Langford and brought in a talented and conscientious Ohio newspaper publisher and amateur scientist, Philetus W. Norris. Norris took the job for nothing—"Mainly," Schurz announced, "in the interest of science." The selection pleased the American Association for the Advancement of Science, which had joined the army in condemning deteriorating conditions in the park. Norris kept meteorological records, documented geyser eruptions, collected flora, and developed a working relationship with the Smithsonian. By 1879, Schurz was able to wean a $1,500 annual superintendent's salary from Congress as part of a first-time appropriation of $10,000 for park improvements. This funding enabled Norris to initiate a primitive trail and road construction effort that won praise from General Sheridan as a worthwhile beginning. But Norris was out of his political element. Ultimately, he was undone by a sequence of greedy machinations that he simultaneously resisted and joined without realizing the full implications of his actions.[53]

Norris's ensnarement began soon after he arrived. By then, the railroads were on the move again. From Dakota, the Northern Pacific under Henry Villard (replacing bankrupt Jay Cooke) had resumed its westward march. At the same time, the Union Pacific under Jay Gould was laying track northward from Ogden, Utah, with the announced intention of providing service into wonderland. It became a race between two storied Gilded Age plutocrats. Norris backed Gould's plan to build a spur eastward into the park from Virginia City, Nevada, which drew the ire of Montanans who felt a proprietary interest in the park and touted Villard's proposed Northern Pacific spur southward from Bozeman. Gold miners along the park's Montana border joined the chorus, calling for a branch line to their mines that would cut through the park, or, as a preferred alternative, they suggested chopping off a chunk of wonderland for their private use. Meanwhile, Villard was both pushing publicly for lines into the park and working behind the scenes with Wall Street mogul Rufus Hatch to establish a company that could steal a monopoly on Yellowstone services. It was all too much for Norris, who grew increasingly hysterical as "land sharks" (his phrase) tore at the helpless park and its equally helpless superintendent. Like Yosemite's Hutchings after him—in an atmosphere of intrigue that resembled Yosemite, that indeed constituted common frontier development practice—Norris fruitlessly sought to channel compulsive excess toward moderation. For his efforts, the Department of the Interior fired him. Poor Norris had already left the scene when the *New York Sun* published an article by a Northern Pacific official that, according to a prominent Yellowstone historian, "attacked the ex-superintendent in a manner so savage as to be almost unbelievable." Unbelievable now, but not when land-subsidized railroads often served as tools for economic speculation on a monumental scale. Norris's replacement, Iowan Patrick H. Conger, was the brother of a Michigan senator with a reputation as a "railroad man." [54]

In supporting these speculative wheelings and dealings, Interior was merely fulfilling its assigned mission to promote frontier settlement through the transfer of public lands to private ownership. Machinations involving railroads and Wall Street financiers were an accepted part of that patriotic process. Besides, Interior lacked financial resources, personnel, practical experience, and cultural imagination for administering a large national park. And the institutional character of Interior contained no protective feeling for the American land, no grounded sense of community with it, that might cause the agency's leaders to spontaneously rise up in the park's defense, no matter how powerful and predatory the threats might be. The only federal agency with those sympathies, and with the means and above all the will to take action in defense of nature, was the U.S. Army.

But what about the reputed connections of Old Army brass with big business, especially railroads? Those ties have been cited in making blanket condemnations of the Old Army as an agent of the powerful against the weak during the Gilded Age. But as with so much else about this misunderstood institution, its relationship with railroads and other business interests (with the natural environment, too, for that matter) belonged in a category that was distinctive within American culture and even within the professional culture of nineteenth-century armies of the Western world. In the Old Army officer corps, those with the closest personal ties to railroads were engineers, many of whom left military service to work for railroads at a time when civil engineers were in short supply. But these elitist army engineers were resented by Old Army infantry and cavalry troops of the line, whose interest in railroads was strategic. Railroads provided beneficial logistics and supply services to troops in the field as well as opportunities for troop concentration that permitted better tactical training; and on these grounds, they drew considerable line support. The railroads' various speculative schemes, with their frequent cash payoffs, meant much less. The most conspicuous badges of wealth in the Gilded Age—the great mansions with their imported statuary, the voluptuous vacations, the imported fashions, and other opulent accoutrements

easily transferable to civilian officials—were rungs on a ladder attached
to another building. To cash in big, Old Army officers would have to
abandon army life.[55]

For a bank clerk or an insurance salesman schooled in the patriotic
virtues of unleashed individualism, changing professions to make more
money produced few if any qualms of personal conscience and virtually
guaranteed an increase in community respect. But for Old Army soldiers,
it was quite different. They had been schooled in self-restraining and self-
deflating bonds of community that made the difference between life and
death in battle. Such ingrained awareness of the dangers of individualism
pushed to the point of community breakdown focused the imagination in
ways foreign to civilian entrepreneurs for whom social fragmentation
was a way of life. Faced with the temptations of individual wealth, Old
Army officers played the game, but rarely to the point of excess so common in the civilian community. They held back not because they found it
morally bad in the commonly accepted sense but rather because it conflicted with civic virtues derived from another source: for Old Army officers, individuality was a subordinate function of community, community
was a matter of individual life and death, and the bonds of national
community incorporated the American land.[56]

No one illustrates that environmentally protective anti–big business
attitude so dramatically with regard to Yellowstone than—of all people,
by current mythmaking standards—hell-for-leather Phil Sheridan. Sheridan's contributions to the park's initial establishment, and then to its protection from early despoilment and exploitation, were monumental.

In 1869, Sheridan was named head of the Division of the Missouri,
the army's largest command. The division extended from Illinois westward into Montana and southward into Texas and was headquartered in
Chicago, the nation's railroad capital. The sybaritic Sheridan enjoyed
many an evening of culinary excess with the city's railroad barons. But
they never bought him (he died a poor man) or undermined his judgment when the public interest was at stake. At one point, Sheridan's social friends at the Texas and Pacific Railroad asked to have forts guarding
the Texas northern frontier moved southward nearer the railroad line, on
the pretext of guarding settlers. Their real objective was to draw unwit-
ting settlers toward their railroad and charge high prices for railroad-
owned land, then pick up the land the settlers left behind for next to
nothing with a view toward its speculative development. Sheridan saw
through the scheme and angrily refused to use the army to "intimidate"
settlers into giving up lands "which in that case may ultimately come into
the hands of the railroad, or to other speculative monopolies."[57]

The plutocrats who drew Sheridan's greatest ire were the powerful
railroad barons and Wall Street investors who sought to extend rail lines

into Yellowstone and monopolize its concessions. Langford sold out to them; Interior caved in to them. Sheridan fought them continuously for more than a decade, first from Chicago, then from Washington after he was named the army's commanding general in 1883. And he defeated them.[58]

Sheridan's central role in creating Yellowstone National Park and preventing its early collapse began in 1870–1871, when he authorized an escort and supplies for the pivotal Washburn expedition, ordered the follow-up Barlow/Heap expedition of the Army Corps of Engineers, and provided an escort and supplies for the parallel expedition led by the civilian geologist Ferdinand V. Hayden. The park proposal growing out of those forays drew Sheridan's enthusiastic support. After the park's establishment and rapid deterioration, he supported proposals for War Department assistance made by Ludlow and Belknap that the Interior Department rejected. He closely followed events afterward, applauding Superintendent Norris's efforts while growing increasingly concerned over reports that the park was too much for Interior to handle. By 1880, close to 10,000 unpoliced visitors were streaming into the park annually, many of them commercial hunters. They were stripping the park of wildlife and natural artifacts. "Every tourist [wrote a Yellowstone historian] seemed to be a vandal throwing stones, sticks, branches, stumps, garbage, and clothing into the geysers and hot springs. . . . Forest fires blazed out of control, often the result of campfires deserted while still burning. People rolled boulders down the precipitous walls of the Grand Canyon of the Yellowstone. Firewood was fetched wherever available and whenever needed." There was no public authority, and no public ethic for visitors to internalize.[59]

In 1881, Sheridan took the bull by the horns. After reviewing a depressing assessment by his aide de camp whom he had sent on a reconnaissance into the park, he led a military expedition of 150 men and three hundred horses and mules into Yellowstone. It was part investigation, part park improvement mission, and part publicity ploy for greater protection. Expedition members cut the first trail along the Snake River from Jackson Hole to Lake Yellowstone—the "Sheridan trail"—that served as the main southern entry into the park until a road was completed over it in 1895. Along the way, Sheridan interrogated everyone he saw. He was appalled at the reports of despoliation and wildlife slaughter.

The worst news came from the railroad construction superintendent who hosted him on a ride on a work train to Billings, Montana, twelve miles beyond the park's border. The Northern Pacific had hatched a Yellowstone Park Improvement Company, under the management of Wall Street financier Rufus Hatch. The new combine had won the support of the acting interior secretary for a plan to obtain illegal leases to large tracts surrounding all the park's principal natural attractions and exclusive rights to operate concessions on them, a monopoly of 4,400 acres of prime parkland with virtually no rules of restraint on its development. This proposal was what Superintendent Norris had been helplessly screaming about. "The improvements in the park should be national, the control of it in the hands of an officer of the government," an angry Sheridan wrote in his report of the expedition. Again, he offered troops to protect nature. He also drew up a plan to expand the park by 3,000 square miles, which he included in his published report, to keep miners and other developers at a safe distance while also incorporating the habitat of Yellowstone's wildlife, which extended beyond the boundaries of the existing park. Shortly afterward, he carried his Yellowstone campaign to Washington when he was named commanding general of the army.[60]

From Washington, Sheridan pursued two main goals: protect Yellowstone against uncaring despoilers and conniving monopolists and expand its boundaries. He orchestrated the "Greater Yellowstone Movement" to implement his park expansion proposal, winning endorsements from the American Forestry Association and other scientific groups and leaders, sportsmen clubs, and especially the resourceful George Bird Grinnell whose *Forest and Stream* served as a pulpit for Yellowstone protection and expansion. In January 1883, Senator George Vest of Missouri, chairman of the Senate Committee on Territories and a consistent park supporter, introduced legislation that incorporated most of the ideas Sheridan espoused, including park expansion, outlawing monopolies, and army protection; but the bill stalled.

Meanwhile, Henry Villard's Northern Pacific launched a lobbying effort to build a spur line into the park. As part of that effort, the railroad's Wall Street front man, Rufus Hatch, seemed on the verge of obtaining the concession monopoly for the Yellowstone Improvement Company whose prospect had outraged Sheridan two years earlier. To build support for their schemes, Villard and Hatch organized separate VIP expeditions into the park for the summer of 1883—government officials, newspaper publishers, dignitaries from London, Paris, and Vienna, a total of nearly four hundred power brokers cavorting in wonderland on a scale of luxury fit for a maharajah. The awed editor of a local newspaper wrote, "We seem to live in an odor of greatness." Sheridan didn't like the smell of it. He organized a counterexpedition that included Senator Vest and other congressmen, cabinet members, and President Chester A. Arthur. The ensuing publicity garnered by the Sheridan group gave Vest the momentum he needed to block the railroad spur line and other schemes to reduce or even eliminate federal control of the park, including angry pronouncements by anti-park congressmen that the government was not meant to "raise wild animals" and should get out of "show business"—that is, close down the park, forget about environmental preservation, and concentrate exclusively on unloading federal lands for private development fast.[61]

Park defenders won that battle, but they were losing the war for Yellowstone's enduring protection because of the Department of the Interior's mismanagement, susceptibility to manipulation by business interests, and stubborn refusal to accept offers of support from the army. In 1883, frustrated park supporters in Congress succeeded with a proviso that $29,000 of the park's $40,000 annual appropriation be used for park improvements carried out under the direction of an army engineer. Congressional appropriators added the suggestion that Interior reconsider accepting the army's offer to protect the park with troops. By then, Norris had been replaced as park superintendent by Patrick Conger, the brother of the Senate "railroad man." Conger surprised everyone, however, including many of his original backers, by opposing the railroad schemes. But like ex-superintendent Norris, his superiors in Washington ignored him and continued to work with the powerful railroads. Eventually, they dumped him. In the president's cabinet, on Yellowstone matters it came down to a battle between War and Interior.[62]

Sheridan had won a beachhead with the 1883 legislation requiring an army engineer to administer Yellowstone road and bridge construction. He lost no time in appointing First Lieutenant Daniel C. Kingman, a thirty-one-year-old honors graduate of West Point stationed at the Omaha headquarters of the army's Department of the Platte. Kingman was detailed from the War Department to the Interior Department with orders to report to the secretary of the interior, whose approval would be required for everything he did in the park. Kingman followed his instructions to the letter. But he also knew that he had Sheridan looking over his shoulder; that he was the first army officer to serve in a national park in an administrative capacity; that he had been sent as part of an effort to save the park; and that every day he would be setting precedents for national park governance. Shortly after arriving on the scene, Kingman let all parties know where he stood by warning that if the park should "become the resort of fashion, if its forests are stripped to rear smooth hotels; if the race course, the drinking saloon, and the gambling-table invade it; if its valleys are scarred by railroads and its hills pierced by tunnels, then it will cease to belong to the whole people and will be unworthy of the care and protection of the National Government." Yellowstone's administrators had a duty, Kingman said, to reject exploitation and develop policies and rules designed "to keep the park as nature made it."[63]

Kingman's assignment was to repair run-down roads and bridges under Interior Department direction. But since there were hardly any roads or bridges in the park and no Interior Department plan for laying them out, Kingman plunged ahead on his own, guided only by his personal responses to the new national park concept. He explained to his civilian superiors that the new road system would be "winding, following the valleys and avoiding the hills, thus by its short views ahead giving the tourist a sense of expectancy, instead of treating him to the long perspective of a monotonous roadway ahead of him." In selecting building materials, he would avoid cutting down trees and rely on wood from an 1882 timber burn. Following those self-imposed guidelines, Kingman spent four years laying out a road system that would remain unchanged in its basic outlines and continuously admired for its environmentally sensitive design to this day and that would serve as a model for future park roadways nationwide. He also joined Conger in protesting exploitive plans for railroads and concession monopolies.[64]

Interior officials couldn't touch Kingman (who went on to become chief of army engineers), but they could get rid of the disappointingly antidevelopment Conger. The new man appointed in 1884, Robert Emmett Carpenter, was a small-time politician on the take who brought national park administration to a new low. His pathetic career reached its climax during a trip he made to Washington in 1885 to lobby for cutting off part of the park as part of a scheme to steal mineral deposits believed to be on park land. The plan called for Carpenter to telegraph his cocon-spirators in Montana as soon as the bill passed so that they could rush in, stake their claims, and pay him off. Everyone knew about it (such schemes were so blatant in those days that they seem in retrospect almost like parodies), and it blew up in his face. This occurred at a time when a well-meaning effort initiated by Carpenter's predecessor to police the park with a team of ten youthful and inexperienced "assistant superintendents" was attracting mounting public ridicule. The governor of Montana called this motley crew as "useful in protecting game . . . as a Sioux Indian would be in charge of a locomotive." They meant well, but they were trying to enforce a concept that hardly anyone understood, much less respected, in a remote frontier region where civil authority was, to say the least, difficult to exercise. In 1886, a fed up Congress cut off all funds for Yellowstone administration, leaving the interior secretary with two choices: abandon the park or hand it over to the army as authorized by Congress and persistently ignored by Interior.[65]

On August 20, 1886, Troop M, First U.S. Cavalry, under Captain Moses Harris, took command of Yellowstone National Park with orders to report to the secretary of the interior. Captain Harris was a hardened twenty-four-year army veteran of many western campaigns who had won a Medal of Honor in an assault on Lee's troops in Virginia during the Civil War. As ordered, he established camp for his fifty-man troop near the park's principal attractions, its geysers. In a sign of things to come, he picked the camp site carefully, reporting to the interior secretary that it was in woodlands out of sight of the geysers so as not to interfere with the view, a spontaneous yet aesthetically based choice that was all the more impressive when compared to the choices then being made in civilian-run Yosemite Valley in California.[66]

Harris had no training in park governance (who had?), but he knew about life on the frontier. He was fair-minded yet hard as nails. He wrote to his civilian boss in Washington that Yellowstone's problems came from "a class of old frontiersmen, hunters and trappers" who inhabited the park's immediate vicinity, and he went after them with armed patrols. He hunted down poachers, kicked out "professional tramps," some of them wanted criminals using the park as a refuge, ordered ramshackle hotels torn down and rebuilt to decent standards, attacked monopolists, and delivered a barrage of regulations—from a ban on selling "taxidermic specimens" (i.e., illegally massacred wildlife) at park hotels to "uniform" transportation rates for unknowing tourists regularly swindled by local stagecoach entrepreneurs. It amounted to a parkwide sobering up after a fourteen-year binge. Harris was probably the harshest park commander Yellowstone or Yosemite would ever have, but he was honest, conscientious to the point of obsessiveness, and apparently the right man at the right time for turning around a very bad situation.[67]

With the arrival of Harris's troop in 1886, Sheridan's fifteen-year battle to create Yellowstone National Park and secure its future was effectively won. The park would be expanded as Sheridan proposed, and army troopers would protect it until the civilian park service he had also proposed could be established, which did not occur until 1916. It is unpleasant to imagine the outcome of the Yellowstone experiment without the army holding the line there for thirty years.

Sheridan was not alone in fighting for Yellowstone, by any means. Senator Vest probably deserves the most credit among the park's many champions. But Sheridan stood out if only because he had no professional reason to be involved and plenty of reasons not to be. Unlike Vest, the chairman of the Senate Committee on Territories, no public position on the park was expected of Sheridan one way or the other. Yet, unbidden, he spoke out strongly against some of the most powerful economic and political interests of his time and backed up his words with actions, repeatedly committing federal resources to the park's defense that were otherwise unavailable. The park had its executive branch sympathizers, notably in the U.S. Geological Service, but USGS had no spare manpower or money and no experience in frontier administration. Almost singlehandedly, Sheridan filled a conservationist power vacuum in the executive branch of government, and, to that considerable extent, he probably saved the park and the nascent preservationist idea it embodied. His most comprehensive biographer, after reviewing how much effort and conviction Sheridan put into Yellowstone with no other motive than a soldierly love of the land, concluded that it "represented his finest hour and greatest achievement." Needless to say, it is also the least remembered.[68]

THE YOSEMITE DECISION

But back then, in 1890, the army's saving role in Yellowstone was well known, as were Interior's limitations. Indeed, a Yosemite role for the army was one point on which the California state commission agreed with its "despicable" adversaries. The same commission report that lambasted John Muir and Robert Underwood Johnson joined them in calling for an army presence in the new national park: "The State of California [should] take measures to induce the Federal Government" to station two companies of U.S. Cavalry in the new national park, the commission recommended in its 1890 biennial report.[69]

Even the Interior Department had revised its position after viewing the army's success in Yellowstone and experiencing the deference to civilian authority of army park commanders. Special investigator Thomas Newsham's distressed report on his initial visit to Yosemite in the fall of 1890 opened with these words: "The first and most urgent need for the preservation of the National Yosemite Park is a strong cavalry force." Interior Secretary John Noble made it unanimous: after obtaining the ready agreement of Secretary of War Redfield Proctor, Noble wrote to President Benjamin Harrison on December 1 formally requesting that cavalry troops be assigned to the new national parks in California. He requested that they "send out scouting parties through all the vast region now within the boundaries of the [Yosemite] national park . . . to prevent timber cutting, sheep herding, trespassing or spoliation of the park in any particular." He added that "the good effect of such a [cavalry] force [for Yosemite] would result as much from the appearance of authority and power to enforce the orders and rules established as from actual arrests that might be made." The interior secretary foresaw a long-term commitment for the cavalry assigned to the California parks, and he urged that the federal government "make their quarters so substantial and comfortable" that they would be willing to remain the whole year.[70]

Noble also apprised Robert Underwood Johnson of his cavalry inclinations in a letter suggesting he had made up his mind on the army even before hearing from Newsham. "As soon as my general inspector reports," he wrote, "it is my intention to write the President" requesting a "cavalry guard" for Yosemite and another for Sequoia. Noble advised Johnson that he had already consulted with Secretary of War Proctor, who promised full cooperation, so that "if I request it, the force will be soon on hand."[71]

On December 23, 1890, President Harrison made it official with a directive to Secretary of War Proctor. The directive, which came in a written communication from the president's private secretary, flowed into Old Army channels according to regulations. It collected endorsements as it wound down the chain of command, going from Proctor to the Army's commanding general, Major General John M. Schofield, for his recommendations. Schofield's crisply worded "1st endorsement" marked the entry of a new and different element into the overheated Yosemite melodrama. The commanding general recommended that the commander of the Division of the Pacific in San Francisco "be instructed to select two troops from the regiment of Cavalry serving in that Division, commanded by discreet officers, to discharge the duty herein indicated." He further suggested that "this selection be made without unnecessary delay, so that the names of the officers selected may be reported to the Secretary of the Interior" for him to promptly relay instructions that would permit their timely deployment; that the troops camp out in the parks during summer and autumn when they were most needed; "and that the commanding officers [of the troops] report after sufficient observation and experience whether it will be advisable and necessary to construct quarters and other buildings with a view to the occupation of the parks during the winter." On January 6, 1891, Proctor notified Noble that two cavalry troops would be assigned to the parks as recommended by Schofield. On January 13, Proctor incorporated Schofield's recommendations in his "2nd endorsement" of the presidential order and had it forwarded to Division of the Pacific headquarters in San Francisco.[72]

The secretary of war added a personal addendum to Schofield's call for "discreet officers." The park commanders will "meet and have to deal with large numbers of visitors and these qualities are particularly necessary," Proctor wrote. He wanted the names of the two troop commanders selected by the Pacific Division commander forwarded to the War Department, accompanied by a personal assessment, before a final decision was made. On February 12, after receiving, reviewing, and approving the division commander's recommendations, Proctor notified Noble of the selections. Proctor told the interior secretary he would be getting "two of the best cavalry officers in the service." Their names were Abram E. Wood and Joseph H. Dorst.[73]

CHAPTER FOUR
Captain Wood Starts a Park

The announcement that the new Yosemite National Park would be run by armed soldiers confirmed local suspicions that there was more to this federal scheme than met the eye. To take 1,500 square miles of American land out of economic circulation for alleged aesthetic purposes made no sense. There had to be another reason. The *Mariposa Gazette* was convinced of it. The Yosemite area included "untold millions" in not only gold and silver but also "marble, limestone, granite, slate" that in their "natural condition" a tourist "will not be able to see"; that is, unless converted into products for the marketplace, nature's "wealth" of beauty would be invisible. Why assign soldiers to stifle free enterprise? Obviously, the park announcement was a "false pretense to cover up the real object of the scheme." The "cold-blooded conspirators . . . whoever they are" intended nothing less, the *Gazette* concluded, than the "extinction" of agrarian capitalism in America. Yosemite National Park was a communist plot so massive that it included the United States Army.[1]

But one need not wholly give way to fantasy, which in that time and place could be the conventional mode of communication, to feel legitimately concerned about the federal government's startling commitment to park enforcement. Whereas Yellowstone was largely unsettled except for Native Americans (whose reality was not denied, merely ignored), the area within Yosemite National Park had been collecting white settlers since the 1850s when Mariposa was the headquarters city for the "Southern Mines" of the California gold rush. Much of the gold had been carried away. The current population in the mountainous Yosemite region consisted of farmers, cattle ranchers, and a few ever-hopeful miners. There were also logging interests filing claims (with increasing frequency in the 1880s) in anticipation of timber sales to railroads. These homesteaders and absentee owner/speculators were joined by sheepherders whose "hoofed locusts," as John Muir called them, ranged freely over the Sierra Nevada. By the time Yosemite National Park was created in 1890, nearly 60,000 acres within its boundaries had been claimed for one entrepreneurial purpose of another. In comparatively unsettled Yellowstone, the challenge was to keep outsiders in line; in Yosemite, the far more complex challenge was to deal with land claimants who viewed the new administrators as intrusive outsiders.[2]

Furthermore, hunters inside and outside Yosemite's boundaries were far more legalistically assertive about their "rights" than the Shoshone in

Yellowstone, and their biblically inspired imaginations could be a lot wilder than "uncivilized" Indians. Reptiles were near the bottom of the list of dangerous animals inhabiting the park, but not in the minds of some white residents. One Mariposan petitioned Congress to repeal the park's ban on hunting because Yosemite was a "monster den of deadly reptiles and devouring wild beasts" that threatened to "overrun our commonwealth." Reptilian imagery reappeared in a letter to Interior Secretary Noble from a resident of Wawona, on the edge of the park, who claimed that the park bill reduced valuable land to a "wilderness" inhabited by "wild beasts and reptiles," and if hunting were banned, visitors would soon need "an armed escort" to fight off these demonic predators.[3]

Not surprisingly, reptiles also populated the imaginations of more domesticated local park supporters, such as Yosemite artist Charles Robinson, for hunting was not a prerequisite for such imagery, only an overexcited moral sense. Robinson and fellow valley moralist George Mackenzie saw the cavalry winding up as agents of the evil "ring." "The Washburn crowd" will make sure that the cavalry are "misled, perplexed, discouraged and muddled," Robinson warned Interior Secretary Noble. Apparently unaware of the state commission's call for cavalry for the new park, Mackenzie told Noble he was "glad" that he could cite the commissioners "whenever I shall begin to attack the military establishment."[4]

Robert Underwood Johnson, a strong army supporter, struggled to bring his volatile allies on board in a letter to Noble that illuminated the probable cause of their hostility: their revolution had been a moral triumph but a material failure. They needed paying jobs. Johnson proposed to Noble, and also to Robinson and Mackenzie, that the revolutionaries find employment with the cavalry as "timber agents." On Johnson's advice, Robinson asked Noble for a letter of introduction to the military commander, grudgingly, after advising Johnson that he would remain on "watch" at Yosemite after the troops arrived. Mackenzie told Johnson he was "satisfied" with the *Century* editor's endorsement of the cavalry, but he also wrote Noble that he would withhold final judgment until after he had observed them in the park, where he would hover over them like a "winged angel." Deadly reptiles and winged angels: a peculiar wilderness of mind was gearing up for the arrival of the uniformed agents of satanic forces, "whoever they are."[5]

1891: THE FIRST CAMPAIGN

On January 27, 1891, the commander of the Fourth Cavalry squadron at the Presidio in San Francisco, Lieutenant Colonel Anson Mills, wrote to Interior Secretary Noble for guidance. Mills advised the secretary that

Troops I and K under his command "have been designated as suitable Troops to constitute the guard requested by your Department for the protection" of certain "Big Tree" parks in the Sierra Nevada. "Will you kindly send me a copy of the late laws, creating the parks," he asked, "with a map or description of the lands embraced in each?" Obviously, Mills knew next to nothing about his squadron's new assignment. Two months later, with scheduled departure only a few weeks away, he was appealing to departmental commander Brigadier General Thomas H. Ruger for an on-site reconnaissance. He still hadn't heard anything about his assignment from Interior.[6]

While Mills tried unsuccessfully to find out what was going on, troop commanders Joe Dorst and Jug Wood went to work. They were used to a government that grew confused when it came to policy implementation. Although they were still in the dark as to their precise assignment, they knew their troops would be camping out in the mountains for six months. Presidio quartermaster records for the early months of 1891 show repeated requests from two officers bound for the Sierra Nevada who knew what they wanted: pack mules, wagons, tentage, utensils, rations, packing crates, "tools and rope for the picket line."[7]

Even Presidio commander Graham laid aside his disputes with the cavalry and went to bat for them. He wrote department headquarters that Jug Wood's I Troop was down to one officer—Jug Wood. Within a few weeks, I Troop got two more: First Lieutenant Alexander Dean, to serve as second in command, and Second Lieutenant Milton Davis, a young man fresh out of West Point who would leave a strong imprint on Yosemite history. Graham also requested an additional cavalry troop for the Presidio to "meet the necessity for some cavalry at this post at all times." The post commander liked using mounted troopers as honor guards for visiting dignitaries. (In April, Wood and Dorst provided honor guards during visits by Secretary of War Redfield Proctor and President Benjamin Harrison.) Graham specifically requested and got Fourth Cavalry Troop B, commanded by Captain James Parker, who happened to be Graham's cousin. Parker, an old comrade of Wood and Dorst, was a graduate of both West Point and the Ranald Mackenzie school of leadership. His troop had been assigned to special duty at Fort Myer, Virginia, just outside Washington, D.C. Like a good cavalryman, Parker recorded the distance of B Troop's subsequent cross-country "march" by train to the Presidio—3,212 miles in an amazing six days.[8]

On May 1, the final countdown began: the Department of California issued Special Orders #38, directing Troops I and K to proceed to Yosemite, Sequoia, and General Grant National Parks for an anticipated duration of about six months under canvas or on patrol. Preparations were by then nearly complete. A week earlier, Wood had submitted a report to post commander Graham listing all his equipment and requesting that it be inspected prior to departure on May 14. On May 9, Wood and Dorst asked that their troops be excused from post drills and other duty to complete final inventorying and packing. Reverting to form, Graham denied the request.[9]

On May 14, on schedule, Wood and Dorst led their troops out of the Presidio. Standard procedure called for them to form in a column and march due east into the Sierra Nevada. They would do that on future departures. But this year, because they were running late and knew next to nothing about what awaited them, they headed into San Francisco and loaded their horses and equipment onto Southern Pacific railroad cars. Late the following afternoon, after descending into the parched San Joaquin Valley and changing trains at Madera, Wood's I Troop debarked at the town of Raymond, 198 miles from San Francisco and about 40 miles southwest of its Yosemite destination. (Dorst's K Troop continued southward beyond Madera to get closer to its assignment at Sequoia.)[10]

Jug Wood did not know it, but the transfer point at Raymond served as an outpost of the notorious Yosemite "ring." The town was the product of an alliance between the Southern Pacific Railroad and the Yosemite Stage and Turnpike Company headed by Henry Washburn, Yosemite's most successful entrepreneur. Washburn's story typified the settlement process in the Sierra Nevada in the post–gold rush era. He was preceded by two brothers who emigrated from their home in Vermont to Mariposa in the 1850s in quest of gold. Unsuccessful as miners, they turned to commerce. Three other brothers, including Henry, joined them from Vermont. By the 1880s, Henry was known as Mariposa County's "transportation king." He and his partners (family members and friends) either constructed or bought out the private roads and stage lines serving the popular "southern route" into Yosemite. This route funneled traffic from the county seat at Mariposa into Wawona, about twenty-six miles south of the state park and eight miles north of Yosemite's Mariposa Big Tree Grove of sequoias that also drew many visitors. The Washburns linked their stage route with the railhead at Merced that brought tourists north from Los Angeles and San Diego. They established another junction at Madera that handled the eastward trade from San Francisco. Competition from two northern wagon routes led Washburn to lobby the Southern Pacific for still another rail junction closer to Wawona to shorten the stage ride; and Raymond was born, just like that, in 1886.[11]

By 1891, when Jug Wood arrived, the town had grown from a tent city into a typical frontier urban agglomeration of dirt streets and rickety wooden buildings, dominated by the Southern Pacific station, four hotels (the largest one built by the Washburns in 1890), and the corrals, barns, offices, and employee housing of the Washburns' Yosemite Stage and

Turnpike Company. From Raymond, after perhaps spending a night in a Washburn hotel, tourists boarded one of the Washburns' "shiny eight- or eleven-passenger stages pulled by well-groomed horses" for the forty-mile ride on a Washburn road to Wawona, where another Washburn hotel waited to serve them at the southern terminus of the Washburn toll road northward into Yosemite Valley. Robinson's "ring" paranoia had some basis in reality, but no more so than for many other entrepreneurial combines that sprouted up on the American frontier during its rapid settlement.[12]

Raymond being a town of limited outdoor diversions, one can assume that a crowd gathered at its train station on the afternoon of May 16, 1891, to watch sixty-three men in blue uniforms lead their restless horses down wooden ramps and pull crates out of freight cars as officers and sergeants hurried about, barking orders. The troop pitched camp for the night near the station. At dawn the next day, the sweet sounds of reveille pierced the canvas and clapboard walls sheltering the town's civilian inhabitants. After the usual morning routine of roll calling, feeding and inspecting horses and men, checking out equipment, and policing the camp area, all with a by-the-numbers precision that was utterly foreign to Raymond's entrepreneuring chaos, the blue-coated aliens mounted up and formed in a long column of twos, Captain Jug Wood at the head. The sound of a trumpet echoed once again through the ramshackle town, and Troop I, Fourth U.S. Cavalry, perhaps the finest frontier cavalry regiment ever assembled, headed up the dusty Wawona road toward the new Yosemite National Park. Its improbable mission: defend nature against humans.

The Yosemite assignment marked an anniversary for Jug Wood. Just thirty years earlier almost to the month—in April 1861—he had launched his military career by joining the Thirteenth Iowa Volunteers at the age of sixteen. Most of those three decades had been spent on the trail across the North American continent. Constant hard-riding exposure to the elements had produced an accumulation of ailments that would have crippled an average person. Now here he was, forty-six years old, still in the saddle, riding into the Sierra Nevada at the head of a troop of U.S. Army cavalry. His immediate superior called him "particularly fitted for the active command of men," the ultimate cavalry compliment. A comrade described him as a "strict disciplinarian . . . endowed with a keen insight in human nature" who had seen "very hard service." A photograph taken several years earlier, when compared to his West Point graduation photo, showed how quickly he had aged. The clean, sharp features were gone. The chiseled cheekbones and jaw now blended into a rounded face that had acquired a uniform puffiness, and the flesh had loosened under his chin. He did not look soft; used might best describe the impression, used hard. His thin lips were nearly hidden

Wood after several years of hard frontier riding. U.S. Military Academy Library.

behind a thick, sculpted mustache extending out from his face on either side that added to an appearance of stern authority. His eyes were still clear and focused on an object close at hand, as at West Point; but now they were brighter and opened wider, as if they had caught some horror and been fixed by it into a permanent expression.[13]

The road leading out of Raymond that Jug Wood and his troop followed for the forty-mile march to Wawona was lined with oak trees. It was smooth and sixteen feet wide—built to handle Washburn stagecoaches. It maintained a level path toward the hazy peaks of the Chowchilla Mountains, twenty miles off, but when it reached that point the path steepened as it climbed more than 4,000 feet to the 6,500-foot summit of the range, whence it abruptly descended 2,500 feet into Wawona's mountain valley, called Pallahchun, or "a good place to stop," by its original Indian inhabitants and renamed Wawona (Indian for "big tree") by the ubiquitous Washburns. Troop I marched at a steady pace for about twenty miles, with intermittent pauses as required by regulations, before pitching camp in the late afternoon in the Chowchilla foothills. Early the next morning, the troopers began their ascent, breathing the crisp mountain air so alluring to dwellers of the hot and dusty San Joaquin Valley that it had made Wawona into a destination in its own right, apart from renowned Yosemite Valley twenty-six miles beyond it. On the afternoon of May 17, Troop I came to a junction where the road from Raymond combined with the road from Mariposa, signaling that they were one mile from their destination.[14]

In a few minutes, the trail-weary troopers rode into a scene from a fairy tale. A bright green meadow framed a long white building two stories high. A circular drive in front of the white building enclosed a well-tended park planted in grass and evergreens. In the center of the park a man-made fountain gushed forty feet into the air. The building itself was encircled by wide covered porches. On the front porch, in rocking chairs, sat several elegantly dressed ladies and gentlemen gazing curiously upon the newcomers. This was the famous Wawona Hotel, pride of Mariposa County. Here the leading citizens of the state of California, the nation, the entire world, came to refresh themselves. Ulysses Grant, John Ruskin, and Lillie Langtry (listed in that order in one proud account) took long walks through the adjacent mountain meadows, dined in the luxurious restaurant (breakfast of beefsteak, ham and eggs, trout, hotcakes, cornbread with homemade preserves, "to be taken in its entirety"), and breathed the invigorating mountain air—at $4 a day, room and board.[15]

At this moment, on the afternoon of May 17, 1891, it would be hard to say who was more startled or enchanted—the dusty troopers resting in their saddles, gazing wonderingly at the hotel and its numerous outbuildings, or the hotel guests in frock coats and hoop skirts looking back at them. A Wawona historian describes the encounter: "Even the springtime roar of the South Fork was diminished by the cadence of hoof beats on May 19 [sic], 1891, when two troops of cavalrymen trotted across the meadow. Their leader, a ramrod-straight officer, halted in front of the main Hotel where a crowd had gathered on the porch. 'Captain A.E. Wood, commander of the Fourth Cavalry and acting superintendent of Yosemite National Park, at your service,' he announced. Wood, a Civil War veteran, West point graduate, and Indian fighter, radiated authority."[16]

A stretch, perhaps, but it no doubt captured the spirit of the occasion. For many Wawonians, the cavalry completed a picturesque tableau they had been assiduously constructing for two decades since the Washburns purchased the primitive inn at Pallahchun that Galen Clark, another knight of the forest, had run since 1856. The Washburns built the white-walled Wawona Hotel on the site of Clark's inn and extended the Mari-posa-Wawona road twenty-six miles northward through the mountains into Yosemite State Park to provide the first direct stage link between Mariposa and Yosemite Valley. The stage line's inauguration was quite an event. The *Mariposa Gazette* printed a list of forty-two local eminences who boarded a fleet of Washburn and Company conveyances and "trav-elled to Yosemite Valley, equipped with 'cordials and restoratives'" on the stage line's inaugural run. The liquid refreshment gave courage during the new road's final and treacherous 2.6-mile descent into the valley, a stretch that became known as "the Washburn slide." That was the begin-ning of what one local resident called Wawona's "Periclean Age," domi-nated by its white Acropolis, the Wawona Hotel, that produced "a civilization second to none." The army's arrival marked a kind of com-pletion for the architects of Wawona's storybook realm. Years later, the wife of a Washburn partner recalled "when the logs were blazing in the office and there were gathered there a United States Senator, stage driv-ers, Indian guides, an East Indian prince, and various army officers. . . . Soldiers lent flavor, charm, and romance to the scene."[17]

Flavor, charm, and romance were not part of Jug Wood's working vocabulary. His immediate concern was to establish camp before night-fall and feed sixty-three horses and men. There is evidence that he al-ready knew where to look. On April 25, three weeks before I Troop arrived, the *Mariposa Gazette* reported that Wood had decided to establish his headquarters near Wawona "after a thorough investigation of the Val-ley." At about that time, Presidio records show a brief simultaneous ab-sence from the post for Dorst and Wood, probably a reconnaissance. Wawona was Wood's logical choice for several reasons: convenience to a railhead; a position astride the most heavily traveled road into Yosemite Valley; an adjacent village where foodstuffs and other supplies could be obtained; and proximity to the county seat at Mariposa, with its tele-graph, mail services, and land records, where a new park administrator would have considerable business. Wawona's only drawback was its lo-cation on the southernmost boundary of the new park, which would complicate patrolling, but that obstacle was not insurmountable for a frontier cavalry troop. In any case, the story is that Wood and his men chose a campsite a mile north of the hotel selected by eight-year-old William M. Sell Jr., who led them there. This unlikely incident made a permanent impression on Sell's imagination, for he recounted it into his old age. It added a nice touch to the tableau, even though Wood already knew where he was going.[18]

Troop I's camp stood in the midst of a peaceful grove of cedars and yellow pines along the banks of the Merced River. (It is still in use today as the "A. E. Wood Campsite.") After signaling a halt, Wood repeated a routine he had followed hundreds of times during his frontier army career. He had the horses fed and picketed, sent men out to gather wood, unpacked gear from wagons and pack mules, and constructed a camp consisting initially of a neat row of white canvas tents. Ever the practical imaginer, he named it Camp Near Wawona. On that first night, we can be sure there was a light burning late at the commander's tent as that hard-riding bureaucrat completed the details of organizing his camp—water, sanitation, food storage, drills, inspections. He was commanding an army post now, smaller but identical in basic organization to the Presidio, and he had to bring it into conformity with army rules and regulations.

Wood's external lines of communications flowed in two directions, to the Presidio in San Francisco and to the Interior Department in Washington. The Presidio channel was straightforward and familiar. During his first days in camp, Wood filled out and forwarded numerous requisitions to the Presidio's quartermaster and subsistence departments for fuel, forage, straw, extra issues of rations, and other supplies. He requested and received copies of army regulation advertisements for local suppliers of fresh beef and mutton. He was ordered to designate a commissary officer to receive army funds for meat purchases and keep receipts and other requisite records. His monthly "post return," completed on a form used by Old Army posts everywhere, went to the Presidio at the end of May as required. With that, the camp in Yosemite was formally plugged into a network of channels through which a uniformed national service corps of 28,000 Americans, most of them concentrated in ninety communal encampments across the nation, communicated, disbursed food and equipment, transferred personnel, and maintained a state of mobilized readiness innate to the institution.[19]

Communication outside military channels was another matter. On May 19 Wood formally reported for duty to the secretary of the interior in his new capacity as acting superintendent of Yosemite National Park (a title borrowed from Yellowstone that would apply to all army national park commanders). His polite and deferential initial communication revealed how little he had been informed about his assignment. It also marked the beginning of a constant struggle for guidance from the civilian officials he dutifully served:

> In obedience to Special Orders No. 38, Hdqrs. Dept of Cal., I moved here with Troop I 4th Cavalry for the purpose of protecting the Yosemite National Park from trespassers etc. I have the honor of reporting to you for such instructions as you may desire to give me for the purposes above mentioned.

I would also respectfully request to be furnished with several copies of the act of Congress creating this National Park, together with the regulations for the government of the same, for distribution among the stockmen who have been in the habit of feeding their stock upon the pasturage of this Park.

Any suggestions in addition to the orders requested above, will be gladly received.[20]

There is no record of a reply from Interior Secretary Noble or any member of his staff, although it appears that Wood somehow obtained a copy of the park legislation from local sources. It was extremely vague on enforcement, which happened to be Wood's mission. The one word with any bite was "trespass." "He [the Interior Secretary] shall cause all persons trespassing upon the [park] . . . to be removed therefrom," the legislation stated. It did not say what constituted a trespass (what about a cattleman leading a herd to his patented homestead within the park, devouring vegetation along the way?), nor did it mention how the trespassers should be "removed." It called upon the interior secretary to "provide against the wanton destruction" of fish and game but did not say how. It invited the interior secretary to issue "rules and regulations" for the park, but it made no mention of penalties for rule breakers. From a legal standpoint, anyone who wanted to could thumb his nose at Yosemite's acting superintendent.[21]

But would they dare? As during previous frontier administration assignments, Jug Wood had one trump to play—the qualities acquired at the Mackenzie school of leadership that rendered him, in the words of his squadron commander, "particularly fitted for the active command of men." Wawona's historian was less circumspect: he "radiated authority."

It was easy to give orders, and in frontier country just as easy to ignore them. The "leadership" Jug Wood had learned meant winning loyalty and respect not by the righteousness of one's ideas but by simple fairness and honesty in daily interactions. Wood knew the people he would face in the Sierra Nevada. He had not yet met them personally, but twenty years of frontier experience with whites who viewed army efforts to enforce laws as a threat to democracy had taught him what to expect and how to act. In frontier law enforcement, how one handled oneself mattered as much as legal authority, as the tenderfoot civilian "assistant superintendents" sent to Yellowstone fresh out of college a few years earlier had learned to their distress.[22]

Two weeks after his arrival, Wood circulated his first public communication. It was addressed to cattlemen and sheep owners of "middle and southern California" who were drawn to Yosemite's cool, watered mountains from late spring until early fall when the lowlands were dry and hot. Wood offered them a "square deal." Herders who owned land within the park, and had surveyed and marked that land, could graze within their marked boundaries. As for everyone else, Wood had his duty:

> This Yosemite Park is to be a Park throughout all time—it is not a temporary arrangement. . . . The time will be when the United States will be possessed of the title to all the lands within its boundaries and in the meantime it would be better if the citizens living near the Park would make arrangements to conform to the new conditions of things, thus avoiding the consequence of a violation of the law.[23]

Wood did not identify the consequences of violating the law. There were none, of course, but he did not announce that either. He was playing frontier poker. Now it was their bet.

While announcing his presence, Wood was also trying to figure out where he was. The park's boundaries were not yet marked. A map widely used for Yosemite Valley that included some portions of the new national park had been completed in 1883 as part of a Sierra Nevada survey directed by a U.S. Army Engineer, Captain George M. Wheeler. There was also a map of the region made in 1873 by the California State Geological Survey. But the best Wood could come up with for his more localized park duties was a map acquired in Wawona entitled "Map of the Yosemite National Park." It was a slapdash effort, displaying a few main roads, rivers, and mountain peaks, obviously rushed into print to trade on public curiosity about the new park. Today it would be called a tourist map. Nevertheless, it became Wood's primary operational map for administering a rugged 1,500-square-mile mountainous area with snow-capped peaks as high as 13,000 feet, deep canyons with sheer granite cliffs, steep wooded valleys, and forests that extended as far as the eye could see. The lack of a satisfactory topographical map would place cavalry patrols at considerable disadvantage in blocking illegal intruders, such as sheepherders who had been working the area for years and could retreat into their hidden network of backcountry trails. But the army would have to live with that until the Fourth Cav's Lieutenant Nathaniel F. McClure completed the first authoritative map of Yosemite National Park in 1896. During the intervening years, troopers picked their way through the park's mountains, forests, valleys, and canyons, filling out the picture as they went.[24]

An equally vexing problem for Wood and his successors was posed by private land claims. The park was honeycombed with hundreds of claims, especially in the southern, southeastern, and western portions closest to Mariposa. Each claim constituted a separate legal tangle. According to the law, claims were invalid if made before federal land was surveyed. Although many of Yosemite's claims predated surveys, their owners claimed they postdated surveys and thus were valid. The correct answer lay in disordered records in Mariposa, Stockton, and other rural land offices. Moreover, U.S. homesteading laws provided for claims to be made in anticipation of a federal survey, provided the boundaries of the claimed land were listed with the land office of the county in question. Were such supposedly binding reservations for future homesteads rendered null and void by the park legislation? Wood was as uninformed as everyone else on that point. Furthermore, most county and/or federal claimants had not marked the boundaries of their claims. Without such markings, how was the cavalry to tell, say, whether cattle were in fact grazing on a privately owned homestead within the park, as its owners would invariably claim? Members of the Fourth Cavalry had to spend many hours in government land offices obtaining correct boundaries for hundreds of homesteads before confirming these boundaries, one by one, in the field. After that, they could begin arguing with the "owners" who invariably disputed negative findings.[25]

Exploration, mapmaking, surveying, trail-blazing, public administration, site investigations, record searches, law enforcement without enforcement authority; in a mountainous wilderness frequented mainly by free-spirited sheepherders, cattlemen, miners, and hunters unaccustomed to taking orders from anyone; on behalf of an idea that few on the scene understood and a government that few on the scene respected: those were among the challenges undertaken by Jug Wood's I Troop from their tent encampment in the Sierra Nevada, with virtually no information or policy guidance from their civilian superiors in the nation's capital three thousand miles away.[26]

Early in June, Wood sent out two expeditions. Second Lieutenant Milton Davis led a party of eleven men on a scouting and mapping patrol into the remote northern reaches of the park that departed on the fifth. Four days later, First Lieutenant Alexander Dean led a party of twenty-one men on a mission to show the flag in the central portion of the park with easiest access to Mariposa that was used regularly by land claimants, many with herds of cattle. Dean returned and delivered his report on June 13, Davis on June 15, the latter after leading his patrol through 195 miles of some of the most rugged mountain territory on the continent. A day later, Wood again wrote Interior Secretary Noble. "I have the honor to state that I am still awaiting instructions & suggestions from the Hon. Secretary regarding my duties as commandant of the Guard for the Yosemite National Park," he began. He had finally received a copy of the park's hazy rules and regulations, but without any explanatory comment, and he wanted particularly to know what penalties he might invoke for breaking the rules against selling liquor, killing fish or game, or setting fires or for violating the sweeping regulation that all "trees, shrubs, plants, timber, minerals, mineral deposits, curiosities, wonders or other objects of interest in the Park . . . shall be retained in their natural condition."[27]

While awaiting instructions from Washington, the commander of I Troop did some investigating. Setting forest fires was a misdemeanor under California state law, he learned. "Can these laws be made applicable to that offense within the limits of this Park?" he asked his silent civilian superiors in Washington. Also, Wood knew from long-standing experience with frontier whiskey salesmen (whom the cavalry loathed for provoking Indians) that federal Internal Revenue laws forbade whiskey sale without a license. He asked whether he could enforce that law within the park since the park rules also forbade liquor sales, and he added, "I have my eye on such a case now."[28]

Wood also reported on an initiative that showed another side of his professional training. He had set out to enlighten local residents on the *idea* of the park: "I have tried, with some success, to impress the public mind with the fact that this Park was set apart, by the Congress, for the purpose of preserving the objects of wonder which nature has scattered with such a prodigal hand, within the limits of this Reservation, & that all, without distinction, are cordially invited to come & visit these wonderful creations, provided they observe the Rules." No one had ordered him to do this, but it seemed like the right thing to do. And as Wood's character might win respect for the law where others with more sophisticated intellectual skills failed, so it might also in the same crusty way win respect for ideas, even the revolutionary idea of preserving and protecting natural beauty.[29]

Interior Secretary Noble finally wrote to Wood on June 19. The reason for the long delay explained a lot about the condition of America's governing institutions on the eve of the twentieth century. The U.S. secretary of the interior was out of town when Wood's letters arrived, and they simply accumulated on his desk with other government correspondence from throughout the nation. Noble enclosed twenty copies of the park's rules and regulations (the first copies Wood had received from Washington) and told Wood they must be "strictly enforced in every particular" so that the parklands could be "restored to their pristine condition." But when it came to those particulars, the interior secretary grew vague. Wood could detain no one for violating the rules, nor could he seize personal property. The most he could do was expel "trespassers" from the park. Under this toothless regime, there was nothing to stop evicted trespassers from immediately returning, including sheepherders and cattlemen with their herds. To discourage such be-

havior, Noble suggested that Wood perform his expulsions "in so em-
phatic and severe a manner that they will not choose to repeat the offense"—whatever that meant.[30]

As for further instructions, such as how to go about managing a national park, Noble shifted the shoe to the other foot: "You are requested
to forward a report upon the nature of the country you have to superin-
tend, its water-courses, game, etc. with any suggestions you may deem
best as to its proper management." Wood's first full report was expected
before the end of August, so that Noble could incorporate its information
into the Interior Department's annual report to Congress for the coming
fiscal year.[31]

Wood's task was not made any easier by his new second in command going off on a drunken binge. He had First Lieutenant Dean arrested immediately and sent that same day (June 18) under guard to the
Presidio for court-martial, even though this left Troop I with only two officers, Wood and Davis. Wood's prompt response made no impression on
Charles Robinson who couldn't wait to tell Robert Underwood Johnson
about the incident when he learned of it two weeks later. Robinson presented the information as his long-sought proof that the army was helpless before the "corrupt Yosemite ring," which, he suggested, was
deliberately drugging I Troop's officers with alcohol when they visited
the Wawona hotel. "I have seen nothing of it [Dean's arrest] in the press,"
Robinson lamented.[32]

The press may not have played up Dean's drunkenness to Robinson's moral satisfaction, but (although he did not mention it to Johnson)
there were articles during this period about other army activities in
Yosemite. The *Los Angeles Herald*, under the headline "Patrolling
Yosemite," reported an encounter by a cavalry patrol with four sheepherders under circumstances that dramatized the cavalry's dilemma. The
patrol, led by Second Lieutenant Davis, had surprised the herders and ordered them to remove their sheep from the park. They obeyed the order,
and Davis and his patrol continued on their way. Returning by the same
route, Davis came upon the men again. They simply had waited until his
patrol had moved out of sight and moved back into the park. This time
Davis arrested the sheepherders and led them to the main camp. There
Wood lectured them before releasing them on $500 bond each, "to appear
for trial if the federal authorities want them." [33]

Wood laid out the problem and his improvised solution in the annual report he wrote a few weeks later: "The last days of May the sheep
commenced their annual migrations to the mountain grazing grounds,
and by the 10th of June there were fully 60,000 of them close to the southern and at least 30,000 near the western boundaries of the park." As the

herds advanced, Wood sent out patrols to meet them. Their orders were to explain the new rules and warn off herders before they could enter the park. Wood contemplated no other action so long as the intruders stayed away. Then the incident reported in the Los Angeles newspaper occurred. "I knew that there was no penalty attached to a trespass upon this Park, but I also knew that the sheep men were not aware of this . . . and . . . decided action upon my part" could stall their parkward march until the grazing season was over.[34]

But Wood had to reach big-city sheep owners as well as their hired herders in the park. After Davis had brought the herders into Camp Near Wawona, "as good fortune would have it" a friend of the man who owned the captured herd was in Wawona, and he telegraphed the owner that the cavalry meant business. Wood also telegraphed for a deputy U.S. marshal and "got this news in circulation." He knew a marshal would not be sent, "nor did I want him, *as this was all for effect.*" The owner of the sheep rushed up to Wawona, where Wood was waiting. Wood released the herders and advised them and their boss that he would take no further action so long as they stayed away from the park. Wood's strategy worked in Yosemite, but it ran into trouble in San Francisco.[35]

On June 26, the U.S. attorney in San Francisco cabled the attorney general in Washington, D.C., advising that "Capt. A.E. Wood Fourth Cavalry USA" had reported arresting four sheepherders who he proposed to prosecute. "Can find no law authorizing Criminal prosecution," the U.S. attorney wrote. Neither could Wood, who never considered it. His words were "all for effect."[36]

The U.S. attorney made no attempt to contact Wood for clarification before cabling Washington; but he did send Wood a "long opinion on the subject of trespass," the cavalry captain reported, concluding "of course" that criminal action could not be pursued. The attorney's need to lecture him on what Wood already knew "was all right and commendable in him," Wood wrote, if he had only stopped there. But he also distributed copies of his communication to Wood to San Francisco's daily newspapers, along with a copy of his cable to Washington and other commentary that made it look as if he had fought off a U.S. Army insurrection. Wood, who had little experience with ambitious urban politicians, was dumbfounded. He had been in the park less than three weeks. Intruders were advancing toward its borders. He had responded with a strategy learned from hard experience that was midway between the two prevailing extremes of frontier law enforcement: unworkable legal abstractions and inhuman vigilante "justice." As Wood said, he expected his adversaries to recognize that he had outfoxed them, but by then the grazing season would be over. He was seeking to buy time for nature and win the respect of hardy mountaineers who played the game the same way. Wood reported that he "had to go to a great deal of trouble" to correct the confusion caused by a U.S. attorney with an inexplicable (to Wood) craving for publicity in far-off San Francisco. He did not realize that, for the U.S. attorney, it was "all for effect" too—his political career.[37]

On the other hand, Wood could engage in legalistic wordplay when he had to, frontier style, as he did with John B. Curtin, cattleman, lawyer, state senator, attorney for concessionaires in the state park, and a national park homesteader. Wood and his army successors would fight a running verbal battle with Curtin for more than fifteen years, including a lawsuit that went to the Supreme Court. Curtin's correspondence with Yosemite's cavalry leaders has been called by one Yosemite historian a "classic expression of the rugged individualism exhibited by western pioneers in resisting the slightest government control." Curtin was rugged; he was also learned and shrewd. His letters read like legal briefs, probing for openings in Yosemite's intellectual defenses. Wood realized that simple sheepherder stratagems would not work with this man.[38]

"My duties are executive or ministerial purely and not judicial in any sense," hard-riding Jug Wood wrote in one of his many legalistic letters to Curtin, avoiding the other's latest attempt to trap him into a debate over the interpretation of various clauses in the act establishing the park. Curtin had every right to challenge the law through the courts, Wood said, but not through the park's acting superintendent, who was merely the law's agent: "The conditions I give you . . . are only the direct orders of the Secretary of the Interior." Moreover, there was nothing in those orders "to prevent you from fully enjoying your property." All Curtin had to do was follow the rules, beginning with marking the boundaries of the park land he claimed to own. If Curtin would do that and so notify Wood, he would be allowed to move his cattle through the park to his land "without molestation." However, once Curtin's cattle had reached his private lands, they "must be kept upon them and not allowed to roam anywhere else." Should they stray into public lands, they "will be ejected summarily by order of the Secretary of the Interior."

As for Curtin's argument that cattle recently caught by Wood's troopers were in the state park, where Curtin claimed their presence was legal, the cattleman was triply wrong: first, state officials had advised Wood that Curtin had no right to be in the state park because grazing cattle there was illegal under state law; second, Wood could not allow cattle to pass through the national park to graze in the state park in violation of state law; third, the grazing area that Curtin claimed was public land in the state park was, in fact, public land in the national park and therefore banned from grazing according to federal law. Wood had never been to law school, but his intellect had been disciplined by two decades of argumentation with legalistic nitpickers like Presidio commander Graham over Old Army rules, regulations, and procedures. It also helped to have studied how to encircle an adversary's position.[39]

In addition to Curtin and his cattlemen colleagues, Wood also established contact with regional kingpins in the sheep and mining industries, such as sheep owner L. U. Shippee of Stockton and A. E. Preciado of Madera, who owned several silver mines within the park. Shippee wrote to Secretary Noble asking for clarification of Captain Wood's authority. Preciado wrote directly to Wood requesting information on what was permissible under the new regime. The communications were tense but civil. They indicated growing local respect for the park idea and the soldier responsible for making it real.[40]

Even the *Mariposa Gazette*, arch foe of the "cold-blooded conspirators" behind the park, "whoever they are," began warming to the Old Army troopers. On June 20, the newspaper reported that an I Troop patrol picking its way through five-foot-deep summer snows in Yosemite's mountainous backcountry had rescued "an old prospector, lost, nearly starved." The daring, disciplined cavalry were a potential rescue force.[41]

In late July, *Mariposa Gazette* editor and publisher F. Angevine Reynolds reported on a pleasantly surprising visit to Wawona: "The soldiers . . . keep themselves busy, looking after trespassing sheep and cattle herders. . . . The effect . . . is already apparent in the myriads of beautiful flowers and abundant growth of grass, which covers the ground where formerly it was bare as a traveled road." Reynolds would remain a critic of the national park "land grab" on principle, but she had only praise for the cavalry, and not only for their environmental restorations: "The officers appear to be very pleasant, quiet gentlemen," she wrote, "and are evident favorites about the hotel." Since I Troop had only two officers (a replacement for the banished Dean did not arrive until mid-August), and Lieutenant Davis was hardly there, the chief charmer obviously was, in yet another guise, Jug Wood. Later that summer, Wood's name appeared at the head of a *Gazette* column called "Wawona Notes," just above a reference to a visiting executive of Levi Strauss and Company: "Captain Wood with a detail of twenty men, is scouting through the National Park, on the lookout for bands of sheep and cattle." Jug Wood had made scouting for park invaders into a social item.[42]

A good part of Wood's success during that crucial initial year at Yosemite, and in his succeeding two years in the park, was due to the support provided by Second Lieutenant Milton F. Davis, I Troop's newest and youngest officer. Davis had a rural background similar to Wood's. He grew up dirt-poor on a farm in Oregon where he was the chief support of his widowed mother. In his spare time he took courses at a local college. He had accumulated two years of college credits when he won an appointment to West Point in 1886 at the age of twenty-two. He graduated in 1890 and was assigned to the Fourth Cavalry. At twenty-six, he was mature for his junior rank, a crack shot, and he loved the outdoors. He and Wood complemented one another perfectly: the older Wood had experience and authority, Davis had legs. While Wood spent most of his time on administrative matters, earning local respect and establishing procedures essential for consolidating the park's identity, Davis was almost continuously on patrol. He would no sooner return to camp from one direction than he was off in another. During his three years at Yosemite under Wood, Davis chased intruders from one end of the park to the other, blazed trails, mapped and surveyed, and climbed dozens of rugged mountains. The patrol that rescued the lost prospector in five-foot-deep snowdrifts was under his command. His legacy includes numerous pioneering maps and sketches of the Yosemite region that wound up in research collections at Yosemite and the University of California at Berkeley.[43]

During the crucial season of 1891, Wood made Davis his field commander for what amounted to a military campaign. Between early June and mid-October, Wood dispatched twenty mounted patrols to every sector of the park for periods of from three days to two and a half weeks each. According to I Troop's meticulous records, the patrols covered a total of 2,027 miles. Davis participated in twelve of the twenty patrols, covering a total of 1,424 miles, commanding ten, and serving under Wood on two others. Davis led the longest patrol in duration—seventeen days, 326 miles, over the entire park. But Wood led the patrol with the best record for miles per day—203 miles in ten days. Wood's average of twenty miles a day for ten days through Yosemite's northern and western mountains secured his hard-riding reputation with any of the younger men under his command who might have harbored doubts. Even more patrolling would be needed to check the persistent sheepherders. But in conjunction with other measures Wood was taking, it marked an auspicious beginning.[44]

On August 31, 1891, the complementary roles of Wood and Davis literally reached a peak of extremes. On that day, Davis became the first person to scale the 12,311-foot summit of the mountain that today bears his name, along with a nearby string of lakes. The preceding night, he later recalled, he "slept out without blankets at the timber-line." Mean-

while, Wood was at his makeshift desk in Camp Near Wawona putting
the finishing touches on a historic first annual report by an acting superintendent of Yosemite National Park, dated August 31 and addressed to
the secretary of the interior.[45]

Considering Wood's virtual zero base of information when he arrived in the park three and a half months earlier, his 1891 report was a
tour de force. He summarized his initial actions, regretting that they had
to be so ad hoc because "up to the 30th of June I had received no instructions whatever from the Department." The instructions, when they finally came, did not help much. New issues requiring adjudication arose
"every day." Wood could have made his life easier and more popular locally, without earning any reprimands from his superiors in Washington,
by keeping quiet and avoiding confrontations. But he never considered
that approach. In his encounters without rules of engagement, Wood relied on "my ideas of equity" acquired in frontier service. The results were
far from perfect, but during a few weeks Troop I had at least succeeded
in getting the word out quickly, making its presence known, warding off
numerous incursions, and above all earning local respect for the park and
its administrators.[46]

Wood then presented the description of the park's topography that
the interior secretary had requested in his letter of June 19—mountains,
rivers, streams, canyons, meadows, roads, trails. The description was extensive, and though still rudimentary in terms of the park's immense
size, a beginning. Wood made an important observation about trails:
many ran through the park, but none were shaped by it. They should be
reconfigured to the shape of the park, building on the network of sheepherder trails that honeycombed the region. To that end, I Troop had initiated a campaign of "searching out and blazing" trails within the park's
boundaries. That campaign would accelerate under subsequent acting
superintendents to become one of the Old Army's most enduring contributions to Yosemite's development into a physically integrated entity.

There followed a report on the park's game. Its population of bear,
deer, grouse, and quail had been decimated by intruders, Wood wrote.
He proposed a wildlife protection campaign. Eviction of trespassing
sheep would help: "As they graze in masses, they trample the nests of the
quail and grouse to pieces, destroy the eggs, or crush the young before
they are able to fly." Wood predicted that with strict patrolling "the possibilities are that [the park] will be alive with game in a few years."

Next, with apologies, came an "incomplete" list of tree species and
their altitudinal locations—nine varieties of pine (2,500–11,000 feet), three
varieties of fir (7,000–9,000), two of spruce (5,500–8,000), and so on. Wood
was obviously a tree lover after Muir's heart. He promised a more extensive report on trees the following year "if I have the honor of being [reap-

pointed] the superintendent of the park," and he made special mention of "the most wonderful natural growth upon this earth . . . the Sequoia gigantea, of which there are two small groves within this park."

A large portion of the report addressed the thorny issue of absent and resident land claimants, whose numbers were "probably much greater than the Congress knew of" when the park was established. These land claimants represented the most difficult administrative problem by far. Wood provided descriptions of thirty-five townships where confrontations with landowners had occurred. The detail suggested that Wood had spent considerable time scouring land office records. The first item on the long list began: "Township 4 south, 19 east: There are some mining claims in the northern portion, the number not known. A very little timber in the southeast corner, but the township is essentially an agricultural country. There are farms upon this township that have been under cultivation for nearly 30 years. The assessors rolls in Mariposa show that 5,400 acres have been taken up. The Stockton land office shows that almost 3,040 acres have been homesteaded, patented, or paid out."

Wood singled out for special mention "about 35 Indians . . . remnants of the Yosemite tribe . . . [who had lived in the region] longer than tradition goes back." They were "quite intelligent." He liked and respected them. They were "more steadfast" than whites and had a "moral right" to the land of a sort that whites could not claim. Even without formal land titles, they belonged.

The report's final section contained three recommendations. First, a survey must be undertaken to replace boundaries for townships and private holdings within the park that are "simply neighborhood traditions." Second, Congress should pass a law making violation of park rules a misdemeanor with a maximum $1,000 fine and six months in jail, with civil courts passing judgment. Third, unless the federal government was willing to buy out all claims, some of those that were creating the worst problems should be excluded from the park; they were undermining the overall protection effort.

Jug Wood adjusted so rapidly to his park assignment in part because, although the park concept was new, the park mission Wood and his men performed was not. The Old Army had been surveying and mapping public lands and evicting trespassers from them for more than a century, from Appalachia across the continent to California. Troop I simply carried those procedures into Yosemite, recording its natural phenomena, blazing trails over its mountains, mapping its terrain, and bringing exploiters of its public lands into line.[47]

Wood's training in hard-riding discipline, scientific observation, and civic virtue came together in his character and work habits. How he handled his Yosemite assignment showed why being "particularly suited for the active command of men" meant much more than the ability to lead a cavalry charge. He was literate (after writing hundreds of reports for more than twenty years) but not intellectually pretentious. He represented the federal government in Washington, but he was no eastern tenderfoot; you could tell that merely by looking him in the eye, if you dared. He was polite, deferential, and well-groomed. At his outdoor table on the banks of the Merced or on horseback on the trail, in personal encounters or through the mails, this blue-uniformed ex–Iowa farm boy who had spent virtually his entire adult life on the frontier conversed with equal facility with businessmen, loggers, attorneys, sheepherders, state officials, drifters, prospectors, Wawona society matrons, and the U.S. secretary of the interior, adjusting his tone and manner as required in each instance.

Charles Robinson found Wood unbearable. He pestered Interior Secretary Noble and Robert Underwood Johnson throughout the summer and fall with letters condemning the troopers who by then had become inextricably linked in his mind with the evil "ring." On August 31—the same day Davis was gasping for breath on the 12,000-foot summit of the mountain that would be named after him, and Wood was hunched over his desk in camp assembling his annual report—Robinson was drafting another tirade to Johnson. Wood had long ago court-martialed and exiled Lieutenant Dean, but not from Robinson's mind. "He *was* beastly drunk," Robinson wrote, adding an underline for emphasis. What's more, even James Mason Hutchings said "the troops are of no earthly use."[48]

Like Robinson, Hutchings, Yosemite's foremost resident publicist, also opposed Wood for self-centered reasons. Within six weeks of Yosemite National Park's establishment, he had dispatched a smooth letter to Interior Secretary Noble, enclosing information about the park, reporting that numerous friends were "kindly and warmly interesting themselves in my behalf for the position of [Yosemite] superintendent" and that Noble would soon be hearing from California senator Leland Stanford on that subject. Hutchings wrote again a few days later. He got nowhere. The cavalry had done him out of a potentially well-paying job.[49]

Secretary Noble used his department's annual report to Congress to publicly announce his satisfaction with Wood's performance. "He has very efficiently performed the duties assigned to him," Noble wrote. He quoted extensively from Wood's report and included the full text in an appendix. He also initiated what would become an annual litany about the need to correct the "peculiar and inexplicable" absence of congressional funding for managing the park or "any penalties for violation of the rules or regulations required to be formulated by the Secretary."[50]

Noble concluded his Yosemite report with comments on California's management of Yosemite Valley. He condemned the state's "carelessness . . . wantonness . . . [and] very great destruction." The contrast with his account of the cavalry in the adjacent national park was very sharp indeed.[51]

Jug Wood's army superiors stayed completely out of park management, leaving it between him and his Interior Department overseers, except for one in-house issue: whether the camp should be made into a permanent post like Yellowstone as the interior secretary had recommended. At a time when such outposts were being closed down throughout the West, the chances of creating a new one in Yosemite were remote. Wood recommended against it on practical grounds. Wawona was the only workable site for a permanent camp outside the state-run Yosemite Valley, and it would be snowbound most of the winter; supplying it over the 7,000-foot-high Chowchilla Mountains would require resources the War Department might not want to commit since Congress had yet to appropriate a cent for park administration. With that recommendation in the mail, its acceptance a foregone conclusion, I Troop pulled up its tent stakes on October 25 and departed by the same route it had arrived, crossing the Merced and marching west over the Chowchillas to Raymond and a train to San Francisco.[52]

Back at the Presidio, life picked up its familiar rhythms. Within days of Wood's return, he and post commander Graham resumed their jousting, like a couple of knights in training. At one point, Wood went too far when he publicly objected to a petty Graham put-down during inspection instead of submitting a complaint quietly through channels. That objection led to a demand from Graham to departmental headquarters that Wood be court-martialed for insubordination. Wood, who would have done the same had one of his subordinates challenged his authority in public, meekly pulled in his horns.[53]

The most novel activity that winter was a new "lyceum" education program for officers, part of a nationwide army initiative. Post Commander Graham organized a series of twenty-four lectures by officers on the post to serve as the Presidio lyceum's centerpiece. Jug Wood led off on February 1, discoursing on "The Proper Employment of Cavalry in War," with Graham probably sitting in the front row eyeing the speaker's uniform for any infraction of the dress code. Other lecture topics falling to the Fourth Cavalry officers ranged from "Some Elements of Discipline" by Joe Dorst (who commanded the Sequoia troop) to "Horse Shoeing" by Yosemite mountaineer Milton Davis.[54]

Wood retained his acting superintendent title while wintering at the Presidio and frequently found himself involved in park affairs. At Interior's request, he participated in overlapping Yosemite state park and national park investigations initiated by Noble. These joint activities marked the beginning of an amicable working relationship on park issues between agents of the Interior and War Departments that continued for the next twenty years while the army ran Yosemite. Perhaps one reason they got along so well was that the army showed no desire to expand its role or challenge the Interior Department's authority. It would not be the same with the U.S. Forest Service after its establishment in the Department of Agriculture under Gifford Pinchot in 1905. As we'll see, Pinchot tried hard to steal the parks from Interior. In those pre–National Park Service days, army engagement in the parks served as a bulwark against Pinchot's imperialistic designs.[55]

1892 AND 1893: SECURING THE BEACHHEAD

The cavalry rode into Yosemite in the spring of 1891 at Interior's urgent request and rode out that fall with the department's expectation that the troopers would be back next year—and, according to the interior secretary, for many years afterward. But that assumption was by no means automatic. There was no legislation authorizing troops for Yosemite or Sequoia, as had been the case for Yellowstone. Instead, there was an informal request from Interior to War. With no involvement in the early exploration of the Yosemite region as with Yellowstone (going back to Lewis and Clark) or long-standing commitment to Yosemite preservation as with Yellowstone (recall Sheridan's central role), there would have been good justification for the army declining to deploy two-thirds of its modest cavalry force in California on a thankless public service mission in the Sierra Nevada. If the army had taken that route, parks that became the crown jewels of our national park system would have been threatened with early collapse; at the minimum, their size would have been drastically reduced. Interior seemed to make the army's choice easier— and the nation's environmental future bleaker—by forgetting to invite the cavalry back.[56]

But the army returned anyway, for reasons that say a lot about its character and role in nineteenth-century America. The process began early in 1892, in the form of stock inquiries from the Presidio quartermaster and Captain A. E. Wood, sent through channels to the commander of the Department of California, who in February queried the army's commanding general in Washington, Would the cavalry be needed for Yosemite and Sequoia in 1892? If so, the Department of California needed to requisition supplies and make appropriate personnel adjustments. The commanding general asked the secretary of war, who contacted the secretary of the interior. "What? Troops for Yosemite and Sequoia?" The unsolicited query jolted a distracted interior secretary into awareness and action. He immediately said yes and drafted the necessary formal request to the War Department, which was approved. Orders were printed and forwarded back through channels to the Department of California and the Presidio, and the commanders of I and K troops (Wood and Dorst) initiated their by-the-numbers preparations.[57]

The detailed Yosemite orders for Wood's troop have not survived, but those of his successor, Captain George G. H. Gale, offer a glimpse into the Old Army's unique contemporary capabilities for frontier assignments like the national parks. For the Yosemite assignment, Wood's Fourth Cavalry successor was authorized to call upon the Presidio quartermaster for three wagons, fourteen team mules, ten pack mules, a standardized complement of camp equipment (tents, shovels, kettles, and so on) for sixty men, and a large hospital tent. Grain and other subsistence stores needed for the march would be shipped by rail to points along the route selected from the standardized itinerary forms completed during previous marches to the Sierra Nevada. Equipment that could not be conveniently carried by wagon would be shipped by rail to Raymond for later pickup for the final leg over the Chowchilla Mountains. Subsistence stores other than fresh beef and vegetables would be shipped directly to Yosemite by the Presidio quartermaster upon their periodic requisition by the Yosemite commander. A packer (for the mules), a hospital corps man, and an army physician would be detailed from the Presidio to serve with the troop during its Yosemite encampment. Medical supplies would be requisitioned from the Presidio as needed, and so on. This comprehensiveness was why nineteenth-century frontier expeditions of every sort sought a "military escort," which was much more than a group of outriders. It provided vital organization and support available at the time from no other source.[58]

No doubt Secretary Noble would have eventually renewed the troop request on his own, but not until later and probably in response to desperate appeals from California preservationists (as in fact occurred when the army was absorbed with the Spanish-American War in 1898 and neglected to remind Interior to issue its park invitation, triggering frantic crisis calls from Muir and others). At this fragile early stage in the institutionalization of the national park idea in the Sierra Nevada, when nationally organized administrative institutions hardly existed, at least with any meaningful supply system or manpower pool, the rhythmically regulated Old Army bureaucracy kept a jerry-built park administration alive. [59]

There was also this added value-based dimension: the character and strength of the Old Army's commitment to the California parks were shaped by the uniquely *grounded* patriotism of its national service ethic.

The idea of a national park resonated with earthy patriotic significance within the Old Army. Jug Wood's reverent description of the trees of Yosemite was circumspect compared to many of his peers, including First Lieutenant John Lockwood, who would be Wood's Yosemite deputy commander in 1892 before moving on to Sequoia. Lockwood later wrote about those experiences in an article for a national magazine that defended not only the advanced idea of national parks in general but also the more sophisticated idea of an American polity in which environmental preservation fostered a sense of national community:

> To roam the virgin forests, watered by the Merced, the Kaweah, and the Kern, to enter into the free natural life of the mountains, to dwell in common with the creatures not yet driven from their native haunts, to partake of the spirit of the national playground, is to receive a greater favor and benefit from *our common country*. One can hardly overestimate the benefit involved. *Secrets of science* else tramped under foot, rare specimens of bird and beast else ruthlessly exterminated, *beauties of nature*, here held superior to brick and mortar, all these things are fostered and encouraged by the wise decision which reserves certain traces of land for plaisances in perpetuity. *Each year of our national life* will add to the value of these reservations.[60]

Nature, beauty, science, and nation were fused in Lockwood's Old Army perspective of the American polity into an institutional outlook unique for its time and place that might be called ecological nationalism. It is worth keeping that culturally distinctive outlook in mind, as this account of the Old Army's return to the parks resumes, beginning with the reengagement process in February when Noble said yes, by all means, send troops to the parks, and orders to that effect passed down the army chain of command, supply requisitions flowed through channels from the Presidio to depots across the West, new recruits checked in, new equipment arrived, old equipment was refurbished, and I and K Troops drilled, submitted to inspections, and delivered reports until May, when it was time once again to move out.

This year—unlike 1891 when Troops I and K left the Presidio abruptly by train—the cavalry followed standard departure procedures. Early on the morning of May 4, after trumpeters sounded boots and saddles and assembly, the park-bound troopers spilled out of their barracks to the post stables, saddled and bridled their horses, and led them out as if for a drill. The Presidio band was already assembled on the parade ground in full regalia before a crowd of onlookers, including wives who would not be seeing their husbands again for several months. The two

troops totaled about one hundred men combined, each with a mount, supported by a train of forty pack mules and six wagons carrying basic equipment. (Food and forage would be shipped ahead to preselected campsites
for the sixteen-day march.) With a sign from the troop commanders, the
men mounted and wheeled into a marching column as the band struck up
the traditional "The Girl I Left Behind Me," and in that fashion, with
Wood and Dorst in the lead, followed immediately by their officers, the
two troops moved off at a walk, headed up the hilly road flanking the eastern boundary of the post, left the military reservation, and cut through
Golden Gate Park, bound for their first encampment twenty-five miles to
the southeast in the tiny rural farm community of San Mateo.[61]

How times have changed. For anyone familiar with San Francisco today, the cavalry's route through San Mateo, Mayfield, and San Jose con-
jures images of twelve-lane freeways, speeding cars, and off-ramps like
roller coasters leading into fields of boxy houses. A century ago, that
same route offered a radically different picture, described by Joe Dorst in
a letter to his wife from "Camp at Gilroy," eighty-four miles and five
days' march southeast of San Francisco. Dorst was in high spirits after a
"delightfully warm and sunshining" march:

> Last night the farmers' brass band serenaded us. They came to
> Wood's tent after he turned in, men, women & boys, played "March-
> ing through Georgia." They gave three cheers for Capt. Wood, with
> rolls on the drums & toots on the horns, & the ladies gave him a bou-
> quet. Then they came to my tent, & called me, & played "Rally
> around the flag"—at its conclusion the front of the tent was opened
> & I stepped forth to be introduced & make a speech & was also given
> three cheers. . . . [Now, after another day's march] we are camped on
> the roadside, & as the weather is pleasant, the whole community &
> fellows with their girls in buggies, carts, and on horseback are out to
> look at us.[62]

The line of cavalrymen swung east from Gilroy toward the Santa
Clara Mountains, which they traversed through Pacheco Pass, at the spot
where John Muir had caught his first glimpse of the Sierra Nevada
twenty-four years earlier and named it the "Range of Light." Like Muir
before them, I Troop descended into the hot and dusty San Joaquin Valley and headed toward "the mighty Sierra, miles in height, and so glori-
ously colored and so radiant, it seemed not clothed with light but wholly
composed of it."[63]

The column of men in blue on horseback moved slowly across the
San Joaquin Valley toward the mountain park they had been assigned to

protect. The temperature of the alkaline air soared. After a march of twenty miles, their mounts were exhausted. They stopped for two nights, resting their horses and waiting for cooler air before resuming their march. Four days later, having traversed the valley and swung south, they parted company at the town of Madera. K Troop continued south toward Fresno and Sequoia. The men of I Troop—the guardians of Yosemite—turned north toward Raymond. With Jug Wood in the lead, they climbed the 7,000-foot-high Chowchilla Mountains, descended 3,000 feet, and rode past the shimmering, white fairy-tale hotel with its gushing fountain to their own simple Camp Near Wawona on the shaded banks of the Merced. They were back home in the heart of what one I Troop officer called "a cavalryman's paradise."[64]

Like the year before, Jug Wood reported to the interior secretary for duty and requested "orders and instructions." Noble asked the chief of his Patent and Miscellaneous Division whether there should be any "new instructions" for Wood. The chief replied that "having looked over the correspondence with Capt. A.E. Wood [Wood's desperate pleas for guidance in 1891] . . . I do not notice any additional instructions that need be given to him." So Noble left Yosemite's puzzled but always deferential acting superintendent as much at sea as he had been the year before.[65]

For Jug Wood, that second summer in paradise would be filled with pain. He had cancer. The first signs of distress appeared early in July, when he hurried back to San Francisco for treatment. "I saw Captain Wood yesterday . . . he is not looking well," Esther Dorst wrote from the Presidio on July 10 to her husband Joe in Sequoia. Jug had lost more than fifteen pounds, she said. He told her it was something in the food at camp, but no one else had reported sick; a few days earlier, Esther Dorst had encountered Second Lieutenant Davis passing through, in perfect health. The Presidio's chief surgeon, Dr. Leonard Wood, told him it was cancer of the tongue. From then until his death two years later, a fellow officer recalled, "he . . . suffered the tortures of the damned" in paradise.[66]

He tried not to show it. During the emergency leave when the dreadful diagnosis was made, Mrs. Dorst invited him and his wife for dinner. Even though he did not look well, "I never saw Capt. Wood enjoy dinner so much or seem so pleasant & chatty," she wrote her husband in Sequoia. Wood joined in singing after dinner and later became so absorbed "looking over your books . . . that at a quarter to eleven when Mrs. Jug thought it time to leave he seemed quite loathe to go."[67]

Wood kept up his brave front after his return to Yosemite later that month. Early in August, perhaps to reassert his authority over himself as well as his men, he led a six-day, 115-mile patrol. But thereafter, except for a few relatively brief forays, he stayed close to camp. His new deputy, First Lieutenant Lockwood, remained with him most of the time, leaving supervision of the incessant patrols to Second Lieutenant Davis.[68]

Even without patrol responsibilities, Wood had plenty to do. The greatest administrative challenge facing the head of Yosemite National Park during the first three years of its existence was to win respect for the park idea and for federal authority. That meant educating sheepherders, cattlemen, miners, timber owners, tourists, arsonists, and other Yosemite visitors and inhabitants. Wood approached each group according to his assessment of its character.

Toward sheepherders he was uncompromising, partly because he hated the destruction of plants and wildlife caused by these "hoofed locusts," but also because he resented efforts by some wealthy sheep owners to mislead the Interior Department. After hearing that they were writing directly to Interior requesting permission to lead their sheep through the park to grazing grounds in Nevada, Wood explained their real object to his civilian superiors—namely, "to graze their flocks along these [Yosemite] trails" until they got close to the Nevada border, then turn around and graze them back again, thus spending the entire season grazing in the park en route to nowhere.[69]

Generally, Wood had been successful in containing infiltrations through the principal southern and southwestern routes, but the mountaineering sheepherders still controlled the park's vast northern and eastern regions beyond the Tuolumne River. That's where Davis concentrated his patrols in 1892. They caught one herd near Mono Pass at an elevation of 12,000 feet on the park's northeastern boundary and another in the mountains beyond the Tuolumne River further north. Still the sheepherders persisted. In 1893, Wood upped the ante by borrowing a tactic from Yellowstone. Although there were no penalties for trespassing other than eviction, whereupon the intruders would return as soon as the troopers moved off, Wood began evicting sheepherders from one boundary and their flocks from another at the opposite end of the park. By the time the herders relocated their flocks, the sheep would be scattered. It was tough work—Wood's troopers had to log long distances over unfamiliar mountain terrain for the strategy to work—but it had its effect.[70]

Initially, Wood showed more patience with cattlemen, who enjoyed higher standing in the West than sheepherders; but once he felt the word had gotten out, he cracked down hard. It was common practice in the spring among cattle owners in Mariposa and adjacent counties to lead their herds into the high country homesteads they used for summer grazing, cut them loose, and come back for them in the fall. The park was created so quickly and without warning that when Wood arrived in 1891 and began to spread the word, he found that many ranchers had already deployed their herds "and to enforce the order against their stock would have subjected them to hardship and pecuniary loss" that he deemed unfair under the circumstances. So he let them off with a warning not to do the same the next year, while telling those who had not yet entered the park to hold off.

One wealthy rancher exploited Wood's goodwill by moving six hundred head of cattle into the park and intermingling them with the herds of small homesteaders. When Wood discovered the ruse, he began herding "the whole outfit" out of the park, but the duped homesteaders "begged so hard for their stock that I had to relent." He also ordered everyone to mark their boundaries, and he established regular procedures for bringing cattle in and out of the park. During the early part of the following season, 1892, he resumed the education process and succeeded in bringing several cattle owners into compliance.

Toward the end of the summer he showed his firm side to those who persisted "in the belief that I would not be severe with them even if they did not do as I wished." He sent his patrols on a sweep through the park, dispersing all the loose cattle they found. Then he went after a rancher who had built two houses on federal land that his cowboys used as a base while openly flouting park rules. Wood ordered both houses burned to the ground. By the end of the season, it had become "generally understood" among cattlemen "that the law forbidding trespass was going to be enforced."[71]

Wood also had to deal with miners stubbornly scratching away at the Sierra Nevada more than forty years after the California gold rush had picked most of the area clean. In 1892, he inventoried mining claims in two of the three main mining districts in the park and founded they totaled 115 (the records were missing for the third district in high mountain country near the eastern border). None of them were profitable, but that did not seem to matter to the miners Wood interviewed.

A miner without hope would be as great a natural curiosity as the Yosemite Valley. This characteristic is so buoyant in its effect that no matter if he only has a trace of the mineral, he firmly believes that when he gets a little deeper he is sure to "strike it rich." . . . A sight · of his hardened hands, strong but soiled clothing, his dry humor, *his clear reasoning from his own standpoint*, and his decided and positive manner when speaking of his claim deprives the subject of its pathos and half convinces the listener.[72]

Wood concluded that the miners' unwavering certainty of one day striking it rich meant that the government could not hope to purchase a miner's claim (as Wood recommended for farmers and cattlemen), "satisfy him, and still keep the expenditure within the bounds of reason." The only alternatives he could see were to exclude the mining districts from the park or keep them as eyesores until the owners and their feverish dreams died out.[73]

Timber owners made up another component of Yosemite's dissonant human ecology. They were a faceless group of nonresident speculators whose greatest danger lay in their potential. There had been little logging as yet. Most of the timber claims were registered in the 1880s in speculative anticipation of the construction of a railroad. Wood recommended that the government move quickly to buy back those lands (his boundary reduction proposals never included forested land) before the dreams of the timber speculators came true and the purchase price grew prohibitive. That recommendation, too, would eventually become policy.[74]

Wood saved his strongest condemnation for people who carelessly or willfully burned the trees he loved. As Stephen J. Pyne, the foremost historian of fire in America, has noted, systematic control of runaway fires on public lands began with the Old Army in national parks: "The Army not only launched federal fire protection but also demonstrated conclusively the techniques by which all wild and forested lands could be managed." This historic contribution could not have been more timely in the face of a new species of tenderfoot camper that was invading the parks and triggering massive conflagrations out of carelessness or sometimes childish maliciousness. Civilian resources were utterly helpless against these destructive sightseers.[75]

The saving efficiency of the Old Army's fire suppression work came from more than technical knowhow and disciplined training. It was infused with an empathetic outlook that Wood captured movingly in his report to the interior secretary. He offered a description of the effects of forest fires on fir trees that was at once scientific and poignant:

> A degree of heat that would not affect the pine will blister the fir, causing the bark to withdraw from the sapwood, the top branches and the tips of the main limbs will die, and although the tree will look green, decay has set in, and in about fifteen years after it has received its wound, without any apparent cause, it breaks and crashes to the ground. . . . [It is] impossible [to fix] even an approximate value [on the damage, for its consequences] reach hundreds of years into the future.[76]

As for the unschooled tourists causing much of the damage, Wood did his best to educate them about the park's inspiring purpose. He had special praise for those "who fit out camping parties and go into the high mountains. . . . I encourage this, for I find that . . . they are impressed with the grandeur of the scenery and the magnificence of the forests, but unlike the [day] tourist, they take a personal interest and pride in the park."[77]

Wood continued to implement his values fairly, firmly, and relentlessly during the 1893 season, his third and last, while his health rapidly deteriorated. In a letter to his superiors he expressed satisfaction with the restoration fostered by his command and called for stepped-up vigilance. He reported on a new campaign undertaken under his personal supervision, with the support of the State of California Fish Commission, to stock the park's largely barren lakes and rivers with trout. He had distributed 25,000 rainbow trout the preceding September, mainly in the Merced River, Lake Ostrander, and the creeks above two of Yosemite Valley's waterfalls. The following September, he received another batch of 7,000 and led a patrol into the Yosemite mountains to distribute them. That fish-planting patrol occurred after another of Wood's hurried visits to the Presidio hospital for medical treatment. He must have felt he was shuttling back and forth between paradise and hell.[78]

Fortunately, his wife Minnie was near at hand. She spent much of the summer at Wawona, along with two other officers' wives and their young children. The excursion was the brainchild of the Presidio's chief physician, Leonard Wood (no relation to Jug), who was treating him and had accompanied I Troop to the park that season as troop surgeon. Leonard Wood was the Harvard-educated soldier-athlete who would a few years later command the legendary Rough Riders (starring Teddy Roosevelt) and be named army chief of staff when Roosevelt became president. The visiting wives and children stayed at the Wawona Hotel and visited Yosemite Valley and other parts of the park with Dr. Wood, whose park duties were minimal, while Jug went about his business and occasionally joined the group for dinner at the hotel.[79]

The lift provided by Minnie and her friends was undermined by perhaps the most unpleasant incident of Jug's three-year Yosemite tenure. It was provoked by Yosemite's irrepressible moralist, Charles Robinson. There had been a change of administration in Washington, and Robinson lost no time in introducing himself to the new interior secretary, Hoke Smith, using Robert Underwood Johnson as a reference. Robinson wrote only to complain, but what could he possibly complain about now? He had to admit that the most widely damaging park intruders, the sheep, were "pretty well excluded now . . . owing to the presence of the military," although he could not resist recommending various redeployments to improve their effectiveness. His chief concerns, however, lay elsewhere. He had received reports, he said, that the troopers were frequenting Indian prostitutes. His informants told him that the prostitutes had settled near the headquarters camp and the purveyors of these "diseased . . . squaws" were also selling the soldiers whiskey. Robinson recommended excluding all Indians from Wawona, where they had been living peacefully for years. But that wasn't all. Robinson had also learned that the loose-living wives of cavalry officers had taken up residence in Wawona, producing an unhealthy "relaxation in discipline." Robinson wanted these temptresses excluded too.[80]

Robinson's letter was forwarded to Wood for comment. The Yosemite commander responded to Robinson's proposals on troop deployments calmly, point by point. When it came to the conjoined references to Indians, drunken troopers, and the corrupting temptations of prostitution and marriage, the acting superintendent delivered a controlled explosion. The Indians were hotel workers who lived in a rancheria about a mile away; "none of them are prostitutes"; to move them away would deprive them of an honest livelihood upon which they had grown economically dependent. Nor were the charges against his soldiers justified. Any member of I Troop had "a better social status . . . more self respect and adhere[d] to the truth closer" than their false accuser. As for the references to his wife by this "brute," Wood was dumbfounded. He began to explain to the interior secretary about "duty" and "honor," but he trailed off; the gulf was too wide.[81]

Robinson's self-appointed role as the conscience of Yosemite declined after that insane outburst, and he grew progressively irrelevant to Yosemite's increasingly promising future under Old Army administration. His actions deserved highlighting because he played an important early role in mobilizing public indignation against conditions in the state-run Yosemite Valley, in serving as an information resource for Johnson and Muir, and now finally because his moral sensitivities stood in starkly instructive contrast to those of Old Army officers. Wood's moral emotions were fed by currents of natural beauty; Robinson's were ruled by perverse imaginings nurtured by puritanical repressions. We see the contrast in Robinson's tub-thumping judgments on Yosemite issues, which, unlike Wood's, never included invocations of the wonders of nature he pretended to defend; and we see it in his final judgment of dying Jug Wood when Robinson's neurotically warring mind, deprived of natural spoliation as a moralistic outlet, erupted in hallucinations of prostitution, drunkenness, and "disease" that he reported with relish to the secretary of the interior of the United States as his righteous duty. There was no way Wood could reach Robinson. He knew that because, throughout his career, vindictive moralists like Robinson had used him and other Old Army officers as scapegoats during their self-redeeming cultural conquest of indigenous peoples identified with "savage" nature.[82]

While Robinson raged against savage "prostitutes" and reptilian "rings," Wood focused his moral concerns on specific individuals, irrespective of their social standing, who were causing the greatest damage to the natural landscape. They included R. U. Shippee, the politically influential president of the Stockton Savings and Loan Society and the largest owner of the flocks of sheep that were devastating Yosemite's mountain meadows. "Mr Shippee is a very rich man," Wood wrote to Interior Secretary Hoke Smith, "and was at one time a prominent candidate before a political convention for Governor of this State, and I am surprised to learn that he is so lacking in public spirit, as to be indifferent to the damage his herds would do this Park if allowed to go to his lands. . . . If the Government wishes to preserve this as a Park, *All* stock must be kept off of it." The public spirit Jug Wood cited in his letter, uncommon for that time and place, was a working concept for park commanders.[83]

Jug spent his last season in Yosemite in constant pain. Late in September 1893, he wrote to army surgeon Leonard Wood who had recently transfered to Georgia. He reported on daily activities in the park and thanked his friend for sending beef soup that was apparently easier for Jug to take down than regular army fare. Before concluding, he presented a clinical description of his condition. He was trying to hide the symptoms of the cancer consuming his inner mouth from his men, but "the swelling interferes materially with my speech." He said he and his wife had decided to follow the advice offered by Leonard Wood several months earlier but resisted by Jug until then, to have surgery to excise the tumorous area in his tongue. As soon he returned to San Francisco, he would apply for two months leave, proceed directly to New York, and "get the operation performed & no one at the Presidio need be the wiser."[84]

But even that brief delay proved impossible to sustain. During the first week in October, Jug suddenly left the park on emergency leave after telegraphing his superiors: "I was in hopes that I could march the command into the Presidio before asking for leave of absence, but I now find that I cannot do so." On October 22, I Troop left Yosemite with Second Lieutenant Davis in command. Wood had rushed east for surgery.[85]

By mid-November, he was back in command of his troop, leading drills and serving on post committees as if nothing had happened. On Christmas Eve, he requisitioned a barrel of beer for his men. On January 29, 1894, he was given the signal honor of leading the cavalry squadron in a full-dress parade of all units at the post. A few days later, he wrote Leonard Wood that he had recovered from his "nervous prostration." The surgeons back east had cut away a large portion of his tongue. "I have no pain—can eat anything without trouble & can talk without much defect."

He attributed his past behavior, such as rushing away for surgery, to "hypochondria."[86]

It was not hypochrondia. On March 2, Department Commander Ruger wrote to his superiors in Washington that Wood was too ill to handle the Yosemite assignment during the coming season. Ruger named a replacement, but on March 22 the secretary of war asked him to reconsider. Might not a summer in Yosemite help Wood's health? Everyone involved with the park wanted him back. The interior secretary personally requested his return. Even cantankerous John P. Irish, the Yosemite state park commissioner who had bitterly attacked Robert Underwood Johnson and Muir, was asking for Wood. General Ruger replied that Wood's return would be "inadvisable."[87]

Almost to the end, Jug Wood insisted on remaining in active command of his troop. Presidio records in March 1894 show him performing all duties expected of a healthy troop commander. But anyone who knew him would have been surprised to see the man who had camped out in subzero blizzards in the Rockies protesting (as he did on March 9) that Presidio parade ground drills should not be so early in the morning during a season of chilling wind from the bay. On March 25, Graham approved a request from Wood to wear a soft hat rather than a regulation forage hat while on duty in order to "alleviate the pain." On April 13, he underwent emergency surgery, and on April 14, at 10:15 A.M., he died. The information was telegraphed to the Fourth Cavalry squadron on maneuvers at Camp Gilroy. A picked detachment of twenty men under Wood's old comrade, James Parker, saddled up and rode all day and night, arriving at the Presidio at 1:15 P.M. on April 15 to serve as an escort for the funeral. Four other Fourth Cav officers and six noncommissioned officers came in by train to serve as pallbearers and coffin bearers.[88]

The funeral was held on April 16, 1894. Jug Wood would have been well satisfied with the proceedings, which were laid out in Presidio Post Order #81. At 1:45 P.M., the cortege formed at Wood's quarters. It included a squad from Light Battery D, Fifth Artillery, with a caisson "properly draped"; the Fifth Artillery Band; the Fourth Cavalry escorts and bearers; and every other officer, noncommissioned officer, and enlisted man on the post, lined up by companies—more than four hundred men. All personnel wore full-dress uniforms, as if for a parade, which it was. At 2 P.M. sharp, the band struck up the funeral march. Regulated by its slow cadence, carefully spaced ranks of soldiers moved down officers' row and up the winding road to the Presidio cemetery and an open gravesite on a hillside overlooking San Francisco Bay and the headlands beyond. Officers barked crisp orders, squads broke from the mass, marched, halted, turned into statues, rifles volleyed in unison, a trumpeter sounded taps, and Jug Wood was laid to rest—strictly according to regulations.[89]

CHAPTER FIVE

Running a Cavalryman's Paradise

*Though the cold of spring and autumn may be biting, though
the life may be lonely, though the work may be difficult—happy
is the soldier whose lines fall amid these scenes of grandeur
and sublimity, where nature has put forth her mightiest efforts. . . .
It's the cavalryman's paradise.*
—Nathaniel F. McClure, First Lieutenant, U.S. Cavalry[1]

Early in 1892, the Sierra Club was established in San Francisco under
John Muir's presidency with a strong commitment to protect Yosemite.
Its impressive charter membership included prominent public officials,
attorneys, professors from the University of California at Berkeley, and
the president of Stanford University. In the summer of 1895, a preliminary draft of the first detailed map of Yosemite National Park went on
display at the club's meeting rooms at the California Academy of Sciences. The historic map-in-progress was the work of club member
Nathaniel F. McClure, an officer with the Fourth U.S. Cavalry regiment.
First Lieutenant McClure was well known at the club. The January 1895
issue of the *Sierra Club Bulletin* featured his account of a patrol he led into
Yosemite's rugged backcountry. McClure's article and map also launched
a secondary career for the young soldier as the Sierra Club's first foreign
correspondent. During the next twenty-five years, he sent dispatches to
the *Sierra Club Bulletin* on his spare-time mountain climbing while based
with the U.S. Army overseas. Before retiring as a brigadier general, Mc-
Clure was awarded a rare honorary life membership in the Sierra Club.
Its *Bulletin* published a glowing tribute to him shortly after his death in
1942.[2]

The Sierra Club's founding intellectuals supported, greatly admired,
and often worked closely with Yosemite's cavalry guardians, and John
Muir's feeling of kinship with them was unusually intense. Why this
deep affinity?

This chapter and the next highlight five representative soldier
guardians of Yosemite and one at nearby Sequoia—who they were, what
they did when they got to the parks, how they got the values undergird-
ing actions that inspired civilian environmentalists. Park activities of
other soldiers are also described. The inquiry into the roots of their environmental ethic is pursued further in subsequent chapters when the ob-

serving lens shifts back onto the Old Army's civilian beholders. We begin here with Sierra Club member Nate McClure.

NATHANIEL F. McCLURE: "IT'S A CAVALRYMAN'S PARADISE"

Nathaniel Fish ("Nate") McClure was born and raised on his family's small tobacco farm in western Kentucky not far from Paducah. His schooling consisted of studies at home in his spare time until he caught the attention of his local congressman, John G. Carlisle, by bombarding Carlisle with correspondence about his dreams of public service. Carlisle was taken with the enthusiastic young farm boy and secured him an appointment at the U.S. Military Academy at West Point. There McClure felt as if he had entered a whole new world of learning and romance. A half century later he described his cadet years in an essay that opened a book he edited entitled *Class of 1887*. McClure recalled that he and his classmates had come to West Point from farms and towns across the nation impelled by a "thirst for exploration and adventure," only to find that "the Regular Army was then but a handful of men in whom the people of the country with few exceptions were not greatly interested." Still, "we helped open the way for the settlement of the West. We have assisted in the restoration of order in hurricanes, floods, earthquakes and other colossal upheavals of nature." Writing in 1938, this seventy-two-year-old retired brigadier general who had commanded a brigade in Europe during World War I was reminding his army colleagues of historic army activities that the selective institutional memory of the "New Army" of the twentieth century had already blurred.[3]

Nate McClure's 1887 West Point graduation photo shows a slim-faced, delicately featured young man, with wide dreamy eyes. He looks fragile and a little lost. Yet that appearance of delicacy, gentleness, and wide-eyed innocence did not prevent him from being an "excellent officer" in the judgment of Lieutenant Colonel S. B. M. Young, his squadron commander at the Presidio and a battle-hardened Civil War veteran who went on to become U.S. Army chief of staff. Presidio commander Colonel William T. Graham, who agreed with Young on almost nothing, seconded his judgment of McClure, whom Graham considered "a superior young man in all respects."[4]

McClure first came to Yosemite in 1894 by an unusual convergence of circumstances. Jug Wood's untimely death was one of them. Jug died only a few weeks before his troop was scheduled to return to Yosemite for a fourth consecutive season. His replacement as I Troop commander was

Nate McClure, Yosemite mapmaker and Sierra Club correspondent, West Point graduation photo. U.S. Military Academy Library.

unprepared for a field assignment so soon. Instead, the Yosemite assignment went to a Fourth Cavalry troop that had arrived at the Presidio the year before—C Troop, under Captain George H. G. Gale. Second Lieutenant Nathaniel McClure was C Troop's third in command. However, his promotion to first lieutenant was due at any moment. When that happened, he would automatically be transferred to another troop because Gale's lone first lieutenant slot was already filled. Shortly after C Troop reached Yosemite, McClure's promotion came through, along with transfer orders to the Fifth Cavalry in Texas. But those orders to move were superseded by orders from the army's commanding general to stay for as long as it took to complete a special task of the highest military priority. McClure's priority assignment was to design the first detailed map of Yosemite National Park.[5]

The map was troop commander Gale's idea. C Troop was on maneuvers at Camp Gilroy, near Santa Cruz, when Gale learned of the decision that "threw management of the park in [my] inexperienced hands." He immediately wrote to the secretary of the interior for "instructions," and in keeping with past Interior practice, he received none. Fortunately, Gale was a hardened frontier veteran, an honors graduate of West Point, and accustomed to command responsibilities under his own initiative. After C Troop reached the park on May 25, Gale quickly concluded that his predecessor had established a solid foundation for authority, and that what was most needed at this point, in order to secure the park's boundaries and permit the construction of an integrative network of trails, was a decent map of the place.[6]

Gale divided the park into several sections based on the limited information he had. He made outline maps of each section and distributed them to picked patrols. Each patrol was ordered to fill in details on its assigned section as it moved over the terrain. The first patrol, nine men, departed on June 4 under McClure's command. Two days after their return on June 13, Gale left for another section with ten men. The patrolling continued throughout the summer and into the fall. After each patrol, the men reported their findings to McClure, whom Gale had named project coordinator. McClure later recalled that he had to start virtually from scratch, since the maps available to him "were unreliable in almost every particular." That fall and winter, after returning to the Presidio, Gale and McClure continued working on the map. Realizing they needed more detail to do the job right, Gale requested that McClure's "detached service" be extended into 1895 and that he accompany the troop assigned to Yosemite that year, which would be Alex Rodgers's (formerly Joe Dorst's) K Troop. The extension was no problem. The Old Army loved frontier mapmakers.[7]

Meanwhile, the Sierra Club had become the focal point for a small but rapidly organizing environmental preservation movement based in the West. The club came into being in San Francisco in 1892 when efforts by John Muir and Robert Underwood Johnson to launch a "Yosemite Defence Association" converged with efforts led by faculty at the University of California at Berkeley and Stanford to establish a Sierra Nevada—oriented alpine club. Muir was the Sierra Club's first president, and its other officers were three professors, a member of the U.S. Geological Survey, and an attorney, all avid mountaineers. The club's membership grew from twenty-seven to more than three hundred within a year. According to a club historian, membership consisted principally of "prominent professors, scientists, politicians, and business leaders . . . the kind of Californians who would be called progressives by later historians." Board members included David Starr Jordan, the president of Stanford University, and Joseph LeConte, the University of California's world-recognized professor of botany, geology, and natural history. This was the readership for Nate McClure's article describing his Yosemite backcountry patrol that appeared in the January 1895 issue of the *Sierra Club Bulletin*. McClure's article had made a powerful impression on a very discerning audience.[8]

It's easy to see why. The soldier's report completed an earlier word picture of the new park drawn by John Muir in 1890. Muir's account had appeared in *Century Magazine* in September of that year as part of the Johnson-Muir campaign for a Yosemite national park. It described a circuit through areas north of the Tuolumne River that the proposed new park would incorporate. But Muir's circuit did not include the rugged mountain terrain extending into the towering crest of the Sierra Nevada that would mark the park's northernmost boundaries. That was the area charted by McClure in his *Sierra Club Bulletin* article five years later, entitled "Explorations Among the Cañons North of the Tuolumne River" (as was common in those days, McClure used the Spanish spelling for canyon).[9]

McClure's descriptions of nature integrated scientific observation and poetic expression in the style Muir had perfected. McClure's article also included four enriching ingredients that Muir's account of Yosemite exploration lacked. First, in contrast to Muir's rambling style, it gave geographical shape to the area it covered. Even today, one can chart the path of McClure's seventeen-day patrol (as a few hardy hikers continue to do, using copies of his still-popular map) as it winds through valleys, into canyons, up the steep sides of mountains, along ridgelines, creeks, rivers, lakes, over glaciers, in a circle north from Wawona, east to west through the park's northernmost reaches, south to Hetch Hetchy Valley, then into Yosemite Valley before returning to Wawona; in that systematic geographical progression, Yosemite's backcountry gradually unfolds like a moving picture tour put to words. By comparison, Muir's article was more like a collection of separate landscape paintings by a grand master.

Second, whereas Muir focused exclusively on the interconnected natural beauty of the region, McClure added a layer of human connections in the form of man-made trails that his patrol either discovered or blazed. He was knitting together the new arbitrarily created park as he moved through it. Third, McClure entwined his patrol's trail-blazing with that of sheepherders then active in the park as well as the Indian trailblazers before them, adding a human history dimension to the region that Muir, who was more interested in geologic history, generally overlooked. Finally, McClure gave his narrative momentum by keying it to an adventurous and often suspenseful pursuit of elusive sheepherders who had made the Yosemite backcountry their personal domain, beyond the reach (until then) of the park's uniformed administrators. Those layered elements were integrated with great sophistication to produce a tale of man and nature that was absorbing, earthy, and informative on several levels at once.[10]

McClure set the military tone of his Sierra Club article in its opening words: "On August 18, 1894, I left the cavalry camp near Wawona, California, with a detachment of the Fourth U.S. Cavalry, consisting of twelve men and five pack-mules, with rations for twelve days, to scout for sheepmen, who were reported to be unusually thick in the vicinity of Tuolumne Meadows." That McClure had an additional objective became evident when the patrol arrived in Tuolumne Meadows the following day. There McClure interviewed a homesteader about a route to Lake Eleanor, almost due east of the Meadows. But McClure wasn't looking for a direct route to the lake. Instead, he requested and obtained a sketch, "covering two-thirds of a sheet of legal-cap paper," that looped northward into the park's most remote terrain—a foreboding mountainous region, sliced by glaciers, with high narrow ridges and deep canyons.

With the homesteader's skimpy sheet of instructions and a crude Sierra Club sketch as their only guides, McClure's patrol set out on the morning of August 20. They began on the well-traveled Conness Trail, but in less than three miles they came to a fork mentioned in the homesteader's description. From there, McClure sent three men up the Conness Trail to look for sheep while he and the others searched the area until they found the blazes marking the sheepherder trail that would set them off on their circuit. They were doing what the Old Army had been doing for a century: mapping and tracking.

The main group zigzagged through the mountains for two miles before coming to a clearing that McClure picked for a campsite. From there he sent two men scouting southward while he continued with three others up a creek bed. After about four miles, McClure rode into a meadow where he found several of the "the enemy's" pack animals grazing. He arrested one sheepherder (another escaped) and returned to camp to find the soldiers there augmented by the squad he had sent up the Conness Trail. The Conness squad had three sheepherders in tow. McClure sent the four "prisoners" back to Wawona under guard and continued his march into the mountains. During the next two days, August 23 and 24, the members of McClure's patrol, "relying on the lay of the land . . . zigzagging across ridges," found their way into a canyon where they discovered two sheepherder camps. The surprised herders fled up the canyon, leaving their supplies and thousands of sheep behind.

On August 24, six days into his march, McClure sent two men back to Tuolumne Meadows to pick up fresh supplies from Wawona while he and the others moved deeper into the forbidding range of mountains and canyons. That same day, while picking his way through a canyon, scanning its western walls for a route his patrol could follow to the next canyon, McClure realized that the homesteader's directions that had set him off were "no longer dependable." McClure was now wholly on his own. He was walled in by a mountain with three jagged spurs on its peak that appeared "as you advance up the cañon, like the teeth of a gigantic circular saw." He could go no further and was forced to make camp: "After a good meal I . . . was lying on my bedding, resting, when all at once, as my eyes were scanning the side of the great backbone that separated me from Matterhorn Canon, I thought I saw a place where a way to ascend might be found. Up I sprang."

After climbing the ridge alone and searching for some time along its backbone, McClure found a route that he marked with piles of stones before returning to camp just before nightfall, "well pleased" with his efforts. The next morning, leaving one man behind to look out for the supply train from Tuolumne Meadows, the cavalrymen struck out, blazing their own trail up the wall of the canyon. They had now joined the Indians, mountain men, and sheepherders as contributors to this remote region's human geography, but with one important difference: McClure's exploring, mapping, and trailblazing were aimed at illuminating and unifying a newly established entity called Yosemite National Park so that its preservationist rules and regulations could be effectively enforced. He was blazing (as would his successors) what the most knowledgeable historian of Yosemite's trail network called "administrative routes."[11]

On the evening of August 25, the supply unit arrived with six more men, five pack mules, and 85 rations; the expedition now had fifteen men on horseback, nine pack mules, and 150 rations. The supply unit reported large concentrations of sheep in Bloody Canyon, back the way McClure had come. McClure split the expedition in half. He directed a sergeant to take seven men with 80 rations back toward Bloody Canyon. The others, led by McClure, pressed on. Their path ran along the jagged crest of the

Sierra Nevada, sometimes climbing, sometimes suddenly descending into deep canyons. They were cut off from their supply line now and could only push ahead.

With that division of McClure's forces also came a division of purpose. Henceforth, his policing role gave way almost wholly to exploring and mapping this "truly sublime" country. He even enlisted one of the "enemy" as a guide, as frontier soldier-explorers before him had enlisted Indians for the same purpose.

McClure's guide was a companion of a sheepherder captured in a mountain canyon on August 26. McClure promised to let his prisoner go if he would show the way westward to Jack Main's Canyon, just north of Hetch Hetchy Valley, through especially difficult terrain. The prisoner said the only man who knew that route had fled when McClure's patrol approached. Find him, McClure said, and you'll go free and so will he if he knows the way to Jack Main's Canyon. Three hours later McClure had a "very willing" guide. He led McClure's patrol not only to Jack Main's Canyon but also into another world heretofore unknown to soldiers patrolling the park.

My guide suddenly turned sharp to the right and began to work up what seemed to be, from below, an impassable cliff, the rocks being bare and steep, with here and there a few scattered tamarack trees and bunches of willows. After going up perhaps a hundred feet, the trail suddenly turns into a seam running up the side of the bluff in the direction of the head of the main cañon. This seam, or inclined ledge, can scarcely be noticed from below.

This was the world, invisible to the outsider, that sheepherders had inherited from the Indians who traversed these mountain lands for hundreds of years. Here and there a pile of stones marked the way. But "there was no well-defined path; and one going over this country must travel more or less by the great cañons, which correspond, in a rough way, with the streets of a mighty city."McClure's guide pointed beyond two of these mighty stone cities toward a pass that seemed "impossible" to reach.

To our left, as we looked toward this pass, was the main range, studded with high, jagged peaks and curving gradually around like an enormous amphitheater, until it reached the saddle through which we were to go, and then extending miles to the northwest. Many snowbanks, and even glaciers, lay along the northern slopes, and from these hundreds of rivulets trickled and tumbled into the two main cañons, cutting the declivities in the most fantastic manner into innumerable arroyos and minor cañons.

McClure's dismounted patrol led their horses in single file behind the guide, picking their way slowly among the boulders, descending into and out of steep ravines, "with an occasional rock pile here and there to mark the route," just as the region's inhabitants had done for centuries before the arrival of Europeans. They finally reached Jack Main's Canyon and said good-bye to their guide. The trail leading out of the canyon toward Lake Eleanor was also from an ancient Indian era, but it soon grew wider, the terrain more compacted, the path made easier to follow by clumps of horse dung left by the mounts of homesteaders living nearby.

The patrol seemed to be moving through time as well as space as it marched out of the deep canyon into the heavily traveled homesteaders' trail. McClure's haunting prose turned prosaic. They trotted past Lake Eleanor, turned onto the dusty stage road leading into Yosemite Valley, and continued from there to Wawona, arriving on September 3.

McClure had concluded a circuit of the park that was both literal and figurative, an odyssey in the classical sense. He had begun his account in strict contemporary military fashion, introducing his "detachment" at the time of its departure. Then, as he moved deep into the mountain wilderness, his imagination plunged into unexplored depths, conjuring integrative images as he jousted with natural forces that could engulf him in an instant. Finally, to complete the archetypal circuit, he returned from that primeval world, both physically and spiritually, with his prize: a wild land domesticated lovingly, empathetically, into a nature park. He had mapped it, named its components, given it a bounded, measurable identity that integrated it with the culture he served—a culture that he also sought to integrate with nature.

That final integration set McClure apart from the region's previous trailblazers. In the article's conclusion, he noted that "almost every sheep-herder has a different name for each of the great cañons north of the Tuolumne River," which "may prove in future a stumbling-block to those wishing to visit this region." He added, in the only italics in the article, "One should never forget that the name he hears spoken may be associated in the mind of his interlocutor with a totally different place from what it is in his own mind." Such domination of empirical observation by folklore was wholly unacceptable to McClure. Here his romanticism ceded to science without surrendering its warm attachment to nature: "In a map which I am preparing on this part of the National Park, I hope to remove much of the confusion existing on this subject, by naming the most prominent features" of a place he clearly loved.[12]

Students of American myths who find so many layers of meaning in the frontier cavalry might profit from a closer look at McClure's cavalry patrol—his embarkation into new territory, his primal discoveries, his rejuvenated return, his integration of new wisdom. McClure's odyssey was fundamentally different from the one-sided experience of Americans on the western frontier who were seeking mainly to overpower, subjugate, and exploit nature. Like John Muir but in a more complex sociopolitical context, McClure had taken a modern abstract idea, Yosemite National Park, and enriched it with precisely detailed form and emotional depth. Experiencing nature at its engulfing primeval core and then, like Homer's Ulysses, returning to the mundane everyday world with his prize (the essence of classical Greek mythopeia), and finally connecting his experience with its opposite contemporary extreme in the empirical world of modern science and sealing the connection with primal feeling—it was that unusual capacity to reopen and rejuvenate an age-old route of heart and mind that gave McClure's patrol a character rare for its time.[13]

McClure returned to Yosemite in May 1895 with Captain Alex Rodgers's K Troop to continue working on the map he initiated under Captain Gale. He had grown deeply attached to the region and tried to arrange a switch with Alexander Dean (the unpopular I Troop first lieutenant whom Wood court-martialed for drunkenness in 1891) in which Dean would take McClure's slot with the Fifth Cavalry in Texas. If that had happened, McClure would have returned to Yosemite again in 1896, but the regiment in Texas wanted nothing to do with Dean. McClure managed only a brief extension through the 1895–1896 winter, to be spent at the Presidio completing revisions of the map by then on display at the Sierra Club headquarters. During that period, McClure also prepared additional notes on his Yosemite explorations for publication in the *Sierra Club Bulletin* the following spring. Finally, in March 1896, he submitted the map's final version to the chief of army engineers, Department of California, whereupon his "detached service" ended and he received orders to depart at once for Fort Bliss, Texas.[14]

McClure's map marked a turning point in the history of Yosemite National Park. There had been maps of the region encompassing the park, notably one by the army-led Wheeler Survey of the 1870s, but none specifically geared to the boundaries of the national public entity created by Congress in 1890. McClure gave the park topographically detailed shape and form for the first time. He also opened the way for effective administration by pinpointing remote areas where sheepherders and other trespassers had escaped detection. Finally, in preparing his map, McClure initiated a process continued by subsequent park commanders and civilian administrators of naming Yosemite mountains, lakes, canyons, rivers, and other natural sites. Many of those new names replaced old names assigned by sheepherders, miners, Indians, and others who had passed through the area over the years. As one astute student of Yosemite history observed, "Place names were also a way of staking claim to territory." Changing place-names and publishing maps that brought those changes into general public usage were ways "of preventing trespass not only by the animals but also by a way of life which national park status had changed." Thus, McClure's map marked the beginning of a distinct historic identity for the new Yosemite National Park. He brought the park into historical time. (The next step, already under way in some quarters, would be to recover and reintegrate the central role of Indian cultures in the human history of national parklands.)[15]

McClure subsequently wrote about his Yosemite experiences for the professional journal of the United States Cavalry Association. In that article, he described the cavalry's duties and accomplishments in Yosemite, intermingling scientific precision with rhapsody as he lovingly recalled the services performed on behalf of its "lakes, rapids, thundering waterfalls, great fissures in the earth's surface, bald granite domes, mighty cliffs . . . beautiful meadows . . . hidden among forests and extend[ing] up the mountain sides far above the timber line," where "thousands of streams come trickling down from the snowbanks and glaciers, and swelling they unite, to go tumbling over beds of boulders on their way to the sea."[16]

CAPTAIN JOSEPH DORST: "ALL THE WORLD LOVES A LOVER"

In 1891 and 1892, Joseph Dorst's K Troop of the Fourth Cavalry administered Sequoia in tandem with Jug Wood's I Troop in Yosemite. Serving under Dorst were a junior officer and an enlisted man profiled later in this chapter who would play critical roles in Yosemite's future, Harry Benson and Gabriel Sovulewski. Dorst was their role model. "He was my best friend and instructor," Benson said; Sovulewski worshiped him. "No matter how many, or how great hardships you put upon me, I am ready to follow your directions with all the honesty and courage at my command," Sovulewski wrote Dorst in one of a series of reverent letters that continued for years after Sovulewski had left the army and was working in Yosemite as a civilian.[17]

Joe Dorst's influence over a generation of Fourth Cavalry troopers, many of whom served in California's national parks, reflected his status as the valedictorian of the Mackenzie school of leadership, Ranald Mackenzie's favorite regimental adjutant. Like his classmate and good friend Jug Wood, Dorst was a superb soldier, but where Wood was a shy, stiff, taciturn man who showed a bluntness toward his subordinates that could be harsh, Dorst was relaxed, warm, self-assured, and openly caring. He wore his heart on his sleeve. A picture of Dorst as a young officer

Joe Dorst, Sequoia's first commander and Ranald Mackenzie's favorite adjutant, seated in the center with the Fourth Cavalry shortly after graduating from West Point. U.S. Military Academy Library.

confirms a classmate's description of a "singularly handsome and well-built" young man, seated at the center of a group of six uniformed comrades gathered outdoors in front of a tent, erect but wholly at ease, his hands draped casually over the arm of the chair, thick well-groomed mustache, frank appraising eyes gazing straight into the lens. He was the only one who did not seem to be posing.[18]

Dorst graduated from West Point in 1872 and was sent directly to the Fourth Cavalry regiment in Texas. Mackenzie took to him at once. The young lieutenant rode alongside the Fourth Cavalry's commander into battle, sat by him in meetings, and kept the regiment's official records as its adjutant. Bolstered by Mackenzie's effusive recommendations, Dorst "obtained his captaincy long before any other member of his [West Point] class." For his part, Dorst worshiped Mackenzie. He wrote the previously cited posthumous tribute that summarized his revered commander's character virtues, concluding that Mackenzie's greatness as a leader lay in his being "an exalted type of the noblest work of GOD, an honest man"—an attribute Dorst took wholly to heart.[19]

During Dorst's two seasons in Sequoia, he and his bride Esther exchanged more than one hundred letters. Besides providing the only extensive personal record of the army's daily activities in the California parks, the letters recount a revealing change in Joe's internal ecology of thoughts and feelings. At the time of his marriage in his mid-thirties, he had spent his entire adulthood in uniform as a cadet at West Point or a soldier in the regular army. Bonding was for him a masculine experience drawing on a military tradition of character virtues created to overcome fear and pull men together on the battlefield. Now his warrior bonds were complemented by the bonds of heterosexual love. On the trail in Sequoia, in his first letters "home" to his bride after nearly twenty years of army bachelorhood, Joe struggled to integrate those sometimes conflicting emotional currents.[20]

The internal struggle that came to a head in Sequoia was prefigured in his courtship. Joe Dorst met Esther Archer and fell in love with her in 1884, but he did not court her until nearly six years later. He explained why with characteristic frankness in a letter to her mother, Catherine Archer, in which he sought her approval for their marriage. "I was restrained," he wrote, because Esther's family "had money." Her father was a wealthy merchant with ties in Denver, St. Louis, and Philadelphia, whereas Joe's father was an ironworker who had a small foundry in New Albany, Indiana, across the Ohio River from Louisville. "I have never courted rich people . . . and I did not wish to put myself in a position where my motives might be questioned," Joe went on in his letter to Mrs. Archer. Also, when he first met Esther during a visit to New York, he was a junior lieutenant stationed in a godforsaken post on the frontier. When he wrote Mrs. Archer six years later, he was a captain assigned to West Point and about to be transferred to metropolitan San Francisco, a step up by his modest standards if not by hers.

Mrs. Archer responded to his statement of intentions with caution. Who, she asked, could speak for Dorst's character? He replied with consternation moderated by that same disarming frankness: "I am but little acquainted with society or society people, as I have but little inclination that way, and also because all my service . . . was on the frontier." He listed army generals who knew him, then the superintendent of the Military Academy, then "all the officers of the Fourth Cavalry," growing more and more flustered as he wrote. He realized those grizzled soldiers would not make the impression on this well-connected society matron that "I would wish," and she probably "would not attach much value" to what they had to say. Feeling himself sinking before her eyes, he suddenly had an inspiration. Retired army commanding general William T. Sherman, a man of high social as well as military standing, knew Joe (the army was so small then that most officers knew one another), and he also might know Mr. Archer. Dorst signed off with a promise to contact the general at once.[21]

The rest, as the Dorst family might say, was happy history. Sherman turned out to be an old friend of Esther's father. "He [Dorst] is one of the finest young fellows in the Army, of most excellent character and reputation," the retired general wrote to Mrs. Archer. "The only rival she may have," Sherman continued, "will be Dorst's horse, which every good Cavalry officer loves more than anything except a wife or child." The letter concluded, "I accept an invitation to the wedding." The old general wrote to Joe the same day. "All the girls supposed you bullet and love proof," he said, but Joe had made the right decision, "for all the world loves a lover."[22]

Esther and Joe married in Denver in August 1890 upon completion of his West Point tour of duty. From Denver they proceeded directly to Joe's new assignment at the Presidio in San Francisco. They had scarcely settled in when Esther's lover left her to camp out in the Sierra Nevada for half a year. She felt abandoned. He felt guilty. During that long 1891 season and the season of 1892, Joe and Esther Dorst exchanged scores of letters.[23]

Leading his troop into camp in Sequoia in 1891, a task he previously would have found exhilarating, Joe was surprised at how much the gyroscope of his feelings had changed. "It is the first time I ever wanted to go back into a post after getting into the field," he wrote after receiving two passionate letters from Esther within days of his arrival at Sequoia. "How utterly miserable I should be were it not for you. . . . every pleasurable thought is connected with you."[24]

In early June, Esther begged him to visit her or to let her visit him. After all, wasn't he in a park that was meant to be visited? He replied at once. For him, a trip back to the Presidio so soon was not in the cards. As for Esther coming to Sequoia, Joe did not think K Troop's preliminary camp at Mineral King, a former mining community near the park's southern border, had much to offer in the way of tourist accommodations. "The ground is bare, stony & bushy, like a sandy sage brush country. The wrecks of old buildings, crushed by snow, are scattered around like dirty drift wood. . . . A few large tents, & twice as many small shelter tents are scattered around over ground smooth enough for the men to sleep on. . . . Dust, dirt, & a general slovenly appearance every where." Sequoia had a way to go as a tourist destination.[25]

In a couple of weeks, Joe wrote, conditions would get even worse: K Troop would move to a point twenty miles off, "on the other side of a gap 10,500 feet high, where only pack mules can go, & where men have to lead their horses." Her letters followed him into the mountains. They reached him in bunches of two and three and four. She never complained about his absence. She just loved him and missed him.[26]

Late in June he obtained a weekend leave and found Esther bedridden. Earlier that month in San Francisco, on an errand, she had fainted and was rushed home in an ambulance. The post physician explained the cause of her symptoms and told her she needed bed rest. She was two months pregnant. Joe was overcome with grief and guilt. She had said nothing of it in her letters; she did not want him to worry. On June 23, on a train returning to Sequoia, he begged her forgiveness for his cruel insensitivity. General John Schofield, the commanding general of the army, was on the same train with him, but Joe had walked right by his car without presenting himself. Who cared about the commanding general? He only felt love for Esther and admiration for her courage.[27]

Joe returned to Sequoia a changed man. His previous professions of love seemed perfunctory compared to what he felt now. A whole new world of human intimacy had opened to him. The scenes of life in camp and on the trail that he had so much enjoyed describing to her now "seem out of place." "Many a time I would have been utterly blue & weary of life," this outdoorsman wrote from one of the most beautiful outdoor sites in the world, "had I not thoughts of my wife in reserve & of her love."[28]

The rest of the summer was sweet torture for the lovestruck cavalryman. He looked forward with wonder and excitement to the birth of their first child. He worried constantly about Esther, sometimes so much that he tossed on the ground all night without sleeping. His union with her had made him "a better man than I have ever been in my life—I owe so much to you." He lived only for her letters.[29]

Dorst was engulfed. In the midst of his personal turmoil, he tried to organize Sequoia. His patrols were beginning to have an effect on intruding sheepherders and cattle drivers, but he needed to pay more attention to those activities and spend more time in the field. As his attention shifted toward the mountains, Esther abruptly pulled him back into camp and out the other way when she overwhelmed his objections and took a train to the nearby town of Visalia toward the end of August.[30]

After Esther's visit, Dorst's turbulent feelings underwent yet another change. His professions of love were as strong as ever, but alongside them there appeared a generalized irritability about his work. He felt indecisive and sedentary. Recently, several of his men had gone off on a spree, and he had to call a summary court-martial at camp. That would not have happened before. On September 9, as if reporting an astonishing discovery, he told Esther that he had not "ridden a horse anywhere since Aug. 15."[31]

At the height of that period of irritability and indecision, Dorst requested in early September through army channels that a young cavalry officer named Harry Benson be assigned to his troop. Benson had impressed Dorst earlier in Arizona as a second lieutenant fresh out of West

Point. Since promoted to first lieutenant, he was assigned to the Fourth Cavalry headquarters in Walla Walla when Joe put in a call for him. Joe asked Esther to help out by lobbying for Benson with squadron commander Anson Mills at the Presidio. The call for Benson indicated that a side of Joe's personality he had neglected was asserting itself.[32]

There were other signs. On September 28, Joe received a letter from Esther reporting a rumor at the post that he was to return on October 15. The rumor was false, he replied; in fact, he had asked to remain in the park through mid-November. It was a matter of professional honor and duty. He discussed the heightened danger of fires, which in the fall did not come only from tourists or campers. There was a new threat from the thousands of sheep and cattle grazing in lands east of the park. When the November snows came, they would withdraw. Without troopers to head them off, the herders would take a shortcut through the park, trampling the vegetation and increasing the risk of fires during this unusually dry season: "The destruction of the Giant Forest would be a calamity that could never be repaired. It is the most remarkable in the world."[33]

In a letter a few days later, his feelings vacillated from one extreme to the other. He reported that the temperature was ninety-eight degrees, and he was more concerned than ever about the expected invasion of sheep and cattle and the spoliation and fires they might cause. At the same time he was "all anxiety" about her because "the last one of your letters was short, & you said you were tired." He was also anxious to have Benson on hand to back him up. He begged her for another letter soon to set his mind and heart at rest about her condition.[34]

On October 9, the two sides of his inner conflict finally confronted one another on the surface. He wrote Esther that he had received orders to return to the Presidio on November 1, and had requested that the return date be extended to mid-November. He hinted that his orders from Department of California headquarters in San Francisco had been influenced by the common knowledge among his colleagues of Esther's condition and his concern about her: "I should regret very much having some disaster occur after my leaving, such as the burning of the Giant Forest, & then have it said that I was so anxious to get home that I failed to make proper representations of what might happen. That would be disgraceful." He added that Benson was on the point of leaving San Francisco for Sequoia. And he concluded: "I am feeling a little blue tonight. . . . I am afraid to go home or to leave camp & go anywhere in the Park where the mail will not reach me. I want to do both." But of course he couldn't.[35]

Three days later, with Benson having finally arrived the day before, Dorst's inner tumult entered a new phase. It showed up in his letters to Esther during the remaining weeks of his tour in 1891 and during the following year when he also commanded the Sequoia troop. He began with a fourteen-page letter (his longest to date) elaborating his responsibilities in detail. Apparently, Esther had been puzzled by his earlier comments about staying on in Sequoia in order to give his men needed "recreation." "My sweetheart, I would not try to keep my troop from leaving here, & delay being with you, solely to give my men a good time," he wrote, and he went on to discuss how what he called "recreation" belonged to the category of training and discipline.

When the men had arrived at the park in May, many of them "had been in the habit of dissipating so much at night time, in San Francisco, that it took several weeks to make them fresh and active." Many were new recruits who knew nothing of service in the field, having spent their first months in the army at the Presidio performing drills that were nothing but "shows." Even worse, by Dorst's standards, these men who had only recently come under his command "had never had any training to develop military aspirations . . . and had no idea what a real soldier was." The park assignment provided an opportunity to whip his troop into shape in the field and also "to get the men who are not soldiers so disgusted . . . that they will buy their discharges or transfer to some other troop when we get back."

That was the context for his remark about "recreation." It was a part of the complicated business of molding his troop into a disciplined unit whose members felt bonds of loyalty that would strengthen their resolve in combat (and perhaps save their lives), hence his efforts to organize "some pleasant incidents to remember, some personal experiences of an agreeable nature" to recall to one another. The letter ended with comments on mules "who had never worked together {and] would not pull together" unless properly trained, and horses who had grown "soft, from lack of work [at the Presidio], & their backs not tough and would soon get sore." Men, horses, mules—after announcing that he was "off tomorrow [October 13] with Benson," he bid farewell to his "darling wife."[36]

The four-day patrol with Benson left Dorst feeling comfortable enough to leave the troop in his new chief subordinate's command and pay a two-day visit to Esther. Following his return, until K Troop's departure on November 16, Dorst was almost constantly on patrol. The Sequoia correspondence he and his wife preserved included only one brief letter for that three-week period, written early in the morning on October 31. He was on the trail, pursuing trespassers, living on bread, bacon, and coffee. "We are to get beef & potatoes tomorrow, but I shall not be here," he wrote. He had to keep up the pressure; he had to keep moving.[37]

During the following season of nearly seven months (from May 6 through November 30, 1892), Joe returned to the Presidio to visit Esther and their baby son Archer only once, in August. There was no less mutual longing in their letters. "I am more nearly homesick than I ever was in my life," he wrote to her in June. But the work the previous year had been "most carelessly performed. . . . There would have been no trouble with sheep all this year, had any detail last year showed one tenth the energy of Benson this year."[38]

He delivered the above assessment after returning from fighting a fire that, he told Esther, had engulfed nearly one-third of the treasured General Grant sequoia grove. Awaiting him was a letter from the secretary of the interior ordering him to station troops in the fire-prone grove and also to investigate allegations of park violations dating "nearly a year back." Fortunately, he had just assigned a detail to General Grant under Sergeant Gabriel Sovulewski, but to have someone in Washington order him to "correct evils that were right under my nose" was humiliating, especially since his superior was "perfectly right. . . . I should have spent a great deal more time about the park . . . instead of loafing my time away in camp. . . . God knows I want to see you and baby badly enough, but I can not do my work properly with my mind always planning how I can manage to neglect a little here, & do a little carelessly there, in order to get time to leave. . . . Please do not try to argue me out of this . . . for it's hard enough for me to stick to it as it is." He need not have worried. "You said it was a sermon," Esther replied, "well, . . . I would rather get a good sound discourse from you, who practise what you believe to be right & who try always to live to the higher better aspirations in man than go and hear anyone whom I am not sure of being sincere & honest."[39]

On July 16, after being in the saddle almost continuously for a month, Joe wrote Esther a long letter while at an overnight camp. He wrote by the light of a forest fire his troops were fighting. He described his patrolling activities and the lay of the land in minute detail. He had fought fires and chased herds of sheep and cattle, in many cases tracking them over mountains and into canyons. Tomorrow, after making sure the fire he was fighting was contained, he would "make one or two detours in this remote corner of the park to let the men get acquainted with the country & learn something more about it myself, particularly with regard to routes traveled by sheep men." Then he would hook up for awhile with Benson, who had been on patrol nearly four weeks without a break. He had also dispatched another patrol to survey the eastern line of the park, cut a trail along it, and chase out whatever sheep and cattle they might find; he needed to review their work. As soon as he returned to the main camp, whenever that might be, after submitting several required reports to the Interior Department and the War Department, "if nothing interferes, I think I shall feel at liberty to go to the Presidio for a day or two." Having laid that all out, he concluded:

> Now darling you must know that I am more anxious to see you & the baby perhaps than you are to see me. . . . It is very painful for me

to feel this, & yet have my sense of duty pulling me away from you, & know I must not think of you at times, but give my whole mind to the many complications that arise here, consider them thoroughly, & be prepared always with a clear & well considered course of action for every emergency. I am dying to see the youngster, & am anxious for you both nearly every minute of my waking hours, when I am not able to get your letters. I have to be active to keep free from fretting. With all my heart, much love.[40]

Esther responded immediately, telling him not to worry. They were reunited finally in late August, and he returned to Sequoia on August 27. He found his command running smoothly and immediately wrote Esther: "I do believe I am loving you more all the time."[41]

Some interpreters of late nineteenth-century American culture have presented the "soldier hero" and the effeminate aesthete as contrasting masculine models. But even if the soldier hero met the emotional needs of large segments of an increasingly urbanized American population, that did not necessarily make him the norm in the Old Army of the frontier. Joe Dorst, bona fide soldier hero, was a masculine warrior, a heterosexual lover, and an extremely sensitive aesthete. He also brought an unusual kind of idealism to his heartfelt marital relationship. Joe and Esther never sought solace and inspiration in visions of material wealth or spiritual salvation. Instead, they found justification for their separations in invocations of national civic duty to a political community functioning for the most part on another wavelength.[42]

HARRY C. BENSON: "I LOVE IT AS I CAN NO OTHER PLACE IN THE WORLD"

No one contributed more to Yosemite National Park during its formative years under army administration than Harry Benson. After a two-year tour in Sequoia under Joe Dorst, Benson served two years as a deputy troop commander in Yosemite (1895–1897) and three additional years as Yosemite's acting superintendent (1905–1908). During the latter period he supervised the complex incorporation of the state-administered Yosemite Valley into the surrounding national park. Throughout the intervening and subsequent years of the army's twenty-five-year Yosemite tenure, Benson stayed involved, informally advising park-based soldiers and Interior Department officials in a constant stream of letters, some mailed from overseas. He even spent his military leaves chasing trespassers through the mountains and canyons of Yosemite backcountry. The dogged sincerity of his commitment disarmed people on all sides of the park issue. John

Harry C. Benson, Yosemite's most steadfast defender, early 1900s. Yosemite National Park Library.

B. Curtin, the attorney-cattleowner–state legislator who fought the army from day one, wrote to his old adversary in 1908 that when he learned Benson had been assigned to the park once again, he advised clients seeking a grazing variance that "while 'hope springs eternal in the human breast,'" they had best postpone their efforts because Benson would never yield to them.[43]

Jug Wood was hard, Nate McClure gentle, Harry Benson perpetual motion. On or off duty, he was always in a rush. He stood only five feet six inches tall, but he created an imposing impression in the saddle with his stiffly erect posture, his stern demeanor behind a closely trimmed mustache, his clipped speaking style, and his superb horsemanship. On the ground up close, when his gentle blue eyes and diminutive height joined the picture, he could inspire softer sentiment. "What an energetic little man he is!" wrote Esther Dorst affectionately, after meeting him for the first time in the summer of 1892. He had been called to the Presidio to testify at a court-martial. Esther was alone at home with her six-month-old baby when Benson suddenly appeared. He "ran in for a few moments," ran out, visited horses he kept across the bay, reappeared for dinner ("Mr. Benson did justice to the meal and was very entertaining"), coaxed her into a horseback ride for the first time since her pregnancy ("I enjoyed it more than I can express"), charmed her baby son ("Mr. Benson . . . knows nursery rhymes which he quotes to him"), walked her dogs, appeared again the next day out of the blue for dinner, led her on another riding excursion along the bay, took her into his confidence on his matrimonial plans, listened sympathetically to her confidences on the mingled joy and pain of a marriage with forced separations—in short, became so involved in so many different aspects of her life during his seven-day visit, while transacting a slew of other business, that Esther might at least partly have been speaking of herself when she wrote to her husband as Benson prepared to return to Sequoia: "Indeed dearest could you really do without him?"[44]

He was probably the only man in the Old Army (or out of it) with a lake, a mountain pass, and a partridge named after him. Benson Lake and Benson Pass in Yosemite National Park commemorate his explorations in Yosemite backcountry. The *Callipepla elegans bensoni* was captured, skinned, carefully packed, and sent to the Smithsonian Institution by Benson while pursuing Apaches in the Sierra Madre in northern Mexico in the 1880s. It was named by the Smithsonian's curator of birds in honor of the many contributions to the museum's collections by this hard-riding soldier-ornithologist.[45]

Harry Benson was born in 1857 in Gambier, Ohio, where his father taught Latin at Kenyon College. He graduated Phi Beta Kappa from Kenyon in

1877 and entered West Point the following year. He graduated in 1882, ranked seventh in a class of thirty-seven. Including his term at Kenyon, that gave this small town midwesterner eight years of higher education by the time he received his second lieutenant's bars and headed west.[46]

Benson's high standing at West Point led to his assignment to the "elite" artillery corps. He began his thirty-five-year army career in 1884 as a member of the artillery garrison at the Presidio of San Francisco. Benson performed well at the Presidio, but he craved a frontier assignment. A year after arriving, his commander reluctantly approved his request for a transfer to the Fourth Cavalry in Arizona Territory. The frontier cavalry suited a temperament that belied Benson's bookish background. He loved the wild outdoors; he loved hard riding; he thrived under punishing conditions; he had to keep active. The Fourth Cavalry in Arizona had all that and more, as Benson arrived in the midst of the infamous Geronimo campaign.[47]

The young officer earned universal praise for his exploits in the vanguard of the campaign against Geronimo and his allies. The campaign commander, General George Crook, commended Benson for bearing "uncomplainingly the almost incredible fatigues and privations as well as the dangers incident" to his prolonged field assignment. When Crook was replaced by General Nelson A. Miles for the final push against the elusive Apache, Benson was part of the picked unit, commanded by Captain Henry W. Lawton, that pursued Geronimo to his hideout and surrender in Mexico. Harry Benson was, by any standard, a brave warrior.[48]

He was also a meticulously honest warrior, astoundingly honest in one prominent instance. In 1890, while on detached service as an instructor at West Point, he received a congratulatory communication from army headquarters. Apparently he was under consideration for a Medal of Honor at the recommendation of General Miles for "gallantry in a perilous ride of 90 miles through a country infested with hostile Apache Indians" during the final pursuit of Geronimo. Miles reported that the heroic deed occurred on July 1, 1886. The letter from Benson's superiors asked for details to fill out the recommendation. The response was classic Harry Benson: "Just what Gen. M. [Miles] means by the 'perilous ride on July 1st', I do not know." He had made no ride, perilous or otherwise, on July 1. Miles could have meant a ride on May 20 or June 26 or perhaps July 28, Benson went on; however, none of those rides had placed him in peril, and none deserved a medal.[49]

Indeed, Benson made no secret of his opinion that the entire Geronimo campaign was overblown, a creation of what today would be called media hype. He could not conceive of celebrating a campaign in which a tiny band of Apaches eluded more than 5,000 soldiers for nearly five years. He was especially annoyed by the attention paid to the final pursuit of Geronimo by him and other members of Lawton's picked force. Although none of the pursuers ever fired a shot, the story had it that they underwent inhuman hardship. To Benson, the hardships of pursuit in the field were part of a cavalryman's job. More than two decades later, when the *Army and Navy Journal* published what Benson considered an inaccurate account of the now legendary chase, he wrote a withering response, calling the claims of privation exaggerated and zeroing in on one of that group who had exploited public misperception to secure "a reputation entirely outside the Army for command and for capacity in Indian fighting and also a medal of honor."[50]

The object of Benson's scorn was a fellow member of Lawton's squadron, the Harvard-educated army surgeon and future chief of staff Leonard Wood. Wood received a Medal of Honor for the Geronimo campaign (the same commendation Benson had summarily rejected as undeserved), belatedly in 1898, to give luster to his first army command as head of Teddy Roosevelt's cinematic Rough Riders. Under Teddy's patronage, Wood's career (and his ego) took off like a rocket. At the time Benson mocked his combat and command credentials, Wood was a major general stationed in Washington, D.C., about to be named army chief of staff. Wood read the article and exploded. Benson's career would never recover, but he remained unrepentent to the end. In a reminiscence shortly before his death, he wrote, "It is needless to remark, that there were no battles, though a medal of honor was illegally given during that campaign." On the other hand: "During that trip, I secured a specimen of the Imperial Woodpecker but one specimen of which had ever before been taken. . . . This created more of a furor than did the capture of Geronimo."[51]

The "furor" Benson created was not front-page news, but it wasn't hot air either. The imperial woodpecker he captured during the Geronimo campaign was "the first ever taken in the United States by a scientific observer," wrote an excited Robert Ridgway, the Smithsonian's curator of birds, on October 12, 1886, in a letter addressed to Benson in Fort Bowie, Arizona, the staging area for Lawton's elite Geronimo pursuit unit. Benson had been sending ornithological specimens to the Smithsonian since shortly after joining the Fourth Cavalry in Arizona in 1884. The practice was common in the frontier army, notably among surgeons who contributed extensively to various museum collections throughout the nineteenth century. Benson's case was special for the dicey conditions under which he carried out his collecting and for his thoroughness and enthusiasm. ("These skins had to be packed fresh and in damp weather and brought 130 miles in rain storms, so that they have not as good a form as I would like," he apologized in one letter from Fort Huachuca.) It was five months after the imperial woodpecker submission that he discovered that the bird would be named after him. "I take great pleasure in informing you that the plumed partridge recently collected by you in Sonora proves to be a strongly characterized new sub-species," Ridgway wrote to Benson on March 1, 1887. Ridgway asked for additional details for the article he was preparing for the next issue of the *Proceedings* of the museum that would announce to the world the discovery of the *Callipepla elegans bensoni*.[52]

Benson's detached appraisals of birds and generals masked a warm-hearted idealism, as Esther Dorst had quickly recognized. Personal ambition figured little in his decision-making. His humility was so unaffected that it never even occurred to him to deploy it, as many others did, as a moral virtue. It simply made no sense to him not to be precise, thorough, and honest, and to choose what he liked doing over what might advance his professional career. He consistently sought outdoor activity even when it meant rejecting opportunities for reward and promotion. He requested a transfer in 1884 out of plush urban assignments with the artillery so he could gallop around Arizona. He asked to be relieved from an assignment under the State Department at the World Columbian Exposition in Chicago in 1893 so he could return to his cavalry troop in the Sierra Nevada. In 1898, after landing a cushy job as a customs inspector in peacefully occupied Cuba, he asked to be transferred to the war zone in the Philippines. His immediate superior in Cuba, none other than future adversary Leonard Wood, had recommended him for a higher administrative post. Benson fought it off by applying for a transfer to the Philippines because, as he wrote a friend, "this [Cuba] is a fine station for some old officer . . . but for a Cavalry officer it is no place. . . . there is no action."[53] Such was the soldier who, in the judgment of a Sierra Club president and Sierra Nevada historian, stood "preeminent" among Yosemite commanders—without whom "our [Yosemite] legacy would have come to us seriously impaired."[54]

Harry Benson made his Yosemite debut in May 1895 as a first lieutenant and second in command of the Fourth Cavalry's K Troop, once Joe Dorst's, then commanded by Captain Alex Rodgers. Benson was McClure in overdrive—"practically continuously in the mountains," as he later recalled and others testified. On his first patrol in the summer of 1895, he followed a route similar to McClure's historic journey but with longer working days and harder chases after sheepherders. During that patrol his men collected 40,000 sheep and forty sheepherders and drove "them all in together, mixing the brands to the horror of the sheep herders." It was Benson's way of introducing himself to his adversaries. And wherever he went, which was just about everywhere in the 1,500-square-mile park, he blazed trails. "On every detail," he later recalled, "each member . . . carried a hand hatchet, hung from the saddle by a leather boot, and wherever there were trees, blazing was done, and were there no trees, the blazing was done by placing rocks along the route." Sergeant Gabriel Sovulewski, who served on many of those patrols, remembered them this way: "[Benson] would keep [us] away from our base of supplies for thirty days at a time. Many times rations were short, and sixteen to twenty hours of action per day, covering sixty miles in the saddle, was not unusual."[55]

In some respects, it was the Geronimo campaign all over again, but this time with a more socially redeeming purpose. One Yosemite historian described Benson's mountain activities as "an endless game of hide-and-seek over an enormous tract of almost inaccessible mountain territory with a formidable number of unterrified, thoroughly resentful, sheepherders [who] always had the advantage" over the army because they knew the country better. Benson compensated with relentlessness; he gave his adversaries no rest.[56]

Compared to the mobile Apache, the sheepherders with their large grazing flocks were more vulnerable to a tracker as experienced and tireless as Benson. They moved their herds secretly into remote mountain canyons and valleys; but once in place, they remained stationary and had to be supplied. Benson and his patrols tracked down the supply routes and staked them out. When Benson spotted a pack mule bringing supplies, he would follow it, blazing the trail as he went for use by future patrols, until he located the herd. He would then scatter the sheep and make the herders lead him out by another route, which he also blazed. By that means, he wrote, "I was enabled to make trails covering entirely that [remotest] part of the Park." The sheepherders didn't like it at all. Benson recalled three of them "who had it given out . . . that they would kill me on sight."[57]

Trailblazing went with chasing trespassers, and both went with mapmaking: "As soon as the day's march was over and we had had something to eat, I at once started over the country on foot and prospected in the vicinity of the camp for several miles around and in this way became acquainted with the mountains and streams." He took copious notes on the terrain, of course, according to Old Army regulations. During the 1895 season, when Benson and McClure served together in the park, Benson contributed to the map McClure was completing. During the next two seasons, after McClure left, Benson refined McClure's effort. He joined the Sierra Club at about this time, where he forged lifelong friendships. Captain Alex Rodgers submitted Benson's new map with his acting superintendent's annual report for 1897. He said a comparison of it with McClure's map "will show corrections made, and will also show the new trails opened and blazed during the past two years." There was considerable progress in both respects.[58]

Benson also prepared another kind of map that was badly needed by the administering troops. According to park rules, private lands within the park that had been registered before the park's establishment could be used for grazing. Park troopers were constantly running to land offices to check out claims. Usually, by the time the troopers dug up enough evidence to move against false claimants, the trespassing herds had grazed down the illegal pasturage and their owners were happy to move on. But that was before Benson. In 1897, after comparing land office and survey-general data with what he found on the ground, he compiled what Alex Rodgers described as "a large scale map, showing in colors all patented lands within the boundaries of the park." Troopers then knew, for the first time, precisely who belonged where among the various claimants using the park. In effect, Benson's patented lands map closed off another "enemy" escape route.[59]

Finally, as Benson had collected birds in Arizona, so he now planted fish in Yosemite—meticulously, relentlessly, in adverse conditions, and with praise-winning thoroughness. For years, local residents had decried the lack of fish in the region's mountain lakes and streams. In 1891, the California Fish and Game Commission shipped trout fingerlings to Jug Wood's troopers for planting around Wawona. In 1895, the owners of the Wawona Hotel, anxious to lure anglers into the region, built a hatchery for the commission.[60]

The new state hatchery seemed timed for Harry Benson's arrival. For the next two seasons, the soldiers on Benson's backcountry patrols carried cans of trout attached to their saddlebags. When suitable sites were located, Benson recalled, "the tops of the cans were removed and the can properly placed in running water so that the fish would neither be drowned or smothered." Not all of the fish came from the hatchery. Sometimes Benson waded up to his neck in freezing streams to net trout "to fill the four cans which I always carried with me" on patrol.[61]

Benson's activities during the 1895–1897 period also served as a preparation for much broader contributions when he returned after the Spanish-American War to serve for four consecutive years as Yosemite National Park's acting superintendent. This was a crucial period of boundary adjustments and integration of the state-run Yosemite Valley into the national park. In managing that complicated incorporation, Benson displayed what the editor of the *Sierra Club Bulletin* called "a prophetic vision" of the park's future. Among other things, he was instrumental in preventing Yosemite's absorption by the U.S. Forest Service, established in 1905 under Gifford Pinchot, a man whose outlook was quite different from that of John Muir and the army's park commanders. But even without those later contributions as acting superintendent, the work of Harry Benson as a young lieutenant in the 1890s in giving shape and form to Yosemite National Park would deserve special mention—not only for what he did with so much thoroughness, precision, and honesty but also for how deeply he felt about preserving Yosemite for future generations.

In 1903, while he was stationed at Jefferson Barracks, Missouri, Benson wrote a long letter to an incoming acting superintendent of Yosemite. The letter discussed every aspect of the park assignment in precise detail: what horses, mules, and equipment to bring; what route to follow from the Presidio; what was needed at the main camp at Wawona; backcountry trails; sheepherder haunts; local residents who could (and couldn't) be trusted. On and on Benson's letter went, more than twenty-five handwritten pages. Near the end, in the midst of a technical discussion on which trails were most in need of repair, he suddenly blurted out: "I wish I might be down with you. I love that place." The deep feeling hidden behind his brisk demeanor and staccato writing style had surfaced, as it had in another instance when he wrote, "I love it as I can no other place in the world."[62]

As with John Muir (and, as noted, Jug Wood), the driving motive for Harry Benson's effective actions on Yosemite's behalf was affective love. For Muir, it was an earthy poet's primal love of nature; for Benson, a warrior's. Both were primarily scientists and lovers and secondarily philosophers of nature.

More will be said about that distinction. For now, it is sufficient to note that the love of nature of John Muir and Yosemite's army commanders, with its distinctive blend of science and sensuality, was fundamentally different from the outlook behind the national park idea in mid–nineteenth-century America. The latter was aptly described by a historian of America's national parks as "monumentalism" or "scenic nationalism," a "reliance on nature as proof of national greatness." It was born of a soaring messianic pride (which often compensated for feelings of cultural inferiority toward Europe) that characterized American nationalism in the nineteenth century. European nationalism found its grandeur in ornate castles and palaces; American nationalism looked to natural wonders like Niagara Falls, the Grand Canyon, and Yosemite Valley. The national park idea promoted natural wonders as cultural icons disconnected from the ecosystems in which they lived. Thus "monumentalism, not environmentalism, was the driving impetus" for the congressional legislation in 1864 establishing in Yosemite Valley the first federally mandated park. When the landscape designer Frederick Law Olmsted tried to introduce a more intimate ecological perspective into the viewpoints of Yosemite's first commissioners, his proposals were rejected. It was not until John Muir began writing about the valley as an intimately interconnected natural community that a sensually and scientifically integrative perspective began to gain currency. Nonetheless, Muir's would remain a minority outlook throughout his lifetime (he died in 1914) even among park enthusiasts—but not among the Old Army officers who served in Yosemite.[63]

GABRIEL SOVULEWSKI: "DEAN OF THE YOSEMITE STAFF"

Gabriel Sovulewski was sixteen years old when he migrated to Chicago from his native Poland in 1882. Six years later, he followed the path of many immigrants lacking professional skills during those boom-and-bust years and enlisted in the U.S. Army as a private. His first assignment was K Troop, Fourth U.S. Cavalry, in Fort Huachuca, Arizona. In spring 1890, his troop transferred to the Presidio in San Francisco. He had by then been promoted to corporal. The following spring, Joe Dorst led K Troop into newly established Sequoia National Park. Sovulewski didn't know it then, but his life had taken a decisive turn.[64]

Sovulewski was a protégé initially of Dorst, then of Harry Benson. They were his models for personal and professional conduct, especially Dorst for whom he showed an almost religious veneration in correspondence that followed Dorst throughout his career. There was less numinousness in Sovulewski's feelings for Benson, more nitty-gritty respect and admiration born of working together for many years. During the 1930s, when Sovulewski was long retired from the army and working for the National Park Service in Yosemite, he told an interviewer, "The National Parks in California, and Yosemite especially, owe more to the late Colonel H.C. Benson than to any man living." He was recalling his long patrols under Benson in the 1890s in Sequoia and Yosemite and his service as a civilian trail-builder and off-season park supervisor after he left the army and was hired by then acting superintendent Benson in the early 1900s. Benson felt the same way about Sovulewski: "Too much credit cannot be given to this man for the development of Yosemite National Park." Through the 1890s and early 1900s, as Benson's authority and involvement in Yosemite steadily increased, so did Sovulewski's as the chief implementer of Benson's unsparing efforts.[65]

Sovulewski was the perfect sergeant. He welcomed authority and knew how to exercise it, but only over a few men for limited ends under the direction of a superior who trusted him to do his assignment honestly and efficiently without requiring constant supervision. He advanced rapidly in the ranks, earning his stripes as a quartermaster sergeant only six years after enlisting. His duties involved overseeing equipment, distributing funds, and keeping accounts. He also proved trustworthy in a command situation, as when, in 1892, he headed a squad assigned to oversee

tiny General Grant National Park adjacent to Sequoia and received a commendation from Joe Dorst for his "tact . . . firmness and thoroughness."[66]

Sovulewski first served in Yosemite with K Troop in 1895. By then, K
Troop's command had passed from Dorst to Alex Rodgers, and Harry
Benson had been elevated to deputy troop commander. From 1895
through 1897, he did yeoman work for K Troop in Yosemite. Following
the outbreak of the Spanish-American War in 1898, K Troop transferred
to the Philippines. But Sovulewski's heart remained in Yosemite, in more
ways than one. During his last prewar year in the park, he met and married Inez Rose Rider of New York. Available records do not indicate
whether she grew up in the area or visited the park as a tourist, but they
both soon decided to make Yosemite their home. In December 1898 in
Manila, after ten years of military service, Sovulewski resigned from the
army and returned to California. He took a job in Yosemite as a packer
and guide. But, with a growing family to support, he was eventually
forced to accept a better paying position as a civilian employee of the
army quartermaster in San Francisco. After Benson returned as
Yosemite's acting superintendent in 1905, he arranged for Sovulewski to
be transferred to the park and put in charge of its winter management
with a raise in pay and the title of park supervisor.[67]

The Benson-Sovulewski alliance expanded quickly into a year-round
working arrangement. When Benson departed for the winter in 1906, he
left Sovulewski a set of instructions that would have kept an entire troop
busy. Besides supervising a pair of civilian rangers and other winter employees, Sovulewski was directed to repair culverts on one road, walls of
the grade on another; remove snow from roofs and bridges; inspect and
reditch three main trails leading to the valley rim; make sure the two main
roads into the valley were in good repair for the opening of the 1907 season; police all campsites; and so on, with the concluding admonition: "It
is expected that you . . . will be daily employed on some work connected
with the repairs of the roads, drains, culverts and bridges in the Valley or
such other work as has been specifically mentioned above." During this
period, of course, Yosemite would be under a thick blanket of snow. [68]

By the time the army left the park for good in 1913, Sovulewski, his
wife, and their seven children were permanent Yosemite residents and local institutions. Gabriel was the knowledgeable and competent old-timer
to whom everyone turned for information and direction. Inez "became
'Mother Sovulewski' to all of Yosemite . . . because of her leadership in
community affairs." During most of the interim administrative period
from 1913 until the formal establishment of the National Park Service in
1916, Gabriel was the park's de facto superintendent while retaining his
old title of park supervisor. He was by far the most qualified person to be
the park's first superintendent under the National Park Service, but he

didn't seek the job. He was most comfortable as the indispensable sergeant—and always would be, even after he left the army—happily removed from the trappings of power that went with a senior management position. Even so, Sovulewski was considered for the coveted superintendent appointment by his friend Stephen Mather, the founding director of the National Park Service. But Mather decided not to go after the reluctant Sovulewski, mainly because of the ex-sergeant's limited formal education at a time when the fledgling Park Service was competing to match the Forest Service's progressivist standards of professionalization.[69]

So with his old title of park supervisor, Sovulewski wound up serving contentedly as chief assistant to Washington B. "Dusty" Lewis. Superintendent Lewis, an engineering graduate of the University of Michigan, came to Yosemite from the U.S. Geological Survey where he enjoyed high professional standing. He held the superintendency for twelve years, with Sovulewski serving under him as park supervisor. Sovulewski continued in a similar capacity for each of Lewis's successors until he retired from the Park Service in 1936. To mark the occasion, Mather's successor, Horace M. Albright, another long-standing Sovulewski fan, presented him with an award for holding "the record" for consecutive employment with the National Park Service. When Gabriel died in 1938, he was laid to rest in Yosemite Valley alongside his wife.[70]

Sovulewski's most enduring contribution during a Yosemite career that spanned forty years was in trail work. Park Service Director Albright called him "one of the greatest trail builders I've ever known." In 1928, a Yosemite National Park journal featured an article on the park's six-hundred-mile network of trails, written by Sovulewski at the request of the park's chief naturalist, Carl P. Russell. The article displayed Gabriel's usual self-effacement. He said the park's most important trail work had been done under the army, especially "Col. H.C. Benson."[71]

During that defining army period in the 1890s—the era of Wood, Benson, and McClure—no funds were available for park improvements. The park's trail system was constructed only from equipment nature provided, as had been done for hundreds of years prior to European settlement. Sovulewski followed what a historian of Yosemite trailblazing called an "intuitive approach," using existing geography to determine the route and building up a trail's natural lines with rocks rather than carving new paths. The availability of funds for trail construction after 1900, and the establishment of scenic views as trail destination points, led Sovulewski to adopt a more systematic technique. But he continued to assign highest priority to his intuitions in completing the network that ultimately encompassed the entire park and would be used by millions of visitors. Sovulewski explained his approach to trail building this way: "Thorough knowledge of the country, love for that kind of work, good cool head with common sense, instinct of a dog to know which way to get home and last but not least, disregard for the time of day, are the principal requisites. . . . In my experience in exploring, wild animals in many cases solved numerous difficult problems for me."[72]

The high value Sovulewski placed on animal intuitiveness, on what he proudly called in reference to himself "instinct of a dog," may help explain the deference that stayed with him after he left the army and joined the ranks of rural westerners known for their rugged independence. Sovulewski called his years in the Old Army "the happiest and most independent" of his life. How could he view that hierachical, regimented, fundamentally communitarian institution as fostering his independence? Apparently, it allowed freer expression to an inward part of his personality that mattered a great deal to him. Sovulewski's was a kind of ecosystem of thought and feeling that aspired above all to balance. His humility reflected an arrangement in which his intellect shared its independence with primal "animal" emotions in the service of a natural world that he—to use a word that appeared again and again when hard-riding soldiers assigned to Yosemite and Sequoia talked about nature—that he, like Dorst, Benson, and McClure, "loved."[73]

ALEX RODGERS: TO YOSEMITE BY WAY OF VERSAILLES, DARMSTADT, AND FORT APACHE

While Harry Benson and Gabriel Sovulewski got their inspiration from Joe Dorst during their 1895–1897 service in Yosemite, they (and Nate McClure also) got their orders from Alex Rodgers. Rodgers was the right man at the right time to give Yosemite's trail-smart young officers the leadership they needed at that stage in the park's development. Plainspoken Jug Wood had the right temperament for introducing federal authority into a rural region of independent-minded homesteaders. But now there was a need for refinements in the formulation of park policy in Washington, D.C., that would consolidate gains made by the cavalry on the ground. Alex "Sandy" Rodgers's patrician background and policy-making duties overseas and in Washington were made to order for Yosemite in 1895.

Rodgers was not only a Mackenzie-era veteran of the Fourth Cavalry like Joe Dorst and Jug Wood, but he also had known and adored Mackenzie since childhood. They were cousins and came from the same hometown, Morristown, New Jersey. Alex was an impressionable eight-year-old in 1862 when his older neighbor and cousin Ranald Mackenzie graduated as West Point's valedictorian and went on to fame and glory in the Civil War. Rodgers followed his boyhood hero to West Point in 1871. His graduation and assignment to Mackenzie's frontier regiment was the fulfillment of a childhood dream.[74]

Rodgers had quite a family pedigree. His father was Admiral Christopher Raymond Perry Rodgers, a distinguished naval commander, diplomat, and superintendent of the United States Naval Academy at Annapolis. A grandfather, George Washington Rodgers, was also a prominent navy officer. A grandmother was the sister of Commodore Oliver H. Perry, hero of the battle of Lake Erie in the War of 1812 ("We have met the enemy, and they are ours"), and Matthew C. Perry, who opened Japan to foreign intercourse in 1853. A great-grandfather commanded a Maryland regiment in the War for Independence. Like his older cousin Ranald, Alex Rodgers imbibed his colorful personal history at family gatherings in Morristown, but he also spent several years of his boyhood in Versailles, France, and in Darmstadt, Germany, where his father held diplomatic postings. There he acquired fluency in French and German, to which he later added Spanish and Portuguese. After graduating from West Point in 1875 (a year behind his good friend Joe Dorst), he joined the Fourth Cavalry at Fort Sill, in Indian Territory (now Oklahoma), a long way from his grammar school in Versailles.[75]

Throughout his career, Rodgers vacillated between the "Indian Territory" and "Versailles" sides of his personality. He loved frontier campaigning, but he also felt wholly at ease in high society. The photograph of him that he preferred seeing in circulation—it appeared in the albums of Joe Dorst and James Parker—was in Romanesque profile rather than the usual full face. Taken around 1880, when he was a first lieutenant in his late twenties, it accented his aquiline nose while reducing the visual effect of his full lips and cherubic cheeks. He was more ornately attired than most of his fellow officers in such portrait photographs, with layers of braids and epaulettes. He looked confident, proud, patrician.[76]

Yet Rodgers spent most of his first decade of frontier service at war with his high-toned background. His influential father had lobbied the secretary of war to satisfy his son's desire to serve in Mackenzie's regiment; but without his son's knowledge, he also engineered Alex's transfer less than three years later to Paris, France, to serve on the staff of the U.S. delegation to the Paris Universal Exposition. Rodgers had no sooner arrived in Paris than he began campaigning to return to Indian Territory. He wrote to the adjutant general of the army asking that, if his regiment became involved in any "troubles," he "be relieved immediately . . . and ordered (by telegraph if possible)" to rejoin his comrades in the field. He also appealed to commanding General of the Army William T. Sherman, to Mackenzie repeatedly, and with increasing insistence to his father. Admiral Rodgers finally gave in and wrote Mackenzie: "I have several let-

Alex Rodgers, Yosemite commander of noble lineage. U.S. Military Academy Library.

ters from Sandy, and two telegrams . . . imploring me to have him ordered back to his regiment. . . . As his life will be spent fighting on the frontier, I think his present employment will do him more good and help to make him a wiser man and a more useful officer. . . . He seems intensely anxious to be with you." Early in 1879, Alex happily abandoned the salons of

Paris and rejoined his regiment just in time to lead a three-month scouting party through the Texas scrublands near the Mexican border.[77] But his father, or someone else in authority, soon went after him again. The following summer he was ordered to report to the romance languages department at West Point. He declined the appointment but was overruled by the West Point superintendent, who knew of his language skills. Again, Rodgers unleashed a barrage of letters, including one to General Sherman, but to no avail. But he kept moving up the ladder until he obtained a Special Order from the secretary of war overruling everyone and ordering him to rejoin the Fourth Cavalry ("at his own request," the order read). Most of the regiment was then with Mackenzie in Fort Garland in the Colorado Rockies, responding to an uprising among Ute Indians goaded by land-hungry whites. Why would a young man flee the comparative luxuries of Paris and West Point for isolated outposts in the arid plains of Texas and the freezing Colorado rockies? James Parker provided part of the answer in this description of daily life in Fort Garland for troops in from patrol:

> All my companions, the young lieutenants of the command, Wentz Miller, Jug Wood, Joe Dorst, Squire Mason, Sandy Rodgers . . . found time for numerous diversions. There were deer and duck in the vicinity, horse racing was a favorite sport, foot races were indulged in. We constructed a primitive gymnasium where we held numerous events. At night it was cold on the mountain plateau, but in our fireplace great pinon logs crackled, throwing out an aromatic odor. There was much singing, under the leadership of Dr. Munn, our surgeon, and Colonel Beaumont, commanding officer of the cantonment. There was considerable card playing, while some of the officers, more studious, utilized the evenings to improve their minds by study.[78]

It was a life that Alex Rodgers always treasured during his thirty-year army career, both for the lighthearted diversions and for the often incredible hardships he shared with his comrades (no matter how isolated the location, Old Army scenarios always featured the group, never the frontier isolato), as Joe Dorst recalled for him during a letter in 1891:

> You yourself in the winter of '78 and '79 in following an Indian trail with a small detachment & returning to your post, travelled at least 1600 miles [in Texas] and at one time were 84 hours without water. At another time in 1882, while five troops were fighting Apaches at Horse Shoe Canyon in Arizona, you were with three troops near the line between Texas & New Mexico on an Old Indian Trail, & your command was 56 hours without water, many animals were lost, and

a number of men were so exhausted that they had to be left behind & were only saved from death by water carried back to them after it was found.[79]

This was the same Alex Rodgers who learned his French at Versailles and his German at Darmstadt—and who, on January 11, 1883, less than a year after that brutal southwestern patrol, could be found waltzing in full-dress uniform in Harrisburg, the capital of Pennsylvania. The occasion was Pennsylvania's social event of the year, the marriage of Alex Rodgers to Virginia Cameron, one of the most sought-after debutantes of that era. Sandy's bride was the daughter of Senator James Donald Cameron, Pennsylvania banker, railroad magnate, secretary of war under President Ulysses Grant, son of former senator and secretary of war (under Lincoln) Simon Cameron, and now father-in-law of First Lieutenant Alex Rodgers.[80]

Alex and Virginia spent most of the next six years with his regiment in the Arizona mountains. In 1890, they moved northward to the new regimental headquarters in Washington State, but not for long. For the ensuing five years, frontiersman Rodgers ceded place to diplomatist Rodgers as he served successively in Rio de Janeiro as a State Department aide and in Washington, D.C., with the Military Information Division, the armed forces' first modern intelligence gathering agency. Then, once again, he launched a barrage of appeals that concluded with his Washington commander reluctantly releasing him to rejoin his regiment. Rodgers arrived at the Presidio on March 1, 1895, to take command of K Troop barely two months before its departure for Yosemite.[81]

"It became apparent soon . . . that there was a general idea that the enforcement of the law against trespassing was going to be very lax this year," Rodgers wrote shortly after arriving in the park. That was partly a residue of George Gale's hurried tenure and self-serving interpretations by land speculators of Jug Wood's recommendations for reductions in the park's size. Wood had sought minimal reductions that would make park administration more efficient by cutting out the most populated parkland. Others, such as the congressman for the Yosemite area, Anthony Caminetti, invoked Wood but went much further in greedily seeking to bring undeveloped park land onto the market.

Caminetti's park reduction bills were defeated in 1893 and 1894 after strong opposition from the Sierra Club and influential Easterners like Robert Underwood Johnson. Caminetti tried again in 1895, this time with support from the San Francisco press. In February 1895, just before Alex Rodgers arrived in the park for the first time, the *San Francisco Chronicle* wrote that Yosemite was chiefly a creation of "'tenderfoot' Easterners," supported by a local group (the Sierra Club) that had recently "cropped up," consisting mainly of "learned professors, gentlemen of elegant leisure." Arrayed against this effete crowd were, as usual, the rugged, honest, hardworking "small settlers" of the Yosemite region who wanted only to exercise their rights to develop the nation's "free land."[82]

Old Army park administrators fit neither category. Their attitudes evolved on a separate plane. The better they got to know the park, the more their commitment deepened, both professionally and personally. They talked less about park reduction, especially after McClure's expedition in 1894 introduced soldiers to the park's awe-inspiring backcountry, the "cavalryman's paradise," and opened the door to effective patrolling and administration across its entire expanse.

The beginning of what Benson would later call a "new [army] era" in Yosemite became fully apparent to local users when Rodgers, Benson, McClure, and a newly commissioned second lieutenant named William Smedberg (a future general and war hero) hit the trail in the spring of 1895. Rodgers sent out his first patrols within three days of K Troop's arrival in Wawona on May 22. A few days later, he dispatched his first letters to local stock owners.[83]

"Your cattle are ranging at will," Rodgers wrote to J. B. Curtin on May 30. "I have the honor to inform you that all patrols leaving here will have orders to eject any of your cattle that may be found outside the limits [of your claim] which you are required to mark to my satisfaction." To "Mr. White," a sheep owner, he wrote: "If you bought your sheep under a misunderstanding, I am sorry for you." But the army's orders from the secretary of the interior were "peremptory." Any sheep White brought into the park would be immediately driven out. Again, to another cattleman: "It is my desire to do everything to facilitate the legitimate business" of ranchers, so long as they obey the rules.[84]

Rodgers was always politely clear about the limits of his authority, but within those limits he left his adversaries no room to maneuver in their accustomed manner. In the above letter to a rancher, he also wrote that the boundaries of his land must be visibly marked and authenticated by Rodgers; that if this procedure was not followed, all his cattle would be removed from the park; that if it was followed and any cattle strayed off his marked land, those cattle would be removed. He could mark his land and stay in it, according to park regulations, or get out.

But it was in dealing with Interior Department officials in Washington that Rodgers's polished manner worked to greatest effect. He began the process within a week of his arrival. Copies of those letters to cattleman Curtin and sheep owner White also went to the secretary of the interior to buttress a letter with broader purpose. "In performing the duties of Acting Superintendent, an officer's efficiency must depend largely on the support given him by the Interior Department in carrying out the regulations,"

Rodgers wrote. He noted that Curtin had flourished a letter from the Interior Department granting him authority to bring in cattle under escort, which he was now interpreting as his right to range those cattle wherever he wished. It would be helpful, Rodgers suggested, if the interior secretary avoided direct communications that might be exploited and instead communicated to park users through the acting superintendent. Referring to sheepherder White's claim to be leasing park land from an unauthenticated property owner, Rodgers recommended a ruling outlawing subleasing as part of an effort to reduce vegetation-consuming park traffic by itinerant herders. The soldier-diplomatist accompanied his recommendation with a statement of subservience that also subtly gave direction: "The force on duty here is small and it is only by hard work and strong support from the Interior Department that it can enforce the regulations."[85]

Rodgers's policies had an immediate impact. Within a month of his arrival, J. B. Curtin angrily demanded that the Interior Department issue a ruling in support of the long-standing practice of Yosemite landowners to graze their cattle anywhere in the park. Curtin argued that ranchers always used adjacent public lands for grazing, and federal parkland should be no exception. Rodgers responded that "such action would entirely defeat the object of the law establishing the park." Instead he called for "firm treatment" without the exceptions that had undermined public lands policy elswhere on the frontier. The park cavalry had "begun to convince people that government ownership and control of land is not a farce"; this was no time to ease up. In July, Rodgers used an Interior Department query on the advisability of cutting timber on private lands in the park to propose a "blanket ban" on timber cutting, or, if that wasn't feasible, a complex series of regulations (marking boundaries, proving ownership to the cavalry, examination of each felled tree at the cavalry's convenience, and so on) designed to make timber cutting so cumbersome that its perpetrators would simply give up.[86]

As Rodgers worked for refinements in park policy in Washington, he came under assault from an unexpected direction, the governor of California. J. B. Curtin was also a state legislator, and he and his allies reacted to Rodgers's success in cutting their lines of influence to Washington by turning to the statehouse. On June 24, Rodgers received a letter from Governor James H. Budd vouching for the integrity of landowners in the park, asserting that their activities did no damage, and suggesting that Rodgers was exceeding his authority. In reply, Rodgers provided the governor with a polite lecture on the national park concept, the importance of Yosemite regulations for its realization, and national civic consciousness in general. "Many of the cattle men are good men," Rodgers wrote, but "some of them are much the reverse." Either way, the law about grazing was clear and applied to all equally.

Moreover, the presence of many herders also affected the wildlife population, since "they [the herders] frequently have firearms and use them in killing game, in violation of the law." Beyond these specific legal infractions, of which Rodgers listed several more, there loomed the larger fact that "Congress created this park for a National purpose, for the preservation of Natural features, forests, game, etc.," and state and local interests should work with the cavalry to make the new concept a reality; "the advantage to the United States and to California of having this park is one that will increase from year to year." There is no record of any further correspondence from the governor of California. The park's army guardians had closed off another invasion route.[87]

With Rodgers using his diplomatic skills to shape park policy in Washington and Sacramento, and his skills as a frontier commander to keep his patrols moving through the park constantly and "systematically," as he put it, Yosemite made rapid progress toward recognition in fact as well as on paper as a protected national public entity. In summarizing his 1895 activities for the interior secretary, Rodgers described how patrols led by Benson, McClure, Smedberg, and himself had gotten into previously inaccessible grazing sanctuaries in Yosemite's rugged backcountry and evicted thousands of sheep and cattle. Although "I have only 46 horses . . . the patrols have been sent out so frequently that sheep men are afraid to go far in, except those who drove over the snow to places heretofore not visited by troops. Efforts are being made to find all such places." The 1895 season, the first of three consecutive seasons Rodgers spent in Yosemite, concluded with trespassers on the defensive as never before.[88]

Next on the scene would be the most imposing cavalryman of all. He was older and higher ranking than the others. Comfortable with power, he found pretension of any kind amusing. With great relish, he took on the entire San Francisco power structure on nature's behalf.

CHAPTER SIX

"He Was No Ordinary Man"

"THERE WILL BE MUSIC"

Jug Wood had only a few weeks to live when he wrote a letter from the Presidio to his friend and former physician Dr. Leonard Wood. It was February 1894, and Jug's cancer had reached an advanced stage. His pain showed through in every sentence until near the end, when the tone abruptly turned buoyant as he reported the arrival of a new commander for the Presidio's cavalry squadron. Presidio commandant William Graham had "tried to bulldoze" the new cavalry leader, Jug confided. The new man responded by charging Graham with "tyrannical & capricious conduct." The battle lines were drawn. "From now until the finish," the dying cavalryman wrote, "there will be music."[1]

The man who brought music into Jug Wood's last days was S. B. M. (Samuel Baldwin Marks) Young, the most imposing of Yosemite's singular commanders. Jug was one of a long and remarkably varied list of admirers that Young acquired during a forty-two-year army career that began with his enlistment as a private during the Civil War in 1861 and concluded with his retirement in 1903 as a lieutenant general and U.S. Army chief of staff. Ranald Mackenzie wrote in 1878 that Young could "discipline and drill cavalry better than any field officer of the cavalry." Teddy Roosevelt, whose Rough Riders served under Young in Cuba, declared in 1899, "General Young was—and is—as fine a type of the American fighting soldier as a man can hope to see." In 1922, nearly three decades after Young served in Yosemite, Francis Farquhar, California historian, two-term president of the Sierra Club, and editor of its *Bulletin* for twenty years, made a pilgrimage to Young's retirement residence in Montana. The lifelong impression Young had made on Farquhar remained vivid even into the 1960s when he published a glowing tribute to Young for his contributions to Yosemite's protection in the 1890s, declaring, "He was no ordinary man."[2]

S. B. M. Young stood six feet two inches tall and weighed 240 pounds during his mature years. He was ruggedly handsome with broad shoulders, thick neck, bushy mustache, and clear blue eyes. Outfitted in a crisp navy blue dress uniform adorned with yellow stripes and gold braid and insignia, with polished boots, an engraved saber hooked to a thick leather belt, and a crest of medals adorning his massive chest, he seemed a "beau ideal," "every inch a soldier," a "fighting man to the fingertips," to use some of the descriptions employed by persons encountering him for the first time. He sent a female reporter for the *Philadelphia Sunday Press* into a prolonged swoon that she recorded in a lengthy article published shortly after Young, a Pennsylvania native, was named army chief of staff in 1903 at the age of sixty-three: "He has what the novelists style a well-knit, powerful body. . . . The towering frame is not covered with extra flesh. . . . Through his thin summer coat one can see the play of splendid muscles across the back and shoulders."[3]

"Well-knit body" aside, Young's appeal to the female reporter was probably due in part to his being wholly at ease in the presence of women, a result of having raised five daughters, two of them on his own after his wife passed away, as well as an Indian girl he adopted who died in childhood. To Teddy Roosevelt he wrote, "I'm fonder of the society of bright and clever women than of anything else"; then he added, as if to reassure his masculinity-obsessed friend, "I much prefer fighting."[4]

Part of the honest affection Young inspired from both sexes came from his willingness to let heartfelt emotions soften his stern facade. In a letter to his eldest daughter, Marjorie, written from a camp in the Philippines, he spoke of the "foolish tears [that] sometimes flow from strong men's eyes." A harp she had sent him soothed his loneliness, he wrote, for without his daughters he felt like "a poor orphan boy." He told her he had just "paid a whole lot of pesos to a peasant for betraying his brother"; explained that he needed the information for his brigade's protection; then anguished over his involvement in this "queer business for a Christian e'en tho' he be a soldier"; then questioned his self-questioning: "It is strange . . . that a large strong man cruel and wicked in the battle field, as I am, should be troubled with sentiment."[5]

The considerable evidence that Young's "sentiment" was not mere sentimentality—that he acted on honest emotions even in the face of the Victorian social conventions of his time—includes his response after a skirmish with Apaches in the 1880s when he found a baby Indian girl trying to nurse her dead mother. He carried her home and adopted her. She remained a member of the Young family for four years until her premature death from illness. A surviving family photograph, taken outdoors, shows his very proper wife seated on the right side of the frame, a baby daughter on her lap, another daughter beside her, both facing their mother; on the other side of the frame, almost as if posing for a separate picture, sits then-captain Young, and clinging to him is his adopted Apache daughter Ogarita.[6]

Young was particularly known for his wry humor, which he often used to deflate pretensions, including those generated by his own commanding manner. The *Philadelphia Sunday Press* interviewer recalled the

S. B. M. Young and family on the Texas frontier, including adopted Indian daughter, Ogarita. U.S. Army Military History Institute.

"delicious twinkle" in his eyes, which seemed to be suggesting, "'You don't really take these pronouncements seriously, do you?'" The Sierra Club's Farquhar, after describing Young's soldierly bearing and his heroic combat exploits in the Civil War and on the frontier, wrote: "Yet there was something in his expression that made one wonder if he was not inwardly chuckling" over the heroic role fate had assigned to him. He appears to have been a remarkably integrated social being, with great zest for life.[7]

Young was born near Pittsburgh in 1840, the ninth of eleven children in a prosperous farming family. Within days of the fall of Fort Sumter in 1861, he quit his job as a surveyor and draftsman and joined the Union army as a private in a ninety-day Pennsylvania volunteer regiment. After the regiment disbanded, he raised a company for the Fourth Pennsylvania Cavalry and was rewarded with its command and the rank of captain. He was a natural cavalry officer—brave, aggressive, coolheaded, adept at managing the rapid movement of large bodies of men racing ahead of their lines of supply. He fought heroically in numerous major engagements (including Antietam and Gettysburg); was twice seriously wounded (one wound left his right elbow in a permanently locked position, and he had to learn to write and use a saber with his left hand); was breveted successivly major, lieutenant colonel, colonel, and brigadier general; assumed command of a cavalry battalion, a regiment, and a brigade; and captured the last flag taken from Lee's army just before the final Confederate surrender.

Then, as suddenly as it began, the war ended, and Young went home, a twenty-five-year-old ex–Union army general bathed in glory, commander of hundreds of men, returning to rural Pennsylvania to work as a draftsman. Within a year, he reenlisted as an infantry private. His war record won him a commission as a second lieutenant. One of his Civil War commanders, Colonel J. Irvin Gregg, had him transferred to Gregg's newly formed Eighth Cavalry regiment to take command of a troop. That also meant promotion to captain, an unusually rapid jump in rank in a post–Civil War army whose size would remain at about 28,000 until the end of the century. Promotion was mainly by seniority then; the army's upper ranks were crowded with Civil War veterans still in their prime. Young did not receive another promotion for seventeen years. In some ways, that was not a bad thing. With limited prospects for promotion, junior officers like Young focused on doing their jobs, while their superiors competed incessantly and often bitterly for the tiny army's few topmost posts.[8]

TEXAS TRACKER AND GARDENER

Young served in the Southwest for most of the next twenty-five years, moving from one remote outpost to another. He gained a reputation as a relentless tracker in the region's small-unit "continuous campaign" (as General George Crook called it) that was more pursuit than fighting. A unit adjutant left behind a log of a sixty-day chase involving 125 soldiers and Indian scouts under Young in southwest Texas in late 1877 that captured his lifestyle. Day after day, Young's men picked their way through gullies, canyons, and jagged mountains, cutting steep trails for their supply wagons, watching pack mules lose their footing and tumble down rocky hillsides, marching in scorching heat by day and camping in freezing temperatures at night, often forced to make "dry camp" with only a few drops of water left in their canteens. The pursuit concluded with a predawn assault after camping without fires, to avoid detection, in a snowstorm. The defining characteristic of that lifestyle was, as Joe Dorst wrote, its physically punishing routine—month after month and year after year without letup.[9]

Like many other Old Army officers, Young kept a daily journal. Often he used it as a workbook. He would copy down drill procedures and rules and regulations, then add commentaries on them from the "General" and "Special" orders continually circulating among the troops on the frontier. A typical journal entry included the full text of a correspondence at several command levels on a fine point in drill procedure that was ultimately resolved by the commanding general of the army with these words: "After the piece has been inspected, returned to the recruit, and the hammer placed on the safety notch, the right hand is not dropped to the side before lowering the piece with the left hand, but it is passed at once directly to 'near the middle band' and the piece lowered to the ground."[10]

That institutional obsession with hierarchical regimented detail, about as foreign to American frontier individualism as one could get, was for Young an important part of his training in developing the disciplined and acutely observant habits of mind required for his frontier duties. The most obvious was the direction of cavalry units. Young's home study routine helped him win a two-year appointment as a cavalry instructor when the army opened an Infantry and Cavalry School at Fort Leavenworth, Kansas, in 1881. "I do not know of any officer in the army who can handle a battalion of Cavalry with more skill than he," wrote the school's commander. Before Young returned to the frontier, he authored a one-hundred-page textbook, *The Care of the Horse,* that became a frontier cavalry standard.[11]

Young's mastery of minutiae was useful in collecting data for the army's numerous environmental monitoring programs. He also applied it to polish his skills as a horticulturalist, botanist, and truck farmer in order to meet additional army requirements to keep his troops supplied with homegrown produce and to beautify the remote outposts where they served. On one occasion, Young wrote to a New York seed supplier to request thirteen species of flowers and twenty-two vegetables for a "trial garden" at his "Godforsaken" new post in Texas. Later, from Fort Hancock, Texas, he submitted an assessment of an earthquake that struck while he was in his post commandant quarters. Here are excerpts from his report:

1. Character of ground: Rio Grande Bottomland. Alluvium with considerable mineral salts and alkaline earths. Heavy sub-stratum of quicksands, salt water found 3 to 6 feet below surface.
5. There was no sudden shock. The windows commenced rattling in their frames, there was a trembling sensation similar to that caused by a heavy freight train passing at a high rate of speed, the

e also performed dutifully as a political philosopher and moralist, as
rmy officers were occasionally requested to do by their superiors. In
ry 1893 an army-wide circular requested the views of officers on cap-
nishment. The issue was being hotly debated in Congress, from pul-
nd in the press, with popular sentiment overwhelmingly in favor.[16]
There is scarcely a subject in governmental ethics which merits
r study," Young's commentary began. At the minimum, there
d be a "Congressional Commission composed of Scholars deeply
l in social sciences and entirely free from political and religious
including foreign experts who could provide comparative cultural
ectives on the death penalty. His own reflections had left him no
on on this complex subject "with which I am entirely satisfied." But
he was under orders, he would endeavor to address the issue by
ing it into three categories—state ethics, state policy, and state ob-
es. As a matter of policy, the state had a right to inflict capital pun-
nt when its officials judged that "the protection of innocent life and
fety of society demand it." However, that right should be exercised
extreme discretion in an emerging nation "having such great diver-
of conditions." There should be an awareness of differences be-
n regions "where society is older and conditions more stable" and
er regions, where society existed "in a formative state." Those dif-
es posed a dilemma for congressional lawmakers who could only
h capital punishment nationwide. To do so, Young thought, would
emature given prevailing conditions in some parts of the country.
hen he added an important qualification. "The killing of a fellow
ure [by the state] as a punishment" was an "abhorrent" practice that
d be viewed as a sign that American society had not yet arrived at
vel of "social advancement" its people claimed to seek. There could
 moral justification for it. State-administered capital punishment
t best a shameful necessity, imposed by social failings for which all
icans shared the blame.
o concluded Major Young's assessment: neither self-righteous nor
ctive, condemning the "abhorrent" practice he felt forced to endorse
emporary expedient, reminding his fellow citizens of their shared
nsibility for conditions contributing to the need for it, arguing from
andpoint of a patriotism unafraid to incorporate self-doubt.
oung delivered his assessment of capital punishment near the con-
on of that period in the U.S. Army's history when soldiers performed
less constabulary duties while based at remote outposts on the west-
ontier. In that unconventional "peacekeeping" and "nation-build-
military environment, he had formed his character and acquired his
ical skills. All in all, they were pretty impressive. At home in a draw-
om or camping out in a blizzard, he was an accomplished horseman,

rattling increased rapidly, and wickedly, for near
then an undulation was experienced similar to a
waves—the motion was distinctly eastward and

7. Clock with pendulum seven inches long on
floor stopped. Clock with same length of pendu
ground floor did not stop. Large picture on east
swung out six inches and struck headboard of
lamp suspended six feet from center of ceilin
ground floor was found swinging six inches (ext
utes afterward. A common glass tumbler half fu
dow sill upstairs in south wall, water was spilled
and west sides.[12]

And so the description went, as the commandant of F
through his quarters applying his acquired coolness
reaucratic nitpicking skills to measure the effects of
had just occurred under his feet.[13]

Young's competence and coolness were bound
Mackenzie. Although he did not join the Fourth Ca
Young served in a combined command under Macke
much of the 1870s. The grueling chase in Texas descr
ried out by Young under Mackenzie's orders. Mac
Young for a number of discrete assignments, includi
gotiation of an agreement with a senior officer of th
settled a border dispute. While commanding at Fort
lowed Mackenzie's policy of strict honesty and fair
taking on influential settlers—as when he condemnec
ulent claim against the Mexican government" by a
to expand his holdings, or when he served as Am
public activities celebrating a bridge connecting the t
Texas and Mexico, a goodwill ceremony that the gov
to attend. Early in 1878, Young wrote Mackenzie th
birth to their first son whom they had proudly nam

In 1891, Young left the Southwest for good when h
mander of the school of instruction at the army's m;
depot at Jefferson Barracks, Missouri. He was by th
jor with nearly thirty years of hard service and an ar
bravery and competence. An inspector general wro
about so many reforms [at Jefferson Barracks], cor
and made so many improvements . . . that he . . . i
out of what was formerly not a very creditable one

rattling increased rapidly, and wickedly, for nearly 30 seconds, and then an undulation was experienced similar to a boat in chopping waves—the motion was distinctly eastward and westward.

7. Clock with pendulum seven inches long on north wall ground floor stopped. Clock with same length of pendulum on west wall ground floor did not stop. Large picture on east wall ground floor swung out six inches and struck headboard of bedstead. Hanging lamp suspended six feet from center of ceiling in dining room ground floor was found swinging six inches (extremes) fifteen minutes afterward. A common glass tumbler half full of water on window sill upstairs in south wall, water was spilled or splashed on east and west sides.[12]

And so the description went, as the commandant of Fort Hancock moved through his quarters applying his acquired coolness under fire and bureaucratic nitpicking skills to measure the effects of an earthquake that had just occurred under his feet.[13]

Young's competence and coolness were bound to appeal to Ranald Mackenzie. Although he did not join the Fourth Cavalry until the 1890s, Young served in a combined command under Mackenzie in Texas during much of the 1870s. The grueling chase in Texas described earlier was carried out by Young under Mackenzie's orders. Mackenzie also selected Young for a number of discrete assignments, including the successful negotiation of an agreement with a senior officer of the Mexican army that settled a border dispute. While commanding at Fort Hancock, Young followed Mackenzie's policy of strict honesty and fairness even if it meant taking on influential settlers—as when he condemned the "false and fraudulent claim against the Mexican government" by a Texas rancher seeking to expand his holdings, or when he served as American coorganizer of public activities celebrating a bridge connecting the twin cities of Laredo in Texas and Mexico, a goodwill ceremony that the governor of Texas refused to attend. Early in 1878, Young wrote Mackenzie that his wife had given birth to their first son whom they had proudly named Ranald.[14]

In 1891, Young left the Southwest for good when he was appointed commander of the school of instruction at the army's main Midwest recruiting depot at Jefferson Barracks, Missouri. He was by then a fifty-year-old major with nearly thirty years of hard service and an armywide reputation for bravery and competence. An inspector general wrote that Young "brought about so many reforms [at Jefferson Barracks], corrected so many abuses and made so many improvements . . . that he . . . is making a model post out of what was formerly not a very creditable one to the Army."[15]

He also performed dutifully as a political philosopher and moralist, as Old Army officers were occasionally requested to do by their superiors. In January 1893 an army-wide circular requested the views of officers on capital punishment. The issue was being hotly debated in Congress, from pulpits, and in the press, with popular sentiment overwhelmingly in favor.[16]

"There is scarcely a subject in governmental ethics which merits deeper study," Young's commentary began. At the minimum, there should be a "Congressional Commission composed of Scholars deeply versed in social sciences and entirely free from political and religious bias," including foreign experts who could provide comparative cultural perspectives on the death penalty. His own reflections had left him no opinion on this complex subject "with which I am entirely satisfied." But since he was under orders, he would endeavor to address the issue by breaking it into three categories—state ethics, state policy, and state objectives. As a matter of policy, the state had a right to inflict capital punishment when its officials judged that "the protection of innocent life and the safety of society demand it." However, that right should be exercised with extreme discretion in an emerging nation "having such great diversities of conditions." There should be an awareness of differences between regions "where society is older and conditions more stable" and frontier regions, where society existed "in a formative state." Those differences posed a dilemma for congressional lawmakers who could only abolish capital punishment nationwide. To do so, Young thought, would be premature given prevailing conditions in some parts of the country.

Then he added an important qualification. "The killing of a fellow creature [by the state] as a punishment" was an "abhorrent" practice that should be viewed as a sign that American society had not yet arrived at the level of "social advancement" its people claimed to seek. There could be no moral justification for it. State-administered capital punishment was at best a shameful necessity, imposed by social failings for which all Americans shared the blame.

So concluded Major Young's assessment: neither self-righteous nor vindictive, condemning the "abhorrent" practice he felt forced to endorse as a temporary expedient, reminding his fellow citizens of their shared responsibility for conditions contributing to the need for it, arguing from the standpoint of a patriotism unafraid to incorporate self-doubt.

Young delivered his assessment of capital punishment near the conclusion of that period in the U.S. Army's history when soldiers performed thankless constabulary duties while based at remote outposts on the western frontier. In that unconventional "peacekeeping" and "nation-building" military environment, he had formed his character and acquired his technical skills. All in all, they were pretty impressive. At home in a drawing room or camping out in a blizzard, he was an accomplished horseman, fleeing winter snows only to be "butchered at leisure by that ignoble band of pot hunters, who . . . hang about the park['s borders] like a band of hungry coyotes." Forsyth added the weight of precedent by pointing out that when a forest reserve was established adjacent to Yellowstone in 1891, it was "placed in charge of the [army] Superintendent of that Park." Why not, he asked, do the same for the Sierra Forest Reserve as a minimum response if Sequoia National Park expansion was not immediately feasible?[22]

Forsyth followed his Sequoia protection proposal with a more comprehensive report that discussed needed "improvements" in both Yosemite and Sequoia. The report described routes for proposed trails, sites for bridges, and road upgrade requirements. Its recommendations for Yosemite included a trail that would circle the park just inside its outer boundaries, with other trails leading inward from it "to facilitate proper patrolling of the interior." Forsyth also called for a formal survey of the park, preferably by the U.S. Geological Survey, and markers along its borders. Finally, he recommended that Yosemite and Sequoia troopers receive "better shelter than can be obtained from canvas" (i.e., that permanent facilities be constructed). [23]

Forsyth used Yellowstone as the model for many of his proposals. He pointed out that permanent facilities existed for Yellowstone troops, that they were stationed in the park throughout the year, and that park improvements were funded through a special annual congressional appropriation. Knowing how hard it would be to get money out of Congress for merely preserving public lands (rather than commercially "improving" them), Forsyth sweetened his request with an offer to contribute army equipment and personnel at no charge.[24]

Finally, on January 21, Forsyth sent a letter to Interior Secretary Smith offering to double the number of cavalry in the California parks from two troops to four (as Young had previously sought). The interior secretary was probably feeling overwhelmed by this outpouring of enthusiasm for environmental preservation from an agency of the federal government with no formal responsibilities in that area and no bureaucratic "interest" in it. He asked Forsyth to submit cost estimates for his park improvement proposals. The instant reply, obviously prepared in anticipation, included detailed breakdowns for, in Yosemite's case, a mess hall and kitchen, a stable for horses, and a water supply system for the army camp at Wawona. The estimates included board feet of construction, architectural drawings, and so on, itemized to the penny. The total for army facilities and park improvements in both Yosemite and Sequoia was $15,100, hardly a budget-busting figure for maintaining national parks in California that had as yet received no financial support from the federal government beyond what the War Department elected to allocate from its own operating funds. By comparison, $535,000 had been appropriated by Congress for Yellowstone since its establishment in 1872, with most of that amount coming during the previous decade, after the army's involvement. Interior Secretary Smith approved Forsyth's pathbreaking proposal and included it in the department's annual budget submission to Congress.[25]

Three days after the interior secretary sent in his budget request incorporating Forsyth's proposal, the pleased California commander invited him to formally ask the War Department to detail four troops of cavalry to Yosemite and Sequoia. The formal query was necessary because, unlike Yellowstone, there was no congressional legislation specifically assigning troops to the California parks. The army commitment had begun in 1890 in response to a personal request from the secretary of the interior to the secretary of war, and War Department procedure required that the request be renewed annually. So once again, after being reminded by the people who were doing him a favor, the interior secretary wrote the secretary of war on March 9, 1896; his army-prompted request was approved by the War Department on March 19; orders went out; and the Presidio cavalry began their park assignment preparations.[26]

While the army intensified its commitment to park protection, others in California intensified theirs to park exploitation. In April, Interior Secretary Smith cabled Forsyth for his views on legislation introduced by Senator George C. Perkins of California for a railroad right-of-way through seventeen and one-half miles of Yosemite National Park that would terminate at the entrance to the state-run Yosemite Valley. Perkins had offered his bill on behalf of the Yosemite Valley and Merced Railway, an embryonic enterprise described in one of its broadsides as representing "vast agricultural, mining and timber interests." Perkins's bill also authorized the railroad wildcatters to cut timber in the park and construct coaling depots, machine shops, sidetracks, and water stations. To head off this potential environmental disaster, Forsyth replied that he was willing to consider a right-of-way, but he flatly opposed the timber cutting, depots, and sidetracks that he knew were needed for the railway to be built and serviced. In any case, he said, all decisions should be deferred until completion of a "careful study with a view to guarding the interests of the nation in this great park." As a first step, he recommended an examination "in detail" of the proposed rail route by "an experienced officer of the [army] engineer corps." With sufficient roadblocks in place to prevent a calamitous decision during that session of Congress, it was now up to the Fourth Cavalry to begin implementing Forsyth's preservationist objectives in "this great park."[27]

S. B. M. Young could not wait to deploy his troops in Yosemite's defense. In December, a touring army inspector general had judged the Presidio cavalry squadron "first class" in all respects. Morale was high. Young had even established a squadron polo team that competed with civilian clubs in the San Francisco area. The park assigment offered a fine opportunity to introduce new recruits to the Old Army mission of protecting public lands and restraining frontier excesses. In March, Young won Forsyth's permission to accompany the squadron and take personal charge of the two troops assigned to Yosemite.[28]

Young's commitment delighted his subordinates. Harry Benson had been bombarding the Presidio quartermaster with equipment requests with limited success. Now Young demanded—and got—"one tent for each officer and one tent for each two men, a guard tent, a bake tent, reading room for the men and a mess tent for the officers," plus numerous other camp luxuries befitting an officer of Young's rank, reputation, and habits of command.[29]

Young had less success with the Department of California quartermaster, a step up the chain of command, from whom he sought permanent facilities, including a stable and a water supply system. The quartermaster refused to authorize those costly improvements until Congress approved the proposal from departmental commander Forsyth included in the Interior Department's annual budget request. Clearly, Forsyth had pushed the army system as far as he could on committing army resources. The rest was up to civilian bureaucrats and politicians.[30]

Young could handle it either way. He was finally back in the field, leading a squadron of cavalry on a six-month expedition into the Sierra Nevada. His equipment may not have been all that he and Forsyth wanted, but it still was superior to Young's many previous frontier expeditions. And the territory was superior too. Instead of scouting a parched wasteland along the Mexican border, he would be defending a lush mountain park—and not from Indians.

They left the Presidio early in May: a long blue line of 250 mounted troopers winding through the noisy streets of San Francisco, two abreast, followed by four swaying horse-drawn ambulances, twenty wagons, and twenty-four pack mules. In suburban San Jose, the squadron halted for four days to perform in parades and public drills during the town's annual floral festival, while its protean commander (who personally arranged this interlude) indulged his personal passion for horticulture, acquired while beautifying desert outposts. Then they mounted up, reformed, and headed west toward the Sierra Nevada. A photograph taken midway through the march shows the bulky, mustachioed Young, in uniform and wearing a field hat at a rakish angle, sitting in a camp chair in front of his tent, burnt-down cigar between his fingers, leaning back, one leg crossed over the other, looking like the happiest man who ever tried to appear stern before a camera.[31]

The photograph was taken by a magazine reporter who traveled with the squadron as part of a dramatic turnabout in the San Francisco media from the staunch opposition five years earlier to a military "takeover" of public land. "Few realize the amount of work, the hardship, and the vastness of the task imposed" by the park mission, the reporter wrote. An editorial in the *San Francisco Examiner* applauded the doubling of the cavalry contingent for the parks and declared, "Woe to the unfortunate trespasser on Uncle Sam's pleasure ground for the coming season." A subsequent editorial hailed the achievements of the Fourth Cavalry in Yosemite, contrasted them with the "squalid" state-run valley, and suggested that handing the valley over to the cavalry "may be the best thing we can do."[32]

Young's Yosemite contingent consisted of Alex Rodgers's K Troop and James Parker's B Troop, the latter minus Parker who was on temporary duty as an instructor at West Point, a total of 113 men. They reached the park on May 19 and occupied the old campsite on the Merced River a mile from the Wawona Hotel, but with far more imposing effect than before. With over fifty tents, some as big as houses, set out in neat rows like streets, soldiers bustling to and fro on foot, groups of straight-backed riders suddenly issuing forth or returning, oil lamps glowing at night, the camp gave off the appearance of an unusually orderly frontier town. Each night taps echoed through the sugar pines and mingled with the sounds of the river as the lights of S. B. M. Young's Yosemite camp town winked out according to regulations.[33]

Not only were there more troops than before, but with Young in charge they performed with more discipline, purposefulness, and visibility. From his Wawona command post, he dispatched patrols in continuous waves through the park. They carried copies of Nate McClure's map with Harry Benson's latest updates, and many of them were led by park veterans Benson and Rodgers. The doubling in troop strength also permitted a strong presence at the main camp at all times, which Young exploited to conduct elaborate drill exercises and present them as public events for a frontier community for whom the army camp offered considerable novelty. The show got grander with the arrival in mid-June of the Presidio's Fifth Artillery Battalion. The weeklong visit was instigated by Forsyth as part of a training mission that included target practice along the Santa Cruz coast, followed by a march into the mountains for a week at Yosemite before returning to the Presidio. Forsyth and Young hoped to make Yosemite an outpost in a field exercise scheme for Presidio-based troops (Santa Cruz for artillery practice, Gilroy for cavalry maneuvers), which would justify the construction of permanent military facilities in the park. That in turn could lead to a more stable year-round troop presence at Yosemite, as at Yellowstone. As part of this environmental defense strategy, Young would later call for a further expansion of the Yosemite garrison, from two troops to three, in order to patrol portions of the Sierra Forest Reserve adjacent to the park.[34]

A high point in Young's campaign to build community support came with the production of one of the most elaborate public events in Mariposa County history—a "Field Day" that lasted a weekend. It began with an evening minstrel show at the Washburn and Company carriage house by Fourth Cavalry troopers, performed before "the largest audience ever assembled in Wawona," the *Mariposa Gazette* reported. They had ridden over the Chowchilla Mountains, 250 hardy citizens, to watch a performance "far above the shows that visit our part of the country" on a stage constructed by soldiers, in a hall that soldiers had decorated with evergreens, while soldier-waiters circulated among the crowd serving refreshments. The next day's activities included syncopated drills, a polo match and other "field sports," a picnic lunch, and a baseball game between soldiers and Mariposans.[35]

After the game, as the sun dipped behind the Chowchillas, visitors and hosts marched into the soldiers' camp. "Here," wrote the *Mariposa Gazette*'s correspondent, "words fail us." Awaiting the visitors was a sumptuous seventeen-course banquet at garlanded tables arranged in a huge hollow square, with every dish prepared by soldier-chefs "who understood how to prepare viands fit for kings," supported by soldier-waiters who showed "remarkable courtesy." Mingling with the guests were Colonel S. B. M. Young, the famous frontier tracker, decked out in full-dress uniform, and other beribboned army dignitaries, such as Alex Rodgers and Harry Benson, brought in from backcountry patrol and spruced up for the glamorous occasion. The banquet was followed by a music performance by soldiers, group singing, speeches, "cheers for both hosts and guests," and finally, at 10:30, a dance that concluded at midnight. It was a wilderness tour de force.[36]

The next morning, troopers organized their Mariposa guests into a caravan and escorted them to the top of the Chowchillas. With much cheerful waving and lusty huzzahs, the two groups parted. "No matter how many soldiers Uncle Sam may have to guard his interests, Troops B and K of the 4th U.S. Cavalry will have first place in the heart of Mariposans," the *Gazette* reported at the conclusion of its account of another coup in the many-sided career of S. B. M. Young, the new social lion of Wawona.[37]

ENVIRONMENTAL POLICYMAKER

Young orchestrated social events like his "Field Day" to win public support for more serious initiatives that would have a lasting influence on national park policy. Until his arrival, park commanders had focused on introducing a rudimentary degree of governmental authority, and giving the park shape and form as an independent administrative entity, by establishing a visible policing presence, making it known to the surrounding community, exploring and mapping, inventorying park users, blazing trails, driving out trespassing herds of cattle and sheep, and keeping the stock of landowners within the park from straying (usually by design) onto public property. Alex Rodgers had sought to refine some of those ad hoc actions into long-term policies. Young went much further. His season in Yosemite provided several textbook examples of Old Army leadership virtues developed during the three decades Young spent dealing with land-obsessed settlers and a remote and distracted national government, now applied to making the national park concept a working reality.

Young got an early chance to stake out a position on broad principles of park policy when he was asked by Interior Secretary Smith to comment on Senator Perkins's Yosemite railway bill. Although General Forsyth had erected several procedural roadblocks to the project, the California senator remained undeterred. He wrote to Smith that he looked forward to "again personally calling upon you" about the railway after Smith had consulted "the officer in charge of the reservation," which was Young. Perkins must have hoped for more sympathy from Young than Forsyth. He got less. "I am strongly of the opinion" that the Perkins bill should be opposed, Young wrote the interior secretary. The railway speculators were incapable of perceiving, much less defending, the fundamental "public interest" given legislative expression in the act creating the California parks. At a time when interpretation of the vaguely worded statute creating the park meant everything, Young concluded that it mandated the park's protectors to oppose all activities that might "mar the scenic, dispel the romantic and despoil the picturesque" in Yosemite. As a matter of policy, he said, the government should grant "no franchise for any railroad within the Park until a definite and stable system of management" for national parks and forest reservations nationwide was established.[38]

Young convinced his civilian superiors to accept a similar unyielding policy against reservoirs, another kind of intrusion that would play a fateful role in Yosemite's history. This policy recommendation came after he was asked to comment on an application for "reservoir rights" for a string of nine lakes in a remote northeastern corner of the park, with the reservoirs to be created by the construction of a series of dams along the lakes' descending path. Young requested that a decision be withheld until he could complete an on-site investigation and file a detailed report. He then contacted the reservoir applicant, proposed a meeting at the lakes in question in early July, and sent Alex Rodgers to the rendezvous as his representative. The applicant, R. U. Graves, failed to show up, but Rodgers surveyed the sites and prepared a report on the reservoir proposal for his commander.[39]

Rodgers reported that there was a drop of several hundred feet between the highest and lowest of the nine lakes, and that "a great deal of water would undoubtedly be stored" if the dams the applicant sought were constructed. He also agreed with the applicant that the location was "little visited" by tourists and that hardly anyone would notice the construction. Nevertheless, he recommended against building the dams and reservoirs. The area was "extremely picturesque," Rodgers said, and "in a few years," once the park idea took hold, it would receive many visitors. Preparing for that future had been the cavalry's long-term aim in driving out backcountry herders, blazing trails, and mapping the rugged terrain. To grant a reservoir concession would undermine those efforts and encourage additional environmentally exploitive initiatives.[40]

Young agreed with Rodgers's assessment. He returned the application with the comment that, "minor and significant as they may seem" at this point, the proposed activities boded ill for the future. They constituted "a violation of the spirit, if not the letter . . . of the act establishing this park." The interior secretary accepted Young's recommendation and denied the reservoir application. But the army's reservoir policy would be upheld only temporarily by Interior. In 1913, with World War I looming and the army on its way out of Yosemite, John Muir and his allies lost a decade-long battle when the park's breathtaking Hetch Hetchy Valley was ordered to be flooded to create a reservoir. A lot more of that sort of thing might have occurred without the committed and often ingenious leadership of Young and his colleagues for the first quarter of a century of Yosemite National Park's existence.[41]

Young adopted the same bluntly preservationist stance toward the controversial issue of private lands within Yosemite and related campaigns by speculators and politicians to reduce the park's size. Cavalry administrators initially found some of the park reduction proposals attractive because they eliminated bothersome landholders and made the park easier to police. But the soldiers had grown increasingly disenchanted with those efforts for two reasons. First, park reduction advocates invariably converted modest park reduction proposals into major land grabs. Second, beginning with McClure, soldiers explored and mapped the park's awesome backcountry and fell in love with it. Furthermore, after a lot of digging in land office files, they understood the extent to which park land claims were fraudulent. Young transformed that hardening preservationist position into a national policy.

Again, Young used a specific case forwarded to him for comment by the interior secretary as a pretext for his broad policy formulation. The case involved a petition signed by thirty Yosemite "landowners" demanding that a 23,000-acre township where they claimed to own most of the land be excluded from the park. Young contacted the U.S. Land Office in Stockton for information on patented lands in the township. Only eleven of the petitions were legitimate, covering a total of 1,800 acres. Thus, the claimants actually owned less than 10 percent of the township they loudly claimed to own in its entirety. Young's recommendation that their petition be rejected included a report by Alex Rodgers on other recently uncovered fraudulent land claims that had caused Rodgers to make unjustified boundary adjustment recommendations the previous year that he now regretted. Reasoning from those documents, Young further recommended against any further "piecemeal" boundary adjustments. Instead, he called for the establishment of a commission of experts to review the entire issue from the standpoint of the park as a whole and come up with a comprehensive boundary plan. Interior implemented Young's antipiecemeal adjustment policy at once. His bipartisan commission recommendation was implemented a few years later, in 1904, when the park's boundaries (minus state-run Yosemite Valley, which would be added in 1905) were assigned contours very close to what they are today.[42]

In another instance, Young used the case of a miner repairing a trail to entice an important policy statement from Interior on timber cutting in the park. The park's rules and regulations forbade timber cutting on public lands, but Interior had been vague on the issue of mines with extensive timber requirements for external facilities and internal supports. Young's initiative in that domain began after a cavalry patrol found a miner clearing a trail and chopping down trees on parkland to support a tunnel inside his mine.[43]

Young addressed a three-part question to his Interior Department superiors: To what extent could the acting superintendent (1) regulate the working of valid mining claims, (2) determine that a mining claim had lapsed due to failure to perform the minimum annual work required by law, and (3) regulate a miner's park activities outside the boundaries of his claim? Young's carefully worded query brought a response from Interior that gave him what he wanted—a formal ruling against timber cutting on parkland comparable to rulings against grazing. This ruling blocked the timber owners' strategy of chopping down trees on parkland surrounding their claims. Six months later, perhaps not coincidentally, a group of timber owners submitted a petition to Congress asking that the federal government purchase all timber claims in the park—precisely what Young had sought to foster in eliciting the timber ruling.[44]

Railways, reservoirs, mines, land claims, boundary adjustments: these attempts to exploit Yosemite's natural resources derived from prevailing values that the federal government for the most part accepted unthinkingly. S. B. M. Young spoke up for a contrasting value system that emphasized aesthetic and scientific considerations within a distinctive patriotic framework. His interpretations constituted a significant environmental policy achievement. In effect, he transformed communal land concepts into national policy in a frontier society where private land ownership was practically a religion.

TAKING ON THE ESTABLISHMENT

Another part of Young's assigned mission was to actively foster Yosemite's development as an accessible visitor destination. In the future, the issue of balancing tourism and preservation would dominate debate over national park administration. But at this embryonic stage, the challenge was to transform an idea occupying the outer fringes of government into pragmatic, mainstream policies that would make a park system—including sophisticated debates about its character—possible. The new park idea could not survive in empty parks. At the minimum, boundaries would shrink drastically unless visitation increased. Young had used the prospect of increased park visitation to stave off boundary adjustments, reservoirs, and other environmentally degrading schemes. But the influence of his vision would evaporate without some increase in the trickle of visitors.[45]

One of Young's environmentally constrained tourism initiatives called for a travel route keyed to repairing the nearly impassable Tioga Road that led through the luxuriant Tuolumne mountain meadows. The route would permit a tour by wagon from Wawona on the park's southern corner westward, northward, and eastward—"about 100 miles through, perhaps, the most beautiful natural park in the world," Young wrote. Tourists could park their wagons alongside the route, set up camp, and strike out over existing trails to some of the region's awesome peaks or its "innumerable mountain streams, glacier meadows, and lawns of luxuriant grass and natural flowers." Yosemite would be on the way toward becoming the *public* nature park it was conceived to be.[46]

But as with his response to other aspects of the park idea, Young also sought to shape the character of park accessibility by launching a parallel initiative that caused widespread public astonishment and consternation—namely, to make visitors more accountable for their behavior.

Tourists who came to Yosemite for spiritual rejuvenation often left garbage dumps behind. Young described the effect in a letter from his Sierra Nevada headquarters to his superiors at the Interior Department in Washington:

> The majority of campers are careless and negligent about . . . policing their camp grounds when leaving. The spectacle of empty tins that had contained preserved fruits, soups, vegetables, sardines, etc., together with offal from the cook fire . . . is detestable anywhere, but is abominable in the superlative degree when incurred in the view of a beautiful mountain stream, skirted with meadows of luxurious grasses and gardens of wild flowers.[47]

Young's appalled reaction was a product of his military background. The Old Army was unique among American institutions in its commitment to policing campgrounds in accordance with highly detailed rules and regulations. Unfortunately, Lieutenant Colonel Young could apply none of those restrictions to frontier individualists who were ever alert to "military despotism" and unaccustomed to being told by the government what to do when camping out in the wilderness. He needed a legitimizing pretext, and he found it in the park's wildlife.[48]

During Yosemite's early years, wildlife did not enjoy the same protective priority as natural vegetation among Yosemite's civilian defenders. Their attitude was influenced by John Muir's personal distaste for the sport of hunting, from whose ranks wildlife protection grew. Other factors were the predominating naturalist and alpinist interests of many Sierra Club founders. There was sympathy for wildlife protection, but not the same commitment as for forests and meadows.[49]

By contrast, Yosemite's cavalry administrators sought to protect both vegetation and wildlife in the California parks from the beginning. As we have seen, Joe Dorst requested permission to protect park wildlife that ranged across park boundaries. Subsequent army park superintendents displayed the same outlook.[50]

Alex Rodgers broadened the wildlife protection context in 1895 when he added the "well-meaning visitor" to the list of wildlife threats that until then had been limited to illegal poachers who hunted mainly for profit. Rodgers reported that visitors interpreted the firearms permit required by park regulations as a permit to hunt. Rodgers proposed that Interior draft an amendment requiring that firearms be left with the park's guardians on entry and reclaimed on departure. Young decided that Rodgers's proposal could be implemented without recourse to Washington simply by transmitting that stipulation to persons applying for permits to bring in firearms. This decision set the stage for an encounter that would pit Young against some of the most powerful citizens of California and also against one of nineteenth-century America's most sacred beliefs—the "right" to carry firearms on remote frontier land whether it was a nature preserve or not.[51]

The issue surfaced even as Young was en route to Yosemite. Reports that the army's California park contingent would double to four troops of cavalry caught the attention of California congressman W. W. Bowers, whose district included Sequoia National Park. Bowers wrote the secretary of war to protest this plot to "harass and outrage American citizens . . . to drive them away from their own lands." And although a more stringent firearms policy had yet to be announced, Bowers saw it coming and he also saw a nefarious reason for it—namely, "to disarm peaceable citizens traveling on the highways through these public reservations . . . [so] that these vast tracts may be held exclusively as the hunting and fishing preserves for the United States troops, their special friends and the especial friends of the Hon. Sec. of the Interior." Without rejecting the earlier perception of the *Mariposa Gazette* that the California parks constituted a federal plot to make agrarian free enterprise "extinct," Bowers embellished it with a complementary scheme to disarm the local citizenry while creating a hunting preserve for the rich and powerful.[52]

A copy of Bowers's outraged communication went to Young. Its effect was like water over a stone. He had been dealing with similar rhetoric from frontiersmen for over twenty years. Within days of arriving in the park, he posted guards at the Wawona entrance and on the Big Oak Flat private toll road, the most traveled northern gateway. One of the guards' chief duties was to confiscate firearms.[53]

Young knew that for his controversial firearms policy to work—and gain his broader objective of winning the respect of tourists for federal law enforcement in Yosemite—he had to be scrupulously fair. There could be no favoritism, no exceptions. Rich and poor, park friends and foes, must all receive the same treatment. When Warren Olney, a Sierra Club founder, applied for a permit to carry a rifle into the park during a camping trip with friends, Young sent his regrets: "Please leave firearms with the guard."[54]

In midsummer, Young refused a firearms permit requested by a surveyor from the U.S. Geological Survey who intended to kill game for his party. This action was unprecedented. Federal agents always killed game for sustenance while working on public lands. The startled USGS surveyor appealed to the secretary of the interior who asked Young to comment. Young replied that his wildlife policy made no exceptions; it applied to cavalrymen on patrol in the park as well as representatives of other federal agencies. His ruling against the USGS official was upheld.[55]

Young's scrupulousness extended even to military dependents. On June 30, he penned a note to an army lieutenant spending his leave at the Wawona Hotel with his family: "It has been reported to this office that a boy, thought to be your son, was seen shooting at game birds or song birds or squirrels within the boundaries of this National Park." This must be a case of "mistaken identity," Young wrote, before suggesting that it would not be in the lieutenant's interest, legally or careerwise, to condone violations of park rules.[56]

In mid-August Young filed a progress report on his new firearms policy. Besides the firearms averted by his mailed denials of permits, more than two hundred weapons had been confiscated at park entrances and other locations. "As a probable resultant, young broods of quail and grouse abound through the park," he wrote, although there were still not as many deer, bear, lynx, fox, and raccoons "as there should be in their natural home in the park." Nonetheless, the new policy pointed in the right direction. Young recommended that the cavalry's arrival in the parks be moved up from May to April so that soldiers could thwart early spring hunters and hasten the day when Yosemite would flourish as a "natural game nursery."[57]

Young's public education campaign reached its apex in an incident in September that reverberated throughout the state. It was preceded by a sequence of events that began on July 17 with a letter to Young from Donald Y. Campbell, a prominent San Francisco attorney. Campbell said he was a charter member of the Sierra Club, knew Harry Benson, had met Young socially in San Francisco, and was a strong supporter of the army's park activities. He would soon visit Yosemite with his two sisters and niece, he said, and he asked Young for a permit to carry a revolver—not to hunt, of course, but merely to protect the ladies. With his gallantry on the line and considering Campbell's affiliations and stated park protection sympathies, Young relented.[58]

On August 14, Young received another request involving Campbell and firearms, but of a wholly different order. John Howard, an officer in several large investment and transportation firms in San Francisco, wrote to General Forsyth stating that he, along with an Oakland banker and the distinguished barrister and Sierra Club member Donald Y. Campbell, were planning a hunting expedition in the Yosemite region. The route to their hunting grounds would take them through the park. They would enter from the west, near a cavalry western outpost, and exit at the park's northern boundary. Howard requested permission to carry firearms through the park with the understanding that they would not be used. Forsyth forwarded Howard's request to Young.[59]

Young replied that he could not "with propriety issue a written permit for the purpose desired." But he also recognized that if the Howard group met Young's requirements and checked their firearms at Yosemite's western entrance, then exited to the north, their stated plans to hunt outside the park would be thwarted, which Young felt would be unfair. So he offered Howard a special accommodation: "If . . . you will inform me in due time of your intended route through the Park, your mode of travel, the point where and exact date when you will be on the boundary line, a patrol party will be directed to meet and escort you through the park." Young's letter went out on August 17; Howard did not reply.[60]

Meanwhile, the outpost on the Big Oak Flat toll road leading in from the western entrance had received the first in a sequence of visits from E. L. Elwell, a local hunting guide. On the first visit, Elwell told outpost commander Sergeant George Goodrich that he had been hired to bring in small group of tourists. He asked several questions about park regulations and followed up a few days later. On August 25, Elwell passed Goodrich's outpost again and mentioned that his clients had abandoned their plans.[61]

On September 1, a toll-taker for the Big Oak Flat Road paused at Goodrich's outpost to ask whether the soldiers had seen a party of hunters led by Elwell. The toll-taker said the hunters had paid a toll for a specific distance on the road, and he wanted to make sure that they had gone no further. From the toll-taker's account, Goodrich deduced that the hunters had left the road shortly before it reached the army outpost and entered the park surreptitiously, as it were, by a narrow mountain trail. A couple of days later a relief detachment replaced Goodrich and his men at the outpost. Goodrich reached the cavalry's main camp at Wawona on September 4 and reported the incidents to his superiors.[62]

S. B. M. Young recognized at once that he had been conned by the upstanding San Francisco businessmen. He sent Lance Corporal James F. Keilty and three privates on a "forced march" ride in pursuit of the intruders. Early on the morning of September 7, after a day's ride, a four-hour rest for their horses, and fourteen more hours in the saddle, Keilty's patrol found the trespassers' camp. It was occupied by nine men—Elwell the guide, two hired packers, and six hunters. Besides Howard and Campbell, the hunters included two heads of San Francisco area import-export firms, the president of a lumber company, and a senior officer of four interlocking utility companies. (The Oakland banker mentioned in Howard's original request had apparently bowed out.) Facing this illustrious lineup across the embers of a campfire on that brisk September morning were four exhausted young soldiers, led by Lance Corporal Keilty, who was in his early twenties. Keilty asked if they had firearms. They admitted having two rifles and three pistols (one of the latter being Campbell's permitted pistol for protecting two sisters and a niece nowhere in evidence), which Keilty confiscated. He told the hunters that he had orders to take them to the army base camp in accordance with procedures for captured trespassers in force for the past five years.

At that point George H. Collins, president of Sanger Lumber Company, leaped on his horse and started to ride off. Keilty asked him to remain. Collins "insisted that I make a display of force," young Keilty later wrote in his report to Young; "I then buckled on my belt, with pistol attached." Whereupon Collins spurred his horse, Keilty grabbed the reins, and Collins called to his comrades "to witness what he called an outrage on a peaceable United States citizen." The other eminent San Franciscans mounted up and (as stated in the complaint they later filed) "were in turn . . . placed under arrest by Corporal Kelty [sic] for attempting to push by him on the trail out of the park." On September 10, after stopping off in hotels to provide appropriate overnight accommodations for lawbreakers of such stature, Keilty reached Wawona and brought his captives before Young. The acting superintendent lectured them on the rules they had violated and sent them on their way. He had no authority to fine or incarcerate them. The long ride to the park commander's camp, which many other trespassers had taken before them, was their punishment.[63]

Five days after the Wawona encounter, duplicate signed copies of a forty-six-page complaint against Young left San Francisco for Washington. Addressed to the secretary of war and the secretary of the interior, it was signed by the fuming San Francisco businessmen who must have begun drafting it on the train home. The complaint came with an equally indignant letter from U.S. senator George Perkins stating: "I have known all these gentlemen for many years. They occupy high positions in this commercial community, and they are all influential men in their respective spheres." Lieutenant Colonel Young's behavior toward them "was hasty, ill-considered, and very reprehensible." Perkins demanded that he be disciplined.[64]

The complaint was long-winded in the manner of the times but not unusually angry in its tone. Rather, it displayed a condescending attitude toward the acting superintendent and his troopers while elevating the complainants with numerous references to their high social standing. True, the complainants had, as Perkins put it, "a few [illegal] firearms," which they had been unable to surrender at the western entrance because, they said, it was "much out of our way." The only error they admitted was a "breach of etiquette" by failing to acknowledge Young's offer of an escort. The complaint concluded with a call for Young's censure, presented less as a demand than an assumption, given the high economic and social standing of the complainants.[65]

The secretary of war washed his hands of the matter after noting that Young was under Interior Department orders. The interior secretary forwarded the complaint to Young for comment. In his reply, Young reviewed the sequence of events, beginning with the fraudulent request by Campbell for a weapon to protect his female relatives and concluding with the trespassers' ludicrous claim that they had been roaming through the park for six days because they were lost. The reason these pious frauds even considered a protest was evident in the tone of their complaint. They assumed that their social stature guaranteed them special treatment. For Young, who abhorred pomposity and had set out to win respect for park authority from all classes, such condescension afforded a golden opportunity.[66]

Shifting from the indefensible substance of the complaint, Young addressed its wordy social stature section. It included an account of the corporations, clubs, and other high society affiliations of the complainants. (Campbell listed the Bohemian Club, the University Club, and the California Bar Association, along with the Sierra Club.) Young responded like a scientist examining an interesting species:

> Admitting specifically that they are severally members of various social and luncheon clubs as stated, and that they are, respectively, members, officers, agents and employees of the several firms, corporations and professions indicated, and admitting further that their social, commercial and financial standing is as high as their respective descriptive lists seem to intimate, I am unable to see that the facts so stated and admired are in any way or in any degree relevant to the subject matter of the complaint. If they are relevant, I might plead in reply a list of clubs and other organizations with which I have had the honor to be associated. This I see no occasion to do. If they believed that by reason of their exalted social, commercial and professional standing the rules of the Park would not be enforced against them, the experience of the complainants should have undeceived them.[67]

The high-minded moguls were no better than anyone else. "The same course was followed with them that is followed with all trespassers and violators of the rules, whether sheep-herders or cattlemen, or gentlemen in professional or commercial life." Young could see "no reason why the rules of the Park should not be enforced against such imprudent persons exactly as they are enforced against obscure trespassers of whom the press takes no notice, and who have not the necessary means to set forth their fancied grievances in voluminous complaints to the Interior Department."

Young then turned to Senator Perkins. Although Perkins's condemnation of an officer performing his civic duty was a "gross injustice," Young was "not . . . concerned about Mr. Perkins' opinion of me or of my official actions . . . except insofar as they shed light on the veracity and character of the complainants" who had solicited Perkins's aid. In that regard, "if I have any doubt as to the character of the complaint and of those by whom it is preferred, it would be removed by their open and scandalous attempt to influence the judicial action of the Secretary by the official influence of a Senator of Congress."

Young's contemptuous response stunned the San Francisco business community. After the interior secretary's denial of the complaint ("inasmuch as [the complainants] knowingly violated the Park regulations"), Campbell filed an apoplectic demand for a "rehearing" on this "untold abuse of power by the Military in this Country." Young reacted by having copies of his statement condemning the intruders reprinted for local circulation.[68]

Young's mocking assessment of the character and values of the San Francisco businessmen seems even more extraordinary in retrospect. Here was a member of a reputedly socially conservative federal institution publicly denouncing reigning social, political, and economic icons on an issue of national policy. He belonged to the power structure he was mocking—including many of the same clubs as the complainants, and when his eldest daughter married in San Francisco a few years later, the city's mayor was among the attending dignitaries—but he did not hesitate to separate himself from that elite group's values, even to ridicule them, when they challenged his sense of fairness in the performance of his duties. His actions offered a "striking example of administrative firmness and forthrightness in public service . . . [in] an epoch in which people were just beginning to recognize the paramount position of the general welfare . . . in the public domain," wrote Francis Farquhar, past president of the Sierra Club and editor of its *Bulletin*, in an introduction to a reprint of Young's lengthy letter to the interior secretary, a booklet entitled *Yosemite in 1896*, that Farquhar brought out in 1962 as an inspiration to a new generation of environmental activists.[69]

The effects of Young's remarks were not limited to metropolitan San Francisco. Especially significant was the reaction in the park's home county of Mariposa. Many Mariposans associated federal park authority with the machinations of remote and powerful "outsiders" such as the plutocrats Young arrested. Like Congressman Bowers in his accusations about a hunting preserve for the rich and powerful, they included the army in that imperial category. But Young had stood Bowers's position on its head. Within days of his summary arrest and eviction of the elite San Francisco delegation, the *Mariposa Gazette* was commenting on the incident's intricate implications. A high-ranking outsider had taken on other high-ranking outsiders on behalf of a local entity managed by the national government: What interest was Young defending? Could it be something new?

"During the first few years in which the troops were placed on guard in the Park no end of trouble and annoyance was given them" by local intruders, the *Gazette* noted, but the army had persisted in its mission. Now, as the park was taking hold as an administrative entity and attracting rich visitors from big cities, the army was demonstrating equal firmness toward the newcomers, regardless of their social standing—and why not? "We do not attempt to justify the [park] regulations," the *Gazette* wrote in its article on the incident, but "we have no option but to obey." The "we" was easier to digest when it included the heads of San Francisco corporations. "Because these people who were arrested happen to be prominent people, bankers, lawyers, etc., they are not privileged from arrest," the *Gazette* concluded in a ringing endorsement of Young's ruling. The army's policy of being incorruptibly fair in administering a new environmental policy, which Young brought to fulfillment in 1896, had won respect for federal park administration from Mariposans of every persuasion.[70]

Young switched from wildlife to trees for his final Yosemite recommendation, in March 1897, submitted from the Presidio just before surrendering his authority as the park's acting superintendent. Juno T. McLean, owner of a toll road running through the Merced Grove of sequoias in Yosemite, had requested permission to bore a passageway through a giant sequoia. McLean made the request, he said, because "tourists visiting the Yosemite regard the drive through a living tree in a stagecoach or passenger wagon as a notable achievement." Young recommended that the request be rejected, noting bemusedly that "experience in cutting roads through the trunks of living trees is too small at present to warrant the conclusion that any tree mutilated for such a purpose will not be impaired in its vitality, perhaps fatally." Then he added:

> I believe that one of the purposes of the Government in setting aside large areas of the public domain as National Parks was to preserve in their natural condition such natural marvels as the Big Trees of California . . . and cannot recommend such a marked departure from that purpose as the petitioner seeks, merely to gratify the very questionable taste of tourists who may be ambitious to report that they have gone through a tree while riding on the top of a Stage Coach. [He underlined "in their natural condition."][71]

Young concluded his Yosemite epitaph with a reference to John Muir: "As Mr. John Muir so aptly remarks, the small reserve, and the first ever heard of, was in the Garden of Eden, and though its boundaries were drawn by the Lord, and embraced only one tree, yet the rules were violated by the only two settlers that were permitted suffrage to live on it." The quote came from the *Sierra Club Bulletin*, Young said, in proudly associating himself with Muir and his environmentalist colleagues. Young had revised Muir's spiritual invocation, however, to include pragmatic references to "rules" and "settlers." After all, he had a job to do.[72]

PART III: INSIDE CONNECTIONS

So great is this vision of cosmic war that it has pervaded the imagination
of millions of people for two thousand years.
—*Elaine Pagels,* The Origins of Satan[1]

CHAPTER SEVEN
A Conquering Nature

They [whites] are not like the Indians, who are only enemies while at war.
—*Buckongehelas, a Delaware chief*[1]

REDEMPTIVE CONQUEST

The settlement of the trans-Mississippi frontier in the nineteenth century was viewed at the time as the fulfillment of America's quasi-divine manifest destiny. Settlers were missionaries for social, economic, political, scientific, and spiritual "progress" on behalf of Western civilization, which was then usually called Christian civilization for its reliance on values derived from the Western world's Judeo-Christian heritage. The recipients of the blessings of progress were America's "virgin" land and its "primitive" indigenous inhabitants. The vanguard of manifest destiny—politicians, businessmen, preachers, engineers—quarreled a lot among themselves, but on the whole they viewed the project they had jointly undertaken to be a manifestly good thing.[2]

The verbal ingenuity employed by America's leaders in pursuing their apostolic aims was dazzling. In 1781, Governor Thomas Jefferson of Virginia, herald of the "scientific" enlightenment, said to an Indian chief with whom he was negotiating, "We desire above all things, brother, to instruct you in whatever we know ourselves." (Jefferson of course sought no instruction in return.) In 1803, then president Thomas Jefferson wrote to Andrew Jackson, an up-and-coming public servant: "In keeping agents among the Indians, two objects are principally in view: . . . preservation of peace . . . obtaining lands." The Indians were not to be told that peace depended on them giving up their lands peacefully.

Religious missionaries could be more blunt about their intentions. In 1819, in Goshen, Connecticut, the Reverend Heman Humphrey delivered the send-off sermon for the first two American missionaries to Hawaii: "The ultimate conquest and possession of all the heathen lands is certain. . . . Jerusalem and the holy city are to be rescued from the hands of infidels. . . . The effeminate Hindoo and the degraded African will be raised to the dignity of men. . . . The wild men of the American forests will be tamed," and so on, from Western believers and atheists alike, toward the same scientifically enlightened and divinely blessed objective: Get heathen land, "improve" it according to enlightened Western values, and "convert" the savages who inhabit it to those values. There might be

185

quarrels over means, but the moral justness of the conquering objective was universally accepted.[3]

The manifest destiny paradigm—uniting material greed, spiritual salvation, and scientific enlightenment in a common upbeat cause—dominated the American memory of nineteenth-century western settlement until the second half of the twentieth century. After World War II, however, manifest destiny came to be viewed increasingly among professional historians as an overromanticized oversimplification of western settlement, a stifling "garden myth" of an ersatz Eden of one-dimensional yeoman farmers and whooping cowboys, less reality than Hollywood dreamscape. Gradually, historians uncovered a richly textured western social fabric that had been largely left out of the story, peopled with many races, ethnic groups, bustling urbanites, even thinking women.[4]

But the correction away from one-dimensional manifest destiny remained basically incomplete. No meaningful interpretation of American settlement by European immigrants could escape assigning central significance to the moralistic character of the enterprise. American secular and religious leaders delivered their expansionist vision with a devout intensity that startled even those in Europe who had spawned it. Early in the nineteenth century, Austrian chancellor Prince Richard von Metternich wrote worriedly of America's intentions "to set not only power against power, but to express it more exactly, altar against altar."[5]

With a cultural heritage of that righteous character, the moral vacuum created by discrediting manifest destiny had to be filled, or the story would be, literally, un-American—and un-western as well. The historian Patricia Nelson Limerick took up the daunting challenge. She produced a meaningful explanation that consolidated the West's distinctive identity in both American history and the history of Western civilization, and made it a major player across that entire spectrum. Her approach was suggested by the title of the book that introduced it, *The Legacy of Conquest*, in which she wrote: "Conquest forms the historical bedrock of the whole nation, and the American West is a preeminent case study in conquest and its consequences. . . . [It] leads . . . toward Western American history as one chapter in the global story of Europe's expansion. . . . [It and other] studies in 'comparative conquests' promise to help knit the fragmented history of the planet back together."[6]

Limerick's conquest concept, although critical of motivations behind the westward march of progress, was wholly in the Western tradition in its moralistic stance. For American history, it exposed the moral flip side, the dark side, of sunny manifest destiny. It gave a different aspect to previously celebrated people and events while retaining their unifying moral purposefulness. It enabled historians to measure accomplishments against stated intentions and get at motivations behind a half-conscious process described by one of the Puritan founding fathers as emanating from a New England "city upon a hill" that was simultaneously pure symbol and pure fact—a regional beehive of human activity and an ideational moral beaon.[7]

Although the Old Army served as an agent of the broad forces of cultural conquest, Limerick's work made clear that it was a minor player in the larger context she employed. The Old Army was hardly mentioned in her pathbreaking study and others that followed in its wake. Soldiers once lionized for "Indian-fighting," then demonized for it, now careened off stage almost entirely—except for an occasional cameo when they were viewed by society (as society so often views soldiers) "either with contempt or exaggerated honor."[8]

It's unfortunate that the overdue contextualizing of the "Indian-fighting" Old Army's place in a culture committed to Indian fighting in multiple senses of the term failed to provoke a reconsideration of the Old Army's character. There can be no doubt that the Old Army dutifully served the cultural conquest policies of its civilian superiors. Yet its unusual heritage and outlook—bridging "wild" nature and "civilizing" westward settlement—set soldiers apart in their responses to the material selfishness and spiritual selflessness guiding continental expansion. Soldiers dealing with both sides at once were more likely than others to notice that the conflicting impulses driving the new nation's development were functionally interdependent, like plus and minus charges energizing an electric circuit. While the disputatious torchbearers of progress seemed blinded by their own redeeming light, the Old Army adjudicated their self-renewing conflicts with open eyes.

Not until the end of the century was the Old Army's differentness recognized as an untapped source of civic virtue. The army's new champions came from an emergent segment of American society stirred by unanticipated insights. "The thing that is not named in Europe without a shudder, anarchy, exists here in full bloom," the future senator and cabinet member Carl Schurz wrote to a European friend upon arriving in St. Louis, gateway to the trans-Mississippi West, in the 1850s. Schurz welcomed American anarchy. But it came at a price that by the end of the century was being felt more and more, which was when pioneering environmental activists, led by John Muir and Charles Sargent, embraced the Old Army.[9]

PRESERVATIONISTS AND THE SARGENT PLAN

> Mr. Pinchot is opposed to the military in the forests—why I don't know.
> —*John Muir to Charles Sprague Sargent*[10]

On November 23, 1895, members of the Sierra Club gathered at the California Academy of Sciences in San Francisco to hear their president and founder, John Muir, report on a six-week "ramble" through Yosemite National Park to study "the results of four years of protection . . . under the Federal Government." Muir had good news: "When I had last seen the Yosemite National Park region, the face of the landscape . . . was broken and wasted [and] now it is blooming again." Muir attributed the transformation to the work of "quiet, orderly" soldiers under "Captain [Alex] Rodgers." He found them everywhere: "In my wanderings . . . I met small squads of mounted soldiers in all kinds of out-of-the-way places, fording roaring bowlder-choked [*sic*] streams, crossing rugged canons, ever alert and watchful . . . unweariedly facing and overcoming every difficulty in the way of duty [to restore the park] in all the fineness of wildness. . . . Blessings on Uncle Sam's bluecoats!"[11]

The soldiers' achievements appeared even more impressive alongside the "frowzy, neglected backwood pasture" that the state-run Yosemite Valley had become. Campers in the valley who thoughtlessly "trample everything . . . need the services of a soldier," Muir said. He recommended handing the state park over to the army.[12]

Muir's comments gave voice to a sentiment rapidly gaining favor among Sierra Club members and other California park enthusiasts as word of the army's successes in Yosemite and Sequoia spread. The other principal speaker at the Sierra Club meeting proposed a significant expansion of the army's environmental defense mission. He was Professor William Russell Dudley of Stanford, a world-recognized botanist specializing in Sierra Nevada vegetation, who had visited the Sierra Nevada region south of Yosemite. He recounted army successes in Sequoia National Park and contrasting civilian nonmanagement in the adjacent Sierra Forest Reserve.[13]

The Sierra Reserve that Dudley visited represented a recent stunning success for this new generation of environmental activists. In alliance with irrigation farmers whose livelihood depended on protecting forested watersheds, environmental activists had induced President Benjamin Harrison to establish fifteen forest reserves before he left office in 1893, totaling more than seventeen million acres, using a little-noticed legislative rider that gave him executive authority to reserve "forested lands" owned by the government. The list included four reserves in California, highlighted by the four-million-acre Sierra Forest Reserve extending south from Yosemite along the spine of the Sierra Nevada past Sequoia almost to Bakersfield.[14]

Sierra Club preservationists had no illusions about the utilitarian character of reserves compared to parks. National forests had been "reserved" for the introduction of "scientific" harvesting methods that allowed for their continual healthy replenishment, as was then practiced in Europe, rather than their exploitation with no thought for the future. Now there could be forest utilization "on a rational, permanent scientific basis," Muir said in his remarks that evening. However, in the absence of a cadre of trained forest managers and with unbridled exploitation so widespread in the West, the new reserves shared with the parks a basic need for protection against trespassers, fires, and other damaging intrusions.[15]

Hence a challenge was born of unaccustomed success: How could the newly created federal forest reserves receive immediate protection without a cadre of federal forest administrators that Congress was not yet ready to fund? Did any federal agency offer the resources and dedication—the frontier toughness and independence from manipulation by speculators—that was needed to fill the breach until a permanent federal forest administration could be established? Hence also an expansion of the Sierra Club's previous park-centered focus took place. The club meeting in November 1895 was publicized under the title, "The National Parks and Forest Reservations."

The meeting's presiding officer provided the context necessary for understanding the full character of the response of Muir and his allies to the forest reserve challenge. He was Joseph LeConte, the widely respected professor of geology, botany, and natural history at the University of California at Berkeley, who had been exploring the Sierra Nevada and studying its natural history for thirty years. Professor LeConte called attention to a phenomenon "unparallelled in the history of the world," under way in America since the first English settlements, that had accelerated at an alarming rate during the nineteenth century: the denuding of what was once a vast continental carpet of timber. LeConte spoke of trees "which Nature has been two or three or four hundred years in constructing, destroyed in a few hours," of forest fires that obliterated hundreds of thousands of acres of old-growth timber at a time, caused by carelessness and greeted with public indifference.

This wholesale destruction reflected a naive assumption that America's natural resources were unlimited, LeConte said, but that willful naivete was energized by something more insidious that had acquired almost sacred status in American society: "Now I know perfectly well in modern times there is a feeling of this sort: that society, and the state, and the government, and the nation are made for the individual." But "the social organism is also an individual, and one whose life . . . is perennial."

Individual freedom had been embraced with such fervor in America, placed so far beyond social restraint, that "this individualism has, as it were, run mad." Somehow, LeConte concluded, an American government committed to land policies that fostered individual freedom must find the means to restrain an individualism "run mad" in its self-destructive conquest of nature. Thus, when Muir said, in reference to the army's performance in Yosemite, "it is refreshing to know that . . . there is one arm [of Government] . . . to be depended on," he was announcing what he and his audience believed to be an important discovery filled with promising possibilities for government-supported environmental protection.[16]

This was the backdrop for the series of recommendations for an expanded environmental defense mission for the army laid out by Professor Dudley in his speech immediately following Muir. The Sierra Reserve was the nation's second largest after the Cascade Reserve in Washington. During the preceding July and August, Dudley had explored its southern half, from Sequoia National Park southward. He delivered a summary account of how he had collected eight hundred species of plants, measured many sequoias, took copious notes on vegetation, trails, and topography, and recorded barometric observations. Then, abruptly, Dudley's dry, didactic tone changed. He grew emotional, at times lyrical, as he described a concluding side trip to the adjacent national park.

"To pass from the trampled meadows of the Reservation to the protected meadows of the National Park was a lesson in patriotrism." He visited a lake in the park bordered by a meadow "whose flowers were grateful all day and all summer long to the protecting army of the cavalry." "There are few honest people who could look on a scene like this and not pray for the increase of the United States Army, and an extension of its administrative powers" to the forest reserves. To that end, Dudley offered a proposal that included withdrawal from sale of all public forested lands until they could be inventoried and a management plan for them developed; assignment of soldiers to protect the forests and assist in the development of a civilian force that would manage the forests on a permanent basis; and support from the U.S. Military Academy at West Point in training the first generation of civilian foresters.[17]

Dudley's proposals gave teeth to a more general resolution, passed by the Sierra Club the preceding December, calling for army protection of the forest reserves on an ad hoc emergency basis. Muir was the driving force behind this earlier initiative. In his introduction of Dudley, he said that "the troops stationed in the Sequoia Parks could also effectually guard the great forest reserve at the same time." There was ample precedent. Dudley and Muir merely proposed to use the army as a bridge to a civilian service as it had already served as a bridge to the U.S. Geological Survey, the National Weather Bureau, and other public institutions; or, with regard to professional education, as the U.S. Military Academy had served as the nation's only four-year college of engineering for nearly half a century and provided the original cadre of faculty for the nation's first civilian engineering schools. In suggesting that the military provide institutional impetus for a civilian forest service, Dudley was advocating a proven and commonly accepted procedure in frontier administration.[18]

He was also echoing a proposal introduced by the nation's foremost expert on trees, the venerable scientist and environmental activist Charles Sprague Sargent. Sargent was professor of arboriculture at Harvard, founder and director of the world famous 250-acre Arnold Arboretum in Boston, author of the first comprehensive survey of the nation's forests (two volumes, appended to the 1880 national census), editor of the foremost national journal on forestry, then in the process of initiating a definitive fourteen-volume study of trees in America, and soon to be named chairman of the National Academy of Sciences' first commission on forestry. In the breadth of his scientific knowledge and public policy activities on forestry issues, Sargent stood alone during the 1880s and 1890s when the forest reserve system that he passionately promoted was born. Yet he is largely forgotten today, or dismissed as ineffectual, mainly for one intriguing reason: in promoting a role for the army in forest administration, Sargent clashed with a protégé of his who would crush him and then rewrite the history of his contributions to forestry to make him look like a fool, a perspective that subsequent historians tended to accept without further inquiry. The man who did Sargent in was Gifford Pinchot, the legendary founding director of the U.S. Forest Service.[19]

In his influential professional autobiography (he called it "my story of how Forestry and Conservation came to America"), Pinchot described Sargent as a bumbling scientist who had no aptitude for politics and public administration. Sargent would have been the first to admit his limitations as a politician, and unlike Pinchot he had no public administration aspirations. But he would have added that the argument between him and Pinchot was not about that deficit. Rather, it was about two categories of civic virtue in government, one embodied in the army and the other in the ascendant Pinchot. And the category embodied in the army and embraced by Sargent lost, and was then subsequently distorted in historical memory.[20] It happened this way:

The Sargent plan, as the proposal presented to the Sierra Club by Professor Dudley in 1895 came to be known, was first introduced by Charles Sargent in 1889. It appeared in two successive editorials in *Garden and Forest*, a publication launched by him a year earlier that served as the primary public forum for national forest policy discussion during its decade of existence. "There is in time of peace no other work of national defense or protection so important as this which the army can perform," Sargent wrote in calling for the army to serve as a transitional agent for a civilian forest service. A few months after Sargent presented his army proposal, it was endorsed by the American Forestry Association in a resolution introduced by Bernhard E. Fernow, head of the recently established Division of Forestry in the Department of Agriculture. Army forest protection then became an integral component of the lobbying effort by the nation's small band of foresters and other supporters of "scientific" forestry. It was included in forest management bills introduced in the Senate in 1892 and the House in 1893; but Congress was unresponsive, not so much to the army as to the whole idea of federal land management dedicated to restraining rather than unleashing individualistic exploitation.[21]

The Sargent plan gained new attention after the first federal forest reserves were established in 1891, and Robert Underwood Johnson used *Century Magazine* to promote forest protection by frontier soldiers. The associate editor of the nation's leading mass circulation magazine had applied this formula before, when he teamed up with John Muir to promote the establishment of Yosemite National Park in 1890. In the manner and spirit of that immensely successful campaign, Johnson fired the first of many army–forest reserve salvos in January 1893 with a lead *Century* editorial endorsing the Sargent plan entitled "The Army and the Forest Reserves." The timing of Johnson's commitment could not have been better.

Century was based in New York, and New York governor Grover Cleveland, a close friend of Johnson, was about to be elected president. Cleveland would name his personal secretary, Daniel Lamont, also a Johnson intimate, as secretary of war. It was almost too easy. By the fall of 1893, after an exchange of letters between the offices of *Century*, the White House, and the War Department, Lamont was assuring Johnson that he would soon implement the Sargent plan, following a request from Interior Secretary Hoke Smith arranged for the sake of formality. Smith submitted the scripted request to Lamont, but the order that might have altered the course of forest administration in the United States was never delivered (for an unanticipated reason that will be discussed later).[22]

Meanwhile, Johnson as usual was advancing on several fronts at once. John Muir, who had supported the Sargent proposal from afar, became its outspoken champion after bonding with Sargent during a memorable stay at the Harvard professor's garden estate in Boston during the summer of 1893, with Johnson serving as matchmaker. Muir excitedly wrote his wife Louie about Sargent's "fifty acres of lawns, groves, wild woods of pine, hemlock, maple, beech, hickory . . . wild flowers and cultivated flowers . . . all the ground waving, hill and dale, and clad in the full summer dress of the region trimmed with exquisite taste." The two scientifically minded nature lovers took to each other at once and would remain lifelong intimates. They corresponded regularly and went on numerous botanizing trips in the United States and abroad. Muir called Sargent a "heaven blessed giant of a man."[23]

While Muir lined up the Sierra Club behind the Sargent plan, Johnson organized an extraordinary "symposium" in the February 1895 issue of *Century*. Covering nine pages of text, it consisted of an opening summary of the Sargent plan followed by generally laudatory comments from thirteen public figures. They included federal and state forestry officials, civic-minded western landowners, Assistant Navy Secretary Theodore Roosevelt, and a young protégé of Sargent's named Gifford Pinchot.[24]

Pinchot had been cultivating Sargent since calling upon him in 1889 for introductions to the leading foresters of Europe, prior to becoming the first American to pursue graduate studies in "scientific" forestry across the Atlantic. Upon his return to America in 1890 (following an abbreviated course of instruction), Pinchot used *Garden and Forest* to gain, as he put it, a "toehold" in the American forestry movement. In 1891 the magazine published a series of three articles by him entitled "Forestry Abroad." Pinchot also cultivated Muir and Johnson after meeting them at a dinner in New York in 1893 hosted by Pinchot's wealthy, well-connected father.

In the spring of 1894 Pinchot wrote respectfully to Muir that he had followed his advice during a visit to Yosemite and struck out on his own into the mountain wilderness. He did not mention that after touring Yosemite he stopped off in San Francisco, met with Muir's arch adversary John P. Irish, praised California management of Yosemite Valley, and made light of the environmental concerns of Muir and Johnson. This typified a pattern Pinchot followed of saying one thing to his patrons Sargent, Muir, and Johnson and something else to their adversaries, to the progressive astonishment of the former, then disenchantment, and, ultimately, in the case of Johnson and Sargent, personal loathing. (Abstract ideas and "evil" combinations drew Muir's righteous contempt, but rarely individuals; he was too much at one with everything that lived.) "It is badly on my conscience that I started him on his career," Sargent wrote to Johnson thirty years after Pinchot had ground him under.[25]

For it was indeed Sargent who launched Pinchot's career in government, with the enthusiastic support of Johnson and Muir. Pinchot was young, bright, enthusiastic, and committed to expanding the national forest reservation system on sound scientific management principles. The decision to include him in the high-level symposium on the Sargent plan published in *Century* in 1895 seemed like an investment in a new and more hopeful future, and he did not disappoint his patrons, at least at first.

"Excellent," wrote Pinchot of the Sargent plan he would later mock. He then outdid everyone, even Sargent, by proposing that national forests be transferred from the Interior Department to the War Department and that temporary army involvement in forest administration as envisioned by Sargent be expanded and made permanent. In retrospect, it is clear that Pinchot did not believe a word of what he was writing. But at that takeoff point in his career, he needed Sargent.[26]

And he also needed Johnson, for complementary reasons. Sargent offered entrée into the forestry movement, Johnson into another domain Pinchot coveted above all others: politics. In September 1895, Johnson teamed up with Pinchot in getting the American Forestry Association to endorse a resolution that they had engineered. It called for the creation by Congress of a core component of the Sargent plan—the national forestry commission that would carry out the plan's objectives. A week later, Muir wrote Johnson about his "six weeks ramble" in Yosemite that confirmed reports about the army's effectiveness in the national parks. Soon afterward, the *San Francisco Call* published a lengthy interview with Muir that lauded the army's "complete success" in Yosemite National Park and proposed extending army protection to the adjacent national forest reserves. Shortly afterward came the Sierra Club meeting where Muir and Professor Dudley won additional support for the Sargent plan.[27]

The stage was set for a final push for Sargent's national forestry commission by the pro-army triumvirate (Sargent, Muir, and Johnson) that Pinchot had made into a foursome. Early in 1896, Johnson and his new political protégé Pinchot maneuvered behind the scenes in Washington to get around Congress, which had considered Sargent's commission proposal for years without acting. They orchestrated a request from Interior secretary Hoke Smith to National Academy of Sciences president Oliver Wolcott Gibbs for the academy to sponsor a forestry commission. The preadvised Gibbs responded that "no subject upon which the Academy has been asked before by the Government for advice compares with it [the forest issue] in scope . . . no other economic problem equals it in importance." The commission would consist of six experts, chaired by Sargent. All but one were prominent academy members. The lone outsider was a personally recommended protégé of Chairman Sargent, Gifford Pinchot.[28]

The academy's commitment stirred Congress to action. By the summer of 1896, commission members were touring the West, thanks to a special $25,000 congressional appropriation. (Yosemite and Sequoia had yet to receive a cent from Congress, despite repeated entreaties.) Muir joined them en route at Sargent's invitation. S. B. M. Young hosted them in Yosemite. In San Francisco, they were feted by the Sierra Club. Early in the fall, the happy band of commissioners, minus Muir, headed east to begin work on their report.[29]

The first hint of discord from Sargent came in a letter to Muir in November; but he added that he wasn't concerned. "I dare say all this will be adjusted," he wrote. He was wrong. Although there was unanimity within the commission on creating new reserves, Pinchot was lobbying hard against the army proposal of his patron that he had previously endorsed. In February, President Cleveland implemented preliminary commission recommendations for thirteen new forest reserves. That single act more than doubled the size of the national forest reserves to just under forty million acres. "Now," wrote Sargent to Muir, "we must bend ourselves to getting the Reserves protected by the military." But he was no match for Pinchot.[30]

A full account of Pinchot's machinations from the base Sargent created for him is beyond the scope of this book. Suffice it to say that the commission's forest administration proposals did not reach Congress until May, when they had become irrelevant (due in part to Sargent's political ineptness), and that Pinchot shrewdly lifted, virtually word for word, a Sargent commission recommendation to give the interior secretary authority to make forest rules and establish an administrative apparatus, and got himself named chief implementer of it as Interior's special forest agent. With that, Pinchot headed west. He said nothing to Sargent. He wrote Muir that he was "both surprised and delighted" at the appointment he had engineered. (Pinchot still needed Muir at that time but eventually would dump him and drive him to despair by playing a leading role in the successful campaign to flood Muir's beloved Hetch Hetchy Valley in Yosemite and build a dam; Muir died in 1914, the year after he lost the battle for Hetch Hetchy.) When Muir finally pieced it all together, he sputtered to Sargent about this "monstrous business" their young friend had pulled on them: "One feeble sixth part of the Forestry Commission has thus been given the work that had already most ably been done by the whole."[31]

Pinchot's legislative triumph marked the end of the prospect for army forest involvement of any kind. A government career that would carry him into Teddy Roosevelt's inner circle and include the establishment of the U.S. Forest Service under Pinchot's direction had begun. He had no further need for Sargent, who later told Johnson that he never saw Pinchot again. As for the commission's report, it awaited only final disposal in Pinchot's autobiography as "so much wasted paper."[32]

Reaching into history's waste bin, let's take a look at the Sargent commission's recommendations with regard to the army and the forests. Although now largely forgotten, this issue lay at the initiating center of the historic split in the environmental community between "utilitarian conservationists" led by Pinchot and "aesthetic preservationists" led by Muir, Johnson, and Sargent. Conceptual differences between the two outlooks have since been exposed as overblown. But for both sides, the army served as a surrogate for a schism that ran much deeper than its superficial pretexts. The deeper issue concerned the fundamental character of public service.[33]

Under the heading "temporary measures," the commission report repeated Sargent's call for the "temporary detail" of troops to protect the forest reserve system "against fire and depredation." Keep in mind that army units already administered national parks adjacent to the new national forests and that no other force existed for this policing assignment nor would there be one, for all practical purposes, for another decade. As a temporary expedient, army administration made sense. For subsequent "permanent forest organization," the report outlined a program of transition from army administration to a civilian forest service, with the War Department filling the gap until Congress and civilian executive agencies got their acts together, as in the national parks. The transition program included inviting a select number of West Point graduates to study at European forestry schools prior to working with selected graduates from civilian universities who had been awarded the same opportunity to establish a civilian national forestry school. Again, this drew on well-established precedent for seeding such civilian endeavors, including the army-managed transition to a civilian National Weather Bureau completed four years earlier.[34]

In any event, the immediate assignment of troops for the unpoliced reserves seemed so patently in the interest of civilian forest reserve supporters that most of the commmission report's argument was aimed at convincing the army that the forest assignment was historically justified. The report noted that with the end of "the state of actual or quasi war" on the frontier, "new conditions" and "new duties" for the army had arisen. "Wide areas capable of supporting an industrious population are threatened with ruin. . . . This danger is no less real than Indian massacre was formerly, and the citizens of the West can only look to the Army for immediate and temporary protection from it."[35]

The operative word was "temporary." It appeared throughout the commission's army references, as in all of Sargent's previous formulations—"temporary detail of troops," "temporary protection," and so on. To remove any doubt, there was a separate section on "permanent" objectives. They involved the establishment of a "forest bureau" in the Interior Department dedicated to scientific forestry, with personnel stationed in each forest reserve to oversee the sale of products "at reasonable prices, under regulations looking to the perpetual reproduction of the forest," a framework that Pinchot later called "right as rain." With that admirable civilian administration objective unambiguously laid out, there seemed no reason for Pinchot to oppose a few manifestly needed temporary protection measures for forest management during a critical period, drawing on resources available from no other source.[36]

The problem, from Pinchot's perspective, was Sargent's underlying rationale. The commission report that Sargent drafted stated that forest administration involved police work, surveying, road construction, the direction of personnel "not easily trained to habits of discipline"—duties that were often "military in character, and should be regulated for the present on military principles." That part of the rationale drew on the Old Army's nation-building tradition. But Sargent took it a significant step further when he immediately added in that same context that "the forest officers must be men of the highest personal character" who would not succumb to economic temptation or political influence. By Sargent's standards, "military principles" included training in Old Army civic virtues developed during a century-long mission to protect the public domain from excessive exploitation, exemplified most recently in army administration of national parks. In the commission report, Sargent contrasted past civilian and current military administration of Yellowstone to emphasize that the army's contributions to the first national park had been "moral" as well as "physical." The chief challenge in that connection, as he saw it, was to use the transition from temporary to permanent forest administration to introduce army civic virtue into a new civilian forest service run by Washington politicos. Professional training for foresters was easily arranged; character training was, in Sargent's view, far more difficult.[37]

For introducing "the highest personal character" into forest administration Sargent looked to the army and especially to West Point. As part of the transition to permanent administration, a select number of army officers would be sent overseas for graduate study at European forestry schools. Upon their return, drawing on their European scientific studies and West Point character training, they would "organize at some convenient place near one of the great reservations a forest school for the instruction of the forest corps and of such civilians as may desire to avail themselves of its privileges."[38]

But why so much emphasis on West Point for inculcating moral standards? Why not one of the great civilian universities—such as Harvard, Yale, Princeton, or Columbia—founded by Protestant churches with long distinguished traditions of moral instruction? Why should Sargent, certified Boston Brahmin, descendant of New England believers, look for moral instruction to the nation's most prominent secular university and the first one to give priority to atheistic science? He did it for two reasons.

First was the need he perceived for specialized training in civic virtue as well as "scientific" professionalism when developing a federal land management agency from scratch in the late nineteenth century. In that regard, Sargent differed from Muir and Johnson as well as Pinchot. The others assumed that civil service "reform," with its selection of officials according to professional standards insulated from politics, would do the job. That might work for awhile, but what about the nation-state's Achilles' heel in terms of moral responsibility—the lure of power? What about the power-enhancing wheeling and dealing for the public good that the "scientific" forester Pinchot loved so much? How far down the chain of command should it go? What would happen as this "efficient," "professional," "scientific" bureaucracy grew and grew and grew? "Civil service rules are all right," Sargent wrote to Johnson, "but . . . soldiers and soldiers only can protect the reservations at the present time." Or as he wrote in *Garden and Forest*, in calling for a military role in the forests, "there is one constabulary force in the country which is thoroughly organized, which has *esprit de corps*."[39]

The esprit de corps to which Sargent referred, the second component of his program to add a character-building moral dimension to scientific forestry training, was not taught at Yale or Harvard, but it was central to West Point instruction. It relied on virtues distinct to the Old Army's military character and heritage. Sargent believed that prevailing Judeo-Christian morality simply was not enough by itself to restrain the Judeo-Christian values underpinning what an astute historian called the "gospel of efficiency" taking control of the administrative levers of power in Washington at the turn of the twentieth century. Besides, how could a "scientific" land management process be scientific—that is, value-free—when its authors had established the dominance of nature as a moral imperative?[40]

Thus, in this era of rapidly expanding federal administration, the dictum that knowledge is power worried Sargent as much as it excited Pinchot and drew Sargent toward the Old Army. While the replacement of amateurism by professionalism in federal agencies made government more efficient, it had no comparably corrective effect on another malady of national government, be it despotic or democratic, that required equal attention: the allure of power. If anything, technically trained professionals who were new to politics were both more susceptible to that allurement and less conscious of it because they were professionally conditioned to consider their judgments value-free. By having the national forestry school established by ex–West Pointers, Sargent was also encouraging the introduction of character training into the program of education for "scientific" forestry, as had occurred uniquely at West Point, where such subjects as "honesty" and "duty" were part of a science-oriented curriculum preparing university students for national service. Without training in public service *character* as in the Old Army, the agents of "scientific" knowledge applied in the service of expanding state power were helpless tools of impulses operating beyond the periphery of their self-deluding "value-free" awareness.[41]

There is, of course, a place for power-mongering in a good cause. In the modern nation-state, it's often the only way to get the job done. Whether or not Pinchot needed to make all the compromises with timber, mining, grazing, and other interests he claimed were necessary to get a national forest program up and running, no one can gainsay his immense achievements. They reached full flower when the man who had replaced Sargent as Pinchot's chief sponsor was elected president. Teddy Roosevelt called Pinchot his "moving and directing spirit" on conservation. By the time Roosevelt left office in 1909, an astounding 151 million acres of national forest reservations had been established on Pinchot's recommendations. They functioned under a U.S. Forest Service that Pinchot created in 1905 after getting all forested federal lands transferred from Interior to the Agriculture Department, where he had taken up residence. It is doubtful that anyone but Gifford Pinchot could have done it.[42]

But in becoming Roosevelt's chief adviser on environmental issues, Pinchot shaped the character of conservation administration in questionable ways that remain a source of contention to this day. (After he left the federal government, Pinchot's narrow utilitarian outlook broadened, but that didn't change history.) The difference between Sargent and Pinchot was not over the validity of economically oriented utilitarian principles in forest administration, as Pinchot made it out to be. The difference was that Sargent did not think, as Pinchot did, that utilitarian principles should be the whole thing. Sargent believed that, as he put it, "the wisest managers of forests" would also be "true lovers of trees," and that a sustainable yield policy conceived on the principle that, as Pinchot would say later, "wilderness is waste," was neither utilitarian nor aesthetic. Ultimately, many members of Pinchot's Forest Service would come to the same conclusion. Forester Aldo Leopold authored the idea of setting up protected wilderness enclaves in national forests. A historian of American forestry observes: "Where Leopold parted company with Pinchot's edict—and where others have parted since—is at the point where economics seem to be the *only* criterion for rationalizing the necessity of the national forests." That was also where Sargent parted with Pinchot. He wanted to introduce the environmental ethic of a scientifically knowledgeable and sensually caring "nature lover" into utilitarian federal forest administration from the start.[43]

To achieve that difficult objective, Sargent sought a federal agency whose members shared his experiential love of nature and his commitment to blending the natural sciences and aesthetics in deepening that love; were philosophically and institutionally detached from both anti-government economic liberalism and progovernment Progressivism; were committed to science as a humbling inquiry into nature's mysteries rather than an ego-inflating tool of bureaucratic power; were schooled in public service in a system that taught civic virtue as well as professional skill and rewarded character as much as competence; were organized, disciplined, and at home in the wild; and were taught to love and protect the American land.

Sargent found a federal agency with all those attributes already on duty in our national parks. That his modest, transitional army proposals aimed at institutionalizing civic virtue in government were crushed so compulsively by the chief representative of the professionalism and efficiency gaining ascendancy at the turn of the twentieth century deserves more reflection than it has so far received. The record of governance based on personal character that the Old Army left behind in our national parks might offer instruction for those who, in one form or another, within government and without, continue Sargent's quest to strengthen a public conscience constructed on moral abstractions and "value-free" socioscientific perceptions that discourage self-awareness and offer little protection from power's self-inflating seductions. For many reasons, it is worth asking: Just where did the Old Army get the *institutional* values that set it apart from civilian local, state, and federal agencies as a frontier administrator?

Before addressing that question, another one left in abeyance a few pages earlier deserves a response. It concerned the failure of the potentially historic effort of Muir, Johnson, Sargent, and their allies to get the army into the forests on a transitional basis in 1893. The influential Johnson had obtained commitments from newly elected President Grover Cleveland and his secretaries of war and the interior, and the Interior Department had sent the formal request to the War Department for troops that was meant to close the deal. What went wrong? Apparently, the new secretary of war, a New York politician who had no experience with arcane army procedure, had failed to take into account the requirement that all civilian requests for army troops must be forwarded to the army's judge advocate general, or JAG, for a ruling.

The JAG replied that the request was unconstitutional because it was merely from one executive branch to another, thereby circumventing the American people through their elected representatives in Congress. Thus, the judge advocate general invoked a statute that the army held sacred, created at General George Washington's insistence to prevent the U.S. Army from ever being used by the executive branch of government to repress American citizens, as repressive European governments had done for centuries. Environmentalists fired with moral idealism had over-looked that restrictive statute, but not the by-the-book JAG. He knew his institution's boundaries in the democratic scheme of government, and he had taken an oath to protect them from executive assault, even if the assault was perpetrated by democratic idealists. From that morally and legally proscribed position lower down American civilization's value chain, the Old Army invoked its culturally subordinate virtues in performing its constitutional duties.[44]

OLD ARMY VIRTUES 1: LOYALTY AND LEADERSHIP

The Loyal Regiment

No civilian government agency or private corporation demands anything like the highly charged loyalty nurtured within military units. Loyalty means so much more in military life because it is essential to survival in combat. Without bonds of loyalty that transcend personal differences and rivalries, the members of a combat unit are doomed. Fourth Cavalry troops who served at Yosemite marched behind a regimental flag displaying a crest emblazoned with the words *Paratus et Fidelis*—Prepared and Loyal.

Loyalty was cultivated in the Old Army through rituals and procedures transmitted mainly by regiments and companies. A regiment of between seven hundred and nine hundred men (the authorized strength of nine hundred was rarely attained in practice) was the right size for managing many of the inclusive symbols of loyalty—campaign banners, crests, mottos, stirring parades. The regiment's elaborate rituals and drills were complemented by the more intimate relationships fostered by its companies. A regiment consisted of twelve companies, usually of fifty-five to seventy-five men each. Enlisted men kept pretty much to their companies. Officers served as the bridge between companies and their regiments, moving freely in and out of both worlds. (Old Army cavalry regiments called their companies troops; that designation became official in 1883.)[45]

The company was the Old Army's basic institutional unit and the common soldier's extended family. Home was the company barracks, where the bunks of enlisted men lined the sides of a long oblong room, and noncommissioned officers, the sergeants, occupied cubicles at one end. Company personnel slept together, ate together (at long wooden tables, using company utensils), worked together, and played together. They drilled and performed their daily chores together. They patrolled and fought together. Their baseball and football teams competed against teams from other companies. The company was also the Old Army's basic financial unit for payroll, supply, and group savings. Privately collected company funds were used to purchase "family" amenities not available through the standardized supply system, such as nonregulation cooking utensils, sports equipment, and magazine subscriptions. Since the Old Army frontier ration rarely included fresh produce, most companies had gardens behind their barracks that were tended by company personnel. On paydays, when enlisted men liked to go on a tear in a nearby town if they could, they went with their company buddies.[46]

The group loyalty inspired by that enveloping communal experience, intensified by the highly ritualized daily routine in frontier forts, was unique in the United States. It stood out in sharp contrast to comparatively fragmented urban as well as rural civilian life where the value-laden concepts of stand-alone private property and democratic individualism shaped everyday life. Old Army soldiers served those governing sociopolitical concepts; but, unlike American civilians, they did not live them.

The Fourth U.S. Cavalry exemplified the difference between the two worlds in the effects of the Civil War on the relationships of its members. The regiment's prewar officer complement included George McClellan, future commander of the Union army in the looming Civil War; Robert E. Lee, future commander of the Confederate army; and James E. B. "Jeb" Stuart, the soon-to-be-famous Confederate cavalry commander. When war broke out, a "de-southernized" Fourth Cavalry fought as a unit of the Union army.[47]

For four years, officers of the Fourth Cavalry led their troops into battle against units of the Confederate army led by former comrades. Yet these uncompromising warrior-antagonists failed to show the same capacity to carry their antagonisms into a postwar world. In ways that will be discussed further, Old Army training nurtured social bonding in its purest, most primal, transpersonal forms so that on the battlefield it might become autonomic, like breathing.

The blind strength of the primal loyalty cultivated by Old Army training placed special demands on the commander responsible for guiding troops into battle, for group loyalty also meant group dependence in matters of life and death. That was where honest leadership, pursued with the same dedication as group loyalty, came into play.

The Honest Leader

As with loyalty, and for similar reasons, there is no counterpart in civilian society for the *institutional* emphasis that the military places on incorporating personal character virtues into skills training for its officer corps.

A poorly led business goes bankrupt; a poorly led military unit is annihilated. That cosmic difference in the stakes involved, along with the nature of the challenge, means that, in addition to expertise, a military leader must also receive special training in character virtues. When combat propels the human psyche into the twilight zone where reason encounters upswelling primal instincts, it is the intangible qualities of character that prevent stark fear and panic from overwhelming cool judgment. Such mastery, so difficult to attain, is only a preliminary stage in the character training of a military leader. By itself, it is indistinguishable from the icy coolness exhibited by criminal psychopaths. For the military leader seeking to inspire troops to sacrifice in battle, it is but a vessel for the humanizing and self-disciplining restraints on conduct known collectively as martial virtues.

Like armies, which go back thousands of years in human history, martial virtues are older than the abstract moral concepts introduced by Judeo-Christian civilization. They represent a stage on the path to "higher" Judeo-Christian morality and are less concerned with ideals that are products of abstract thought, such as justice and freedom, than with personal conduct in the heat of battle. In early Western civilization, martial virtues flowered in pagan Greece. Homer's *Iliad* was on one level a lecture on the warrior Achilles' failure to show martial virtue in calling an adversary an animal, in denying burial to a dead foe, and in performing other "inhuman" acts. Humanizing martial virtues had the effect of restraining berserk impulses, and berserk leaders, through the reasoned cultivation of emotion-based qualities of character that constituted primitive expressions of what we now call a moral sense. During that early phase in the moral development of the human animal, the honesty displayed by a leader had a powerful educating effect because it could be verified directly by the emotions that link leaders and loyal soldiers through humanizing reciprocal bonds of trust. If a commander inspired loyal trust through honesty, then those trusting bonds upon which the life of the group depended also could be broken by dishonest behavior; it was up to the commander. This evolution marked a major advance in moral development: to the primal leadership qualities of strength and bravery (physical courage) was now added the far more sophisticated quality of honesty (moral character).[48]

Martial virtues came to the United States by way of Europe, where they had undergone considerable refinement under feudalism and monarchy, little of it for the good. They had become the property of an officer corps that reflected the values of a trans-European aristocratic caste. In Great Britain, "the screen of constitutional arrangements served to maintain the gentry in the enjoyment of its practical monopoly of providing officers for the army and navy"; in Prussia, "the military schools

. . . were little more than 'golden bridges' for the sons of the nobility." Leo Tolstoy, serving as a Russian artillery officer during the midcentury Crimean War, disgustedly mocked his army's aristocratic values: "In the eyes of Captain Obzogov, Lieutenant-Captain Mikhailov is an *aristocrat* because he is wearing a clean greatcoat and gloves, and for this reason he finds him insufferable. . . . In the eyes of Lieutenant-Captain Mikhailov, Adjutant Kalugin is an *aristocrat* . . . and for this reason he is not entirely well disposed towards him, even though he fears him. In the eyes of Adjutant Kalugin, Count Nordov is an *aristocrat*, and he is forever cursing him in silence and inwardly despising him because he is an aide-de-camp to the Tsar."[49]

America's European settlers considered their society a living rejection of the overbearing class distinctions that permeated civilian as well as military life across the Atlantic. During the colonial era, frontier-bred militia officers chafed under the high-toned manners of the occupying British officer corps. Following independence, the American commitment to making the values of its army more reflective of America's democratic society, rather than "aristocratical" Europe, were institutionalized. This approach produced a purification of the Old Army's European inheritance (as discussed earlier with reference to West Point), a stripping away of its aristocratic conceptual regalia.[50]

America's democratization of martial virtues addressed only half of the problem inherited from Europe, however. Equally dangerous to democratic values and public institutions was the lure of political power to a uniformed commander of armed and loyal troops. Napoleon's humble background provided no check against his lust for power and his willingness to sacrifice entire armies of his compatriots to satisfy personal ambition. In its response to that danger, American democracy broke new ground. The Old Army of the new United States, to an extent unprecedented among armies of its time (including institutionally democratic but nonetheless class-bound England), handed over responsibility for determining its mission to democratically elected civilian leaders.

That is the broader contextual significance of the institutionalized subordination of the military to civilian authority in American government, intensified in the U.S. Army by its originating association with the army's first and most revered commander, George Washington. No concept stood higher on the Old Army's scale of values than Washington's fundamental insistence on military subservience to civilian authority. Under its influence, American military leaders accepted civilian domination to an extent unique for the armies of its time. In 1889, a West Point commencement speaker, U.S. senator Cushman Davis, reminded graduating seniors of what had already been drummed into their heads during four years at the Military Academy:

You are soldiers, but above all you are citizens. The authority with which you are dressed is subordinate to the civil law, of which you are but the chosen champion and protector. There is not a justice of the peace in the land who, within his jurisidiction, is not your superior officer. You are part of civil government. To conceive of yourselves otherwise is to make you outlaws.[51]

The Old Army's unequivocal subordination to civil authority placed extraordinary demands on frontier commanders engaged more in adjudication than in combat. In evicting white civilian squatters, controlling white civilian whiskey dealers, mediating the encounter between white settlers and Indians, and other similar tasks, soldiers submitted to civilian overseers who were often more interested in protecting citizens who flouted the law than those who sought to obey it, especially in dealings with Indians who stood in the way of rip-roaring "progress." Some officers developed an awareness of human self-contradictions—a rough-edged, Shakespearean sense of tragedy—that contrasted sharply with the moral certainty of civilian leaders who considered conquest of the American continent to be the fulfillment of a devoutly pursued manifest destiny.[52]

This process also produced a two-tier value system in government application of continental expansion policies. The upper tier was occupied by the values of a civilian government that, although it called itself secular, relied for its governing principles on Western civilization's Judeo-Christian heritage of morality derived from abstract concepts (liberty, freedom) that, among other things, spiritualized individualistic entrepreneurial impulses (manifest destiny) and even "scientific" professionalism (the "gospel of efficiency"). The lower tier was occupied by the character virtues of the subservient Old Army (honesty, loyalty), inherited from Europe and purified of aristocratic overlays to bring them closer to their primal roots. Thus, for Old Army officers, the decision on whether they should get a particular mission was determined by civilian leaders guided by abstract politico-religious concepts such as redemptive entrepreneurship and divinely ordained "civilizing" of "savages." The subordinate ethical challenge facing Old Army commanders concerned how to conduct themselves in carrying out the policies of an expanding nation of spiritually, economically, and politically contentious individualists armed to the teeth.[53]

To meet that challenge, Old Army leaders looked for ethical guidance mainly to interpersonal virtues applied to the peformance of their duties under civilian orders. In civilian politics, a person could be (often felt morally obligated to be) both righteous and vindictive in good conscience. Old Army officers, on the other hand, faced with the responsibility of implementing rather than formulating the policies developed by civilian keepers of the public conscience, found themselves drawing on other inspirational sources. As one consequence of this two-tiered arrangement, Old Army officers served America's worthiest ideals while living outside the compulsions that self-righteously manipulated those ideals in nineteenth-century civil society.[54]

OLD ARMY VIRTUES 2: CIVILIZATION AND INDIANNESS

From the beginning of white settlement in North America, "civilization and Indianness were [perceived as] inherently incompatible." "Savage" Indians were human incarnations of "wild" nature and thus lead actors in "the American theme, of Nature versus civilization." This moralistic conflict in which civilized European settlers sought to subdue, convert, and redeem—that is, conquer—a land and its indigenous inhabitants had an inward personal dimension that influenced its expression. While settlers subdued nature, they also struggled to subdue "wild" and "savage" impulses within themselves that their guiding value system rejected as immoral. The two dimensions—external conquest and internal self-conquest—continually interacted in influencing settler attitudes and actions. As a result, internal imaginings purposefully colored external perceptions, and the American landscape vibrated with symbolical meaning for European settlers as much as for Indians: "For the Puritan the Indian as well as himself was part of the cosmic drama willed by God to reveal His sovereignty and His grace. . . . each event, trivial or great, displayed His secret will . . . [and] became for the devout Puritan . . . symbols or metaphors of life's real meaning." In battling over their differences, whites and Indians saw what they believed.[55]

The Old Army patrolled the border of that literal/metaphorical conflict as it progressed westward across the continent. Although the shooting wars between soldiers and Indians grabbed the headlines and dominate popular memory today, they constituted only a small part of the army's role in Indian-white relations. The major part involved mediating the relationship between Indians and two categories of whites—those who sought to exploit Indians brazenly or by manipulation of the law, usually in pursuit of land, and members of the white "Indian reform" movement, an increasingly dominant force during the second half of the nineteenth century, who sought to replace "barbaric" Native American values with the values of what a post–Civil War secretary of the interior responsible for Indian administration called, employing common usage, "higher Christian civilization."[56]

It is important to emphasize the complementary effects on Native American civilization of selfish whites who sought to obtain Indian land

and otherwise exploit them economically and selfless whites who sought to save Indian souls. For even as corrupt speculators and redeemed reformers fought over Christian morals, they were united in a desire to crush pagan Native American civilization. Religious reformers might oppose speculative excesses in the pursuit of Native American lands, for instance, but those same reformers rejected traditional Indian communal ownership of land, and the communal value system it engendered, because it was incompatible with a society based on private property that promoted the individuality essential for absorbing a Christian value system. "If civilization, education and Christianity are to do their work, they must get at the individual . . . one by one," wrote the prominent Indian reformer Merrill E. Gates, president of Amherst College and head of the national Board of Indian Commissioners, in 1885, stating a "humanitarian" viewpoint that was at war with Indian values.

A centerpiece of the self-described humanitarian effort was the Dawes Act of 1887 that carved communal Indian lands into individual homesteads. The legislation simultaneously promoted white spiritual values and provided a bonanza for white economic speculators while reducing the Indians' land base by two-thirds, or ninety million acres. A recent study of the triumph of the humanitarians concluded that the civilizing program of Gates and his associates meant "a commitment to the values of individualism, industry and private property . . . acceptance of Christian doctrine . . . acceptance of the idea that man's conquest of nature constituted one of his noblest accomplishments." The outcome could only be, according to a historical anthropologist's account of this same phenomenon, "a kind of cultural genocide." It reached its peak in the 1880s when speculators and reformers joined forces in successfully promoting privatizing legislation that destroyed the tribally based relationship with savage nature that defined the character of Indian religious *and* economic life. In white relations with Indians, the business of obtaining land and saving souls was a joint stock company.[57]

Soldiers joined civilians in mouthing the language of Indian extinction, which most soldiers viewed as inevitable under the circumstances. But soldiers were only ephemerally involved in its culturally encompassing pursuit and never shared the devout sense of triumph of the conquerors. Indeed, soldiers were barred from cultural extinction command centers because of their "uncivilized" cruelty toward Indians in the eyes of those running the show for whom the Old Army served as a cathartic scapegoat. Phil Sheridan was as ruthless in Indian warfare as he was in laying waste to the Shenandoah Valley during the Civil War, but there is no evidence that he ever uttered the phrase most often attributed to him and through him to the Old Army as a whole—that "the only good Indian is a dead Indian." Still, it fit the image and it stuck. Largely forgotten were these confirmed words from a published report by Sheridan: "We took away their country and their means of support, broke up their mode of living, their habits of life, introduced disease and decay among them and it was for this and against this they made war. Could anyone expect less?"[58]

Similarly, a historian writing in the 1980s about Indian extinction sentiments among whites in the nineteenth century quoted Old Army colonel John Gibbon as calling the Indian a "wild animal" who was "bound to disappear." This same blunt-spoken officer, whose anti-Indian outbursts often came following a battle when his soldiers lay dead on the ground, also wrote: "There is no question in my mind that the Indians on this continent are the worst-abused people on the face of the globe . . . cheated, defrauded, and encroached upon in such a way that, sooner or later . . . every peaceful tribe upon this continent will turn hostile; and I would have no opinion of their manhood if they did not."[59]

In the preceding account of white desires for Indian extinction, Old Army lieutenant C. E. S. Wood also is cited in the same judgmental manner as Gibbon for his comments on the impending doom of Indian civilization. Not mentioned is that this same Lieutenant Wood was so appalled by the cultural repression of Indians that he resigned from the army to devote his life to writing poetry celebrating Indian culture and deploring white conquest of North America. His poetry echoed the sentiments of Old Army soldiers throughout the nineteenth century, including those ordered to direct the infamous removal of the southern tribes to Indian Territory west of the Mississippi in the 1830s, when General John E. Wool attacked the Alabama legislature for attempting to wreck the Indians' way of life; General Winfield Scott, the army's most prominent pre–Civil War commander, called the entire operation shameful; and his aide Erasmus D. Keyes said he regarded himself as a "trespasser . . . one of a gang of robbers."[60]

Far more than is recognized, soldiers struggled to meliorate the effects of the policies they were constitutionally required to carry out. One of the most persistent themes of Old Army reports was that Indians should not be forced to complete in a generation a process of cultural evolution that took lording whites centuries to pull off for themselves. "What's the hurry?" Old Army officers asked of the whites who rushed in after the battles to claim Indian land and Indian souls. Two successive southwestern departmental commanders under whom the Fourth Cavalry served just prior to the regiment's transfer northward into Yosemite and Sequoia in 1890 were particularly outspoken in their condemnations of redemptive conquests.[61]

The first was General George Crook. Like Mackenzie, Crook was both a vaunted Indian fighter and an admirer of Indian communal values, singling out their commitment to truthfulness and their emotional attachment to nature. As for whites, Crook wrote that "greed and avarice on the part of the whites . . . is at the bottom of nine-tenths of all our Indian trouble." That "greed and avarice" was directed toward what Indians had that whites wanted most—American land.[62]

Powerless to overrule his self-righteous white overseers, Crook urged soldiers to at least show where the army stood by being fair and honest in their day-to-day dealings. "Let the Indian see that you administer one law for both the white-skinned and the red-skinned, that you do this without regard for praise or censure, and you will gain his confidence because you have shown yourself worthy of it," Crook said in a West Point commencement speech he delivered in 1884 with two future national park commanders and one deputy commander in the audience.[63]

Crook was succeeded in 1888 (after a brief interval during the Geronimo campaign) by Benjamin H. Grierson, a former small-town music teacher, Civil War hero, and commander of one of the two African-American cavalry regiments formed after the Civil War, the famous "Buffalo Soldiers." In a career that took him from one end of the continent to the other, he pretty much had seen it all, and he had no use for economic greed, self-righteous soul-saving, or military vainglory. He commanded the Department of Arizona until his retirement from the army in 1890.[64]

Grierson's final report prior to his retirement reads like a final judgment. In it he moved knowledgeably and compassionately from reservation to reservation—the Hualpais, the Jicarilla Apache, the Navajo—describing their efforts to construct better lives while "avaricious" whites "skulk and roam" about the reservations like "hungry wolves." Here are excerpts:

> The excitement . . . gotten up by false reports [of a Hualpais uprising was] based on the desire of the people adjacent to get rid of the Indians in order to occupy their land. . . .
>
> [The Navajo] have been peaceable all year, although encroachments have been made upon them as usual. . . . There probably can not be cited another instance on the face of the globe where 20,000 people have lived so quietly and well-behaved as those Indians. It is an astonishing commentary on the civilization of our country, as hardly a day passes that murders and other serious crimes are not committed [by whites that go unpunished]. . . .
>
> [Reports of marauding Indians from the San Carlos agency] are purely false, *in toto*, and are mainly put into circulation by alarmists and certain interested parties who hope, by such methods, to cause

the removal of the Indians and the opening up of their reservation to settlement.[65]

Yet even in his final bitter tirade, Grierson, like Crook and Mackenzie, lauded "decent" whites who treated Indians fairly and resisted the lure of instant wealth. But the sheer unregulated number of new settlers after the Civil War was enough to swamp even the most rooted institutions, much less the fragile ones in place at the time. In 1880, spurred by Arizona's booming silver mines, the Southern Pacific Railroad came to Tucson. At the dedication ceremonies, the company executive sent to hammer in the last spike drew cheers and also gasps—the spike was made of pure silver bullion drawn from the mines around Tombstone. A local civic leader followed the man with the silver spike to the podium to urge that "in the whirl of excitement incident to the race after the precious treasure embedded in our mountain ranges, our last request is that you kindly avoid trampling in the dust the few remaining monuments of the first American settlement of Arizona." The poor man was grasping at straws. Another value system was guiding western development. The town father's self-restraining civic sentiments took second place to those of the lusty, confident railroad mogul and his gleaming symbol of wealth for the taking. Where could honest hearts find salvation?[66]

One place they could not find it, Old Army officers believed, was in the tides of religious revival that swept across the frontier throughout the nineteenth century. Soldiers were as detached from the religious aspects of manifest destiny as they were from the materialistic ones. In 1874, only thirty of three hundred military installations had chaplains. The leading scholar of the Old Army reported that references to spiritual matters in the correspondence of West Point cadets "were derogatory [and] the waves of religious enthusiasm that swept other segments of the population in the nineteenth century made no impact."[67]

Correspondingly, the only segment of white society that felt greater antipathy toward the Old Army than lawless frontier land-grabbers was composed of the zealous pursuers of Indian souls. Throughout the nineteenth century, the Old Army fought a running battle with Christian missionaries that the army could not conceivably have won because the missionaries embodied the moral underpinnings of the civilization that soldiers served. In the immediate aftermath of the Civil War, President Ulysses S. Grant, in what became known as his "Peace Policy," parceled out administration of most of the nation's Indian reservations among missionary societies. "The missionary authorities," the secretary of the interior announced, "have an entire race placed under their control." The army had hankered for similar responsibilities on the grounds that it invariably wound up dealing with Indian excesses erupting in reaction to the humanitarian "civilizing" process. But influential humanitarians believed army administration "would mean only policing the Indians, not reclaiming and civilizing them."[68]

That is precisely the point. "Only policing" was the aspect of army ideology that appealed most to Indians at the largest reservation in the Fourth Cavalry's Arizona Territory (spilling into New Mexico), that of the Navajos. A recent scholarly study comparing army and missionary regimes during that era offers some revealing insights.

Previous army administrators of the reservation had won the support of Navajos because, "mostly concerned with keeping their charges out of war," they had worked out a number of ad hoc arrangements. For example, they looked the other way when Navajos hunted outside reservation boundaries, so long as they did not directly offend whites; made sure promised supplies were distributed fairly; and gave chiefs the responsibility for returning goods stolen from whites by rambunctious braves. The missionary-administrators, on the other hand, focused single-mindedly on moral education as they interpreted it, which meant the eradication of core Indian values. They immediately alienated most of the tribe by driving out an honest and popular white subagent because he had married an Indian woman in a ceremony officiated by a Navajo medicine man. The education of Indians into the ways of "higher" morality was a full-time business. Under its ascendancy, supplies went undelivered and problems with surrounding whites unaddressed. Small wonder that Navajos preferred army administrators who were "more interested in solving immediate problems than in demanding ideological transformations."[69]

It was no different northward where the Fourth Cavalry would be assigned after Arizona, except that the cultural war front broadened. In the 1880s, Old Army troops occupied Omaha, Nebraska, Seattle, Washington, Rock Springs, Wyoming, and other western towns in order to put down riots of whites against Chinese who came as railroad laborers and stayed to pursue the American dream too effectively for their own good. Major General Oliver O. Howard, whose Division of the Pacific oversaw California and the Pacific Northwest, wrote in his 1887 divisional report of "a serious element of [anti-Chinese] disturbance [existing] in nearly every city and town on this coast." He said of events in Seattle, Tacoma, Washington, and Rock Springs: "The well-known feeling of hostility toward the Chinese existing among certain classes of our people is likely at this time to find expression in riots such as these. Then only prompt action on the part of those whose duty it is to maintain the laws can avert destruction of life and property." The division commander's report included a review of the situation in Tacoma from his subordinate, the previously cited John Gibbon, then a brigadier general overseeing the

Department of the Columbia in the Northwest. Gibbon reported that "no one indicted for a crime connected with the anti-Chinese movement can by any possibility be convicted by any jury that can be had here" even though their "rights of American citizenship have been so grossly violated." The Old Army departmental commander was referring to the rights of Chinese Americans, which the army defended as best as it could in hostile territory.[70]

At the same time that the commander of the Old Army's Division of the Pacific was reporting on the need to control white racists rioting against Chinese Americans, he was also condemning white injustices against Indians in the same region. "The Indians in the departments of California and the Columbia have been peaceable for some years, and . . . are generally improving their condition," General Howard wrote in his annual report. But, he continued, "their efforts in this direction are, as usual, beset with many obstacles." They included the illegal sale of whiskey ("without the whites being prosecuted as they should be"), encroachments on Indian reservations by land-hungry settlers, and exploitation of Indian laborers through a "system of peonage" operated by reservation contractors.

The Pacific Division commander singled out for special condemnation a horde of whites who, having taken over "thirty-three thirty-fourths" of the Round Valley Reservation in northern California in the latest phase of a persistent landgrab, got local courts to issue an injunction against the commander of the Old Army unit sent to evict them and another injunction against the division commander himself. The frustrated Old Army troops, who as always bowed before a civilian legal injunction, be it local, state, or federal, had to withdraw. When the division commander got the case transferred to a federal court, the local whites withdrew their complaint, leaving him with no case and the white intruders still in illegal possession of the reservation. The division commander pleaded for congressional action to halt this "outrage upon the Indians." During the 1890s many of the cavalrymen based at the Presidio of San Francisco alternated their time in the field between protecting nature at Yosemite National Park and protecting Indians at the Round Valley Reservation.[71]

And so it went. White reformers with their commitment to celestial virtues could not see, as soldiers marching under their orders could, that the sophisticated manipulation of someone's mind might cause as much damage as turning his or her body on a rack. "Have you ever seen a disturbance, or anything harmful, that has been caused by our Sun-dance?" a Blackfoot Indian leader asked of the uncomprehending white missionaries who insisted on banning the ritual because of its "barbaric" administration of physical pain.[72]

Army officers like Colonel Richard Irving Dodge, an admirer of Ranald Mackenzie, understood what the Blackfoot leader meant. Sounding more like Freud or Foucault than a frontier infantry officer, Dodge wrote in 1881: "Barbarism torments the body; civilization torments the soul. The savage remorselessly takes your scalp, your civilized friend as remorselessly swindles you out of your property." Or there was that other Mackenzie colleague, John Gibbon, complaining that white reformers were absorbed with "elevating [the Indian's] soul" while paying insufficient attention to his "bodily wants."[73]

Bodily wants? Torments of civilization? To be sure, not all army officers showed that much cultural awareness, perhaps not even a majority. The Old Army reflected American prejudices and predilections more than it did not. But the point is that a large number of officers held views comparable to those who governed at Yosemite, and their values came from institutionalized character virtues that opened the eyes of soldiers to widespread manipulation of the ideals they served. The flaws in that value system seemed obvious to so many Old Army soldiers largely because they stood outside the field of projections that shaped most white perceptions of "wild" nature and its "savage" inhabitants.[74]

This was the multidimensional "Indian frontier," encompassing human nature and its external environment, that the Old Army patrolled under civilian orders. Occasionally, shooting wars erupted that provoked outcries from humanitarians and cheers from land-grabbers. But in reality, there was no peace here, ever, and never could be as long as "civilization" stood at an opposing pole to "savagery" within and without. Americans might embrace these archetypal forces or struggle heroically against them, create a richly textured cultural overlay, mingle races and ethnic groups from the four corners of the globe, temporize and humanize, but they could not escape the conflict that energized their value system. War was the culturally defining metaphor that held them together even as it cut them off from deeper bonding resources within their human natures accessible to reason through suggestive, emotion-charged metaphor, which is the subject of the following chapter.

CHAPTER EIGHT

The Military Metaphor

Some certain significance lurks in all things, else all things
are little worth, and the round world itself but an empty cipher,
except to sell by the cartload.
—*Herman Melville*, Moby-Dick[1]

IMPOSED IMAGES

From national wars on poverty, drugs, and cancer to "Onward Christian
Soldiers, Marching as to War," Americans have looked to war and the
regimented military for representative symbols of peacetime political, social, economic, and religious activity.

The Progressive Era at the turn of the twentieth century marked a
high point in military symbol expropriation, as the federal government
expanded its hierarchical power and imperial reach. Civilian Progressives ranging from Theodore Roosevelt to philosopher William James
saw social benefits in military values and regimented procedures as antidotes to the self-centered corruption of the Gilded Age. Sometimes the
antidotes competed. James's famous essay "The Moral Equivalent of
War" argued for a pacifistic equivalent of "militarism . . . the great pre-
server of our ideals of hardihood . . . [because] human life with no use for
hardihood would be contemptible." James sought his "moral equivalent
of war" with its "heightened sense of community" partly as a counterweight to the Roosevelt-supported military "preparedness" movement
that was committed to a policy of "peace through strength" featuring
peacetime national mobilization programs run by the military.

The preparedness movement, which became something of a cult, involved the subordination of professional military manpower administration and policies to a concept of manliness with racist undertones that had
nonmilitary sources, thus constituting yet another, particularly insidious,
sociopolitical expropriation of military symbols. The leader of the movement was Roosevelt's close friend Leonard Wood, Harvard-educated surgeon, athlete, socialite, and Rough Rider, who was elevated by Roosevelt
to U.S. Army chief of staff. Wood employed many of James's arguments
about the need to teach military discipline and "martial virtues," but
without James's pacifist context. Wood was not popular among Old Army
veterans, and many of them considered him a dishonest opportunist. Joe
Dorst, the first commander at Sequoia National Park, found Wood un-

bearable, and Dorst's career suffered badly for it. His successor at Sequoia, James Parker, was bemused by the self-promoting amateurism of the Rough Riders' sporty founders and rejected Wood's invitation to join them. Harry Benson, who commanded at Yosemite longer than anyone and won higher praise, also, as has been noted, saw his career crash after he insulted Wood's carefully groomed manhood. But Wood controlled the symbols that shaped American memory.[2]

As social and political Progressive reformers exploited the military metaphor for often competing purposes, so did philosophers of both capitalism and socialism. The trusts and monopolies that Teddy Roosevelt attacked aspired, like he did, to "military" efficiency. A prominent economist, in a book published in 1889, described a corporate leader as a "general of industry . . . [who] corresponds in position and function to the general of an army." That writer also pictured modern factories as "military organization[s], in which the individual no longer works independently . . . but as a private in the ranks, obeying orders, keeping step as it were, to the tap of a drum." This same expropriated military drum found an echo in Edward Bellamy's utopian dreams of an "Industrial Army" and Henry George's linkages of such dreams with "science and invention," not to mention the "armies" of workers marching through the imaginations of Marxists everywhere. From capitalists to communists, they all loved military symbols.[3]

In similar fashion, the Progressive Era's civilian "generals" of industry discovered new literal as well as metaphorical possibilities in an institution they once mocked. Those proud commanders of new "armies" of workers were, after all, the direct descendants of the "business pacifist" moguls of the Gilded Age who had viewed war as an inferior form of Darwinian competitiveness that business competition would replace. Without entirely giving up those esoteric views, corporate generals also sought practical benefits from the turn-of-the-century global arms race that had its first major culmination in World War I. Public opinion became polarized over the "armaments industry." And once again the army, whom conservative arms manufacturers looked down upon as lacking in entrepreneurial initiative and liberal pacifists attacked on moral principle, got it from both sides.[4]

For the historic Old Army it was even worse. They got it from three sides, the third side being the U.S. Army itself. The Spanish-American War marked the replacement of the blue-coated frontier constabulary that was "scarcely an army at all" by a global New Army organized to support America's new role as an activist world power. New Army reformers were pleased to see the quaint Old Army pass into history and showed no interest in celebrating its civic contributions beyond the battlefield that are the subject of this book. If anything, the sooner they could be forgotten, the better. The U.S. Military Academy's centennial celebration in 1902 featured a parade of distinguished orators, including the president, the secretary of war, and a bevy of generals, who had next to nothing to say about the peacetime frontier duties constituting more than 90 percent of the U.S. Army's history up to that point. Military memory of the Old Army focused instead, when it focused in that direction at all, on Indian-fighting, in the process reinforcing misguided civilian stereotypes of the Old Army's character both pro and con.[5]

By the 1930s, the layers of externally imposed symbols ran so deep that the public could not recognize even the benign reality of a monumental army contribution to environmental protection in America that drew on a noble yet historically degraded army tradition. Franklin Roosevelt put the Civilian Conservation Corps (CCC) on his inaugural One Hundred Days agenda for 1933, promising that it would be up and running by July. The original plan called for the Labor Department to select the men, the Agriculture and Interior Departments to select the work projects, supervise work, and administer the camps, and the War Department to enroll, feed, clothe, house, transport the men to the camps, and condition them. But Interior, Labor, and Agriculture could not handle their assignments. In a desperate effort to prevent the CCC from collapsing in confusion before it even got off the ground, the White House directed that the army's CCC role be expanded to include building and administering the camps, while the responsibility of civilian agencies was restricted to supervising the work projects, with all logistical support (transportation, food, and equipment) provided by the army.[6]

On May 10, when the army took over the new arrangement, the CCC was in disarray. Barely seven weeks later, on July 1, FDR reported that the government had met its promise to put 250,000 men in 1,300 CCC camps nationwide. In only a few weeks the army had assembled the largest peacetime government labor force in American history. Each CCC camp was run by an army reserve officer and supplied and kept in repair by the army's Quartermaster Corps. The CCC soon grew to a national "Tree Army" of 500,000 men. Eventually, 2.5 million young Americans served in the CCC under army management. They constructed a legacy that included half the forest planting in the history of the nation, more than 30,000 wildlife shelters, and countless other environmental improvements.[7]

In keeping with national tradition, the CCC's army managers came under constant attack from all sides of the political spectrum. Leftists accused them of introducing America's youth to fascism in "regimented" camps. Rightists accused them of promoting communism in "communal" camps. Civilian preparedness advocates sought to turn the camps into military training centers. Isolationist opponents of preparedness accused the army of plotting to use them to prepare young men for war. Civilian government agencies jockeyed for expanded CCC management roles that would enhance their authority and enrich their budgets at the army's expense.[8]

Meanwhile, the army, virtually alone among the parties involved, struggled to keep the program on its original targeted course of providing employment during temporary hard times while supporting environmental protection. When jingoistic congressmen sought to make military training part of the CCC, senior officers testified against the proposal. When power-hungry civilian agencies fought among each other and some tried to make the CCC permanent, the army high command, which had never been enthusiastic about what it viewed as a distracting public works assignment, delightedly offered to hand the whole thing back. But FDR, who knew that the operation would collapse without army support, said no. The CCC was eventually phased out during World War II mobilization. With that, the army's indispensable role in the most successful environmental program in American history virtually disappeared from public memory.[9]

Then came the Cold War with its revived memories of the Old Army cavalry in a reprise of the "civilization" versus "savagery" theme, this time in Cinemascope. Even Ranald Mackenzie returned to duty, played by John Wayne in the 1950 film directed by John Ford entitled *Rio Grande*. The movie's inspiration was a daring mission led by Mackenzie into Mexico in 1873 from his post near the Texas border. Since Mackenzie was unknown to the American public (unlike Custer who was far less admired than Mackenzie within the Old Army but a darling of American mythmakers outside it), Ford lyrically renamed him Kirby Yorke. The movie went like this: Indians, depicted without sympathy or shading, had been using Mexico as a safe haven for raids against peaceful Texas settlers. General Phil Sheridan visited Yorke/Mackenzie to deliver illegal unwritten orders for the Fourth Cavalry to launch a raid across the border. If Yorke failed, Sheridan promised that his court-martial would be packed with men who "rode with us down the Shenandoah" and would surely acquit him. The decision was clinched by the brazen kidnapping of several army dependents by savage Indians. Shortly after entering Mexican territory, the cavalrymen discovered the dead body of a kidnapped soldier's wife. She had been raped and mutilated. Military savagery now became a moral imperative. Yorke/Mackenzie and his crusading troopers rescued the women and children and massacred the Indian monsters.[10]

The reality of this historical episode was quite different. Several hundred Kickapoos had fled their oppressive Texas reservation into Mexico, and a few young braves were launching cross-border raids. Mackenzie's raid was intended in large part to head off a hell-for-leather invasion of Mexico by Texas settlers that could have triggered a war with Mexico. Mackenzie's raid could not be publicized and had to be lightning fast so as not to embarrass the government of a neighboring nation that feared and resented American intrusions with good reason. Mackenzie's troops completed the raid in sixty sleepless hours. There were no rapes or mutilations of soldiers by Indians; and most of the Indians Mackenzie's troops encountered were brought back as prisoners.

As usual, Mackenzie fought under civilian orders efficiently but with moral ambivalence and a commitment to fairness toward his delegated adversaries. He took special pains to ensure that they would be well cared for and protected from vindictive whites. He sent them to San Antonio, which had better facilities than his own Fort Clark. He wrote to his departmental superior in San Antonio to urge that the Kickapoos be allowed to camp in the open and cook their own food "so as to change their mode of living as little as possible in order to preserve their health." He also contacted the federal commissioners who had been negotiating fruitlessly for the Kickapoos' return to Texas. The Indians did not trust the commissioners' assurances that they would be safe from retributive settlers. Mackenzie wrote, "No [white] citizen will be allowed to say a cuss word to them or claim a pony." That was a promise no civilian commissioner could make and expect to be believed. Soon afterward more than four hundred Kickapoo warriors and their families returned from across the border. It was Mackenzie's reputation that brought them in, a reputation that would extend westward and northward across the continent. In a world too often offering Indians a choice between vigilante violence and verbal sleight of hand, here at least was an honest warrior who kept his word to his adversaries and was prepared to enforce it against his own people.[11]

Rio Grande appeared shortly after the Korean War broke out in 1950, which may explain its inspiration. Cultural historian Richard Slotkin gives it special attention in the concluding volume of his trilogy on the frontier myth in American culture. He interprets the movie as contributing to an effort by political leaders to build a public consensus for tough anticommunist policies. Cloaking Yorke/Mackenzie's raid in illegal secrecy and casting it as a "choice between willingness to engage in the toil and strife of the 'world's work' and the loss of membership among 'the great fighting races'" gave symbolical reinforcement to the Truman administration's handling of the Korean crisis "by methods similar to Sheridan's." The movie's vividly depicted kidnapping, rape, and mutilation of white women and children by savage Indians assured that "democracy and nation are now entirely identified with the military" in a Cold War confrontation with foreign heathen in Asia. This analysis of the workings of John Ford's imagination may have been accurate; but either way, whether from Ford's celebratory perspective or Slotkin's critical one, Mackenzie and the Old Army suffered from distortion.[12]

Slotkin then carried *Rio Grande*'s metaphorical message forward from the Truman administration in the 1950s to the Reagan-Bush era in the 1980s with this concluding comment: "Yorke clearly lives by Oliver North's dictum that the essence of a Lieutenant Colonel's function is to charge when his commander tells him to charge—whether the order is legal or not. Though both are soldiers, they also play the role of the vigilante who breaks the rules for the sake of a higher law identified with the interests of the state."[13]

The progression from Ranald Mackenzie to Oliver North typifies the complementary role played by popular mythmakers and their learned critics in burying Old Army reality. It guarantees against recovery of inherent values and the myths that nurtured them. Instead, we are left with conflicting cartoons of nineteenth-century American soldiers employed as symbolic weapons in an ongoing cultural war with which Old Army values themselves have virtually no connection.

THE OLD ARMY'S LOST MYTH

Did the regimented Old Army have myths of its own apart from the military metaphors imposed by civilian society? The singular character of Old Army society points in that direction. The Old Army's distinctive procedures and virtues—regimented drill, orders, channels; communal loyalty, battle-tested honesty, unself-righteous fairness—clearly did not originate in the individualistic "higher" scheme of abstract values that the Old Army served. Since the American army modeled itself organizationally on the armies of Europe, it might seem that the source would have been in contemporary Europe. But European standing armies served systems of monarchy and aristocracy against which democratic Americans rebelled, and Americans deliberately purged their own regular army of such "aristocratical" potential. Besides, regimented military procedures did not originate with European armies. In order to learn where and how the symbolical myths informing Old Army values originated, one must go back further than the European experience, much further.[14]

Indeed, the Old Army's guiding myths may not have been recognized even by those who lived by them because they were so *old*. They were older than Western civilization, reaching down further into layered human nature than Judeo-Christian morality. They came from ancient pagan times. Put another way, in terms of the values of nineteenth-century America, the Old Army's guiding myths were rooted in heathen blasphemy.

Consider the symbol-laden empirical facts, beginning with those cataloging the regimented Old Army's blasphemous riot of color. In the *Regulations for the Army of the United States* for 1889, one of the longest sections (Articles 85 and 86, sixteen pages, eighty-four numbered paragraphs) was on the army uniform. Another shorter section (sixteen numbered paragraphs) featured "Flags, Colors, Standards, Guidons, Field Music." The Old Army was awash in color—outrageously bright colors, scarlet and gold, set off by rich tones of blue, often textured in lustrous silk and soft velvet. A typical officer's blue dress uniform was embroidered with colorful braids and stripes and festooned with gold buttons and insignia; displaying ribbons and medallions of every hue, it featured a crimson silk sash, a sword belt of red leather with gold embroidery, a silver-gilted belt buckle, a polished steel sword and scabbard, and shiny black boots with golden spurs. And atop this splendidly glittering human animal sat a magnificent plumed helmet, which, if the officer was mounted, presented itself thusly, according to regulations: "Body: Of cork or other suitable material, covered with black cloth, or of black felt, at the option of the wearer. Trimmings: Cord and tassels, top-piece and plume sockets, chain chin-stream and hooks, eagle with motto, crossed cannon, rifles, or sabers, all gilt, with the number of the regiment on the shield in white; plume of buffalo hair—white for infantry, yellow for cavalry, and red for artillery." If the officer happened to be the army's commanding general, that resplendent ensemble was topped additionally with three black ostrich feathers. This wildly colorful uniform was worn in America at a time when the typical frontier garment was homespun, when government leaders wore drab frock coats, when comparable costumes could be found mostly among morally corrupt urbanites, including the inhabitants of garish fleshpots in red light districts, and, of course, among those living embodiments of heathenism, Indians.[15]

Along with color, equally sensuous music pervaded Old Army life to an extent unmatched by any other public or private institution in nineteenth-century America, so much so that its rhythmic presence made clocks superfluous for regulating a day's scheduled activities. Instead, the Old Army had buglers. They were dispersed down to the smallest unit, the ten-man squad. Wherever troopers went, whatever they did, musical notes filled the air, organizing their activities into ordered harmonies. An officer's wife wrote that the bugle "was the hourly monitor of the cavalry corps. It told us when to eat, to sleep, to march." In the morning, soldiers awakened to the melodies of reveille; at night, they drifted off to sleep to the plaintive strains of taps and tattoo. During the hours in between, they might be drilling on the parade ground or repairing a wagon or writing a report in an office when a sudden burst of music would cause all troops to stop what they were doing and proceed to new prescribed tasks. A trooper without an ear for music would have been useless in the Old Army. The bugler even told soldiers what to wear. There were musical bars for full-dress uniforms and musical bars for overcoats, and woe to the man who missed the notes.[16]

Music and color joined forces during the elaborately choreographed dress parade that marked the concluding high point of each day at frontier posts across the land. This was not a special event (like a frontier harvest celebration) but a daily occurrence integral to Old Army frontier routine—a pagan ritual of colorful horsemen marching to the beat of drums under a setting sun.[17]

And there was also dancing: Skill at ballroom dancing was as much a part of an Old Army officer's public persona as drilling. Off-duty Old Army social life included an extraordinary number of balls and dances, with music provided by regimental bands. They brought together troops from scattered outposts and also frontier farmers and townsfolk. An officer returning to his prairie post in Kansas from a scouting expedition described this welcoming scene: "The band, in neat summer dress, were grouped around the flag staff, while the strains of 'Soldaten Lieder' thrilled through the soft evening air, and fairly carried away by the cadence of the sweet music, a party of young ladies and officers . . . were waltzing upon the green carpet of the parade ground."[18]

Concerts also were popular and well attended. Classical music was not unusual for the concert halls in cities like Chicago and Denver, but the Old Army brought it to mountains and prairies. When the band of Ranald Mackenzie's Fourth Cavalry was stationed at Fort Hays, Kansas, in 1879–1880, it gave weekly open-air concerts, one of which inspired a local editor to write: "The rendition of airs from the opera Martha by the Fourth Cavalry band last Monday was remarkably fine. At the Sunday concert some rare melodies from 'Tannhauser' called forth unbounded praise from judges of good music." This was as close as many frontier homesteaders would get to Wagner's music, and, at the hands of a band of soldiers at large in a vast expanse of prairie, probably as close as *Tannhäuser* would ever get to nature in the raw. Walt Whitman wrote this poem after attending a concert of the Seventeenth Infantry Regiment Band in Dakota Territory;[19] he called it "Italian Music in Dakota:

> Through the soft evening air enwinding all,
> Rocks, woods, fort, cannon, pacing sentries,
>   endless wilds,

In dulcet streams, in flutes' and cornets' notes,
Electric, pensive, turbulent, artificial,
(Yet strangely fitting even here, meaning
    unknown before,
Subtler than ever, more harmony, as if born
    here, related here . . .)
Rayed in the limpid yellow slanting sundown,
Music, Italian music in Dakota.
While Nature, sovereign of this gnarl'd
    realm,
Lurking in hidden barbaric grim recesses,
Acknowledging rapport however, far remov'd,
(As some old root or soil of earth its last-born
    flower or fruit),
Listens well pleas'd.[20]

Nature listens, well pleased. We are a long way from the "industrial armies," "preparedness" camps, and other civilian expropriations of military imagery. There was no parallel in contemporary civilian society for all that colorful plumage or those exquisitely regulated rhythms, but there was parallel in abundance in nature—in the primal rhythms and colors of our "wild" landscape, the bright plumage of "wild" animals, the ceremonial attire and rhythmic rituals of "savage" Indian warriors.

The world historian William H. McNeill examines those ancient sources in a study entitled *Keeping Together in Time: Dance and Drill in Human History*. Before human individuality could take root, McNeill writes, the dominance of the animal herd had to be broken by distinctively human communities held together by socially coordinated rhythms and gestures: "No one doubts that what makes us human is our participation in communication networks—linguistic primarily, but supplemented mathematically and digitally at one end of the spectrum and gesturally and emotionally at the other." The gestural and emotional components of human community came first, and they found expression in dance and drill. Again, "Successive levels of communication—muscular and gestural, then vocal and verbal, then written and mathematical—are what made Homo Sapiens the dominant species it has become." Thus, human community is rooted in rhythmic "muscular bonding" activities that were progressively augmented by abstract ideas of government.[21]

McNeill dates the close-order drill practiced by the Old Army—"a tamer version" of the muscular bonding war dances that were instrumental in creating early human communities—from the rise of warrior kings in Mesopotamia around 3000 B.C. The first kings arose in competition with a ruling priesthood. The priesthood had won the worshipful loyalty of the population by claiming exclusive access to a spirit world that everyone feared. Sumerian warrior kings wrested some of that emotional loyalty away from the priesthood by uniting their warrior followers through the rhythmic cadences of close-order drill. These muscular bonding rituals "dissociated [the followers of the warrior king] from surrounding society" dominated by the priesthood and opened the way to a "separation of throne from altar" that introduced a new channel for human individual and social development in which emotions responded with more sympathy to the independent efforts of the reasoning intellect.[22]

"Feelings aroused by moving together in unison" were subsequently employed in the service of secular concepts of social organization during the emergence of democratic government in classical Greece, which helps explain why the full rights of citizenry in Athens and Sparta were limited to the militarily active segment of the population. In an era when intellection was far more infused with emotion than now, rhythmic drills and dances built emotional support for new reasoned ideas and may also have helped draw them out from emotional depths. Although Greek philosophy, history, and drama "reach us in literary dress," stripped of originating emotions, the "notions of political freedom and equality could not have blossomed so enduringly in practice or been expressed so eloquently as in fact they were . . . without being rooted in the experience of keeping together in time."[23]

Two thousand years later, during the emergence of the modern nation-state on the European continent, another major development in the history of muscular bonding occurred. Maurice of Orange, captain general of Holland, broke down drill procedures into minute-by-minute and even second-by-second increments. Simultaneously, he introduced a regimented workday that kept armies in almost constant activity, creating an "artificial primary community, promoting comradeship in good times and bad," guided by a rythmic "central nervous system" of rules and regulations. As a result, men enlisted by nation-states for increasingly abstract objectives "who had no obvious stake in the outcome, and did have very obvious private reasons for wishing to get out of the path of enemy bullets, nonetheless risked their lives in innumerable battles . . . even when sent to fight in distant, alien lands. . . . We are used to such extraordinary behavior, but it was only possible because, behind and beneath the goals and glories that explained and justified European wars, lurked the primitive solidarity of muscular bonding."[24]

For the Old Army, the main lines of progression are clear. Old Army rules and regulations reached back in a direct line to the emergence of the modern nation-state in the sixteenth century (when rituals originating in primitive times ceased to be a restraint on power and became its tool); back two thousand years more to the social and political rituals of classical Greece; back another two thousand years to the separation of church and state in Mesopotamia; back ultimately to the beginnings of human community before recorded time. This long continuous line of development inherited by America's frontier army vibrated with primal feelings activated by muscular bonding and disciplined for specific tasks that reflected the status of human civilization at the time. Those tasks—now called missions—were determined by leaders and institutions who, as the modern nation-state asserted itself, gradually became detached from and superordinate to the army institution itself (from warrior kings to civilian monarchs to republican legislatures). This was how the two-tier civilian-military value system cited in a previous chapter developed, with the top tier occupied by the ruling moral values of modern Western civilization and the lower tier housing older character virtues drawn from a muscular bonding heritage that guided military units in the performance of their assigned duties. In Europe, the two systems often competed for power, with mutually corrupting results. In the United States, the military component ceded authority to more historically recent "higher" values governing civilian society.[25]

In recounting that historical progression, McNeill delivered an important observation on the relationship between the muscular bonding of military life and the societies military institutions served. He began by pointing out that the careers of modern leaders like Adolph Hitler offered "a dark and ominous proof of how keeping together in time can unite and barbarize a whole nation, *regardless of how well educated, highly skilled and sophisticated it may be.*" But he further noted that diabolical manipulators like Hitler owed much of their success to the devaluation by modern civilization of introspective ties to the deeper emotional roots of what "remains the most powerful way to create and sustain a community." That is, "contemporary disregard of this aspect of human sociality," its neglected development compared to abstract thought, left society prey to such extreme manipulations of mass emotions as Hitler's shrewdly barbaric distortion of military symbology.[26]

Those conclusions deserve special emphasis. The devaluation of emotionally based modes of expression by Western civilization, their relative disconnection from intellectual development, leaves them highly vulnerable to manipulation that confirms the fears that generated this self-defeating process in the first place, a circular trap. By contrast, as McNeill points out, the writings of Hebrew prophets and Greek dramatists that originally shaped the moral values of Western civilization were direct products of the cultivation by Hebrew and Greek political leaders of ecstatic "Dionysian" rituals of song and dance, of "keeping together in time." We celebrate the "verbal embodiment" of Hebrew prophecy and Greek drama in the moral codes of modern society, but we forget their "ecstatic muscular origin."[27]

These developments provide a meaningful context for understanding and evaluating the military metaphor as it was lived by the Old Army performing its duties on the American frontier. The regimented Old Army's ponderously detailed rules and regulations, its labyrinth of "channels," and the virtues generated by those procedures dated from primeval times when the working connections between airy thought and earthy feeling were far more consciously direct than they are now. Human values emerged during that era in the form of rhythmic imagery. This primal foundation for human ethical formulation was also an inward gateway to an interior natural world that self-conquering "higher" civilization sought to seal off. The Old Army was unusual among governmental institutions of its era in its inherited commitment to keep those age-old working relationships active while also retaining another layer of commitment to modern civilization, including civilian authority and empirical science. This engagement with two radically different, often oppositional worldviews affected Old Army perceptions of surrounding society and its so-called natural environment.

THE VIEW FROM THE INSIDE OUT

The British military historian John Keegan, in comparing European and American armies, wrote: "It is impossible to recreate in the imagination what England must have looked like before the forest went four thousand years ago; it is impossible in America not to feel the power of the forest or the desert or the rivers lurking at the edge of what man has wrought in two hundred years."[28]

That Keegan (author of the seminal *A History of Warfare*) should make the immediacy of nature a distinguishing feature of American military history gives additional significance to the Old Army's inherited ties with the natural world. By the nineteenth century A.D., those blood ties had grown superficial on a European continent where, Keegan wrote, "every field has a name, every patch of woodland surviving from the primeval forest that was disappearing before the Romans came is pruned and coppiced, every farm is primped and cosseted and mown and gardened." But for the Old Army on the North American continent the situation was quite different.[29]

It was different for civilian soceity too, but not in the same way. The

American continent was hardly the wilderness settlers imagined. American Indian cultures were extremely complex and sophisticated, but most white settlers could not see that. Indian culture had developed along a separate continuum, in a more "natural" state, which to devoutly divided Western minds rendered it more a receptacle for projected imaginings than an independent reality. At the same time, there was no place here for the comparatively cautious, testing, evolutionary relationship between man and nature that until then had guided the development of Western civilization. Instead, on the civil side, there was a stark confrontation with nature by a society of technologically advanced individualists who had shattered social hierarchies and introjected moral absolutisms based on the conquest of "nature." On the military side, the experience awakened a different set of impulses. As the Old Army's rhythms blended with those of its wilderness homeland, channels blocked by centuries of layered Western "progress" away from instinctually bonding roots were reopened, and a highly original and important exchange of communication was initiated.[30]

In this case, there was no parallel in either American Indian or white society. Old Army contact with nature produced no wild upsurging of raw instinctual feeling, as when land-hungry frontier vigilantes activated natural energies in order to feed unnatural appetites; nor was there identification with urbanites at the other extreme who romanticized the American wilderness into a glorious abstraction or with missionaries seeking to conquer the "savage" soul of nature's perceived human incarnations and convert them to a value system based on self-conquest.

But even as the Old Army rejected those outlooks held by its compatriots, it did not wholly align itself with Native Americans whose complex cultures, although more attuned with nature's rhythms and closer to the Old Army's sensual roots, lacked the army's disciplined engagement in science and linear time. The Old Army adopted a stance apart from all those groups. It neither declared war on nature nor abstractly romanticized it nor evangelized its savage influence, nor adopted a pagan naturalism that rejected the progressive ideals and scientific achievements of western civilization. Instead, drawing on ritualistically fostered character virtues inherited from an ancient past, it assumed an intermediary role as a protector of nature against the excesses of Western progress, an educator of America's individualistic civilizers on the social need for self-restraint, and an educator of inward human nature as well. Their intermediary stance might be called ecological nationalism, with the proviso that this ecology had human social and corporeal dimensions. Rendered publicly invisible by stereotype and prejudice, it guided the behavior of the soldiers who ran Yosemite National Park. The following comments summarize some of its inherited influences and consider how they were imaginatively reshaped in the American crucible.

An Army of Sensual Natural Scientists

The Old Army's institutionalized commitment to "scientific" exploration and study of the American land was described in detail in previous chapters. It ranged from surveying and mapping to the systematic collection of geological specimens and the protection of the public domain from intrusive exploitation. This unconventional military mission reflected the triumph of Jefferson's continental development vision over Alexander Hamilton's global power aspirations in response to America's continental needs and inclinations at the time. For example, Congress rejected a Hamilton-conceived national military academy dedicated first and foremost to the philosophy and art of war while accepting Jefferson's concept for a military academy that doubled as a national scientific school. "In the lonely years of Army duty on the frontier, some officers became amateur geologists, paleontologists, zoologists, botanists, and ornithologists," writes an Old Army historian; and the information they gathered flowed into the Old Army's myriad "channels" leading up the chain of command to the regnant powers in Washington who oversaw a field of operations that was also a modern nation rapidly taking shape in a forested continent.[31]

In its commitment to scientific observation and exploration, the Old Army shared Thomas Jefferson's perception of the American nation as a geographically integrated body of land, his continental consciousness. Like him, they made the scientific study of the American land an integral part of their civic duties. In a description that came close to capturing a basic aspect of the outlook of Old Army officers who administered Yosemite, a student of Jefferson's attitudes toward the natural environment wrote: "Insofar as nature symbolized America in its entirety, nature *was* America for Thomas Jefferson. His interest in nature and his use of the word are therefore a form of nationalism."[32]

It was in the corporeal realm of human nature that fundamental differences between the values of Jefferson and the Old Army arose. Jefferson got his values from the scientific Enlightenment and the moral prescriptions of Judeo-Christian tradition (without the latter's institutionalized rituals). Nature was for him a repository of empirically verifiable information, a creation of inspiring beauty, and in its American incarnation a prize that invoked great pride. But Jefferson's values buttressed a sophisticated intellect that dominated his feelings. Old Army officers joined Jefferson in embracing intellectually detached reason and its great gift of empirical science, but they also held onto commitments to a primal world of sensual rhythms rooted in nature. They got their values and their lifestyle from their blood. Drums beat for them that were completely foreign to Jefferson's makeup, and that brought Old Army officers closer to nature's rhythmic harmonies than Jefferson could ever hope to come in the magnificent harmony of another kind he constructed in Monticello.

Jefferson's attitude toward Indians, those unfortunate living symbols of a side of himself Jefferson repressed, gave him away. He admired their civilization, but primarily as an artifact. Indians could survive in his imagination as living social entities only if converted into "newly-made Americans" as part of "our [white civilization's] final consolidation." The cultural conceit shaping Jefferson's Indian policies came from a compulsion discussed by the author of a revealing study on those policies: "The central paradox of Thomas Jefferson's character, a paradox that helps to account for at least some of the apparent contradictions in his beliefs and behavior toward Native Americans, is that he, the apostle of liberty, had a deeply controlling temperament." This was also the central paradox of a cultural value system dedicated both to continental conquest and to self-conquest as it fought "primitivism" within and without. Jefferson's cultivated harmonies visibly consolidated a victory won in a culturally initiated conflict fought within himself—a conflict that the Old Army, with its feet in both camps, devotedly sought to bridge.[33]

The Old Army's Integration of Raw Nature and Abstract Absolutisms

During a period of feverish messianic expansion across a continent viewed as either Canaan or Mammon depending on the character of one's aspirations (for besieged Indians, it made no difference; the results were the same), the Old Army interacted with white settlers, Indians, and the American land. Year after year, Old Army troopers moved back and forth over the landscape in every kind of weather. The resulting experience of nature as an inseparable combination of breathtaking beauty and almost continuous physical pain (a condition as remote to transcendentalist nature philosophers as life on the moon) produced a brutally intimate respect and affection for the natural world that often turned Old Army reports describing exploitation of nature into sensual laments. By the same token, the constant public scapegoating of the Old Army to justify self-serving greed and self-serving righteousness heightened the awareness of its officers of the imperfections in white American society and the contrasting virtues in Indian society. From those turbulent experiences, the Old Army forged an institutionally unique capacity for kinship with the natural environment, Indians, and their inwardly conflicted conquerors—an ecological system of the heart and mind incorporating civilization and the natural world.

In instructive contrast, during this same period in American history, the transcendentalist philosopher Ralph Waldo Emerson described nature as an intellectualized "symbol of the spirit." For him, the study of nature led ever upward beyond earth's gravity, beyond physicality itself, into a celestial "supernatural" kingdom of "universal soul" inhabited by a cosmically abstract "Spirit . . . the Creator," also known as "the FATHER," who dominated inferior nature with wise words.[34]

Emerson and his neo-Platonist colleagues had enough soaring wisdom to keep many American intellectuals in a trance to this day. The words were (are) marvelous and can inspire the intellect; but they devalue passionate feeling. Among America's few intellectual Ishmaels who delivered their wisdom from throbbing emotional depths such as Herman Melville, the outlook represented by Jefferson and Emerson generated ambivalence alternating between admiration and bitter frustration. It is captured in Melville's marginalia of his Emerson readings, as when he wrote "a noble expression" and "bully for Emerson!" but also "What does this man mean?" and "self-conceit so intensely intellectual and calm that at first one hesitates to call it by its right name."[35]

Another American intellectual in communion with reason's primeval roots, John Muir, responded in a similar fashion in the margins of his own edition of Emerson's work. Muir interspersed intellectually appropriate awe and admiration with heartfelt exasperation over Emerson's unconscious conceit, as when Emerson wrote, "The squirrel hoards nuts, and the bear gathers honey, without knowing what they do," and Muir underlined the last phrase and scribbled, "How do we know this?" Or Emerson wrote, "Trees are imperfect men, and seem to bemoan their imprisonment," and Muir responded, "No." Or Emerson wrote, "Flowers so strictly belong to youth, that we adult men soon come to feel, that their beautiful generations concern not us" and again Muir responded, "No!" When Muir's Boston Brahmin friend Charles Sprague Sargent got a little stuffy, Muir tweaked him by calling him a "Jamaica Plain Transcendentalist." Sargent, who destroyed most of his correspondence, saved that.[36]

Muir and Melville were the Old Army's civilian comrades in spirit. It was in bonding feelings of community derived from primal emotional sources that Muir and Melville forged their art. But whereas the Old Army institution fostered such partnerships between "primitivism" and "civilization," Melville and Muir struggled to them on their own.

The Old Army As a National Communal Society of Adaptive Individuals

The Old Army's communal character, which it shared with armies everywhere, stood out in America for its extreme contrast with surrounding society and its extreme affinity with the surrounding natural environment. A fundamental difference between Ranald Mackenzie and virtually every other civilian American hero of any persuasion, including both exploiters and defenders of the natural environment, was in the extent to which

Mackenzie's life was part of an integrated group experience organized nationally. John Muir had his Sierra Club, John Wesley Powell his U.S. Geological Survey, but those organizations did not envelop Muir and Powell as the Old Army enveloped Mackenzie while exposing him to profoundly heretical perceptions by prevailing American standards. Even the most sacred and culturally defining American institution, private property, existed in the communally structured Old Army only as an extracurricular pursuit.

The environmental historian Donald Worster has perceptively observed that in America, a land of "nonadaptive individualism," it is extremely hard to accept the mere idea of environmental adaptation. This is because "it would contradict the idea running deep in American culture that the individual is, or ought to be, free of all restraints, whether it comes from genes, climate, microbes, one's own inventions, government, all forms of authority, or fate." In the Old Army, an organization of adaptive individuals organized communally according to rhythms inspired by nature, it was not that hard.[37]

Physical Geography and Physical Experience in the Old Army's Mission

For the Old Army, far more than for its European counterparts, physical geography rather than political boundaries shaped institutional and strategic experiences. During most of the nineteenth century, European armies either fought one another across national boundaries or conquered and helped to administer vast overseas empires. With the principal exceptions of a brief venture into and quickly out of Mexico in the 1840s, a few isolated border raids, and the pacific administration of Alaska, the Old Army's field of operations throughout its 114-year existence (1784–1898) consisted of contiguous continental territory. The Old Army organized logistical systems and field commands mainly in terms of the developing American nation's natural configurations (Department of the Platte; Division of the Missouri). An Old Army officer spent his entire professional career, usually more than thirty years, moving back and forth over the American land from coast to coast. No group of Americans, not even Native Americans, had a more comprehensive physical experience of the American nation as a physical entity or organized themselves continentally according to the natural configurations of the American land as did the Old Army.

The Public Domain and Indian Lands

During the nineteenth century, most Americans thought of their nation as a body of laws and institutions designed to protect individual freedom and promote individual initiative. The American republic had no cultur-ally integrative physical identity comparable to the sacred words en-shrined in the Constitution and in common law. Insofar as the Republic was perceived as existing physically (rather than as a unifying ideologi-cal concept), it consisted of fragmented private lots or potential private lots united by a common democratic idea.[38]

Again, the Old Army saw America differently. Beginning with its first mission as protector of the Appalachian "public domain," officers of the Old Army acquired a far more sensually integrative perspective of the American nation than did most of their civilian compatriots. Protection of the public domain came to include protection of public "reservations" set aside by the government for Indian habitation and ultimately protection of national parks. This responsibility added to the Old Army's perception of a national land to be defended not only against foreign invasion but also, and most commonly, against exploitation by white Americans.

Armed combat with Indians did nothing to change that perception. The Old Army's "Indian wars" were carried out under civilian orders; and unlike the unceasing war for Indian land and souls pursued by the civilian community, the army's Indian wars ended when the shooting stopped. At that point, as previously described, soldiers refocused their efforts toward protecting the integrity of federal Indian reservations from incursions by greedy whites. By the end of the nineteenth century, pro-tecting Indian lands had become the Old Army's chief Indian-related con-cern. It produced contempt for white provocateurs that reached a peak of intensity as the century drew to a close, as indicated in the reports of de-partmental commanders from Arizona, California, and the Pacific North-west cited in the preceding chapter.[39]

It is well worth noting that the soldiers who protected the public do-main from incursions also lived on it. Each Old Army encampment or fort was a public entity on public land. Like Indians, soldiers lived on federal reservations, called military reservations, in communal societies.

Thus, at every level of the Old Army's experience of the American polity, there was a connection with deeply bonding emotions unique to the army's inherited institutional character. Although the federal govern-ment established an Interior Department midway through the nineteenth century to administer public lands, the institutional character of Inte-rior's engagement with the natural environment could not compare. When a colorful cavalry regiment formed in the evening on a parade ground at a lonely outpost on the western frontier after having passed smartly in review while the regimental band played; and the regiment's ordered ranks grew still at parade rest, a cannon boomed, trumpets sounded retreat, three hundred men in blue snapped to attention as the stars and stripes fluttered down from their perch against the darkening sky, and the blood-red sun descended behind a line of purple mountains far off to the west, then something nationalistic stirred that was beyond politics—disciplined, proud, yet humble before nature; a reverent ecological nationalism.[40]

The authenticity of the Old Army's primal bonds was validated by the institution's self-image. Ties with nature welled up spontaneously in response to the civic mission assigned to the Old Army, through channels kept open by its institutional heritage. But Old Army soldiers hardly seemed to notice them. In their own eyes, they were warriors, not environmentalists. They won medals for courage in battle, not for holding land-grabbers at bay. They looked longingly across the Atlantic at the splendid armies of Europe marching off to battle with one another, studied them, and after midcentury set out to emulate them while condemning their own military system as inefficient and antiquated. When at the turn of the twentieth century a global New Army replaced the continental Old Army in America and a general staff system inspired by Prussia was adopted, it was with overwhelming support from the army's officer corps.

And yet even though Old Army officers did not celebrate their unconventional mission, and many of them couldn't wait for it to end, and few if any understood its full significance—still, it happened and it produced some extraordinary men. They included brave nation-building warriors like the members of Ranald Mackenzie's Fourth Cavalry—Jug Wood, Joe Dorst, Alex Rodgers, Harry Benson, and others—who would carry their frontier experiences into our national parks. Their environmental achievements are not celebrated in army lore (where warfare is king) or in civilian lore (where the army is stereotyped to fit the biases of the moment). But the inspiration for their overlooked contributions came from elsewhere anyhow. It came from deep within their nature.

Epilogue

The army ran Yosemite until World War I, but after the Spanish-American War in 1898 it wasn't the same. The army was changing, along with the civilian government it served. New global concepts of geopolitics were taking hold. The war concluded with an army occupation force in the Philippines and a navy buildup under way in response to events in Europe and to Teddy Roosevelt's contagious enthusiasm for global power and naval display. A military assignment running national parks seemed quaint, incongruous, a vestige of a past era.[1]

Fortunately for Yosemite, the army stayed on until 1914, when a two-year transition to a civilian National Park Service was finally initiated. For the most part, despite changing army priorities the post-1897 acting superintendents performed well. The Spanish-American War years were the most difficult because of the constant turnover in park personnel as troopers rushed from Yosemite to the Presidio to fill gaps in units boarding transports for the Philippines. During the seven-year prewar period, Yosemite had four acting superintendents; during the 1899 season alone, it had three. During the prewar period, all Yosemite officers and units came from the Fourth Cavalry; during the Spanish-American War, they came from other regiments and also various branches of the service (infantry, artillery, and cavalry). In 1900, consistent cavalry administration was restored, but disruptive yearly changes in park regiments and commanders continued: 1900, Sixth Cavalry; 1901, Fifteenth; 1902, Third; 1903, Ninth.[2]

Inevitably under those transient circumstances, park administration deteriorated. It was made worse by the establishment throughout the park of fixed three- or four-man outposts manned by noncommissioned officers and enlisted men. Left to their own devices far away from the main camp, knowing that their officers were preoccupied with merely finding their way around, and realizing that they would leave for good in a few weeks anyway, troopers at the three- or four-man outposts were easy prey for invading stock owners offering them whiskey or fresh mutton to look the other way.[3]

The situation came to a head in 1903 when the new director of the Sierra Forest Reservation adjacent to Yosemite unleashed a blind-side attack on army administration of the park. The attacker was Charles Howard Shinn, a man of many careers, including journalist, amateur

233

botanist, and California historian who wrote a book on frontier mining communities as representing the fulfillment of America's democratic ideal. Shinn assembled critical information on Yosemite's outposts without the knowledge of the park's acting superintendent, Lieutenant Colonel Joseph Garrard. The Sierra Forest manager then delivered his findings to his superiors in a series of letters filled with insulting remarks about the army's performance. The interior secretary forwarded the damning letters to Garrard and the Department of California commander for comment.

During the army investigation that followed, many of Shinn's "witnesses" (homesteaders, sheepherders, and others from the region) denied comments attributed to them, but there can be no doubt that the army outpost system wasn't working or that Shinn was seeking to use those failings to have all or part of Yosemite placed under forest reserve jurisdiction. Had Shinn succeeded, Yosemite would have been inherited by Gifford Pinchot's U.S. Forest Service when that agency was established in 1905 to take over administration of all federal forest reserves, a chilling thought considering Pinchot's views on natural preservation.[4]

As it was, the high command of the rising New Army eagerly sought a pretext to get out of the national parks and responded to Shinn's anti-army campaign with delight. Departmental commander Major General Arthur MacArthur recommended that a transition to a civilian ranger force be initiated at once. MacArthur's recommendation went to the secretary of war who referred it to the interior secretary for comment. Secretary Ethan Allen Hitchcock replied that Interior could not support a civilian park force and that continued deployment of cavalry was necessary "for the purpose of protecting the reservation(s)," and "also for supervising the work of constructing roads, bridges and trails there."[5]

The interior secretary had recent history on his side. In 1898, the army's Department of California commander, pressed by demands for troops for the Philippines, obtained War Department permission to reduce the Yosemite contingent to eleven men, then held off on sending even them. Word got out quickly, and vast herds of sheep invaded the undefended park. George Mackenzie, Robert Underwood Johnson's man on the scene, sounded the alarm in May in a communication to the *New York Times*, reporting that "the absence of troopers this year . . . threatens to invite the destruction of almost all that has been gained." Interior Secretary Cornelius Bliss was hit with a barrage of panicky letters from California environmentalists and local residents, plus a full-fledged assault by Johnson. Bliss appealed repeatedly to the War Department to rescue the "overrun" park before winning the emergency deployment of troops in July as the result of a personal directive by the secretary of war. But considerable damage already had been done. Joseph LeConte Jr., camping in Yosemite's Tuolumne Meadows in June, wrote to his wife that invading sheep had "cleared off every green thing from the face of the country." Park supporters did not want to go through that again. Despite the army high command's eagerness to accede to Shinn's power play, Interior insisted that the troopers stay on.[6]

Thus, departmental commander MacArthur saluted and went back to work. An inspector general was ordered to evaluate conditions at the park. He echoed the calls of past commanders for improvements in on-site facilities, including housing, offices, proper storage for records, and other upgrades that would give the park's administrative apparatus substance and continuity. At the top of his list of recommendations was the need to keep the same commander in the park for a minimum of four consecutive years. In arguing for command continuity, the inspector general invoked the example of Harry Benson, who "was on duty in the Yosemite and Sequoia Parks for several years and he must have been . . . exceedingly efficient . . . for he is most hated by all the . . . hangers on about the park." Administrative wheels were set in motion for Benson's return.[7]

As an immediate stopgap, Yosemite got a topflight new commander in 1904. Major John Bigelow Jr. was more than Shinn's match intellectually as well as managerially. The son of a former New York secretary of state and ambassador to England, Bigelow was the renowned author of *Principles of Strategy,* the first study of its kind by a U.S. Army officer (published in 1890 and still in print). He plotted Yosemite's terrain as if it were Gettysburg or Shiloh, preparing special maps that identified principal redoubts of his adversaries (sheepherders, cattlemen), and he consulted extensively with Shinn on coordinating strategies. "I don't think now, as I used to, that the soldiers do not want to get the sheep out," Shinn said after spending a summer working with Bigelow, although that did not make the ambitious forest manager covet Yosemite less. But Bigelow held him in check through astute management and the fine field work of troopers he had officered during two previous decades of frontier service—Troops K and L of the Ninth Cavalry, one of the army's two black regiments (who had white officers in those days), the famous "Buffalo Soldiers."[8]

Bigelow was also responsible for establishing the first arboretum and botanical garden in a national park. He conceived and constructed this remarkable seventy-five-acre facility in his spare time during the brief summer allotted to him, drawing on his frontier experience and hurried correspondence with horticulturalists on the East Coast. His arboretum had "the first marked nature trail in the national park system," with log seats and neatly painted signposts identifying plants by their Latin species names. Bigelow told the interior secretary that he hoped his pioneering facility would serve as the foundation for a full-scale Yosemite "nature museum" and education program such as would in fact eventually be undertaken by the National Park Service nationwide.

Unfortunately, Bigelow's prophetic initiative got lost in the underbrush, literally: a boundary adjustment a year later excluded it from the park. Log benches decayed, and signposts disappeared beneath untrimmed foliage that also spread over the trails. Many years later, National Park Service naturalists stumbled on the overgrown pathways and Latin signposts of Bigelow's forgotten arboretum, announcing its discovery as if it were an artifact of a lost civilization. (The ruins are still there, across the Merced River from the A. E. Wood campsite.)[9]

Shortly after Bigelow's departure in the fall of 1904, the inspector general's recommendations were reaffirmed by Major Hiram Chittenden, chairman of a commission established by Congress to adjust Yosemite's boundaries. Chittenden was another Old Army man for all seasons. An engineer, he had spent several years in Yellowstone completing the model improvements initiated by Captain Dan Kingman. In his spare time, he wrote frontier histories that are still used as academic sourcebooks, including the first published history of Yellowstone National Park. Major Chittenden was appalled at the constant changing of the guard at Yosemite and the makeshift tent encampment where troopers lived six months of the year compared to the heated barracks and stable governance he had known at Yellowstone. But Chittenden's draft recommendations echoing the inspector general's call for facility upgrades and command continuity met with bitter opposition from one of the two other members of his commission, Robert Bradford Marshall, a geographer with the U.S. Geological Survey.[10]

On the surface, Marshall's reaction did not make sense. Although he worked at USGS headquarters in Washington, D.C., his home was in California; he was a Sierra Club member, a dedicated preservationist, and a friend of John Muir. He visited Yosemite and Sequoia often, and most of the army park commanders were his friends. But by 1904, Marshall's idealism had incorporated careerist ambition and the self-rationalizing compulsions that go with it. He saw himself as Yosemite's indispensable savior and the army as conniving to block the fulfillment of his destiny while dragging the park down to ruin. Marshall's desire for power to do good was intensified by the knowledge that the Chittenden commission's Yosemite boundary adjustment would be followed by incorporation of Yosemite Valley into the national park, so he hatched a plan to place Yosemite under civilian administration.

Marshall's park plan included transferring him to Interior to run the park. Only the unknowing army stood in his way. He wrote fellow commissioner Frank Bond of Interior that Chittenden's proposal to upgrade army facilities in Yosemite was "biased" in favor of the army. Apparently,

Marshall did not realize (or did not want to realize) that the army was a competing agency only in his self-rationalizing mind. The Old Army of the frontier was passing into history. The New Army replacing it would have been more than happy to leave the park, but as long as soldiers were stationed there in a forced transitional capacity under civilian orders, conscientious officers like Chittenden would try to do the best possible job. After beating back Chittenden's proposal for upgrades, Marshall saw his campaign to put Yosemite under civilian administration, with him in command, rejected by Interior for predictable "lack of resources" reasons. He then commenced complaining about unsanitary conditions in the makeshift army camp that park commanders hated and whose continued awful existence he had personally ensured.[11]

During the next several years, Marshall maintained his close relationship with Yosemite's army superintendents, exchanged warm letters and gifts with them, and continued to spread derogatory comments behind their backs as his campaign to run Yosemite expanded into a campaign to run all the national parks. Ultimately, he succeeded and failed at once. In 1915, on the eve of the establishment of the National Park Service, Stephen Mather, who would become the first Park Service director, named Marshall to the newly created post of superintendent of national parks—and then fired him soon afterward. Marshall had turned out to be an incompetent and unpopular administrator. Horace Albright, Mather's assistant and eventual successor, reported that he alienated workers and tourists alike by his "pomposity" and "heavy-handed" management style.[12]

Like Charles Robinson, Charles Howard Shinn, James Mason Hutchings, and other job-seeking Yosemite saviors, Marshall was well-intentioned but limited in competence and emotional stability, and above all unable to taste federal power without getting intoxicated. Watching them come and go during the army's Yosemite tenure leaves a retrospective observer with a better appreciation of how rare the personal qualities and institutional capabilities the Old Army mobilized for environmental preservation were for that era. During the first shaky decades of the national park system, there were simply no administrative structures inside or outside of government comparable to the army's nor individuals of sufficiently disciplined character and detached commitment to ensure that a National Park Service would have a park system worth administering, much less an admirable model for governance, when its time came.

The army's crowning contribution to Yosemite's enduring future came in the person of Harry Benson, who replaced Bigelow in 1905 for the extended tour recommended by the inspector general. The timing could not have been better. Benson ran the park during a critical five-year period highlighted by its absorption of the state-run Yosemite Valley in final fulfillment of the idea hatched by John Muir and Robert Underwood

Johnson while camping in Yosemite's backcountry in 1889. Benson was the perfect man for the job. No one was more incorruptibly committed to Yosemite's protection. While the Yosemite boundary commission was deliberating in 1904, Benson wrote its chairman that "not one foot of the park should be cut off." But the commission was mandated by Congress to eliminate lands that were privately owned or that showed commercial potential, which turned out to be about one-third of the original park.

After that reduction was followed during the same year by the addition of Yosemite Valley, Benson took charge with a vengeance. "The place has, during the last few years, come to resemble Coney Island," he wrote as he transferred the army's park headquarters into the valley and went to work cleaning it up. That meant dismantling a governing network of personal relationships involving state overseers and park guardians and other valley dwellers, developed during nearly a half century of entrepreneurial settlement and state administration and incapable of reversing the imploding status quo it had manufactured. Saving change for Yosemite Valley could only come from the outside, from someone who knew the park, cared about it, yet who also could write (as Benson did) of a locally popular civilian park employee born and raised in the valley: "Ranger Leidig never searches for trespassers as most of the trespassers about this part of the country are personal friends of his." That judgment, like many of Benson's, was harsh yet necessary. "I love Yosemite better than life," he wrote at the conclusion of a letter minutely detailing transgressions by a "pack of thieves" seeking to get "water and power rights" in the park. His was very tough love—just what nature needed to clear out the accumulated well-meaning ineptitude engulfing it.[13]

Perhaps the most significant achievement of Benson and his handpicked successor, West Point classmate William W. Forsyth (1909–1912), was to effectively block Gifford Pinchot and his new commercially oriented U.S. Forest Service from taking over Yosemite. Not that Pinchot didn't try. He began campaigning to get hold of Yosemite even before he had a forest service to run it. In 1904, John P. Irish, arch foe of John Muir and former head of California's Yosemite Valley Commission (whom Pinchot had cultivated behind Muir's back in the 1890s), lobbied for transferring both Yosemite Valley and the surrounding national park to Pinchot's then landless Bureau of Forestry in the Department of Agriculture rather than incorporating the state-run valley into the national park as proposed by the Chittenden commission. Pinchot was "possessed of artistic feeling and could benefit the national park," Irish said. In October of that year, again before the valley was handed over to the federal government, Galen Clark, the chief valley guardian whose residence in the area went back further than anyone, to the 1850s, joined Irish in proposing to transfer Yosemite Valley to Pinchot's imperial-minded Forestry

Troop F, Sixth Cavalry, William W. Forsyth commanding, on a fallen sequoia at Yosemite National Park, circa 1909. Yosemite National Park Library.

Bureau. The kindly old-timer was undoubtedly unaware of the machinations under way. Irish had once employed Clark and solicited his endorsement of Forestry Bureau management of the park as part of the type of initiative that Pinchot was so good at orchestrating. But a proven army alternative already on the ground in Yosemite enabled Interior to hold Pinchot off.[14]

Coincidentally, the U.S. Forest Service was established under Pinchot and given jurisdiction over all national forest reserves in February 1905, the same month that the transfer of Yosemite Valley from state to federal control was authorized. Two months later, Robert Underwood Johnson wrote to Pinchot expressing concern about reports of the national parks also being transferred from Interior to Agriculture and placed under his control. The Forest Service chief replied candidly: not yet, but he was working on it. He reassured Johnson that he had only the best preservationist intentions. While Pinchot displayed one side of his "artistic feeling" for Yosemite in correspondence with Johnson, another side came to light in correspondence with San Francisco officials. He offered "any assistance which lies in my power" to their efforts to flood Hetch Hetchy

Valley in Yosemite in order to provide San Francisco with water and income from a power generation plant, a project that, as Pinchot well knew, Johnson and Muir and other park protectionists violently opposed. In December 1905, President Theodore Roosevelt proposed in his annual message to Congress that national parks adjacent to federal forest reserves (i.e., the Yosemite, Sequoia, and Yellowstone crown jewels) be transferred to Pinchot's Forest Service, a proposal inconceivable without Pinchot's initiating involvement.[15]

Pinchot's bureaucratic assault on Yosemite included retaining Charles Howard Shinn to head the Sierra Forest Reserve when it was transferred to the new Forest Service. The grateful Shinn nipped away at Yosemite on Pinchot's behalf. After the army moved its headquarters to Yosemite Valley in 1906, Shinn claimed the land under the old army camp near the park's Wawona entrance. But Harry Benson held Yosemite's ground, literally and figuratively. In rejecting a demand by Shinn for boundary adjustments to remove "constant friction," Benson simply declared: "There has been no friction." Although Shinn kept trying, Benson would not surrender an inch of the park placed under his command.[16]

A number of factors blocked Pinchot's efforts to capture Yosemite and other national parks. Preservationists like Muir and Johnson, for whom experiencing Pinchot was like taking a timed-release capsule, became increasingly resistant to him. Also, support for the national park idea was growing nationwide, thanks in large part to J. Horace McFarland's American Civic Association and other sympathetic civic groups mobilized by the Hetch Hetchy controversy: if commercialist predators could invade sacred Yosemite, what next? That public upswelling in turn influenced Teddy Roosevelt to listen to others on the national parks issue, including Muir, with whom he had camped in Yosemite in 1903. Finally, there was the army everyone took for granted. Pinchot had bureaucratic momentum; his Forest Service was growing by leaps and bounds. The National Park Service would not even be created for another decade. Without a working alternative in the persons of Old Army stalwarts like Harry Benson on patrol in Yosemite, Sequoia, and Yellowstone, the conquest of the national parks by Pinchot's public lands juggernaut would have been difficult to avoid.[17]

In terms of day-to-day administration (apart from holding the line against Pinchot), the army's post-1900 mission in Yosemite was, to use military terminology, more of a mopping up operation than a campaign. By 1905, thanks largely to the army, resistance to the concept of federal authority over Yosemite had virtually evaporated, and preservationist principles of park governance enjoyed broad public support. The post-1900 period was mainly one of consolidation and refinement.

A highlight of consolidation was Harry Benson's management of Yosemite Valley's incorporation into the national park. This was an extremely complex and delicate process, involving legal transfers, rewriting concessions, and the construction of an integrated infrastructure ranging from power facilities to trails and telephone lines. Benson oversaw the entire process with aplomb, winning praise for his efforts from the Sierra Club and other park supporters. One of his first acts was to hire ex–Fourth Cavalry sergeant Gabriel Sovulewski to serve as resident park supervisor during the army's annual six-month absence, with primary responsibility for maintenance and trail construction. Thus began that modest man's career of three consecutive decades of service at Yosemite, including two decades with the National Park Service before his retirement with honors as the longest-serving Park Service employee in 1936. Sovulewski attributed his accomplishments to the training in character and discipline he received in the Old Army in the 1890s; he viewed his thirty years of Yosemite trail building as merely completing a mission laid out for him by Major Benson.[18]

Typical of the army's post-1900 refinements were the installation and operation of a telephone system in Yosemite, beginning with one line in 1907 and extended continually until the army's departure in 1914. For that initiative, Army Signal Corps personnel were assigned to Yosemite to supplement the cavalry. In keeping with a century of tradition, soldiers maintained the park telephone lines until civilian agencies were judged up to the task; then the facilities were transferred to them free of charge. The army also gave the park a power plant and a small hospital to provide emergency treatment for the park's growing number of visitors.[19]

Throughout this period, park commanders maintained their commitment to preservationist principles espoused by John Muir even as the civilian environmental movement split into two warring camps over Hetch Hetchy Valley, with Muir spearheading the effort to preserve it and Pinchot throwing his considerable influence behind the ultimately successful drive to flood it. "I strongly recommend" that Hetch Hetchy be kept in its natural state, Benson wrote in testimony submitted to a hearing on the issue in Washington, D.C., harking back to the unequivocal opposition of Alex Rodgers and S. B. M. Young to proposals for reservoirs in Yosemite backcountry in the 1890s. But in those earlier days, the interior secretary normally supported the recommendations of his acting superintendents. Now, in addition to the powerful array of economic constituencies mobilized for Hetch Hetchy, there was Pinchot himself, installed at the Agriculture Department as head of the Forest Service, with a direct line to the White House and to the president's other senior appointees. In 1909, Interior Secretary James R. Garfield wrote Sierra Club Secretary William E. Colby that he wholly supported constructing a reservoir in Hetch Hetchy Valley and that it was "useless to further continue" correspondence on the issue.[20]

That same year Benson was transferred to Yellowstone, but his successor, Major William W. Forsyth, picked up where he had left off. Faced with the interior secretary's opposition, Forsyth tried indirect tactics to block preliminary surveying for Hetch Hetchy and delay work on a possible alternative reservoir and dam at Lake Eleanor. He got a ruling preventing the San Francisco city engineer from surveying for Hetch Hetchy on the grounds that the city was not authorized "to do any work whatever on the Hetch Hetchy reservoir site until the Lake Eleanor project has been developed and proven inadequate." Forsyth then tried to delay the Lake Eleanor project by invoking a government ruling against the construction of permanent structures on government land in the park, but he was overruled by officials more skilled than he at using the legal system to their advantage.[22]

When high-profile hearings on Hetch Hetchy were held in Washington in 1910, virtually the entire upper echelon of the civilian preservation movement—Muir and William Colby of the Sierra Club, McFarland and Edmund A. Whitman of the American Civic Association, and others—joined in urging Interior Secretary Richard A. Ballinger to summon Harry Benson from Yellowstone to testify. (Muir thought Benson's presence was "very important," Colby cabled Ballinger.) This was part of a larger successful effort by the same group of preservationists to convince the Interior and War Departments to set up a board of army engineers to evaluate Hetch Hetchy. McFarland expressed "great confidence in the [Board's] breadth and fairness."[23]

The preservationists got Benson to the hearing, but they didn't reckon on army protocol. By then, the army board of engineers had been assembled, Benson was outranked, and he mainly provided input to army testifiers who did not want to appear biased in advance of their inquiry. Benson was joined in that advisory capacity by Forsyth, who attended subsequent Washington hearings in 1912, as both officers maintained their steadfast opposition to the Hetch Hetchy reservoir and power plant. As for the army engineer board, it confounded Hetch Hetchy promoters by concluding that, from an engineering standpoint, there were "several [other] sources of water" available to San Francisco (promoters had claimed that the Hetch Hetchy option was unique), and that the issue was essentially political and therefore outside the army's judgmental authority. And that's where and how Hetch Hetchy was decided—politically, against the park preservationists whose ranks included on this issue, as on all previous national park issues, the army officers involved in park administration.[23]

The Hetch Hetchy defeat produced important positive by-products for the national park movement. It sharpened public awareness of the differences between preservation and commercially oriented "mixed use," broadened public support for the former in the parks, and made clear that, with Pinchot's Forest Service committed to mixed use principles that included commercial exploitation of natural wonders, the national park system needed a separate civilian agency to administer it. In 1912, in an indication of how things had evolved since Charles Howard Shinn had campaigned against Yosemite sheep encroaching on his forest reserve in 1903, Lieutenant Colonel Forsyth complained that cattlemen were using grazing permits from the forest reserve (now under Pinchot's jurisdiction) to justify illegal grazing in Yosemite. "As Forest Service officials take no apparent action on these flagrant violations of the conditions of the grazing permits," Forsyth wrote to the interior secretary, "it is recommended that the attention of the Secretary of Agriculture be called to the matter."[24]

But the army's time was running out. It had accomplished its primary mission of getting the new national parks up and running administratively, accepted publicly, mapped, cleared of most encroachers, and provided with an appropriate infrastructure of roads, footbridges, and trails. It was time to pass the torch to civilian administration, as had occurred with the National Weather Bureau and other frontier services the Old Army had initiated. In 1907, a detailed plan for such a transfer was developed by S. B. M. Young, the 1896 hero of Yosemite who went on to become army chief of staff. Young retired from the army in 1903 but subsequently went to Yellowstone as acting superintendent at President Theodore Roosevelt's personal request to assess conditions. Young reported that a military force was no longer necessary due to the military's sucess in establishing administrative policies, constructing a park-integrating infrastructure, and reducing lawlessness. He drew up a plan to replace the army force in Yellowstone with a cheaper and smaller "civil guard" under Interior Department authority, recruited initially from discharged soldiers who had served in the parks. Young's proposal, if implemented, would have surely developed into a civilian national park agency. But Interior continued to insist that it was not yet up to the assignment and that the parks still needed the army for administration and protection.[25]

The patience of the army high command was wearing thin. Fewer and fewer staff officers had experiential ties with the Old Army of the frontier; besides, they had their eyes on Europe as it moved toward a major conflagration that could lead to U.S. involvement. Additionally, in Yosemite's case, there was an immediate demand in the Department of California for cavalry to meet pressures on the Mexican border. A series of internal army memoranda and communications between the secretary of war and the secretary of the interior (who fought to the end to keep the army) concluded with a War Department ultimatum early in 1914: army troops would not return to Yosemite.[26]

Troops passing in review at Yosemite, undated. Yosemite National Park Library.

The transition to civilian administration in Yosemite was under way whether Interior was ready or not. The year before, the interior secretary had for the first time named a full-time assistant secretary for national park administration, Adolph C. Miller, but Miller had no staff. He named an able superintendent for Yosemite, Mark Daniels, who hastily cobbled together a small ranger force. But Daniels's knowledge and resources were limited. The next two years of "transition" would have been administrative chaos were it not for the steadying presence of Gabriel Sovulewski, who stayed on as park supervisor. Additional help came from Major William T. Littebrant, who had commanded at Yosemite in 1913 and was sent to the park alone in 1914, at his personal request, to manage the transfer of military facilities and equipment that civilian administrators desperately needed to get started (phone system, hospital, fire fighting equipment, storage facilities, and so on), but it was Sovulewski, the ex–Fourth Cavalry supply sergeant, who more than anyone kept things on an even keel during the rushed transition.[27]

At Yellowstone, where there was an elaborate year-round post garrisoned by four troops of cavalry, the army was more involved in the transition to civilian administration and in getting the new National Park Service off the ground. At one point, with Interior still pleading inadequacy, a resigned army high command directed the establishment of a special "Yellowstone detachment" of cavalry for indefinite duty in the park. It would have consisted of volunteers who were serving or had served in Yellowstone. An armywide call for volunteers went out. Yellowstone's acting superintendent, Colonel Lloyd Brett, processed scores of applications from around the country from enthusiastic army veterans of Yellowstone service. At the last minute, the army was relieved of that unwanted duty, but twenty-one of those uniformed volunteers ultimately resigned from the army to become the Yellowstone nucleus of the civil guard S. B. M. Young had called for in 1907 when it was finally established as a National Park Service in 1916.[28]

That long-sought development occurred following the replacement of Adolph Miller as assistant secretary for national parks. The new man was an independently wealthy, civic-minded marketing genius named Stephen T. Mather, ably assisted by youthful Horace C. Albright. Mather and Albright were Berkeley graduates and Sierra Nevada aficionados. They pushed through the legislation establishing the Park Service in 1916. Mather was named Park Service director, and he and Albright (who would replace him as director in 1930) went on to mold the agency into an effective counterweight in government to Pinchot's mixed use concepts for federal land reservations.[29]

The army was not directly involved in that inspired bureaucratic struggle leading to a national park system that is the envy of the world. But without soldiers holding the line in the parks while civilian preservationists got their act together, it would not have been possible. As the new agency took shape, it drew on the policy precedents the park troopers set, the infrastructure they built, the governing procedures they instituted, the environmental ethic and national service spirit they embodied, even the trademark army-style Park Service uniforms. Yet to this day, virtually no one remembers how it all began.

FAREWELL

And now, Companions:
"There are bonds of all sorts in this world of ours,
Fetters of friendship, and ties of flowers,
　　And true lovers' known, I ween
The boy and girl are bound by a kiss,
But there's never a bond, old friend, like this,
　　We've drunk from the same canteen.

"It was sometimes water, and sometimes milk,
Sometimes applejack fine as silk,
　　But whatever the tipple has been,
We shared it together, in bane or bliss,
And I warm to you friend when I think of this:
We have drunk from the same canteen."

—*From an address by Brigadier General S. B. M. Young
San Francisco, March 19, 1902.*[30]

ABBREVIATIONS USED IN THE NOTES

Note: Other archival sources are cited in full in the notes.

National Archives and Records Administration

NARA	National Archives and Records Administration
RG	Record Group

Records of the Department of the Interior, Washington, D.C.

RG 79	Records of the National Park Service, Parks, Reservations, Letters Received by the Office of the Secretary of the Interior Relating to National Parks, 1872–1907
National Park Service Central Files	Central Files, 1907–1916
Yosemite Corr	Records of the Office of the Secretary of the Interior Relating to National Parks, 1872–1907, Letters Received by the Office of the Secretary of the Interior Relating to National Parks, Yosemite National Park
Yellowstone Corr	Letters pertaining to Yellowstone
Yosemite Annual Report	Annual Report of the Acting Superintendent of the Yosemite National Park to the Secretary of the Interior
Yellowstone Annual Report	Annual Report of the Acting Superintendent of the Yellowstone National Park to the Secretary of the Interior

Yosemite National Park

YNPL	Yosemite National Park Library (a division of the National Archives)

Records of the Department of War, Washington, D.C.

RG 92	Records of the Office of the Quartermaster General
RG 94	Records of the Office of the Adjutant General
ACP	Appointments, Commission, and Personal File
Yosemite Post Returns	Post Returns, Camp Yosemite, Presidio of San Francisco (and other posts as denominated)
Muster Rolls	Muster Rolls, "B" Troop (etc.), regiment as denominated
PRD	Principal Record Division Document File, 1890 (beginning in 1890 and continuing several years beyond it)
RG 393	Records of the U.S. Army Continental Commands
Presidio LS	Register of Letters Received, Presidio of San Francisco, 1890–1913: Letters Sent Letterbooks, Presidio, 1890–1913. (Copies of letters received and sent.)
Presidio Orders	Post Orders, Presidio, 1890–1898
Presidio Register	Registers of Correspondence, Letters and Telegraphs Received, Camp Yosemite, 1908–1913 (complements Presidio LS; much Presidio documentation is lost or oddly filed due to the earthquake of 1906)
RG 107	Records of the Office of the Secretary of War
LS, LR	Letters sent and received

West Point, N.Y.

RG 404	Records of the United States Military Academy

Other Abbreviations

Cleveland Papers   Grover Cleveland Papers, Library of Congress

Colby Papers   William E. Colby Papers, Bancroft Library, University of California, Berkeley

Cullum Register   George W. Cullum, *Biographical Register of the Officers and Graduates of the U.S. Military Academy at West Point, N.Y., from its establishment in 1802 to 1890; with the Early History of the United States Military Academy.* 3 vols. (Boston, 1891)

Dorst Papers   Joseph H. Dorst Papers, U.S. Military Academy, West Point

Farquhar Papers   Francis P. Farquhar Papers, Bancroft Library

G&F   *Garden and Forest Magazine*

Lamont Papers   Daniel Lamont Papers, Library of Congress

Leonard Wood Papers   Library of Congress

Marshall Papers   Robert Bradford Marshall Papers, Bancroft Library

Muir Papers   John Muir papers on Yosemite and related issues, Bancroft Library

Muir Papers CH   Chadwyck-Healey, Inc., microfilmed comprehensive edition of John Muir's papers

NAS Report   Report of the National Academy of Sciences, upon the Inauguration of a Forest Policy for the Forested Lands of the United States, to the Secretary of the Interior, May 1, 1887, National Academy of Sciences

Pinchot Papers   Gifford Pinchot Papers, Library of Congress

Ridgway Letterbooks	Robert Ridgway Letterbooks, Smithsonian Archives, Washington, DC
Roosevelt Papers	Theodore Roosevelt Papers, Library of Congress
RUJ Papers	Robert Underwood Johnson papers on environmental issues, Bancroft Library
Russell Papers	Carl Parcher Russell Papers, Bancroft Library
Sargent Papers	Charles Sprague Sargent Papers, Arnold Arboretum, Boston
Young Papers	S.B.M. Young Papers, U.S. Army Military History Institute, Carlisle Barracks, PA

NOTES

PREFACE

1. Herman Melville, *Mardi: And a Voyage Thither* (New York, 1849), chap. 169.
2. The founding of the Sierra Club, Yosemite National Park, and the federally mandated Yosemite Valley state park, which the national park eventually absorbed, are discussed in Part II.
3. For introductions to self-questioning New Western History, see Patricia Nelson Limerick, Clyde A. Milner II, and Charles E. Rankin, eds., *Trails: Toward a New Western History* (Lawrence, KS, 1991), William Cronon, George Miles, and Jay Gitlin, eds., *Under an Open Sky: Rethinking America's Western Past* (New York, 1992), and other summary citations early in Chapter 7.
4. For a spirited defense of the American West against reimposition of perceived stereotypes, including some attributed to a New Western viewpoint, see Stewart L. Udall, Robert R. Dykstra, Michael M. Bellesiles, Paula Mitchell Marks, and Gregory H. Nobles, "How the West Got Wild: American Media and Frontier Violence," *Western Historical Quarterly* 31, 3 (Autumn 2000): 277–296.
5. Robert M. Utley, *Frontiersmen in Blue: The United States Army and the Indian, 1848–1865* (Lincoln, NE, 1967).

PART I. AN ARMY LIKE NO OTHER

1. Alfred Vagts, *The History of Militarism: Romance and Realities of a Profession* (New York, 1937), 96.
2. 4th Cavalry Muster Rolls, Troop "I." April 30–June 30, 1890, box 977, RG 94, NARA. General Orders No. 5, Headquarters, Division of the Pacific. Robert W. Frazer, *Forts of the West* (Norman, OK, 1972), 9–10. Robert G. Ferris, ed., *Soldier and Brave: Historic Places Associated with Indian Affairs and the Indian Wars in the Trans-Mississippi West* (Washington, DC, 1971), 70–71. Cornelius C. Smith Jr., *Fort Huachuca: The Story of a Frontier Post* (Washington, DC, 1977). For a brief period during the mid-1880s, Tombstone was a major commercial center, with a population over 10,000, until the silver ran out. See John Myers, *The Last Chance: Tombstone's Early Years* (New York, 1950), 38–58. In Tombstone, Myers writes, as in many other American boom towns during the nineteenth century, "a credulous optimism lurked so near the surface that they were willing to believe any rumor that suggested good fortune" (p. 43). See also Jug Wood's comments on miners, Chapter 4.
San Francisco was named the Golden Gate by Lieutenant John C. Frémont when in 1846 during the Mexican War he and his men rowed from Sausalito through the entrance to San Francisco Bay and spiked the Mexican cannon at the Presidio. He proclaimed in his hyperbolic memoirs that he called the bay entrance "*Chrysopylae* or GOLDEN GATE; for the same reasons that the harbor of . . . [Constantinople] was called *Chrysoceras,* or GOLDEN HORN." Whatever, the name stuck. See John Charles Frémont, *Memoirs of My Life* (Chicago, 1887), 512.

In Old Army documents, cavalry troop designations are bracketed in quotes, as in Troop "I"; that awkward style is forsaken here except in direct footnote citations. A cavalry troop is equivalent to an infantry company.

CHAPTER 1. BIZARRE BEGINNINGS

1. Adrienne Koch and William Peden, eds., *The Life and Selected Writings of Thomas Jefferson* (New York, 1993), 25. Richard H. Kohn, *Eagle and Sword: The Federalists and the Creation of the Military Establishment in America, 1783–1802* (New York, 1975), 40.

2. Some scholars suggest that, as with so much else in America's revolutionary experience, opponents of an American standing army drew their philosophical arguments from their oppressors—in this case, a strong tradition in Britain of opposition to standing armies. But the parallel can be overdrawn. Armies reflect the societies in which they live, and eighteenth-century Britain, for all its parliamentary trappings, was a profoundly class-bound society and would remain so for some time. For the British parallel, see Marcus Cunliffe, *Soldiers and Civilians: The Martial Spirit in America 1775–1865* (Boston, 1968), 31–62. It is also worth noting that the standing army syndrome came to the fore rather late in American colonial history. During most of that era, Americans welcomed the security and assistance provided by British troops as settlers expanded into Indian lands. But as American urban society in particular grew more sophisticated and self-assured and acquired interests distinct from, often in conflict with, its rulers, and as the numbers of British troops garrisoned in American cities expanded considerably from the 1760s onward, the uniformed enforcers of increasingly unpopular British rule seemed more and more oppressive. See John Shy, *Towards Lexington: The Role of the British Army in the Coming of the Revolution* (Princeton, NJ, 1965), 393–398.

3. Kohn, *Eagle and Sword*, 17.

4. Dave R. Palmer, *1794: America, Its Army, and the Birth of the Nation* (Novato, CA, 1994), 3–15. Russell F. Weigley, *History of the United States Army* (Bloomington, IN, 1984), 74–94.

5. Kohn, *Eagle and Sword*, 27.

6. Robert K. Wright Jr. and Morris J. MacGregor Jr., *Soldier-Statesmen of the Constitution* (Washington, DC, 1987), 190. The letters that provoked Washington are remembered as the "Newburgh Addresses."

7. Kohn, *Eagle and Sword*, 39.

8. Washington's response to Newburgh lives on in the U.S. Army as an identifying emblem. The 1994 edition of the U.S. Army Field Manual, the army's principal doctrinal statement, opens with a summary of Newburgh and this prideful reminder: "We are an Army that is rooted in the traditions of democracy" (Department of the Army, Field Manual 100–1, *The Army* [Washington, DC, 1994]).

9. George Washington, "Sentiments on a Peace Establishment," May 2, 1783, in Wright and MacGregor, *Soldier-Statesmen of the Constitution*, 193–200.

10. Alexander Hamilton, "Report of a Committee to the Continental Congress on a Military Peace Establishment," June 18, 1783, in Wright and MacGregor, *Soldier-Statesmen of the Constitution*, 200–202. Hamilton's political weakness was a product of his intellectual strength. Some of the principles he elaborated were more relevant to the twentieth century, when America took on a global role, than they were to Hamilton's own time. Jefferson, Madison, and Washington

leavened their patriotic nationalism with strong emotional ties to parochial localism, and the difficult business of constructing civic virtue incrementally from the
ground up, whereas Alexander Hamilton, whose ego was fused with the abstract
idea of the nation-state to a far greater extent than the others, was uncomfortable
with messy intermediaries slowing the development of his beloved nation-state
idea in the making. That temperamental difference made Hamilton stronger
when composing issues for political discussion and weaker in the sphere of political action, where his judgment was often confused by an unbalanced combination of intellectual sophistication and emotional immaturity. Examples of the
latter were the Newburgh fiasco, schemes of imperial conquest, or his impetuous
desire for nationally appointed state governors with powers to veto state legislation. He was at his best as a more restrained and constrained adviser, especially
to Washington, who had superb judgment but lacked Hamilton's intellectual
rigor and compositional skills. (For a good example of that creative symbiosis applied to the composition of Washington's farewell address, see Felix Gilbert, *The
Beginnings of American Foreign Policy: To the Farewell Address* [New York, 1961]),
115–136.)

In an important study on his contributions to American political thought,
Karl-Friedrich Walling, *Republican Empire: Alexander Hamilton on War and Free
Government* (Lawrence, KS, 1999), captures Hamilton's contradictions while clar-
ifying his often underrated legacy. But in some instances, Walling errs as Hamilton did, on the side of applying soaring political abstraction to unpredictably
messy day-to-day activities, as in concluding (pp. 64–65) that Hamilton did not
intend to use force during Newburgh, only the threat of it, without noting, as
down-to-earth Washington did, that a national army is a dangerously unpre-
dictable instrument to play with in this way. As students at West Point are taught,
"means"—how one conducts oneself in specific instances—are the foundation of
martial virtue.

11. Quoted in John Bakeless, ed., *The Journals of Lewis and Clark* (New York,
1964), vi.

12. The texts of the resolutions are in Wright and MacGregor, *Soldier-Statesmen of the Constitution*, 193, 200–202. For a summary account of colonial militia,
see Daniel J. Boorstin, *The Americans: The Colonial Experience* (New York, 1958),
343–372.

13. Ray Allen Billington, *Westward Expansion: A History of the American Fron-
tier*, 3d ed. (New York, 1967), 199–245. William B. Skelton, *An American Profession
of Arms: The Army Officer Corps, 1784–1861* (Lawrence, KS, 1992), 5–6. Edward M.
Coffman, *The Old Army: A Portrait of the American Army in Peacetime, 1784–1898*
(New York, 1986), 4–6; this remains the benchmark study of the peacetime Old
Army.

14. R. Douglas Hurt, *The Ohio Frontier: Crucible of the Old Northwest,
1720–1830* (Bloomington, IN, 1996), 143–152.

15. Michael L. Tate, *The Frontier Army in the Settlement of the West* (Norman,
OK, 1999), 237–240. Tate's recent study on the peacetime Old Army came to my
attention after this book was in final draft. It is an important contribution to an
underexplored topic, especially its sections on Old Army contributions to farming and public health.

16. Weigley, *History of the United States Army*, 90–92. Francis Paul Prucha,
*Broadax and Bayonet: The Role of the United States Army in the Development of the
Northwest, 1816–1860* (Madison, WI, 1953; Lincoln, NE, 1955), 65–80, a landmark
study.

17. Robert H. Berkhofer Jr. discusses Washingtonian "expansion with honor" in his *The White Man's Indian: Images of the American Indian from Columbus to the Present* (New York, 1979), 140–153. Old Army attitudes and affinities regarding Indians are discussed further in Chapters 7 and 8.

18. Francis Paul Prucha, *The Sword of the Republic: The United States Army on the Frontier, 1783–1846* (New York, 1969), 199–202.

19. Ibid., 10–15, 42–45.

20. Wright and MacGregor, *Soldier-Statesmen of the Constitution,* 211.

21. Zachary Taylor to Thomas S. Jesup, Sept. 18, 1820, quoted in Prucha, *Broadax and Bayonet, 104.*

22. For this segment on exploration, I have relied on the extensive writings of William H. Goetzmann, including *Army Exploration of the America West* (Lincoln, NE, 1959, pbk. 1979), 3–64, 262–341, which focuses primarily on the Army Corps of Topographical Engineers, a select group of never more than thirty-six scientific explorers operating from 1838 until the Civil War; *Exploration and Empire: The Explorer and the Scientist in the Winning of the American West* (New York, 1966, pbk., 1978), 3–79, 265–331; and *New Lands, New Men: America and the Second Great Age of Discovery* (New York, 1986), 97–127. "Wants of civilized life" is from Henry Adams, *The United States in 1800* (1889; Ithaca, NY, 1966), 1.

23. Goetzmann, *New Lands, New Men,* 126.

24. Prucha, *The Sword of the Republic,* 182–192. Coffman, *The Old Army,* 44.

25. For army road-building activities, see Carter Goodrich, *Government Promotion of American Canals and Railroads: 1800–1890* (New York, 1960), 19–48; Forest G. Hill, *Roads, Rails, and Waterways: The Army Engineers and Early Transportation* (Westport, CT, 1977), 37–86, and *The Centennial of the United States Military Academy at West Point, New York: 1802–1902,* vol. 1 (Washington, DC, 1904; Westport, CT, 1969), 835–874. As the century progressed, civilian engineers replaced the army in road and canal activities more and more, and army engineer attention shifted toward harbors and flood control.

26. Weigley, *History of the United States Army,* 596. Prucha, *The Sword of the Republic,* 63–80, 193–210.

27. Prucha, *Broadax and Bayonet,* 117, 122, 150–153, 158, 175, 185–187, 197. Tate's *The Frontier Army* has chapters on farming, disaster relief, meteorology, public health, and related topics.

28. Prucha, *Broadax and Bayonet,* 200–222. Tate, *The Frontier Army,* 193–213.

29. Tate, *The Frontier Army,* 21, 111.

30. The enlistee's lament is from the *Army and Navy Chronicle,* May 17, 1838, quoted in Prucha, *Broadax and Bayonet,* 105; emphasis in the original.

31. Washington, "Reflections on a Peace Establishment," 200, Hamilton, "Report of a Committee to the Continental Congress," 202, both in Wright and MacGregor, *Soldier-Statesmen of the Constitution.*

32. Merrill D. Peterson, *Thomas Jefferson and the New Nation* (1970; New York, 1975), 941–943. Albert Jay Nock, *Jefferson* (1926; New York, 1965), 190–191, in which Jefferson is quoted as saying that "if a nation expects to be ignorant and free . . . it expects what never was and never will be" and "the most effectual means of preventing the perversion of power into tyranny are to illuminate . . . the minds of the people" through formal education.

33. Peterson, *Thomas Jefferson and the New Nation,* 856–860. Volume 4 in Dumas Malone's six-volume biography, *Jefferson the President: First Term, 1801–1805* (Boston, 1970), has a chapter entitled "Presiding Scientist."

34. Typically, the indexes of Peterson's 1,000-page study and Malone's six-

volume work contain no primary or secondary references to West Point, although both authors have a great deal to say about Jefferson's other activities in science and education.

35. Stephen E. Ambrose, *Duty, Honor, Country: A History of West Point* (Baltimore, 1966), 12–15. Jefferson to Dr. Joseph Priestley, January 18, 1800, in Adrienne Koch and William Peden, *The Life and Selected Writings of Thomas Jefferson* (1944; New York, 1993), 506–507.

36. Skelton, *An American Profession of Arms,* 167–180. For a thorough discussion of the transition to a more traditional military education system than Jefferson's, a system also viewed as more "modern" in its military outlook, see Carol Reardon, *Soldiers and Scholars: The U.S. Army and the Uses of Military History, 1865–1920* (Lawrence, KS, 1990), and Timothy K. Nenninger, *The Leavenworth Schools and the Old Army: Education, Professionalism, and the Officer Corps of the United States Army, 1881–1918* (Westport, CT, 1978). William T. Sherman led the effort to elevate the troops of the "line" over the engineers inside and outside of West Point. The influence of the Prussian military curriculum model—philosophy of war, tactics, strategy, and organization for war—from the last third of the nineteenth century onward, was also substantial.

37. This account of Williams draws on Arthur P. Wade, "A Military Offspring of the American Philosophical Society," *Military Affairs* 38, 3 (October 1974): 103–107, and Sidney Forman, *West Point: A History of the United States Military Academy* (1950; New York, 1952), 14–32.

38. Forman, *West Point.*

39. Hill, *Roads, Rails, and Waterways,* 37–86. On engineering schools' influence, see George S. Pappas, *The Point: The United States Military Academy, 1802–1902* (Westport, CT, 1993), 275–276. "Marvel of innovation" is from Frederick Rudolph, *The American College and University: A History* (New York, 1962), 229.

40. Unless otherwise cited, comments on West Point curriculum and organization in this section reflect the consensus views of Ambrose, *Duty, Honor, Country;* Forman, *West Point;* Pappas, *To The Point;* and *The Centennial of the United States Military Academy at West Point,* 2 vols. (hereafter cited as *USMA Centennial*). The conclusions on environmental perspectives are my own.

41. For Ludlow's recommendations, see Aubrey L. Haines, *The Yellowstone Story: A History of Our First National Park,* vol. 1 (Yellowstone Library and Museum Association, 1977), 204. Ludlow's description is cited in Kenneth H. Baldwin, *Enchanted Enclosure: The Army Engineers and Yellowstone National Park* (Washington, DC, 1976), 3.

42. For John Muir as prophetic "intuitive ecologist," see Stephen Fox, *John Muir and His Legacy: The American Conservation Movement* (Boston, 1981), 3–27, 290–329.

43. Skelton, *An American Profession of Arms,* 154–180. West Point ledger books meticulously recording cadet backgrounds are at the National Archives facility at West Point; see *Lists Relating to Economic and Social Status of Cadets' Parents,* RG 94. Vagts, *The History of Militarism,* 107–110. The Totten quote is from Coffman, *The Old Army,* 46. Tough West Point entrance exams worked against applicants from new frontier communities, but the student body was still broad-based compared to other universities of that era; and the curriculum emphasis on serving the republican institutions of the newly formed American nation was, of course, unique.

44. "Frontiersmen in blue" is drawn from Robert M. Utley, *Frontiersmen in Blue: The United States Army and the Indian, 1848–1865* (Lincoln, NE, 1967). For

"misfortune," see Richard White, *"It's Your Misfortune and None of My Own": A New History of the American West* (Norman, OK, 1991). White's panoramic account brings the frontier's varied social groups to life, except the army, which appears only as a faceless agent of a remote government. Despite the current commitment to incorporative diversity in New Western and other American history fields, this oversight of a major American social community is typical. Although many frontier army officers were not West Point graduates, the Academy set the institutional standards for officer conduct.

CHAPTER 2. EARTHY PATRIOTS

1. For the first four paragraphs of this section, see *Lists Relating to Economic and Social Status of Cadets' Parents, 1842–1910,* RG 94, NARA facility at West Point, NY; *Roster and Record of Iowa Soldiers in the War of the Rebellion, Together with Historical Sketches of Volunteer Organizations, 1861–1866,* vol. 2, 9th–16th Regiments, Infantry (Des Moines, 1908), 555–563; Lurton Dunham Ingersoll, *Iowa and the Rebellion: A History of Troops Furnished by the State of Iowa to the Volunteer Armies of the Union, Which Conquered the Great Southern Rebellion of 1861–65,* 3d ed. (Philadelphia, 1867), 229–245; Frederick H. Dyer, *A Compendium of the War of the Rebellion,* vol. 2 (Dayton, OH, 1979), 170–171; *War Sketches and Incidents, as Related by Companions of the Iowa Commandery, Military Order of the Loyal Legion of the United States,* vol. 1 (Des Moines, 1893; Wilmington, NC, 1994), 115–156; and William T. Sherman, *Memoirs* (1875; New York, Da Capo Press, 1984), 334, 377–378.
2. Abram E. Wood ACP, RG 94, NARA. *Cullum Register,* 2:189.
3. Wood's graduation photo is on file at the U.S. Military Academy Library, West Point, NY.
4. Wood's Civil War recollection is a memorandum dated Dec. 1, 1888, in Wood ACP, hereafter cited as Wood ACP Memorandum.
5. Anson Mills, *My Story* (Washington, DC, 1918), 216–217. Although Mills did not hook up with the 4th Cavalry until late in his career, the cavalry branch in which he and Wood served was a small component of a very small army, and they crossed paths frequently throughout the post–Civil War era. Mills commanded a squadron of three 4th Cavalry troops at the Presidio in 1890–1891, one of which was led by Wood; see Chapter 4.
6. For listings of continental odysseys of other Old Army officers, see Francis B. Heitman, comp., *Historical Register and Dictionary of the United States Army, from Its Organization, September 29, 1789, to March 2, 1903,* 2 vols. (Washington, DC, 1903).
7. Districts existed only during Reconstruction. For a good breakdown of the shifting maze of continental commands, see Raphael P. Thian, *Notes Illustrating the Military Geography of the United States: 1813–1880,* addenda ed. by John M. Carroll (Washington, DC, 1881; addenda ed., Austin, TX, 1979).
8. The distinctive influence of physical geography on the American army complemented another major difference with its European counterparts: contrasting commitments to standing (Europe) and citizens' (U.S.) armies. The latter difference is discussed in Alfred Vagts, *The History of Militarism: Romance and Realities of a Profession* (New York, 1937), 185–189.
9. James A. Huston, *The Sinews of War: Army Logistics, 1775–1953* (Washington, DC, 1988), 168–169. Odin S. Johnson, "History of the Development of the Communications System in Yosemite National Park," *Yosemite Nature Notes* 35, 5 (May 1956): 12–16.

10. Major General Henry C. Corbin and Raphael P. Thian, *Legislative History of the General Staff of the Army of the United States from 1775 to 1901* (Washington, DC, 1901), 611–622.

11. Erna Risch, *Quartermaster Support of the Army: A History of the Corps 1775–1939* (Washington, DC, 1962), 453–515. Huston, *The Sinews of War*, 253–269. *Quartermaster General of the Army, U.S. Army Uniforms and Equipment, 1889: Specifications for Clothing, Camp and Garrison Equipage, and Clothing Equipage Materials* (Philadelphia, 1889). When there were settlements nearby, units purchased most of their daily supplies, including foodstuffs, from local suppliers but always according to national specifications. Often, army post purchases sustained and even created nearby civilian communities. See Darliss A. Miller, *Soldiers and Settlers: Military Supply in the Southwest, 1861–1865* (Albuquerque, NM, 1989).

12. Robert M. Utley, *The Indian Frontier of the American West: 1846–1890* (Albuquerque, NM, 1984), 41.

13. *Report of Colonel James W. Forsyth, 7th Cavalry, Enclosing Maps, Itinerary and Diary of the March Made Under His Command by the Headquarters and Troops "C" "D" "G" and "M" 7th Cavalry from Fort Meade, Dakota, to Fort Riley, Kansas, From July 25, 1887, to September 8, 1887.* The original is at the U.S. Army Military History Institute, Carlisle Barracks, PA.

14. A typed twenty-two-page copy of Dorst's report is in Dorst Papers, Box 1.

15. John G. Bourke, *On the Border with Crook* (New York, 1891; Lincoln, NE, 1971), 177–178.

16. For a summary of Bourke's career, see Joseph C. Porter, "John G. Bourke," in *Soldiers West: Biographies from the Military Frontier*, ed. Paul Andrew Hutton (Lincoln, NE, 1987), 137–156.

17. Sherman, *Memoirs*, including introduction by William S. McFeely, viii–ix, 17.

18. Wood ACP, RG 94, NARA. A copy of Wood's memorandum is in Young Papers.

19. *USMA Centennial*, 581. John Bigelow Jr., *On the Bloody Trail of Geronimo* (1887; Los Angeles, CA, 1968), 10–12, 175–176, 221. "Abram E. Wood," *Annual Reunion, United States Military Academy, June 12, 1894* (West Point, NY, 1894), 85–89.

20. Nelson A. Miles, *Personal Recollections and Observations of General Nelson A. Miles*, vol. 2 (1896; Lincoln, NE, 1992), 533–545. Bigelow, *On the Bloody Trail of Geronimo*, 89.

21. Wood ACP, RG 94, NARA.

22. Ibid. 4th Cavalry Muster Rolls, Troop "I," RG 94, NARA. Promotion in the Old Army until 1890 was strictly by seniority and limited to rare vacancies within one's regiment (despite excellent ratings, Wood had by 1988 received only two promotions in fifteen years) unless application was made for a vacancy in another branch of service. Still, health and the chance of promotion probably would not have been enough to drive stoic, taciturn Wood to request a transfer. A third factor, perhaps decisive, may have been his marriage in 1886. His wife, the daughter of an Episcopal minister in Chicago, would have found his health problems much more shocking than he did.

23. Joseph Dorst to Alex Rodgers, Feb. 19, 1891, Dorst Papers.

24. Ibid.

25. Frontier army winter campaigning was initiated under Phil Sheridan after the Civil War. See Utley, *Frontiersmen in Blue*, 142–162. Dorst to Rodgers, Feb. 19, 1891, Dorst Papers.

26. William Shakespeare, *Hamlet*, act 5, scene 2.

27. *Cullum Register,* 189–190; Wood ACP, RG 94, NARA.

28. Joseph H. Dorst, "Ranald Slidell Mackenzie," *Journal of the United States Cavalry Association* 10, 39 (December 1897): 367–382. Dorst's article first appeared in the *Twentieth Annual Reunion of the Association of Graduates of the United States Military Academy at West Point* (West Point, NY, June 12, 1889).

29. This summary of Mackenzie's life and career relies unless otherwise noted on Dorst's biographical article and on Michael D. Pierce, *The Most Promising Young Officer: A Life of Ranald Slidell Mackenzie* (Norman, OK, 1993), and Charles M. Robinson III, *Bad Hand: A Biography of General Ranald S. Mackenzie* (Austin, TX, 1993). (Mackenzie got the Indian name Bad Hand because his right hand was disfigured by the loss of two fingers from a Civil War wound.) Grant's evaluation of Mackenzie is in Grant's *Memoirs* (1885; Library of America, 1990), 772. The full quote reads: "I regarded Mackenzie as the most promising young officer in the army. Graduating at West Point, as he did, during the second year of the war, he had won his way up to the command of a corps before its close. This he did on his own merit and without influence."

30. "he whipped . . ." is from Robert M. Utley, *Frontier Regulars: The United States Army and the Indian, 1866–1891* (Lincoln, NE, 1973, pbk., 1984), 209. Post–Civil War demobilization numbers are from Allen R. Millett and Peter Maslowski, *For the Common Defense: A Military History of the United States of America* (New York, 1994), 248, and Russell F. Weigley, *History of the United States Army,* enl. ed. (Bloomington, IN, 1984), 598. The precise numbers are 1,034,664 and 54,302. General Lawton is quoted in James Parker, *The Old Army: Memories, 1872–1898* (Philadelphia, 1929), 93.

31. See the representative scholarly assessments of Custer's post–Civil War career by Paul Andrew Hutton, ed., *The Custer Reader* (Lincoln, NE, 1992), 93: "Without the constant crucible of battle to overawe his soldiers, [Custer] could never win his regiment's devotion." The assessment of Mackenzie ("was looked upon") was made by Captain John G. Bourke, General George Crook's aide, who crossed paths frequently with the 4th Cavalry on the frontier; cited in Sherry L. Smith, *Sagebrush Soldier: Private William Earl Smith's View of the Sioux War of 1876* (Norman, OK, 1989), 31.

32. Pierce, *The Most Promising Young Officer,* 53–65; Robinson, *Bad Hand,* 41–54. In 1869, the 41st was combined with the 38th Infantry Regiment of black soldiers to create the 24th Infantry Regiment under Mackenzie's command.

33. Robinson, *Bad Hand.* For desertion rates, which were running at 33 percent when Mackenzie took command of the 41st, see Jack D. Foner, *The United States Soldier Between Two Wars: Army Life and Reforms, 1865–1898* (New York, 1970), 223.

34. *Fourth Cavalry United States Army, 1855–1935* (unsigned unit history, Fort Meade, SD, 1935); *The History of the Fourth United States Cavalry: Prepared and Loyal* (unsigned and undated unit history extending through 1991, Fort Riley, KS); *The Cavalry Journal* 18, 1 (March 1994), dedicated to the 4th Cavalry; Mary Lee Stubbs and Stanley Russell Connor, *Armor-Cavalry, Part 1: Regular Army and Army Reserve, Army Lineage Series* (Washington, DC, 1969), 4–39.

35. For Sheridan and Reconstruction, see Paul Andrew Hutton, *Phil Sheridan and His Army* (Lincoln, NE, 1986), 20–27. For Custer, see Charles Braden, "The Yellowstone Expedition," *Cavalry Journal* (October 1905), reprinted in *The Yellowstone Expedition of 1873,* ed. John M. Carroll (Mattituck, NY, 1986), 43–66.

For a firsthand account of army life in Texas during Reconstruction, including daily tedium and personal excesses, see H. H. McConnell, *Five Years a Caval-*

ryman, or Sketches of Regular Army Life on the Texas Frontier, 1866–1871 (Jacksboro, TX, 1889; pbk., Norman OK, 1996), esp. 101–125. McConnell condemned Texas Rangers as often behaving like legalized outlaws, and he showed equal distaste for morally righteous and economically corrupt agents of the Freedmen's Bureau.

36. Dorst, "Ranald Slidell Mackenzie," 376.

37. Pierce, *The Most Promising Young Officer*, 142–179; Robinson, *Bad Hand*, 179–194; and Dorst, "Ranald Slidell Mackenzie." Many officers opposed the extermination of the buffalo and sympathized with Indians forced (in the words of one officer) to "sit idly by and witness the disappeance of their meat supply at the hands of heartless skin-hunters." Others such as Phil Sheridan looked at it the same way he looked at the Shenandoah Valley: destroy their food supply and they'll be easier to defeat in battle. After the battles ended, however, Old Army officers across the spectrum condemned economic exploitation of the peace, including the indiscriminate slaughter of wildlife. See Sherry L. Smith, *The View from Officers' Row: Army Perceptions of Western Indians* (Tucson, AZ, 1990), 117–118, and Hutton, *Phil Sheridan and His Army*, 246, 416.

38. This account, including the aftermath, is unless otherwise cited from Utley, *Frontier Regulars*, 267–284; Pierce, *The Most Promising Young Officer*, 180–194; Robinson, *Bad Hand*, 209–238; and Dorst, "Ranald Slidell Mackenzie."

39. Smith, *Sagebrush Soldier*, 88.

40. Pierce, *The Most Promising Young Officer*, 192–193. Robinson, *Bad Hand*, 233–235.

41. Pierce, *The Most Promising Young Officer*, 210–233.

42. Wood, Dorst, Rodgers, Parker, and Young ACPs, RG 94, NARA. Dorst, "Ranald Slidell Mackenzie." Pierce, *The Most Promising Young Officer*, 197–198, 259. *The Old Army*, 28–45, 85–90, 123–137. Young to Mackenzie, April 31, 1878, Young Papers.

43. Bigelow, *On the Bloody Trail of Geronoimo*, 144. Fort Huachuca, Post Returns, March 1886, RG 94, NARA. The high stockade with spiked walls and wide-swinging gate, disgorging galloping troops or admitting fleeing wagonloads of settlers, was largely a later creation of Hollywood set designers.

44. Smith, *Fort Huachuca*, 15–38.

45. This description is a composite. Parts of the day at Fort Huachuca are described in Smith, *Fort Huachuca*, 38–41. I've also drawn on General Orders No. 51, Dakota Territory, Oct. 1, 1879, cited in Don Rickey Jr., *Forty Miles a Day on Beans and Hay* (Norman, OK, 1963), 90, and Post Orders No. 64, March 15, 1891, Presidio of San Francisco, RG 393, NARA. The 1879, 1886, and 1891, components of the composite, deliberately chosen to cover an extended period, show no basic variation.

46. *Drill Regulations for Cavalry, United States Army* (Washington, DC, 1896), 103.

47. Smith, *Fort Huachuca*, 30–45. Gregory J. W. Urwin, *The United States Cavalry: An Illustrated History* (Dorset, England, 1983), 134–163.

48. Army regulations were revised every few years but without much real change during the second half of the nineteenth century. These remarks rely on the revised *Regulations for the Army of the United States* (Washington, DC, 1889).

49. *Drill Regulations for Cavalry*, 383–388.

50. For an institutional summary of the bureaus' development during the nineteenth century, see Major General Henry C. Corbin and Raphael P. Thian, *Legislative History of the General Staff of the Army of the United States (Its Organization, Duties, Pay, and Allowances), from 1775 to 1901* (Washington, DC, 1901); for Subsistence and Quartermaster Departments, see 229–235.

51. When a trooper traveled as an individual on special assignment, he had the option of a cash allowance calculated down to the penny. For instance: "Liquid coffee may be furnished in lieu of the coffee and sugar portion of the ration, provided the cost thereof does not exceed twenty-one cents per man per day. The accounts therefor (Form No. 14) will show that coffee and sugar were not drawn for the time for which the liquid coffee was furnished, and by what officers the other portion of the ration were issued." It was easier to stick with the regular ration. See Corbin and Thian, *Legislative History*, 151–153.

52. *Drill Regulations for Cavalry*, 373–383.

53. Ibid. Regulations also provided instructions for marches and camps. The regulations for encampments remained pretty standard throughout the second half of the nineteenth century. By common understanding, they were applied less strictly during a chase. See, for comparison, *Revised Regulations for the Army of the United States, 1861* (Washington, 1861; Harrisburg, PA, 1980), 79–80. There are good descriptions of southwestern camps in E. Lisle Reedstron, *Apache Wars: An Illustrated Battle History* (New York, 1990), 48–55.

54. 4th Cavalry Troop "I" Muster Roll, April 30–June 30, 1890; Wood ACP, both in RG 94, NARA.

55. 4th Cavalry Troop "I" Muster Roll, April–June 1886, RG 94, NARA.

56. RG 94, NARA. For all practical purposes, these adjutant general records are bottomless.

57. 4th Cavalry Troop "I" Muster Roll, April 30–June 30, 1890, RG 94, NARA; *Compilation of General Orders Circulars and Bulletins of the War Department, Issued Between February 15, 1881, and December 31, 1915* (Washington, DC 1916). Jug Wood was buried on April 16, 1894, under Presidio of San Francisco Orders No. 81, Presidio Post Orders, 1890–96, vol. 12, RG 393, NARA.

PART II. THE CALL

1. John Noble to Robert Underwood Johnson, November 26, 1890, Box 4, RUJ Papers.

CHAPTER 3. "THIS WONDERLAND"

1. The size of the army held steady through the 1870s and 1880s at between 25,000 and 30,000 men, while the nation's population increased from 40 million to 63 million.

For the 4th Cavalry's trans-Mississippi chronology, see unit histories on file at the U.S. Army Military History Institute, Carlisle Barracks, PA: *Fourth Cavalry, United States Army, 1855–1935* (Fort Meade, SD, n.d.); First Lieutenant John G. Kelliher, *History of the 4th United States Cavalry* (through 1957); and *The History of the Fourth United States Cavalry, Prepared and Loyal* (through 1986). Also see *The Cavalry Journal* 18, 1 (March 1994), devoted to the 4th Cavalry.

The Old Army's mediating activities between Indians and white settlers in California during the decade before the Civil War, with army sympathies usually on the side of the Indians, is described in William F. Strobridge, *Regulars in the Redwoods: The U.S. Army in Northern California, 1852–1861* (Spokane, WA, 1994).

2. Strobridge, *Regulars in the Redwoods*. Wood ACP, Dorst ACP, RG 94, NARA. Some army units re-created earlier nation-building roles during the fran-

tic development of Alaska following the 1897 Klondike strike. In 1904, the War Department reported that Army Signal Corps units working in temperatures sixty degrees below zero had completed a telegraph system through the Alaskan wilderness consisting of 2,261 miles of cable, 1,497 miles of land lines, and 107 miles of wireless, linking isolated settlements with one another and with the rest of the nation through Seattle. See *Annual Report of the War Department*, 1890, vol. 1, 21–23 (administration); 1890, vol. 1, 21–23 (infrastructure work); 1913, 29 (transfer to civilian administration).

3. *Historical Statistics of the United States: Colonial Times to 1970*, vol. 1, (Washington, DC, 1975), 8. Francis Paul Prucha, *A Guide to the Military Posts of the United States 1789–1895* (Madison, WI, 1964). Russell F. Weigley, *History of the United States Army*, enl. ed. (Bloomington, IN, 1984), 598. *Annual Report of the War Department* (Washington, DC, 1891), 16, 419.

For post–Civil War anti-army attitudes by white southerners toward army enforcement of Reconstruction, eastern reformers toward cruelty toward Indians, western settlers toward showing too much sympathy for Indians, Gilded Age businessmen toward the army symbolizing an inferior form of competition, and so on during this period remembered by many military historians as "the Army's Dark Ages," see William F. Ganoe, *The History of the United States Army* (1942; rev. ed., Ashton, MD, 1964), 298–355 (with a chapter entitled "The Army's Dark Ages"), and Samuel P. Huntington, *The Soldier and the State: The Theory and Politics of Civil-Military Relations* (Cambridge, MA, 1957, pbk., 1985), 224–226. See also Robert F. Utley, "The Contribution of the Frontier to the American Military Tradition," *The American Military Frontier: Proceedings of the Seventh Military Symposium, U.S. Air Force Academy, 1976* (Washington, DC, 1978), 3–13, *Frontier Regulars: The United States Army and the Indian, 1866–1891* (Lincoln, NE, 1973), and *The Indian Frontier of the American Western, 1846–1891* (Albuquerque, NM, 1984). Also see Paul Andrew Hutton, *Phil Sheridan and His Army* (Lincoln, NE, 1985), esp. 28–144 for campaigning; John G. Bourke, *On the Border with Crook* (1891; Lincoln, NE, 1971), 136–157, 180–201; Robert Wooster, *Nelson A. Miles and the Twilight of the Frontier Army* (Lincoln, NE, 1993), 57–111; and Paul Andrew Hutton, *Soldiers West: Biographies from the Military Frontier* (Lincoln, NE, 1987).

For the reform process leading to the global New Army of the twentieth century, see Weigley, *History of the United States Army*, 271; Timothy K. Nenninger, *The Leavenworth Schools and the Old Army: Education, Professionalism, and the Officer Corps of the United States Army, 1881–1918* (Westport, CT, 1978), 3–31; Stephen E. Ambrose, *Duty, Honor, Country: A History of West Point* (Baltimore, 1966), 127, 193; Carol Reardon, *Soldiers and Scholars: The U.S. Army and the Uses of Military History, 1865–1920* (Lawrence, KS, 1990), 1–50; Jack D. Foner, *The United States Soldier Between Two Wars: Army Life and Reforms, 1865–1898* (New York, 1970); and Chester Winston Bowie, "Redfield Proctor: A Biography" (Ph.D. diss., University of Wisconsin, 1951), 162–224. Emory Upton's program for reform was nearly completed when he committed suicide in 1881. It was talked about for years among reformers and finally published, and many of its proposals were implemented by Secretary of War Elihu Root. See Emory Upton, *The Military Policy of the United States*, with an introduction by Root (Washington, DC, 1904), and Stephen E. Ambrose, *Upton and the Army* (1964; Baton Rouge, LA, 1992), 112–135.

For army professionalism in the context of emergent Progressivism, see Allen R. Millett, *The General: Robert L. Bullard and Officership in the United States Army, 1881–1925* (Westport, CT, 1975), 3–15; Stephen Skowronek, *Building a New American State: The Expansion of National Administrative Capacities, 1877–1920* (New York,

1982), 85–121, 177–212; and Huntington, *The Soldier and the State*, 220–289, 466. William B. Skelton shows how the commitment to professionalism dates back to before the Civil War in *An American Profession of Arms: The Army Officer Corps, 1784–1861* (Lawrence, KS, 1992), 238–259, although the reformist zeal that took hold around 1880 remains distinctive.

4. For Fort Verde, see Constance Wynn Altshuler, *Starting with Defiance: Nineteenth-Century Arizona Military Posts* (Tucson, AZ, 1983), 61–62, and Robert W. Frazer, *Forts of the West* (Norman, OK, 1972), 14. Altshuler reports that the post was abandoned in June 1890, Frazer says April; the discrepancy is probably due to differently dated communications as the abandonment order moved down the chain of command. For Troop K's line of march, see Fourth Cavalry Troop "K" Muster Roll, 1890, RG 94, NARA. The muster roll was signed by Second Lieutenant James E. Nolan, Dorst being on temporary assignment as an instructor at West Point. But in a typical Old Army touch, the unit was identified in reports as "J. H. Dorst's Troop."

5. 4th Cavalry Troop "I" Muster Roll, 1890, RG 94, NARA.

6. The Old Army's departmental and divisional map changed constantly. Erwin M. Thompson compiled a list of commanders for the Division of the Pacific and the Department of California in *Defender of the Gate: The Presidio of San Francisco, a History, 1846–1995*, a book-length National Park Service study that he kindly made available to this writer prior to its publication. The list is in an appendix. A key date is July 3, 1891, when divisions were discontinued; the Division of the Pacific was broken up into the Departments of Columbia, California, and Arizona. Departments reported directly to army headquarters in Washington, D.C. *Defender of the Gate: The Presidio of San Francisco, a History from 1846 to 1995* (Denver, CO, 1997).

7. Donald B. Dodd, *Historical Statistics of the United States: Two Centuries of the Census* (Westport, CT, 1993), 443–462. The opium den count is from Rand Richards, *Historic San Francisco* (San Francisco, 1993), 115.

8. Rudyard Kipling, *American Notes: Rudyard Kipling's West* (1891; Norman OK, 1991, pbk., 1993), 15–27. Kevin Starr, *Americans and the California Dream: 1850–1915* (1973; New York, 1986), 124–126, including the "Paris of America" reference. Richards, *Historic San Francisco*, 130. "Brightest sun" is from Richard White, *"It's Your Misfortune and None of My Own"* (Norman, OK, 1991, pbk., 1993), 391. "Fairyland" is from Edward M. Coffman, *The Old Army: A Portrait of the American Army in Peacetime, 1784–1898* (New York, 1986), 290.

9. Parker's comments are from his memoirs, *The Old Army: Memories, 1872–1898* (Philadelphia, 1929), 196–197. Mills recalls the Presidio in *My Story* (Washington, DC, 1918). Joe Dorst's views are in Dorst Papers and are discussed further in Chapter 5. Jug Wood's marriage is noted in his ACP file, RG 94, NARA. Esther Dorst called Jug Wood's pious father-in-law "a dreadful man" in a letter to her husband Joe on Aug. 4, 1892, in Dorst Papers.

10. Reports on the post's population during the early 1890s vary according to the source and the units tabulated—i.e., the approximately 100 men at Fort Point, a coastal defense installation on the Presidio grounds (still standing directly under the Golden Gate Bridge), were sometimes counted as belonging to a separate entity. See *Annual Report of the War Department* (Washington, DC, 1891), 419. In May 1891, after three 4th Cavalry troops moved in, total strength was listed as 598 officers and enlisted men, plus 21 civilian employees, in that month's Presidio Post Return, RG 94, NARA, of which 193 belonged to the 4th Cavalry. The strolling colonel was Emory Upton, quoted in Thompson, *Defender of the Gate*,

115. Hitchcock (named after his grandfather, the Revolutionary War hero) recalled his San Francisco days in his memoirs, *Fifty Years in Camp and Field: Diary of Major-General Ethan Allen Hitchcock*, ed. W. A. Croffut (Freeport, NY, 1909), 389–408; his Presidio comment (p. 394) is dated April 18, 1852. Hitchcock bought a piece of property, common practice on a posting in those days (as it is now), but he never succumbed to the contagious speculative fever like some of his uniformed contemporaries. Prior to leaving for San Francisco, he was told by the army's commanding general that the gold rush threatened army organization and discipline in the Pacific Division. Enlisted men had deserted in droves for the gold fields. To avoid disintegration, the local commander, Brevet Brigadier General Persifor F. Smith, encouraged his officers to take side jobs, mainly as engineers and surveyors. Some went for the main chance. The chief quartermaster in San Francisco, Captain Joseph L. Folsom, reportedly made over $1 million in land speculation. William T. Sherman, a San Francisco–based captain, resigned from the army and became a San Francisco banker, not to return to military service until the Civil War. See *Memoirs of General William T. Sherman* (1875; New York, 1984), 9–83; Coffman, *The Old Army*, 86–87.

11. For the pre–United States era, see John Phillip Langellier and Daniel Bernard Rosen, *El Presidio de San Francisco, a History Under Spain and Mexico, 1776–1846* (Denver, 1992).

12. See Thompson, *Defender of the Gate*, for the Jones plan and for city efforts to establish a public park that culminated in the Presidio being declared an "open post" in 1874 by then–Pacific Division commander Brigadier General John M. Schofield. Also see Lisa M. Benton, *The Presidio: From Army Post to National Park* (Boston, 1998), 20–39.

13. Thompson, *Defender of the Gate*. *Annual Report of the War Department*, vol. 1 (Washington, DC, 1891), 519–520.

14. *Annual Report*, 1:117, 125–141, 172.

15. The "largest complement" is from John M. Gates, "The Alleged Isolation of U.S. Army Officers in the Late 19th Century," *Parameters* 10, 3 (September 1980): 32–45. Leonard Wood's diary is in the Leonard Wood Papers. Wood arrived at the Presidio in June 1889 and remained there, loving it, until September 1893, when he was transferred to a "dull, stupid" post in Georgia, from which he quickly extricated himself through his Washington connections. The *Daily Alta California*'s Jan. 16, 1887, report on Presidio hops is quoted in Thompson, *Defender of the Gate*.

16. Sidney Forman, *West Point: A History of the United States Military Academy* (1950; New York, 1952), 3–35. George S. Pappas, *To the Point: The United States Military Academy, 1802–1902* (Westport, CT, 1993), 3–22. "A certain element" is from Parker, *The Old Army*, 196–197. For the Presidio's complement in that period, see Presidio of San Francisco, Post Returns, RG 94, NARA, which in May 1891, with Wood's, Dorst's, and Parker's troops on hand, showed six artillery batteries and a headquarters staff totaling a little over four hundred officers and men.

17. Parker, *The Old Army*, 198. Thompson, *Defender of the Gate*.

18. Wood admonished by Graham, Nov. 22, 1890, Presidio LS, vol. 14, 685, RG 393, NARA. Graham's "'Full dress . . .'" order is dated June 19, 1991, in "Compilation of Post Orders Published Showing Daily Routine," a periodic booklet put out by Graham summarizing recent daily orders, in Presidio Orders, RG 393. Graham to Assistant Adjutant General, Department of California, Jan. 21, 1891, Presidio LS, vol. 14; Graham to Adjutant General, Department of California,

March 18, 1891, Presidio LS, vol. 15, both in RG 393. Usually, a letter from an adjutant amounted to a letter from his superior and opened with an "I am directed by the Commanding Officer."

19. Graham to Assistant Adjutant General, Department of California, Sept. 3, 1891, Presidio LS, vol. 15; Presidio Adjutant to Wood, Nov. 6, 1891, Presidio LS, both in RG 393, NARA.

20. For the Sequoia campaign, see Douglas Hillman Strong, *Trees—Or Timber? The Story of Sequoia and Kings Canyon National Parks* (Three Rivers, CA, 1986), 20–29; Larry M. Dilsaver and William C. Tweed, *Challenge of the Big Trees* (Three Rivers, CA, 1990), 61–109; and Larry M. Dilsaver and Douglas H. Strong, "Sequoia and Kings Canyon National Parks, One Hundred Years of Preservation and Resource Management," in *Yosemite and Sequoia: A Century of California National Parks,* ed. Richard J. Orsi, Alfred Runte, and Marline Smith-Baranzini (Berkeley, CA, 1993), 13–18. Alfred Runte, *National Parks: The American Experience,* 2d ed. (Lincoln, NE, 1987), 60–64, discusses Sequoia in the context of the origins and early evolution of the national park system.

21. Stephen Fox, *John Muir and His Legacy: The American Conservation Movement* (Boston, 1981), 3–26, 54–99. Linnie Marsh Wolfe, *Son of the Wilderness: The Life of John Muir* (New York, 1945; Madison, WI, 1973), 103–250. Emerson's invitation is in his letter to Muir from Concord, Feb. 5, 1872, Muir Papers. Muir's September 1877 *Harper's Weekly* article is quoted in Fox, *John Muir and His Legacy,* 56. "Where do you want to go?" Muir recalls someone asking him upon his arrival in San Francisco, to which he replied, "To any place that is wild." See John Muir, *The Yosemite* (New York, 1912; San Francisco, 1988), 1.

22. "Artificial canyons" is quoted in Wolfe, *Son of the Wilderness,* 244.

23. After Yosemite's establishment under state authority, Congress and eventually the U.S. Supreme Court rejected private land claims in Yosemite Valley, thereby reaffirming California's "inalienable" obligation to hold the valley as a public trust. See Alfred Runte, *Yosemite: The Embattled Wilderness* (Lincoln, NE, 1990), 13–60.

24. Ibid. Muir is quoted on "frowsy, backwoods" in Shirley Sargent, *Yosemite: The First Hundred Years* (Yosemite, CA, 1988), 24. See also Fox, *John Muir and His Legacy,* 86–99, and Wolfe, *Son of the Wilderness,* 245–246. Olmsted's fascinating report, so far ahead of its time, was rediscovered nearly a century after it was written by Laura Wood Roper, who had it reprinted with her valuable historical notes in *Landscape Architecture* 43, 1 (October 1952): 12–25. See also Victoria Post Ranney, ed., *The Papers of Frederick Law Olmsted,* vol. 5, *The California Frontier, 1863–1865* (Baltimore, 1982), 464–517.

25. Wolfe, *Son of the Wilderness,* 245–246. Muir became known as the father of the Yosemite idea. But a year before his death he magnanimously reminded posterity that Johnson "invented the famous Yosemite National Park" in a letter to George H. Plimpton, Dec. 9, 1913, for an homage to be read at a testimonial to Johnson in New York; RUJ Papers, Box 4.

26. Johnson kicked off the public campaign in his article "The Case for Yosemite Valley," *Century Magazine* 39 (January 1890): 478, the first of a series that continued throughout the year. Muir's articles appeared in *Century* 40, 4 (August 1890) and 40, 5 (September 1890). The September article, entitled "Features of the Proposed National Park," outlined an area that was almost identical to the one incorporated in the final legislation. Olmsted's open letter was reprinted in the *Sierra Club Bulletin* 29, 5 (October 1944): 61–66. See also Runte, *Yosemite,* 52–56, and *National Parks,* 62; and Fox, *John Muir and His Legacy,* 103–109.

27. See Richard J. Orsi's convincing "'Wilderness Saint' and 'Robber Baron': The Anomalous Partnership of John Muir and the Southern Pacific Company for Preservation of Yosemite National Park," *Pacific Historian* 29, 2 and 3 (Summer/Fall 1985): 137–156. The issue was introduced in Runte, *National Parks,* 61. Douglas Hillman Strong adds the motive of increasing the commercial value of railroad-owned timberlands by getting timber owned by competitors incorporated into Sequoia National Park; see *Trees or Timber?* 29–30.

Other agents for the new national park were the governor of California and probably even the maligned Yosemite State Park Commission. On Aug. 13, 1890, the governor wrote Interior Secretary John W. Noble suggesting "that the government establish its protective power for thirty miles in and around Yosemite Valley" in order to protect it from intrusion by sheepherders whose flocks were denuding valley vegetation. The governor's letter was cited by William Stone, acting commissioner, General Land Office, Department of the Interior, in a letter to Noble, Sept. 27, 1890, file no. 8413, box 89, Yosemite Corr, RG 79, NARA. In a report released at the end of 1890, the state commission claimed to have been behind the Yosemite national park legislation. See *Biennial Report of the Commissioners to Manage Yosemite Valley and the Mariposa Big Tree Grove, 1889–90* (Sacramento, CA, 1890). A likely scenario is that Muir, Johnson, Stewart (of Visalia) and his local allies, the state commission, the governor of California, Congressman Vandever and some of his colleagues, Southern Pacific agents, and a few others, for various motives, all had a hand in bringing about the national park legislation in 1890. That would be typical of the American political "system."

28. For a provocative account of the role of mining in the development of San Francisco, see Gray Brechin, *Imperial San Francisco: Urban Power, Earthly Ruin* (Berkeley, CA, 1999), 13–121.

29. *Mariposa Gazette,* Dec. 20, 1890. *Tulare Valley Citizen,* Jan. 1, 1891. *Delano Courier,* undated. The latter two items were assembled together in the RUJ Papers, box 1. The *Mariposa Gazette* from this period is available on microfilm at YNPL. See also Runte, *Yosemite,* 48–50.

During the nineteenth century, park supporters sought to overcome opposition by stressing the patriotic "monumentalism" and "economic worthlessness" of parklands. "Well, it is about a mile [long]; it is a gorge in the mountains," said the chairman of the Senate Committee on Public Lands, in heading off a query from a suspicious colleague about taking Yosemite Valley out of economic circulation initially in 1864. Monumentalists invoked national pride; America did not have castles like Europe but did have unsurpassed natural grandeur. See Runte, *National Parks,* 11–64, and Hans Huth, *Yosemite: The Story of an Idea* (1948; Yosemite, CA, 1984), 15–40.

30. *San Francisco Chronicle,* Dec. 20, 1890. Anti-park motivations are summarized in H. Duane Hampton, "Opposition to National Parks," *Journal of Forest History* 25, 1 (January 1981): 37–45. They included "materialistic values," antielitism (only the rich could afford to get to the remote parks), bureaucratic opposition (from the Forest Service and other natural resource agencies), philosophic opposition (questioning the right to establish parks on public lands), localism and generalized antigovernment sentiment, logger unions from the early twentieth century onward; and sportsmen who supported parks in the nineteenth century but later grew disenchanted with federal hunting and firearms regulations.

31. "Charges against the Board of Yosemite Commissioners preferred by Chas. D. Robinson at the Cal. State Legislature, of 1889," typescript in box 89,

Yosemite Corr, RG 79, NARA. The issue is also discussed in Runte, *Yosemite*, including the legislature's findings.

32. John Muir to Robert Underwood Johnson, Sept. 13, 1889; March 4, April 19, April 20, May 8, June 9, 1890, RUJ Papers.

33. A representative Mackenzie statement is his "Destructive Tendencies in Yosemite Valley," *Century* 34 (January 1890): 475–476. Linda Wedel Greene, *Yosemite: The Park and Its Resources, a History of the Discovery, Management, and Physical Development of Yosemite National Park, California*, vol. 1 (Denver, CO, 1987), 304–309, part of a three-volume National Park Service Historic Resource Study with maps, descriptions of facilities, and design plans.

34. For Johnson's involvement in the Yosemite Valley resolution, see Johnson to Noble, Sept. 30, 1890, file 2272, box 89, Yosemite Corr, RG 79, NARA. The Yosemite investigation resolution of Sept. 22 is cited in full in Secretary Noble's report delivered to Congress in January 1890. For a year-by-year summary of Noble's Yosemite Valley inquiry, including enabling legislation, see Letter from the Secretary of the Interior, Senate Committee on Public Lands, Jan. 5, 1893, 52d Cong, 2d Session, Senate Doc. No. 22.

35. Noble to Musick, Oct. 13, 1890, box 89, Yosemite Corr, RG 79, NARA. Johnson to Noble, Oct. 20, 1890, file 2445, ibid.

36. Newsham to Noble, Nov. 24, 1890, file 2679, ibid. This letter and the one that followed the next day were written from San Francisco after Newsham had returned from his reconnaissance.

37. For Hutchings, see Runte, *Yosemite*, 13–18, 23–26, 224; Carl Parcher Russell, *One Hundred Years in Yosemite: The Story of a Great Park and Its Friends* (1959; Yosemite, CA, 1992), 47, 55–96. Robinson's proposed triumvirate is described in Muir to Robert Underwood Johnson, Sept. 13, 1889, RUJ Papers.

38. Newsham to Noble, Nov. 25, 1890, file 828, Yosemite Corr, RG 79, NARA.

39. Typescript summaries of Newsham to Noble, Dec. 6, 7, 8, 10, 17, 1890, ibid. Newsham was too judgmental regarding the state commission, whose members served without pay and meant well. But the paranoia and bickering he described were real.

40. *Biennial Report of the Commissioners*. Much of the report's strong language came from commissioner John P. Irish, a Bay Area businessman and politician, who had made similar charges in a letter to the *Oakland Tribune* that prompted a reply from Muir stating he was employed by Hutchings only for one month and that Hutchings only used wood from fallen timber: "I never cut down a single tree in Yosemite, nor sawed a tree cut down by any other person there." See Wolfe, *Son of the Wilderness*, 258–260.

41. Muir, *The Yosemite*, 2.

42. The Yosemite region was then honeycombed with trails laid out by Indians and (later) sheepherders and others. The reconfiguration of these trails to the contours of the new park, essential for the latter's administrative identity, was an army contribution.

43. Muir to Johnson, March 4, 1890, RUJ Papers. *Century Magazine* 34 (January 1890). Aubrey L. Haines, *The Yellowstone Story*, 2 vols. (Yellowstone, WY, 1977), 2:453–454.

44. As noted previously, Yosemite Valley was the first federally *mandated* park, in that it was established by Congress in 1864 and transferred to California to run, whereas Yellowstone was the first federally *managed* national park.

45. Hiram Martin Chittenden, *The Yellowstone National Park*, ed. Richard A.

Bartlett (1895; Norman, OK, 1984), 3–52. Chittenden, an army engineer, served two tours in Yellowstone, 1891–1893 and 1899–1906. An accomplished historian, he also authored standard works on fur traders and other early Far West explorers. See also Haines, *The Yellowstone Story*,1:3–81.

46. Chittenden, *The Yellowstone National Park*, 65–75. Haines, *The Yellowstone Story*, 1:84–138. Folsom worked for Washburn in the surveyor general's office, and his stories got Washburn interested. Washburn left the Civil War army with the rank of brevet major general and was called "General Washburn." His background helped get army support for the expedition.

47. Chittenden, *The Yellowstone National Park*; for "masterly," see p. 74. Haines, *The Yellowstone Story*; for "remarkably thorough," see 2:432.

48. Haines, *The Yellowstone Story*, 1:167, has a side-by-side comparison of the Yosemite and Yellowstone bills. Doane's sobriquet is cited in ibid., 2:432.

49. Haines, *The Yellowstone Story*, 1:177–196. Nathaniel P. Langford to Secretary of Interior, Feb. 27, 1873, Feb. 6, 1874 (two among many on the same theme), Yellowstone Corr, RG 79, NARA. Haines reports on the possible Langford-Cooke scheme on p. 214.

50. For background on Ludlow and the full text of the report, see *Exploring Nature's Sanctuary: Captain William Ludlow's Report of a Reconnaissance from Carroll, Montana Territory, on the Upper Missouri to the Yellowstone National Park, and Return Made in the Summer of 1875*, Engineer Historical Studies (Washington, DC, 1985). Ludlow's party entered the park on Aug. 14, 1875, and left it thirteen days later. He submitted his report from St. Paul to the chief of engineers in Washington, D.C., in March 1876. For an analysis of the report's literary merit, including extended excerpts, see Kenneth H. Baldwin, *Enchanted Enclosure: The Army Engineers and Yellowstone National Park, a Documentary History* (Washington, DC, 1976), 67–84.

51. Ludlow, *Exploring Nature's Sanctuary*, 26, 36–37.

52. General W. E. Strong, with an introduction by Richard A. Bartlett, *A Trip to the Yellowstone National Park in July, August, and September, 1875* (Washington, DC, 1876). Haines, *The Yellowstone Story*, 1:206–207.

53. H. Duane Hampton, *How the U.S. Cavalry Saved Our National Parks* (Bloomington, IN, 1971), 42–44. Haines, *The Yellowstone Story*, 1:216–218, 244–252.

54. Haines, *The Yellowstone Story*, 1:260.

55. Ulysses S. Grant dramatically illustrates the point. Grant's martial virtues provided little protection during his presidency in a Gilded Age of corrupt political manipulation by unregulated economic interests. His worst character flaws as president derived from his almost willful political innocence pursued with personal loyalty and honesty that meant everything morally in military life and nothing morally in the civilian power center into which he carried it. Everyone around him got rich, but he died a pauper. Matthew Josephson, muckraker of the Gilded Age, called him a "blind old lion," "a sad, puzzled figure" (*The Politicos* [New York, 1938]), 196–205; see also Josephson, *The Robber Barons* (1934; New York, 1962), 141–148. (How and when Old Army martial virtues worked best in civic assignments is discussed in Chapter 7.)

56. Officers who left the Old Army were more inclined to enter public service or the liberal professions than business. A survey of West Point graduates who left the army from 1802 to 1902 shows that only 984 out of 2,371 entered business, including 230 farmers and planters, 228 civil engineers, 122 merchants, and 77 manufacturers. There were also 200 lawyers, 14 physicians, 21 clergymen, and 179 authors. Most of the remaining 1,000 alumni held positions in national, state, and local government. See *The Centennial of the United States Military Academy,*

West Point, New York, 1802–1902, vol. 1 (1904; New York, 1969), 483–484. The comparatively limited amount of corruption in the Old Army during the Gilded Age, in the traditional form of kickbacks and misuse of public funds, is striking. There were considerable problems of unduly harsh discipline and inefficiency, with supply mismanagement during the Spanish-American War provoking a sensational congressional investigation, but even that investigation uncovered incompetence rather than graft. See Weigley, *History of the United States Army*, 299–312, and Jack D. Foner, *The United States Army Between Two Wars: Army Life and Reforms, 1865–1898* (New York, 1970), 13–77. My own conclusion, after reviewing boxes of archival records, is that for the Old Army, with its nitpicking inspector generals and bean-counting quartermasters, honest bookkeeping had been honed by habit into a compulsive bureaucratic fetish. Misplaced pennies generated correspondence lasting months.

57. Hutton, *Phil Sheridan*, 173–175. The issue of the use of troops to break strikes under Sheridan in 1877 and after him in 1894 was more problematic, in that many officers sympathized with corporations against "mobs" of strikers as they might sympathize with commanders against unruly troops. On the other hand, had there been no federal troops available, leaving only relatively undisciplined state militia and local police to be deployed, the strikers would have fared a lot worse. Domestic strike assignments were not popular in the Old Army and often came about as a result of pressure from local and state officials seeking to avoid responsibility and also avoid losing votes in public elections. See Jerry M. Cooper, *The Army and Civil Disorder: Federal Military Intervention in Labor Disputes: 1877–1900* (Westport, CT, 1980), 3–24, 75–143, 210–270; Robert W. Coakley, *The Role of Federal Military Forces in Domestic Disorders: 1789–1878* (Washington, DC, 1988), 314–349; and Clayton D. Laurie and Ronald H. Cole, The *Role of Federal Military Forces in Domestic Disorders: 1877–1945* (Washington, DC, 1977).

58. Railroads played a key role in the creation of the first national parks and often in their constructive development, particularly during the early twentieth century when the railroad emerged as a less intrusive alternative to the automobile. But through most of the nineteenth century, when railroads were often both transportation systems and engines of speculative development, their influence could be pernicious. Such was the case in early Yellowstone and with some early speculative ventures in Yosemite. See Runte, *National Parks*, 90–101.

59. Richard A. Bartlett, *Yellowstone: A Wilderness Besieged* (1985; Tucson, AZ, 1989), 35.

60. Hutton, *Phil Sheridan*, 354–355; Haines, *The Yellowstone Story*, 1:263.

61. Bartlett, *Yellowstone Besieged*, 46. Haines, *The Yellowstone Story*, 1:274–282. H. Duane Hampton, *How the U.S. Cavalry Saved Our National Parks* (Bloomington, IN, 1971), 31 ("show business"), 60–65. Hampton's groundbreaking book concentrates on army administration of Yellowstone.

62. U.S. *Statutes at Large* 22 (1883): 626. Hampton, *U.S. Cavalry*, 53–69.

63. Dan C. Kingman, ACP. Bartlett, *Yellowstone Besieged*, 76–79. *Cullum Register*, 2:239. The Kingman quote is from Chittenden, *The Yellowstone National Park*, 16.

64. Bartlett, *Yellowstone Besieged*, 75–79.

65. U.S. *Statutes at Large* 24 (1886): 240; and 22, 627. Secretary of War to the Secretary of the Interior, Aug. 10, 1886, Yellowstone Corr, RG 79, NARA. Haines, *The Yellowstone Story*, 1:292–306, 311–318. See Bartlett, *Yellowstone Besieged*, 237–239, for assistant superintendent descriptions, and Hampton, *How the U.S. Cavalry Saved Our National Parks*, 65, for the Montana governor comment.

66. Richart A. Bartlett, "The Army, Conservation, and Ecology: The National Park Assignment," *The United States Army in Peacetime: Essays in Honor of the Bicentennial, 1775–1975,* ed. Robin A. Higham and Carol Brandt (Manhattan, KS, 1976), 47–50. For Harris's Medal of Honor citation, see "Medal of Honor Recipients, 1863–1963," a report prepared for the Subcommittee on Veterans Affairs, Committee on Labor and Public Welfare, U.S. Senate, 88th Cong., 2d sess. (GPO, 1964). Harris to Secretary of War, Oct. 8, 1886, Yellowstone Corr, RG 79, NARA, in which he reports that his tents "obstruct [n]either the view or approaches of the Hot Springs formation."

67. For Harris's all-out offensive against lawbreakers, see his letters and reports to the interior secretary, especially Aug. 26, 1886; March 8, April 14, May 23, July 10, Aug. 2, Aug. 5, 1887, Yellowstone Corr, RG 79, NARA. In addition to coming down hard on white "frontiersmen, hunters and trappers," Harris also went after Indians, notably Shoshone hunters occupying a reservation near the park's northern boundary. The "problems" with the Shoshone in Yellowstone belonged to a duplicitous nationwide practice of getting Indians to "sell" lands on the mistaken assumption that they would retain hunting rights on them. This issue is informatively discussed with particular reference to national parks in Mark David Spence, *Dispossessing the Wilderness, Indian Removal and the Making of the National Parks* (New York, 1999), with references to Harris on pp. 108–109.

It is important to note that Harris and other army park commanders did not single out Indian hunters, as Harris's actions against white hunters and trappers indicated, and that, overall, army park commanders were quite evenhanded in going after whomever violated park regulations on hunting or anything else. Harris, in keeping with his hard nature, seemed harder on everyone than other superintendents, whereas Jug Wood in Yosemite sympathized openly with Indians, whom he found more trustworthy than whites. (Harris even got into a bitter dispute with fellow soldier Kingman, the engineer, over the width of park roads.)

Also, Yellowstone had a much greater variety of wildlife than Yosemite, and Yellowstone hunters of every class and ethnicity were bound to have a tougher time of it because of the former's special identity as a wildlife refuge. See John F. Reiger, *American Sportsmen and the Origins of Conservation* (New York, 1975), and George Bird Grinnell, ed., *Hunting at High Altitudes: The Book of the Boone and Crockett Club* (New York, 1913).

68. Hutton, *Phil Sheridan,* 360.

69. *Biennial Report of the Commissioners,* 27.

70. Newsham to Noble, Nov. 25, 1890, Yosemite Corr, RG 79, NARA. Noble to Harrison, Dec. 1, 1890, file 37148, filed with 14573, PRD, Yosemite Consolidated File, RG 94, NARA.

71. John Noble to Robert Underwood Johnson, Nov. 26, 1890, box 4, RUJ Papers.

72. E. M. Halford, Private Secretary to the President, to Proctor, Dec. 23, 1890, file 7652B, PRD, Yosemite Consolidated File, RG 94, NARA. John T. Schofield, 1st Endorsement to Halford-Proctor, Dec. 30, 1890, ibid. Redfield Proctor, 2nd Endorsement Jan. 13, 1891, ibid.

73. Proctor endorsement, ibid. Proctor to Noble, Feb. 12, 1891, Yosemite Corr, RG 79, NARA.

CHAPTER 4. CAPTAIN WOOD STARTS A PARK

1. *Mariposa Gazette*, Dec. 20, 1890; April 23, May 2, Aug. 29, 1891. Yosemite National Park had some local sympathy from the start. Ironically, it was based on local feuding. For years, Mariposa County residents had complained about the main privately owned toll road into state-run Yosemite Valley (the work of Robinson's hated "ring") and had sought state support for a "free" road; now they hoped the federal government might build one into the valley through the national park that encircled it. See *San Francisco Examiner*, Jan. 17, 1891. The "free road" continued as a separate issue through the life of the state park.

2. For Mariposa during the gold rush and 1880s, see Carl Parcher Russell, *One Hundred Years in Yosemite* (1959; Yosemite, CA, 1992), 9–15, and Alfred Runte, *Yosemite, the Embattled Wilderness* (Lincoln, NE, 1990), 49–50. There was also a small Indian community in the relatively populous state-run valley. I am indebted to James Snyder, Yosemite National Park historian, for a summary of settlement trends during the 1880s.

3. John Conway to John Noble, Jan. 28, 1891; Mrs. A. V. Bruce to Noble, July 30, 1891, box 89, Yosemite Corr, RG 79, NARA. *Mariposa Gazette*, April 23, May 2, 1891. Conway built some of the best trails in Yosemite state park, but he later became embittered against state park officials and, perhaps by extension, against the national park. See Russell, *One Hundred Years in Yosemite*, 77–78, 102, 215, 217.

4. Mackenzie to Noble, March 20, 1891; Robinson to Noble, March 26, April 12, 1891; Yosemite Corr, RG 79, NARA.

5. Johnson to Noble, May 5, 1891, Box 89, ibid.

6. Anson Mills to John Noble, Jan. 27, 1891, file 267, box 89, ibid. Presidio Register, Jan. 28 and 31, 1891, files 184 and 215, RG 393, NARA. (Letters-received logs sometimes contained references to letters sent.) On Jan. 30, 1891, Congress got a Yosemite park update from Interior Secretary Noble that condemned conditions in the Yosemite state and national parks. Noble's office was good at investigation; on-site management was another matter. Letter from the Secretary of the Interior, Jan. 5, 1893, 52d Cong., 2d sess., Senate Ex. Doc. No. 22, containing a copy of the January 1891 and 1892 reports.

7. See, for example, Presidio Register, Feb. 22 (file 260), April 2 (file 657), April 3 (files 664, 672, 674), April 6 (file 688), April 20 (file 831), April 23 (file 854), April 27 (file 884).

8. Graham to Adjutant General, Department of California, March 20, 1891, file 136, Presidio LS; Presidio Orders No. 81, April 6, 1891 (Proctor), and No. 99, April 27, 1891 (Harrison), all in RG 393, NARA. 4th Cavalry "I" Troop Muster Roll, April 30–June 30, 1890; "B" Troop Muster Roll, April 30–June 30, 1891, both in RG 94, NARA.

9. Presidio Register, April 23, May 5, 1891, files 393 and 1011, RG 393, NARA.

10. 4th Cavalry "I" and "K" Troop Muster Rolls, April 30–June 30, 1891, RG 94, NARA.

11. Shirley Sargent, *Yosemite's Historic Wawona* (Yosemite, CA, 1979), 17–43. Linda Wedel Greene, *Yosemite: The Park and Its Resources, a History of the Discovery, Management, and Physical Development of Yosemite National Park, California*, vol. 1 (Denver, CO, 1987), 107–109. Carl Russell, *One Hundred Years in Yosemite*, 62. C. Frank Brockman, "Development of Transportation to Yosemite," *Yosemite Nature Notes* 22, 6 and 7 (June and July 1943), 49–63, 57–63.

12. For "shiny eight," see Sargent, *Yosemite's Historic Wawona*, 43.

13. The superior was Colonel Anson Mills, in Wood ACP, RG 94, NARA. The comrade's account is in "Reminiscence," Major General William Church Davis (ret.), Jan. 26, 1946, Acting Superintendent Files, YNPL. The photographs of Wood are in the U.S. Military Academy Library, West Point, NY.

14. Greene, *Yosemite Historic Resource Study*, 109. Hank Johnston, "The Great Yosemite Roadbuilding Race," in *Yosemite's Yesterdays*, vol. 2 (Yosemite, CA, 1991), 31–63.

15. Sargent, *Yosemite's Historic Wawona*, 50.

16. Ibid.

17. Ibid., 41, 49.

18. *Presidio Orders* No. 85, April 10, 1891, RG 393, NARA. *Mariposa Gazette*, April 25, 1891, YNPL. Sargent, *Historic Wawona*, 49–51. A. E. Wood mentions an advance visit in his 1891 *Annual Report*.

19. Presidio Register, May 23 (file 1150), June 3 (file 1263), and June 6 (file 1292), 1891, RG 393, NARA.

20. Wood to Noble, May 19, 1891, Yosemite Corr, RG 79, NARA.

21. *United States Statutes at Large* 26 (1890): 651.

22. For the Yellowstone assistants, see Aubrey L. Haines, *The Yellowstone Story*, 2 vols. (Yellowstone, WY, 1977), 1:292–326.

23. Capt. A. E. Wood to "Stockowners," June 7, 1891, Record of Letters Sent, 1891–1900, YNPL.

24. Greene, *Yosemite Historic Resource Study*, 65–66. Francis P. Farquhar, *History of the Sierra Nevada* (Berkeley, CA, 1965), 189–193. The Wheeler map was part of the series "Geographical Surveys West of the One Hundredth Meridian." The tourist map was by Dewey and Company, "Mining and Scientific Press," *Map of the Yosemite National Park* (San Francisco, 1891), in box 89,Yosemite Corr, RG 79, NARA. A version of McClure's map was published in 1895, but he did not complete it until early 1896.

25. *Yosemite Annual Report*, 1891. Greene, *Yosemite Historic Resource Study*, 69–77.

26. For a summary of the troop's mission in the park, see Lieutenant N. F. McClure, "The Fourth Cavalry in the Yosemite National Park," *Journal of the United States Cavalry Association* 10, 37 (June 1897): 113–121.

27. Wood to Noble, June 16, 1891, file 1659; "Rules and Regulations Prescribed for the Yosemite National Park," Oct. 23, 1890, typescript signed by John W. Noble, Secretary of the Interior, both in Yosemite Corr, RG 79, NARA.

28. Wood to Noble, June 16, 1891, ibid. For a good summary of the sheepherder problem, see Douglas H. Strong, "A History of Sequoia National Park" (Ph.D. diss., Syracuse University, 1964), 54–58. The issue of fires was controversial then and still is. Controlled burning of some vegetation is necessary to prevent accumulation of tinder that can trigger major forest fires. Before departing the region for the season, sheepherders frequently set fire to shrubs and trees in order to capture more sunlight on the ground and ensure more grassland the following season. In one sense, that could be good. But when the sheep returned to eat the grass and flowers in a public park "down to the roots," the good turned bad.

29. Wood to Noble, July 16, 1891, Yosemite Corr, RG 79, NARA..

30. Noble to Wood, June 19, 1891, typescript copy, Army Administration Papers, YNPL. Noble's letter probably crossed in the mail with Wood's of June 16, cited above, and also of June 17. See Wood to Noble, June 17, 1891, Yosemite Corr, RG 79, NARA..

31. Noble to Wood, June 19, 1891, ibid.

32. Lieutenant Colonel William Graham to Adjutant General, Department of

California, June 19, 1891, Presidio LS, file 325, RG 393, NARA. Robinson to Johnson, July 3, 1891, box 5, RUJ Papers. Robinson to Noble, Feb. 13, 1891, box 89, Yosemite Corr, RG 79, NARA. 4th Cavalry "I" Troop Muster Roll, April 30–June 30, 1891, RG 94, NARA, shows Wood absent at the Presidio and Davis in command of the troop, effective June 28.

33. *Los Angeles Herald,* June 28, 1891, loose item in box 89, Yosemite Corr, RG 79, NARA.

34. Wood's account summarized here is in *Yosemite Annual Report,* 1891.

35. Ibid.; emphasis added.

36. Copy of cable from Chas A. Garter, U.S. Attorney, San Francisco, to W. H. Miller, Attorney General, Washington, D.C., in box 89, Yosemite Corr, RG 79, NARA.

37. *Yosemite Annual Report,* 1891.

38. Holway R. Jones, *John Muir and the Sierra Club: The Battle for Yosemite* (San Francisco, 1965), 48–49, 79. Farquhar, *History of the Sierra Nevada,* 209. Curtin's opposition to federal authority peaked in 1906, when as a member of the California state legislature he unsuccessfully tried to have the national park incorporated into the state park.

39. Capt. A. E. Wood to John J. Curtin, July 2, 1893, Acting Superintendent Letterbooks, Letters Sent, YNPL.

40. L. U. Shippee to Hon. John W. Noble, June 24, 1891, file 1640; A. E. Preciado to Captain Wood, June 28, 1891, file 1770, both in Yosemite Corr, RG 79, NARA.

41. *Mariposa Gazette,* June 20, 1891, YNPL.

42. *Mariposa Gazette,* Aug. 1, 1891, YNPL. The undated "Wawona Notes" fragment is in a late summer 1891 file at YNPL. Camp Near Wawona, Post Return (hereafter Yosemite Post Return[s]), August 1891, microfilm 617, reel 1485, RG 94, NARA. The National Archives post return file uses the name Camp Yosemite for the entire 1891–1913 period of army administration, although that name was not adopted until 1906, when state and national parks were integrated and a new camp established.

43. Davis's only absences were for army rifle competitions where he was a frequent prizewinner. In 1895, he served on a pioneering survey down the Colorado River into the Grand Canyon that almost got him killed. For rifle competitions, see Yosemite Post Returns, August 1892, July 1893, RG 94, NARA. Davis served in Sequoia National Park in 1896. According to his army peers, he was on the way to the top when a heart ailment forced his retirement in 1909. From then until his death in 1938, he headed the New York Military Academy in Cornwall-on-Hudson, NY. See his biography in the *Annual Report, Association of Graduates of the United States Military Academy* (West Point, NY, June 10, 1939), 195–206, and his obituary in the *New York Times,* May 31, 1938.

44. 4th Cavalry Troop "I" Muster Rolls, April–October 1891. Yosemite Post Returns, April–October 1891, microfilm group 617, both in RG 94, NARA.

45. The origins of Davis Mountain and Davis Lakes are described in Peter Browning, *Yosemite Place Names* (Lafayette, CA, 1988), 31; Davis's namesakes were moved out of the park into Inyo National Forest during a boundary adjustment in 1905.

46. This summary, extending through succeeding paragraphs, is from *Yosemite Annual Report,* 1891.

47. Yosemite troopers would even make topographical maps of their line of march across north-central California to and from the parks and submit copies to

the chief of engineers in Washington for incorporation into an Old Army topographical study of the American land that had been under way continuously for one hundred years. For an example, see references to James Parker mapping portions of the San Joaquin Valley en route to Sequoia National Park in 1893 and later being asked for more detail by the chief of engineers, in Presidio Adjutant to Adjutant General, Department of California, Nov. 17, 1893, file 2919, and notation on Nov. 22, 1893, file 2960, Presidio Register, RG 393, NARA.

48. Robinson to Johnson, Aug. 31, 1891, and others in July and August, folders 1 and 2, box 5, RUJ Papers.

49. Ibid. Hutchings to Noble, Nov. 7, 1890, file 2581, box 89, Yosemite Corr, RG 79, NARA. The interior secretary's correspondence contains no communication from Stanford on Hutchings. During the 1890s, Hutchings spent late spring, summer, and early fall in Yosemite Valley and the rest of the year in San Francisco.

50. "Report of the Secretary of the Interior," *Interior Department Annual Report* (Washington, DC, 1891), 139–142. A knowledgeable Yosemite historian wrote that "paradoxically . . . [Wood's 1891] recommendations [to cut the park's size] made sense" because keeping too much disputed land caused damage to the rest of the park. See Runte, *Yosemite*, 69.

51. "Report of the Secretary of the Interior," 1891.

52. See the log of letters received, Sept. 6, in the September 1891 Yosemite Post Return, RG 94, NARA. For a copy of Wood's recommendation of Sept. 7, see file 2887, with Secretary of War Proctor to Secretary of the Interior Noble, Sept. 25, 1891, Yosemite Corr, RG 79, NARA. 4th Cavalry Troop "I" Muster Roll, October–November 1891, RG 94.

53. Wood to Graham, Aug. 6, 1890, file 1850, Presidio Register, RG 393, NARA. Presidio Adjutant to Graham, Aug. 18, 1891, file 428; Graham to Assistant Adjutant General, Department of California, Sept. 3, 1891, file 473; Presidio Adjutant to Wood, Dec. 14 (file 673), Dec. 24 (file 690), Dec. 30 (file 702), 1891, all in Presidio LS, RG 393.

54. Graham to Assistant Adjutant General, Department of California, Jan. 2, 1892, file 74, Presidio Register, RG 393, NARA. The lyceum program was part of an armywide reform effort that was gradually transforming the Old Army of the frontier into the New Army of the transoceanic twentieth century. Graham to Assistant Adjutant General, Jan. 25, 1892, Department of California, file 71, Presidio LS, RG 393. For educational reform, see Carol Reardon, *Soldiers and Schools: The U.S. Army and the Uses of Military History, 1865–1920* (Lawrence, KS, 1990).

55. "Directions for Instructions to Capt. John S. Stidger," March 15, 1892, General Land Office Memorandum, box 89, Yosemite Corr, RG 79, NARA. Letter from the Secretary of the Interior, Jan. 5, 1893, 52d Cong., 2d sess., Senate Ex. Doc. No. 22. This document includes Noble's reports of investigations in 1891 and 1892. "Copy of endorsement on letter of the Secretary of Interior to the Secretary of War of March 26, 1892," file 841; Stidger to Noble, May 18, 1892, file 1535m, both in Yosemite Corr, RG 79, NARA.

56. As noted in an earlier chapter, four-mile-square General Grant Park was eventually incorporated into Sequoia, and Sequoia is used here for both entities for convenience. The informal, extralegal arrangement between the Interior and War Departments for the California parks continued until 1900, when, after the War Department expressed concern, Congress made it official. *U.S. Statutes at Large* 31 (1890): 618.

57. Ruger to Schofield, Feb. 3, 1892, AGO 25326, with file 946; Noble to Secretary of War Elkins, Feb. 15, 1892, Elkins to Noble, March 15, 1892, file 764, all in

Yosemite Corr, RG 79, NARA. Adjutant General to Commanding General, Department of California, Feb. 24, 1892, file 26178 AGO w/14573 PRD 1890, RG 94, NARA.

58. Special Orders No. 40, Department of California, April 20, 1984, filed with AGO/PRD 1890, file 14573, RG 94, NARA. George Gale to Interior Secretary, April 22, 1894, Yosemite Corr, RG 79, NARA. 4th Cavalry Troop "C" Muster Roll, April 30–June 30, 1894, RG 94.

59. Noble seemed pleasantly surprised by the army's initiative. He later asked the chief of his Patent and Miscellaneous Division (his adviser on legal issues) whether he needed to do anything "new" to keep such a remarkably responsive service going; the answer was no, so far as the chief knew. Noble to Thomas H. Musick, April 26, 1892, box 89; Noble to Musick, May 23, 1892, and Musick to Noble, June 3, 1892, file 1603, Yosemite Corr, RG 79, NARA.

60. Captain John A. Lockwood, "Uncle Sam's Troopers in the National Parks of California," *Overland Monthly* 2d ser., 33 (1899): 356–367; emphasis added. By the time he wrote this article, Lockwood had been promoted.

61. 4th Cavalry Troop "I" Muster Roll, April 30–June 30, 1892, RG 94, NARA.

62. This description is from Joe Dorst to his wife Esther, May 8, 1892, Dorst Papers.

63. John Muir, *The Yosemite* (1915; San Francisco, 1988), 2–3. The incandescent descriptions in this book were composed at the age of seventy-three, during the last year of Muir's life.

64. "Cavalryman's paradise" is from First Lieutenant Nathaniel F. McClure, "The Fourth Cavalry in the Yosemite National Park," *Journal of the United States Cavalry Association* 10, 37 (June 1897): 121. As noted, in official army documents, the base camp came to be called Camp Yosemite, but those stationed there preferred Camp Near Wawona. After Wood's death, it was renamed Camp A. E. Wood. See *Annual Report of the War Department* (Washington, DC 1892).

65. Noble to Thomas H. Musick, April 26, 1892, box 89; Noble to Musick, May 23, 1892, and Musick to Noble, June 3, 1892, file 1603, all in Yosemite Corr, RG 79, NARA.

66. Harry Benson to Chester Versteeg, June 23, 1924 (a reminiscence), Acting Superintendent File, YNPL. Esther to Joseph Dorst, July 10 and 15, 1892, Dorst Papers. Yosemite Post Return, July 1892, RG 94, NARA.

67. Esther to Joseph Dorst, July 11, 1892, Dorst Papers.

68. Patrols are listed in Fourth Cavalry "I" Troop Muster Roll, April 30–June 30, July 1–Aug. 31, Sept. 1–Oct. 31, 1892, RG 94, NARA.

69. *Yosemite Annual Report*, 1892.

70. *Yosemite Annual Reports*, 1891, 1892, 1893. The sheepherder story was not all black and white. Sheepmen used an allotment system for grazing that produced a measure of environmental preservation that has not been sufficiently credited. But the park idea also had an aesthetic dimension, and there was no question that what sheep did to park flowers and other vegetation close to the ground was grotesque. Also, there was the issue of federal law, which sheepherders (along with others) persistently violated. The army spent more time on them because they were more pervasive and resourceful, but never to the exclusion of other violators. Thanks again to Jim Snyder of the Yosemite National Park Library for sharing his research on the complex web of local alliances, rivalries, prejudices, and social strata that was painfully disrupted by the park's establishment.

71. Ibid.

72. Ibid.; emphasis added. Mark Twain describes comparable experiences among silver miners in Nevada in *Roughing It* (1872; New York, 1980), 146–303.

73. *Yosemite Annual Report*, 1891.

74. *Yosemite Annual Report*, 1892. Runte, *Yosemite*, 46–49.

75. For an assessment of the Old Army's role in fire protection, see Stephen J. Pyne, *Fire in America: A Cultural History of Wildland and Rural Fire* (1982; Seattle, WA, 1997), 219–230, 295–296.

76. *Yosemite Annual Report*, 1892. Wood's judgment on fir tree fire resistance has since been proven wrong—firs are actually more fire resistant than pines—but his ecological outlook combining empathy and science was still ahead of its time.

77. Ibid.

78. *Yosemite Annual Report*, 1893. The second fish planting was reported in A. E. Wood to Leonard Wood, Sept. 27, 1893, carton 26, Leonard Wood Papers. The potentially adverse impact of indiscriminate fish planting is better understood now than it was among naturalists in Wood's day.

79. Leonard Wood's "Diary," carton 2, Leonard Wood Papers. Joe Dorst to Esther Dorst, Presidio to Wawona, June 12, 13, 19, 20, 27; July 2, 10, 20, 24, 25, 26, 30, 31; Aug. 8, 9, 1893, Dorst Papers. This summer of 1893—before he underwent what a biographer called a "transformation" from "a young medical officer full of excitement for life . . . into a man mostly full of himself"—Leonard Wood was a robust thirty-three years of age, recently married to the niece and ward of U.S. Supreme Court Justice Stephen Field. Leonard's bride Louise came to Yosemite with their newborn son, along with Esther Dorst and her infant boy and Minnie Wood, Jug's wife. For Wood's "transformation," see Jack C. Lane, *Armed Progressive: General Leonard Wood* (San Rafael, CA, 1978), xv.

80. Charles Robinson to Hoke Smith, May 12, 1893, file 1509, Yosemite Corr, RG 79, NARA. Robinson also was apparently the unattributed author of a petition by Yosemite Indians requesting $1 million in damages from the government. Wood mentioned the petition in his 1891 report and expressed concern that local whites would fleece the Indians out of any money they might gain. One can only guess what Robinson, who could trumpet Yosemite Indian rights and condemn them as pimps and prostitutes with equal moral zeal, had in mind. See Mark Spence, "Dispossesing the Wilderness: Yosemite Indians and the National Park Ideal, 1864–1903," *Pacific Historical Review* 40, 1 (February 1996): 42–43.

81. Wood to Smith, June 24, 1893, box 90, Yosemite Corr, RG 79, NARA.

82. The depth and character of this gulf in values is discussed in Chapters 7 and 8.

83. Shippee owned about 60,000 head of sheep navigating in and out of the park. See Shippee to Noble on company letterhead, June 24, 1891, file 1640; A. E. Wood to Hoke Smith, July 11, 1893, file 2331, both in Yosemite Corr, RG 79, NARA. Young's encounter is described in Chapter 6.

84. Yosemite Post Returns, July, August 1891; 4th Cavalry Troop "I" Muster Roll, June 30–Aug. 31, Aug. 31–Oct. 30, 1891, both in RG 94, NARA. "Diary," entry dated Aug. 9–15, 1893, carton 2; A. E. Wood to Leonard Wood, Sept. 27, 1893, carton 26, both in Leonard Wood Papers.

85. On Nov. 3, writing from Westville, Connecticut, Wood applied for a two-month extension of his leave. It was granted, but Wood did not exercise it. Instead, he headed back to the Presidio to report for duty. Application for leave, Oct. 2, 1893, Wood to Adjutant General, War Department, Nov. 3, 1893, ACP Wood; 4th Cavalry Troop "I" Muster Roll, Aug. 31–Oct. 31, 1892, all in RG 94, NARA.

86. Presidio Register, Nov. 20 (file 3035), Nov. 29 (file 3057), 1893, RG 393, NARA. A. E. Wood to Leonard Wood, Feb. 9, 1894, carton 26, Leonard Wood Papers.

87. Ruger to Adjutant General, March 2, 1894, AGO 1030; Assistant Adjutant General H. C. Corbin to Ruger, March 22, 1894, AGO 1030; Ruger to Adjutant General, April 2, 1894, copies with Patents and Miscellaneous Division, Interior Department, file 1449; John P. Irish to Hoke Smith, March 8, 1894, file 1063, all in Yosemite Corr, RG 79, NARA.

88. Wood to Assistant Adjutant General, Department of California, March 9, 1894. Department Commander, Department of California, to Wood, March 17, 1894, files 684 and 683, Presidio Register, RG 303, NARA.

89. Presidio Orders, vol. 12, no. 81, April 15, 1894; Graham to Commanding Officer, 4th Cavalry, April 17, 1894, file 264, Presidio LS, both in RG 393, NARA.

CHAPTER 5. RUNNING A CAVALRYMAN'S PARADISE

1. Lieutenant N. F. McClure, "The Fourth Cavalry in the Yosemite National Park," *Journal of the United States Cavalry Association* 10, 37 (June 1897)" 113–121; see 120.

2. Professor Joseph N. LeConte Jr. of the University of California at Berkeley, a Sierra Club founder and board member for more than forty years, relied on McClure's article and map in completing his own detailed map of the park in 1896. For the map, see Sierra Club, "Map of the Central Portion of the Sierra Nevada Mountains and of the Yosemite Valley," Sierra Club Pub. No. 12 (Berkeley, CA, 1896), at YNPL. For LeConte, see LeConte Family Papers, box 4, Joseph N. LeConte Papers, Bancroft. Membership Records, carton 309, file 21, Sierra Club Records, Bancroft. N. F. McClure, First Lieutenant, 5th Cavalry, "Explorations Among the Canons North of the Tuolumne River," *Sierra Club Bulletin* 1, 5 (May 1895): 168–186. The best history of the Sierra Club for this period is Holway R. Jones, *John Muir and the Sierra Club: The Battle for Yosemite* (San Francisco, 1965); for the club's establishment, see 7–11; also Michael P. Cohen, *The History of the Sierra Club, 1892–1970* (San Francisco, 1988), 1–38. The Sierra Club tribute to McClure is by Francis P. Farquhar: "Nathaniel Fish McClure, 1865–1942," *Sierra Club Bulletin* 27, 3 (June 1943), 96–98. McClure's articles for the *Bulletin* include: "Ascent of El Yunque" [Puerto Rico], 3, 2 (May 1900): 127–134; "How Private Burns Climbed Mount Pinatubo" [Philippines], 5, 1 (January 1904); and "The 35th Division in the Vosges Mountains [France]," 11, 2 (January 1921): 175–180. There was also a letter from the Philippines to his fellow club members regretting that he had not yet had an opportunity to place on a "prominent peak" the two club record boxes entrusted to him; see "Letter from Capt. N.F. McClure," 4, 2 (May 1902).

3. Nathaniel F. McClure, *Class of 1887, United States Military Academy: A Biographical Volume* (Washington, DC, 1938), 1–17. McClure died in 1942. In an obituary for West Point's alumni journal, a former colleague called him one of the "outstanding exemplars of the 'Old Army,' now largely traditional" (Brigadier General E. D. Scott [ret.], "Nathaniel Fish McClure," *Association of Graduates, U.S. Military Academy* [West Point, NY, January 1943], 10–11). Congressman Carlisle served as Speaker of the House of Representatives and also as Grover Cleveland's treasury secretary.

4. McClure's graduation photo is at the U.S. Military Academy at West

Point. The assessments by Young and Graham were on his application to the adjutant general for an extension at the Presidio to complete his map, Jan. 31, 1896, file 387, Presidio Register, RG 393, NARA.

5. Gale graduated tenth in his class at West Point and he later taught mathematics there. Muster Rolls for 4th Cavalry "B," "C," "I," and "K" Troops, 1893–1894, RG 94, NARA. *Yosemite Annual Report*, 1894. Gale ACP, RG 94. Constance Wynn Altshuler, *Cavalry Yellow and Infantry Blue: Army Officers in Arizona Between 1881 and 1886* (Tucson, AZ, 1991), 136–137.

6. Special Orders No. 40, Department of California, April 20, 1894, filed with AGO/PRD 1890, file 14573, RG 94, NARA. George Gale to Secretary of the Interior, April 22, 1894, Yosemite Corr, RG 79, NARA. 4th Cavalry Troop "C" Muster Roll, April 30–June 30, 1894, RG 94.

7. Lieutenant N. F. McClure, "The Fourth Cavalry in the Yosemite National Park," *Journal of the United States Cavalry Association* 10, 37 (June 1897), 113–121; see 120. Joe Dorst went from Sequoia to Vienna, Austria, where he served as military attaché at the U.S. Embassy. Muster Roll, 4th Cavalry "K" Troop, 1893–1894, RG 94, NARA.

8. Jones, *John Muir and the Sierra Club*, 7–11. Cohen, *The History of the Sierra Club*, 8–14. Membership Records, carton 309, file 21, Sierra Club Records, Bancroft. McClure's membership was awarded on May 27, 1895, although his submission of an article to the *Bulletin* in 1894 indicated earlier contacts.

9. John Muir, "Features of the Proposed Yosemite National Park," *Century Magazine* 40, 5 (September 1890): 656–667. McClure, "Explorations Among the Canons North of the Tuolumne River," 168–186.

10. McClure's article, along with his map of the park and supplementary notes in the *Sierra Club Bulletin* that came a year later, remain a "constant travelling companion" for contemporary backcountry explorers, according to James B. Snyder et al., *Wilderness Historic Resources Survey, 1989 Season Report* (Yosemite, CA, 1990), 4–5. This account of McClure's expedition, including the quoted passages, draws directly on the *Bulletin* article unless otherwise noted.

11. Snyder et al., *Wilderness Historic Resources Survey*, 4–5.

12. Many of the names McClure assigned are still in use. Jack Main's Canyon, which he named, has been shortened to Jack Main Canyon. Some old-timers claim that McClure misunderstood the pronunciation of the Basque sheepherder who led him to it and that it should be named after Jack Means. McClure would welcome that information as proving his point about name confusion. See Peter Browning, Yosemite Place Names (Lafayette, CA, 1988), 68.

13. McClure's admired article was not fundamentally different from hundreds of patrol reports prepared during the Old Army's century-long march across the American continent. For a preliminary introduction to the archetypal experience that Joseph Campbell called the "mythological round"—the "descent" into primal depths and the return with treasure after overcoming numerous obstacles—see *The Hero with a A Thousand Faces* (New York, 1949; Cleveland, 1970), 40–246, and Mircea Eliade, *The Myth of Eternal Return, or Cosmos and History* (1954; Princeton, 1991), 1–34. Perhaps the best-known epic on that theme is Homer's *Odyssey*, in which virtually the entire story recounts the return. Unlike Homer and other authors of ancient myths, modern romantics sometimes believe it is enough to uncover primal affective roots, in part because modern civilization has buried them so deep that merely gaining access to them can be psychologically enriching. But in ancient times, it was the return to the banal present with new wisdom that counted most.

14. Editor's note, *Sierra Club Bulletin* 1, 7 (January 1896): 288. Adjutant General, Washington, DC, Jan. 31, 1896, McClure ACP, RG 94, NARA. Department of the Army, Special Order No. 38, Feb. 15, 1896, Department of California, RG 393, NARA.

15. The "Wheeler Surveys," led by Captain George M. Wheeler of the Army Corps of Engineers, are appended to the chief of engineers' report in the *War Department Annual Report, 1877–79* (Washington, DC). McClure ACP, RG 94, NARA. See also Francis P. Farquhar, "Nathaniel Fish McClure, 1865–1942," *Sierra Club Bulletin* 27, 3 (June 1943): 96–98. Browning, *Yosemite Place Names.* "Place names were also a way" is from Snyder, *Wilderness Historic Resources Survey,* 99.

For an example of reintegration, see William Poole, "Return of the Sinkyone: The Northern California Coast Returns to Its Roots with an Intertribal Park," in *Sierra* 81, 6 (November/December 1996): 52–55, 72, in which primal bonds with nature are reconstituted and empirical faculties recover emotionally charged values worth serving. The article also demonstrates how the process is both circular and progressive, in that the point of departure and return for the intertribal park is the modern nature park concept. Other examples include the reestablishment of Indian names for many sites within national park boundaries and according other recognition of the place of Native Americans in the history of these "natural" preserves that have been inhabited continuously for thousands of years. For Indian dispossession, see Mark David Spence, *Dispossessing the Wilderness: Indian Removal and the Making of the National Parks* (New York, 1999).

16. McClure, "The Fourth Cavalry in the Yosemite National Park," 113–121.

17. Joseph H. Dorst, "Ranald Slidell Mackenzie," *Journal of the United States Cavalry Association* 10, 39 (December 1897): 367–382. Michael D. Pierce, *The Most Promising Young Officer: A Life of Ranald Slidell Mackenzie* (Norman, OK, 1990), 141, 205, 222. "Joseph H. Dorst," *Annual Report of the Association of Graduates, U.S. Military Academy* (West Point, N.Y., June 12, 1916). Benson to Esther Dorst, Feb. 26, 1916, upon Joe's death, Sovulewski to Joseph Dorst, Dec. 6, 1892, Dorst Papers.

18. Dorst ACP, Wood ACP, RG 94, NARA. See also Cullum Register, 2:189. Although Dorst and Wood were classmates, Wood was five years older, having served as an enlisted man during the Civil War, then studying in Iowa before gaining admittance to West Point. The group photograph from the 1870s is in the Dorst Papers.

19. Dorst ACP, Wood ACP, RG 94, NARA. "Joseph H. Dorst," *Annual Report.* The tribute to Mackenzie, originally published in 1889 in the West Point reunion journal, is accessible in its original form in Dorst, "Ranald Slidell Mackenzie," 367–382.

20. The military experience has been mined extensively for its alleged homoerotic significance. Without taking sides on that bottomless issue, it's still possible, it seems to me, to discuss masculine bonding and heterosexual love in the Old Army on their own terms. Bonds influenced by the sensory-based instincts that govern at least 99 percent of the human animal's nervous system can be, but do not have to be, erotic.

21. Joseph Dorst to Catherine Archer, March (undated) 1890, March 27, 1890, Dorst Papers. *Lists Relating to Economic and Social Status of Cadets' Parents, 1842–1910,* RG 94, NARA facility, at West Point, NY. Obituaries of John Dorst from local newspapers are in the Dorst Papers.

22. William T. Sherman to Catherine Archer, March 28, 1890, Sherman to Joseph Dorst, March 28, 1890, Dorst Papers.

23. 4th Cavalry "K" Troop Muster Roll, September–December 1890, May–June 1891, RG 94, NARA. Dorst Papers.

24. Joe Dorst to Esther Dorst, May 25, May 30 1891, Dorst Papers.

25. Ibid. Larry M. Dilsaver and Douglas H. Strong, "Sequoia and Kings Canyon National Parks," in *Yosemite and Sequoia: A Century of California National Parks,* ed. Richard J. Orsi et al. (San Francisco, 1990), 19–20. For general background, see also Douglas Hillman Strong, "A History of Sequoia National Park," (Ph.D. diss., Syracuse University, 1964), although its treatment of the army is superficial.

26. Joe to Esther Dorst, June 10, 12, 1891, Esther to Joe, June 5, 7, 10, 11, Dorst Papers.

27. Ibid., June 15, 17, 23, 1891.

28. Ibid., August 17, 1891.

29. Ibid., June 26, July 17, Aug. 3, Aug. 17, 1891.

30. Ibid., July 9, Sept. 2, 1891.

31. Ibid., Aug. 31, Sept. 2, 4, 9, 1891.

32. Ibid., Sept. 7, 9, 1891.

33. Ibid., Sept. 28, 1891.

34. Ibid., Oct. 6, 1891.

35. Ibid, Oct. 9, 1891.

36. Ibid., Oct. 12, 1891. I'm focusing on Dorst's side of the relationship not because it was intrinsically more important than Esther's—it wasn't—but because of its direct relevance to this study of Old Army values.

37. Ibid., Oct. 17 (cable from Visalia confirming departure for Presidio), Oct. 31, 1891. 4th Cavalry Troop "K" Muster Roll, Aug. 30–Oct. 31, 1891, RG 94, NARA.

38. Joe to Esther Dorst, June 14, 1892, Dorst Papers.

39. Ibid., June 15, July 3, 1892.

40. Ibid., July 16, 1892.

41. Ibid., Esther to Joe, July 18; Joe to Esther, Aug. 27, 1892.

42. Ibid., June 30, 1890. For a summary of the hero-aesthete contrast, see Mary W. Blanchard, "The Soldier and the Aesthete: Homosexuality and Popular Culture in Gilded Age America," *Journal of American Studies* 30 (April 1996): 25–46. It is worth noting, with the preface that an in-depth examination is beyond the scope of this book, that this contrast was itself an expression of a masculine paradigm rooted in Western religious tradition that still pervades popular culture despite enormous advances in gender studies—the competing brothers, the intellectual and the animal, the good guy and the bad guy, the bad good guy (a corrupt politico) and the good bad guy (a renegade cop fighting the system), and so on and on, with a woman choosing one over the other for various reasons that are often statements about a ubiquitous paradigm that has conflict built into it. In subsequent chapters, the divided root and self-renewing character of that archetypal conflict are discussed.

43. Typical laudatory assessments of Benson are in Francis P. Farquhar, "Colonel Benson," *Sierra Club Bulletin* 12, 2 (1925): 170–175; and the one by Gabriel Sovulewski quoted in C. P. Russell, "Gabriel Sovulewski, Dean of the Yosemite Staff," undated typescript in Gabriel Sovulewski File, YNPL. J. B. Curtin to Benson, April 22, 1908, J. B. Curtin/J. T. McLean Papers, box 4, in Army Administration Papers, YNPL. Yosemite Corr, 1894–1909, RG 79, NARA.

44. Esther to Joe Dorst, Aug. 4, 6, 7, 8, 9, 10, 11, 1892, Dorst Papers.

45. Peter Browning, *Yosemite Place Names,* 10–11. Robert Ridgway, "Descrip-

tion of a New Plumed Partridge from Sonora," *Proceedings of the U.S. National Museum, 1887* (Washington, DC, 1888), 148–150. The Smithsonian Institution was also called the U.S. National Museum. Benson ACP, RG 94, NARA.

46. Ibid. "Harry Coupland Benson," Annual Report, Association of Graduates, U.S. Military Academy (West Point, NY, June 11, 1925), 174–176.

47. Benson ACP, RG 94, NARA. Top West Point graduates went to the Corps of Engineers or the artillery during the Old Army era, reflecting Jeffersonian scientific and technical priorities for military education.

48. Benson was cited for bravery by General George Crook in a report filed from Fort Bowie on April 10, 1886, a copy of which is among Benson's Geronimo campaign papers in the Acting Superintendents files, YNPL. See also General Nelson A. Miles, *Personal Recollections* (1896; Lincoln, NE, 1992), 488. Benson ACP, RG 94, NARA.

49. "Case of 2nd Lieut. Harry C. Benson, 4th Cavalry," unsigned memorandum, Adjutant General's Office, Benson ACP, RG 94, NARA. Unsigned memorandum, War Department, re Benson-led scouting expedition, Nov. 7, 1885–April 17, 1886, Acting Superintendent's files, YNPL.

50. Major Harry C. Benson, "The Geronimo Campaign," *Army and Navy Journal*, July 3, 1909. In the concluding quote, Benson put "outside the Army" in parenthesis, which I have omitted to avoid the suggestion that they were not his words. Two of the more reliable summaries of the campaign are in Robert M. Utley, *Frontier Regulars: The United States Army and the Indian, 1866–1891* (1973; Lincoln, NE, 1984), 369–396, and Robert Wooster, *Nelson A. Miles and the Twilight of the Frontier Army* (Lincoln, NE, 1993), 144–162.

51. Harry C. Benson to Chester Versteeg, June 23, 1924, Francis P. Farquhar Papers, Bancroft.

52. See Robert Ridgway to Second Lieutenant Harry C. Benson, Oct. 12, 1886, March 1, 1887, Ridgway Letterbooks. Benson to Ridgway, Feb. 11, 1887, Accession Records, Office of the Registrar, U.S. National Museum, Smithsonian Institution Archives. Benson's namesake in the partridge family is announced in "Description of a New Plumed Partridge from Sonora," *Proceedings of the U.S. National Museum, 1887*. The initial contact for Benson and many other Old Army ornithologists was Captain Charles E. Bendire, a retired army surgeon, author of a two-volume history of North American birds, and an honorary curator at the National Museum from 1884 until his death in 1897. See Charles Emil Bendire Papers, Smithsonian Archives, and Edgar Hume, *Ornithologists of the U.S. Army Medical Corps* (Baltimore, MD, 1942). Geronimo's final surrender was on Sept. 4, 1886; Utley, *Frontier Regulars*, 389.

53. Benson's career-long efforts to avoid staff assignments are documented in correspondence in his ACP file, RG 94, NARA, which includes the supportive letter from Leonard Wood to the army adjutant general in Washington, D.C., Dec. 1, 1898. "There is no action" is from a personal note in that file of March 19, 1899, to "my dear Johnston," along with State Department communications of May 30 and June 6, 1893.

54. Francis P. Farquhar, "Colonel Benson," *Sierra Club Bulletin* 12, 2 (1915), 175–179. See also Farquhar, *History of the Sierra Nevada*, 201–217.

55. Benson to Versteeg, June 23, July 17, 1924, Farquhar Papers. Russell, "Gabriel Sovulewski, Dean of the Yosemite Staff."

56. Benson to Versteeg, July 17, 1924, Farquhar Papers. Linda Wedel Greene, *Yosemite: The Park and Its Resources*, vol. 1 (Washington, DC, 1987), 370–373.

57. Benson to Versteeg, July 17, 1924, Farquhar Papers.

58. *Yosemite Annual Report*, 1897. See list of members enrolled after 1894 in *Sierra Club Bulletin* 2 (January 1897).

59. *Sierra Club Bulletin* 2 (January 1897).

60. Greene, *Yosemite: The Park and Its Resources*, 1:374–377.

61. *Yosemite Annual Report*, 1896, 1897. Benson to Versteeg, July 17, 1924, Farquhar Papers. 4th Cavalry Troop "B" Muster Roll, April–June, 1896, RG 94, NARA. Alfred Runte, *Yosemite, the Embattled Wilderness* (Lincoln, NE, 1990), 65–66. The troopers' fish planting under state aegis should be considered in the context of the time. Had they known in the 1890s what ecologists know in the 1990s, it is doubtful they would have pursued the effort with the same zeal. More relevant in that context is the parallel introduction by park soldiers of the then novel practice of enforcing regulations controlling fishing in wildland rivers and streams.

62. Francis P. Farquhar, "Colonel Benson," *Sierra Club Bulletin* 12, 2 (1924): 174–179. Benson to "My dear Major," Feb. 27, 1903, Acting Superintendents file, YNPL. In 1903, Lieutenant Colonel Joseph Garrard commanded at Yosemite. The letter may have been to Major John Bigelow Jr., another troop commander who expected the command in 1903 and got it in 1904. Benson served with Bigelow in Arizona in the 1880s. The single-spaced typescript copy, when considered alongside examples of Benson's handwritten correspondence, amounted to more than twenty-five pages in the original. *Yosemite Annual Report*, 1905–1908, RG 79, NARA.

63. Alfred Runte, *National Parks, The American Experience*, 2d ed. (Lincoln, NE, 1987), 11–47. Elie Kedourie, *Nationalism* (New York, 1960), 9–19.

64. Charles P. Russell, "Gabriel Sovulewski, Dean of the Yosemite Staff," typescript, 7 pages, Sovulewski biography file, YNPL. 4th Cavalry "K" Troop Muster Roll, 1888–1892, RG 94, NARA.

65. Benson to Versteeg, July 17, 1924, Farquhar Papers. Russell, "Gabriel Sovulewski."

66. Presidio Orders No. 73, May 1, 1894, RG 393, NARA. *Sequoia Annual Report*, 1892.

67. C. Frank Brockman, "Administrative Officers of Yosemite," *Yosemite Nature Notes* 23, 6 (June 1944): 53–57. *Yosemite Annual Report*, 1906.

68. Benson to Sovulewski, Nov. 5, 1906, Sovulewski file, YNPL.

69. For "Mother Sovulewski," see Brockman, "Administrative Officers of Yosemite."

70. Horace M. Albright, *The Birth of the National Park Service: The Founding Years, 1913–33* (Salt Lake City, UT, 1985), 64. When Inez Sovulewski died in 1928, she was laid to rest in Yosemite Valley, a rare tribute.

71. Albright, *The Birth of the National Park Service*, 64. Gabriel Sovulewski (introduction by Carl P. Russell), "The Story of Trail Building in Yosemite National Park," *Yosemite Nature Notes* 7, 4 (April 1928), 25–28.

72. Albright, *The Birth of the National Park Service*, 64. Runte, *National Parks*, 102–103. James B. Snyder, *Historic Wilderness Survey*, 72–73.

73. Russell, "Sovulewski, Dean of the Yosemite Staff." Sovulewski's reference to independence appears in a letter to the Sierra Club acknowledging his honorary life membership award, in *Sierra Club Bulletin* 21 (February 1936): 85–86.

74. Michael D. Pierce, *The Most Promising Young Officer: A Life of Ranald Slidell Mackenzie* (Norman, OK, 1993), 6–8, 222. Charles M. Robinson III, *Bad Hand: A Biography of General Ranald S. Mackenzie* (Austin, TX, 1993), 2–3.

75. Robinson, *Bad Hand.* Rodgers ACP, RG 94, NARA. Matthew C. Perry's wife was Mackenzie's aunt.

76. The photograph in profile appears in an album kept by Joe Dorst in Dorst Papers, and in James Parker, *The Old Army: Memories, 1872–1898* (Philadelphia, 1929), 33.

77. The flurry of communications regarding the Paris expo are in Rodgers's ACP file, RG 94, NARA.

78. Ibid. For life in Fort Garland, see Parker, *The Old Army,* 126. See also Robert W. Frazer, *Forts of the West* (Norman, OK, 1965), 36–37, 146.

79. Joe Dorst to Alex Rodgers, Feb. 19, 1891, Dorst Papers.

80. Leonard White, *The Republican Era, 1869–1901: A Study in Administrative History* (New York, 1958), 138. Matthew Josephson, *The Politicos* (1938; New York, 1963), 87–90, 239, 279, 444.

81. See Ambassador E. H. Conger to Secretary of State James G. Blaine, Nov. 13, 1891; and endorsement of Rodgers's 1894 transfer request by Assistant Adjutant General in Charge of Military Information Division, November 1894, Rodgers ACP, RG 94, NARA. For the Military Information Division, see Graham A. Cosmas, *An Army for Empire: The United States Army in the Spanish-American War* (1971; Shippensburg, PA, 1994), 25–27. The Washington assignment put Rodgers in on the rudimentary beginnings of a "general staff" planning function in the U.S. Army comparable to that of the Prussian Army that had won the admiration of American military reformers.

82. *Yosemite Annual Report,* 1895. Jones, *John Muir and the Sierra Club,* 11–14. *San Francisco Chronicle,* Feb. 23, 1895.

83. "William R. Smedberg," obituary, *Assembly* 2, 2 (July 1943): 6–7.

84. Rodgers to J. B. Curtin and to "Mr. White," May 30, 1895, and to C. C. Smith, June 23, 1895, Acting Superintendent Letterbooks, Yosemite National Park Museum.

85. Rodgers to Secretary of the Interior, May 30, 1895 (file 2978), Yosemite Corr, RG 79, NARA.

86. Ibid., June 23 (file 3625), July 18, 1895 (file 3821).

87. Rodgers to Governor of California, June 27, 1895, Acting Superintendent Letterbooks, Yosemite National Park Museum.

88. *Yosemite Annual Report,* 1895. Rodgers to Interior Secretary, Nov. 2, 1895 (file 5045), Yosemite Corr, RG 79, NARA.

CHAPTER 6. "HE WAS NO ORDINARY MAN"

1. A. E. Wood to Leonard Wood, Feb. 9, 1894, carton 26, Leonard Wood Papers.

2. Mackenzie's assessment, in a letter to General Edwin O. C. Ord in 1878, is quoted in Barry C. Johnson, "Young's Fight on Thanksgiving Day," *Brand Book* 16, 3 and 4 (London, April–July 1974): 33–48. For Roosevelt, see Theodore Roosevelt, *The Rough Riders* (1899; New York, 1928), 73. Francis P. Farquhar recalled his 1922 visit in a letter to Young, May 7, 1923, in Young Papers. "No ordinary man" is in Francis Farquhar, ed., *Yosemite Complaint Against S. B. M. Young* (Tamalpais, CA, 1962), x.

3. "Every Inch a Soldier" is the title of a profile of Young in *Sunset Magazine* (August 1913): 350–355 (copy in Young Papers). "Beau ideal" is from A. B. White to Young, Oct. 5, 1903, Young Papers. "Fighting man" is from Jacob A. Riis, *Theo-*

dore Roosevelt: The Citizen (New York, 1904), 270. A photograph of Young relaxing in a camp chair en route to Yosemite in 1896 appears in James F. J. Archibald, "A Cavalry March to Yosemite," *Illustrated American* 20 (Nov. 28, 1896): 718–721, and a good oil portrait, by Marion Potter Sharpe, is reproduced in William Gardner Bell, *Commanding Generals and Chiefs of Staff, 1775–1991* (Washington, DC, 1993), 93. Harrydele Hallmark, "An Observant Woman's Impressions," *Philadelphia Sunday Press*, undated clipping in Young Papers.

4. The letter to Roosevelt is quoted in William R. Roberts, "Choosing the First Army Chief of Staff: Lieutenant General S.B.M. Young," (N.p., 1994), 6.

5. S. B. M. Young to Marjorie Young, March 21, 1900, Young Papers.

6. The photograph is in Young Papers. The story behind it is in Sherry L. Smith, *The View from Officers' Row: Army Perceptions of Western Indians* (Tucson, AZ, 1990), 73 n. 205.

7. Hallmark, "An Observant Woman's Impressions." Farquhar, *Yosemite Complaint.*

8. This summary of Young's career is, unless other indicated, from Adjutant General's Office, War Department, July 15, 1902, "Statement of the Military Service of Major General Samuel Baldwin Marks Young," Young ACP, RG 94, NARA. Roberts, "Choosing the First Army Chief of Staff," and Edgar F. Raines, "Samuel Baldwin Marks Young," *Dictionary of American Military Biography*," vol. 3 (Westport, CT, 1984), 1221–1226. In his career summary, Young claimed two years' attendance at Jefferson College in Pennsylvania, but that school's records contain no mention of him. His college was the army.

9. Johnson, "Young's Fight."

10. S. B. M. Young Journal, Aug. 2, 1881, Young Papers. Young's "Individual Report" for 1891, Young ACP, RG 94, NARA.

11. Young ACP, RG 94, NARA. Otis's assessment is dated May 25, 1883, in Young ACP.

12. Young to John Lewis Childs, Queens County, N.Y., Feb. 12, 1886; "Circular No. 2," May 1887, both in Young Papers.

13. Ibid. Young copied his replies to the earthquake inquiry into his journal on May 16, 1887.

14. Young transferred from the 8th to the 3rd Cavalry in 1883 when promoted to major and to the 4th in 1893 when promoted to lieutenant colonel and assigned to the Presidio. His Mexican mission was authorized under Special Order No. 72, Sept. 8, 1878, signed on Mackenzie's behalf by adjutant Joseph Dorst. That and Young's report of Sept. 22 are in ibid. The agreement Young negotiated allowed Americans the right of pursuit across the border so long as they notified the Mexican army during the operation, an unusual concession reportedly attributable to the personal relationship Young developed with his Mexican counterpart. For other Texas activities, see Young to Assistant Adjutant General, Department of Texas, Nov. 25, 1886; Governor D. H. Stanley to Young, March 30, 1889, ibid. Young wrote Mackenzie of the birth of his namesake on May 31, 1878; see ibid. The boy died in early childhood.

15. A copy of the inspector general's report, by Colonel E. M. Heyl, dated March 2, 1893, is in ibid.

16. Young copied his capital punishment remarks into his journal in an entry marked January 1893, in ibid.

17. Presidio Orders, para. 5, Nov. 12, 1893; Young to Commander, Department of California, Feb. 27, 1894, Presidio Register, both in RG 393, NARA. 4th Cavalry Muster Rolls, Troops "B," "C," "I," "K," January–May 1894, RG 94,

NARA. Roberts, "Choosing the First Army Chief of Staff," 6–11. Young replaced Colonel Anson Mills who was close to retirement. Mills spent his next and final army year in Walla Walla as commander of the 4th Cavalry. See his autobiography, *My Story* (Washington, DC, 1918).

18. Presidio Orders No. 31, Feb. 9, 1894, RG 393, NARA. Other illustrations of the continuous clashes are Presidio LS Dec. 1, 1893 (file 610), Jan. 1 (file 82), Feb. 7 (file 110), Feb. 9 (file 123), March 6 (file 166), March 19 (file 185), 1894, RG 393, and Presidio Register, March 23, 1894 (file 903), for "It is not a joint command."

19. For Department of California commanders and their dates of service, see memorandum in Department of California miscellanous file, AG 698, roll 185, RG 94, NARA. Dorst to Assistant Adjutant General, Department of the Army, March 21, 1893 (file 705), and endorsement by Ruger, March 23 (file 718), in Presidio Register; Young to Adjutant General, War Department, Feb. 26, 1894, cited in Young to Ruger, March 5, 1894, in Presidio Register of that date (file 700), all in RG 393, NARA. Young annoyed Ruger by making his request directly to the War Department in Washington, although park commanders were authorized to use that procedure because they were also communicating directly with the secretary of the interior.

For Forsyth's Sheridan connection and previous park activities, see Paul Andrew Hutton, *Phil Sheridan and His Army* (Lincoln, NE, 1985), 163–165, 354–360. George Forsyth, "James W. Forsyth," *41st Annual Reunion, Association of Graduates of the United States Military Academy at West Point* (New York, June 4, 1910), 44–57. California was Forsyth's last posting before retirement. His forty-year career was marred by a tragic incident that would dominate memories of him. He commanded—more precisely, failed to command—the troops at Wounded Knee in December 1890, when a confrontation escalated within seconds into a massacre: 144 Indians (including 44 women and 16 children) and 25 soldiers were killed, and 51 Indians and 39 soldiers were wounded (of whom 7 Indians would die). Forsyth was condemned by his commander, Nelson A. Miles, who tried to drive him out of the service, but an army board of inquiry, although critical of him, exonerated him of deliberate maliciousness. His failure to recognize the situation's explosive potential appears to have been due mainly to the lack of hard-edged command experience of a soldier who spent most of his career riding in a general's suite. See Dee Brown, *Bury My Heart at Wounded Knee: An Indian History of the American West* (1971; New York, 1972), 413–418; Robert Wooster, *Nelson A. Miles and the Twilight of the Frontier Army* (Lincoln, NE, 1993), 185–194; and Robert M. Utley, *Frontier Regulars: The United States Army and the Indian, 1866–1891* (1973; Lincoln, NE, 1984), 405–410.

20. William Graham to Adjutant General, Department of California, Oct. 24, 1895 (file 820), Presidio LS; Presidio Register, Jan. 1, 1896 (file 25), both in RG 393, NARA.

21. Forsyth to Hoke Smith, Jan, 16, 1896, file 274, Yosemite Corr, RG 79, NARA. Douglas Hillman Strong, "A History of Sequoia National Park" (Ph.D. diss., Syracuse University, 1964), 151–153; 193–195. Christopher M. Klyza, *Who Controls Public Lands? Mining, Forestry, and Grazing Policies, 1870–1990* (Chapel Hill, NC 1996), 68–69. *Sequoia Annual Report*, 1891–1892.

22. Lockett to Forsyth, Dec. 20, 1895, file 274,Yosemite Corr, RG 79, NARA.

23. Forsyth to Hoke Smith, Jan. 16, 1896, ibid.

24. Ibid. Forsyth took another try at a USGS survey of Yosemite early in 1896, but the request was again rejected for lack of funds. See C. Walcott to Interior Secretary, returning Forsyth request, March 9, 1896, file 909, ibid.

25. "Letter from the Acting Secretary of the Treasury," 54th Cong., 1st sess., H.R. Doc. 261. The Yellowstone total is in an undated memorandum entitled "Appropriations by Congress for Roads, Bridges, etc., in the Yellowstone National Park," in Yosemite Corr, RG 79, NARA.

26. Forsyth to Hoke Smith, Feb. 29, 1896, file 855, Yosemite Corr, RG 79, NARA. Secretary of the Interior to Secretary of War, March 9, 1896, file 3128 w/14573, AGO PRD, RG 94, NARA. Secretary of War to Secretary of the Interior, March 19, 1896, Yosemite Corr.

27. Forsyth to Acting Secretary of the Interior, April 22, 1896, Yosemite Corr, RG 79, NARA. Senate Bill 2770, "A Bill Granting to the Yosemite Valley & Merced Railway Company a Right of Way," 54th Cong., 1st sess.

28. The inspector general's praise is noted in a memorandum to Young's squadron from the Adjutant General, Department of California., Jan. 2, 1896, file 10, Presidio LS, RG 393, NARA. For 1895 training, see "Report of Cavalry Drills for the Year," Colonel William Graham to Adjutant General, Department of California, Dec. 24, 1895, file 820, ibid. Young's request for permission for the cavalry squadron to march to Burlingame to witness a polo match between the "Riverside Club" and the "4th Cavalry Club" is in Presidio Register, April 4, 1895, RG 393. For Young's park reconnaissance and request, see Young to Forsyth, March 31, 1896, file 1017, ibid.

29. Young endorsement on Benson's returned request, April 30, 1896, file 1450, Presidio Register, RG 393, NARA.

30. Forsyth endorsement on Benson requisition, May 1, 1896, file 1482, ibid.

31. 4th Cavalry Troop "K" Muster Roll, May–June, 1896, RG 94, NARA. James F. J. Archibald, "A Cavalry March to Yosemite," *Illustrated American* 20 (Nov. 28, 1896): 718–721.

32. Archibald, "A Cavalry Ride to Yosemite." *San Francisco Examiner*, March 21, April 23 (approx.), 1896. The April editorial was located attached to a letter that John Muir sent to Robert Underwood Johnson on April 23, in RUJ Papers. Archibald, "A Cavalry March to Yosemite."

33. 4th Cavalry Troops "B" and "K" Muster Rolls, 1896, RG 94, NARA.

34. Colonel William Graham to Forsyth, responding to Forsyth's order, May 19, 1896, file 482, Presidio LS, RG 393, NARA. The communication includes the line of march. *Yosemite Annual Report*, 1896.

35. "Field Day at Wawona," *Mariposa Gazette*, Aug. 15, 1896.

36. Ibid.

37. Ibid.

38. Perkins to Smith, April 23, 1896, file 1264; Young to Smith, typescript dated "June" 1896; Yosemite Corr, RG 79, NARA.

39. Young to Interior Secretary, June 15, 1896, referring to application by R. U. Graves of May 15, 1896, forwarded to Young by the interior secretary, file 2180, ibid.

40. Young to Interior Secretary, July 24, 1896, ibid.

41. For a summary of the Hetch Hetchy issue see Samuel P. Hays, *Conservation and the Gospel of Efficiency: The Progressive Conservation Movement, 1890–1920* (Cambridge, MA, 1959), 189–198. Greater detail is provided in Holway R. Jones, *John Muir and the Sierra Club: The Battle for Yosemite* (San Francisco, 1965), 83–169. See Epilogue herein for reactions to Hetch Hetchy by post-1900 Yosemite commanders.

42. Young to J. Walter Smith, Register, U.S. Land Office, Stockton, Calif., May 24, 1896, Acting Superintendent Letterbooks, YNPL. Rodgers to Young, June 8,

1896, Army Administration Papers, Patrol Reports, YNPL. Young to Interior Secretary June 18, 1896, Yosemite Corr, RG 79, NARA.

43. Young to A. Cordes, Sept. 16 and Oct. 19, 1896, filed with file 2741, Yosemite Corr, RG 79, NARA.

44. Young to Interior Secretary, Oct. 20, 1896; Memorandum by Commissioner, General Land Office, Nov. 11, 1896, file 2741, Petition by Robert Reed et al., Dec. 9, 1896, all in ibid.

45. For a recent summary of the tourism-preservation issue with its science versus landscaping subplots, see Richard West Sellars, *Preserving Nature in the National Parks: A History* (New Haven, CT, 1997). The landscape design dimension is discussed in Ethan Carr, *Wilderness by Design: Landscape Architecture and the National Park Service* (Lincoln, NE, 1998), and Linda Flint McClelland, *Building the National Parks: Historic Landscape Design and Construction* (Baltimore, MD, 1998).

46. *Yosemite Annual Report,* 1896.

47. Ibid.

48. Complaint filed by George H. Bernhard, Oct. 21, 1896, file 2689, Yosemite Corr, RG 79, NARA.

49. When Muir and Robert Underwood Johnson first discussed forming a "Yosemite Defence Association," an idea that would evolve into the Sierra Club, Johnson proposed an alliance with the Boone and Crockett Club, a wildlife-oriented Yellowstone protection group founded by Teddy Roosevelt and George Bird Grinnell in 1887, but the outlooks of the two constituencies didn't match. See 1890–1891 letters between Grinnell and Johnson, especially Grinnell to Johnson, Jan. 19, 1891, in RUJ Papers. For the underrated role of hunters and fisherman in early environmental protection, see John F. Reiger, *American Sportsmen and the Origins of Conservation* (New York, 1975). The relatively brief history of the small but influential Boone and Crockett Club is described in George Bird Grinnell, ed., *Hunting at High Altitudes: The Book of the Boone and Crockett Club* (New York, 1913), 435–491. For a good portrait of the remarkable Grinnell, see Sherry L. Smith, "George Bird Grinnell and the Vanishing 'Plains Indians,'" *Montana: The Magazine of Western History* 50, 3 (Autumn 2000): 20–31.

50. *Sequoia Annual Report,* 1891–1892.

51. *Yosemite Annual Report,* 1895.

52. Bowers sought to block the hunting preserve scheme that existed only in his imagination by disarming the park troopers. His demand was forwarded to army commanding general Nelson A. Miles, who rejected it out of hand. Bowers to Secretary of War, May 6, 1896; Miles endorsement, May 12, 1896; file 37148AGO w/14573, PRD 1890. The plot to make agrarian free enterprise "extinct" was reported in *Mariposa Gazette,* Dec. 20, 1890, and discussed here in Chapter 4.

53. *Yosemite Annual Report,* 1896.

54. Young to Olney, July 18, 1896, Acting Superintendent Letterbooks, YNPL.

55. *Yosemite Annual Report,* 1896. Young to Interior Secretary, Aug. 16, 1896, enclosing correspondence with H. W. Turner, file 2254, Yosemite Corr, RG 79, NARA.

56. Young to First Lieutenant Geo Chase, June 30, 1896, Acting Superintendent Letterbooks, YNPL.

57. *Yosemite Annual Report,* 1896.

58. Young to Interior Secretary, "In the matter of the Complaint of John L. Howard, against Colonel S.B.M. Young, U.S.A. Superintendent of Yosemite National Park," Nov. 30, 1896, including Young's response and copies of relevant correspondence (hereafter cited as Young Response), file 2928, Yosemite Corr, RG

79, NARA. D. Y. Campbell, 119 Bush Street, San Francisco, is on the list of Sierra Club charter members in Jones, *John Muir and the Sierra Club*, 170.

59. Howard to Forsyth, Aug. 14, 1896; Howard to Young, Aug. 17, 1896, Young Response.

60. Young to Howard, Aug. 17, 1896, ibid.

61. Goodrich report to Young, Sept. 18, 1896, ibid.

62. Ibid.

63. 4th Cavalry Troop "K" Muster Roll, August–November, 1896, RG 94, NARA. Keilty report to Young, Sept. 18, 1896, Young Response. John L. Howard et al., separate copies to Daniel Lamont, Secretary of War, and David Rowland Francis, Secretary of the Interior, Sept. 15, 1896, file 2528 (hereafter cited as Howard Complaint), Yosemite Corr, RG 79, NARA.

64. Perkins to Lamont and Francis, Sept. 14, 1896, Howard Complaint.

65. Ibid.

66. War Secretary Lamont to Interior Secretary Francis, Oct. 14, 1896, file 5644; Francis to Young, Oct. 20, 1896, Yosemite Corr, RG 79, NARA.

67. This and succeeding quotes unless otherwise noted are from Young Response.

68. Donald Y. Campbell to Interior Secretary, Feb. 27, 1897, file 634, Yosemite Corr, RG 79, NARA. Campbell's petition includes references to Young distributing copies of his report "in the offices, Clubs and other places" of San Francisco. A printed version of Young's response from that era was obtained many years later by Francis P. Farquhar and reproduced in *Yosemite in 1896* (Berkeley, CA, 1962). Interior Secretary David Francis to Perkins, Feb. 12, 1897, Yosemite Corr.

69. Farquhar, *Yosemite in 1896*. The wedding of Young's daughter was reported in the *San Francisco Examiner*, Sept. 3, 1901. Under the headline "Wedding Flowers on War Trophies When General Young Surrenders His Daughter," the reporter expressed amazement at the variety of flowers garlanding the interior of Young's home and its grounds. The reporter would have been even more amazed to learn of Young's frontier sideline as a horticulturalist.

70. *Mariposa Gazette*, Sept. 19, 1896.

71. Feb. 22, 1897, McLean to Interior Secretary, March 20, 1897, Young to Interior Secretary, file 528, Yosemite Corr, RG 79, NARA.

72. *Sierra Club Bulletin* 7, 1 (January 1896): 276. Young rephrased the concluding words of Muir's comment: "embraced only one tree, yet even so moderate a reserve as this was attacked."

PART III. INSIDE CONNECTIONS

1. Elaine Pagels, *The Origins of Satan* (New York, 1995), 182. Pagels is the Harrington Spear Pain Professor of Religion at Princeton University.

CHAPTER 7. A CONQUERING NATURE

1. Quoted in Anthony F. C. Wallace, *Jefferson and the Indians: The Tragic Fate of the First Americans* (Cambridge, MA, 1999), 232.

2. Introductory discussions of manifest destiny are in Albert K. Weinberg, *Manifest Destiny* (Chicago, 1935); Frederick Merk, *Manifest Destiny and Mission in*

American History (New York, 1963); and, for the complementary "garden myth," Henry Nash Smith, *Virgin Land: The American West as Symbol and Myth* (New York, 1950), 138–305. For the western frontier as a regenerator of democratic institutions and an inspiration to the noble yeoman spirit, see Frederick Jackson Turner, "Significance of the Frontier in American History," paper read at a meeting of the American History Association, Chicago, Illinois, July 12, 1893, in F. J. Turner, *The Frontier in American History* (1920; Tucson, AZ, 1986), 1–38. The wide-ranging debate over Turner's significance is summarized to a recent date by Patricia Nelson Limerick, "Turnerians All: The Dream of a Helpful History in an Intelligible World," *American Historical Review* 100, 3 (June 1995): 697–716.

3. Wallace, *Jefferson and the Indians*, 221, 277. Heman Humphrey, *The Promised Land: A Sermon* (Boston, 1819); the copy I used is at the Newberry Library in Chicago. As Robert F. Berkhofer Jr. observes in *The White Man's Indian* (New York, 1979), "The separation of church and state in the United States was never meant by its proponents to eliminate the moral and spiritual foundations of American society. Government officials joined missionaries . . . in subscribing to the same basic version of Christian civilization. . . . Americanism rested upon a firm religious and moral groundwork in the opinion of all policy makers" (p. 140).

4. Pioneers in the historical reassessment, which had antecedents before World War II, were, for economic history, Charles Beard, *An Economic Interpretation of the Constitution of the United States* (New York, 1913), and for diplomatic history, William Appleman Williams, *The Tragedy of American Diplomacy* (New York, 1959), especially 15–50, for the period from the 1890s forward. Williams prefigured the "New Western History" that flowered in the 1980s in *The Contours of American History* (New York, 1961). For good introductions to the self-questioning New Western History, see Patricia Nelson Limerick, Clyde A. Milner II, and Charles E. Rankin, eds., *Trails: Toward a New Western History* (Lawrence, KS, 1991), and William Cronon, George Miles, and Jay Gitlin, eds., *Under An Open Sky: Rethinking America's Western Past* (New York, 1992). The central role of aridity in western development is explored by Donald Worster, *Rivers of Empire: Water, Aridity, and the Growth of the American West* (New York, 1985); of the underexamined role of the federal government by Richard White, *"It's Your Misfortune and None of My Own": A New History of the American West* (Norman, OK, 1991), 55–178; of global capitalism by William G. Robbins, *Colony and Empire: The Capitalist Transformation of the American West* (Lawrence, KS, 1994); and so on across the spectrum of western experience.

5. Metternich's remarks are from a letter to Count Carl Robert Nesselrode, Jan. 19, 1824, cited in Dexter Perkins, *A History of the Monroe Doctrine* (1941; Boston, 1963), 27, 56.

6. Patricia Nelson Limerick, *The Legacy of Conquest: The Unbroken Past of the American West* (New York, 1987), 25–38.

7. "City upon a hill" is from John Winthrop's sermon "A Model of Christian Charity," delivered aboard the *Arabella* in 1630, reproduced in Perry Miller, ed., *The American Puritans: Their Prose and Poetry* (New York, 1956), 78–84. The full phrase is: "For we must consider that we shall be a city upon a hill."

8. One reason New Western historians overlooked the Old Army, I suspect, was that most of them came of age during the culture wars of the Vietnam era and held, shall we say, an unsympathetic attitude toward things military. For the conflating of the Vietnam War and the Indian wars typical of historians and many others of my generation, see Donald Worster, *Under Western Skies: Nature and History in the American West* (New York, 1992), 11. "Either with contempt" is from Alfred de Vigny, *The Military Necessity* (1935; London, 1953), 5. The author, a poet,

served in the French army from 1814 to 1827. My translated copy of his account of life in a peacetime army does not give the original date of publication.

9. Schurz is quoted in George M. Fredrickson, *The Inner Civil War: Northern Intellectuals and the Crisis of the Union* (1965; New York, 1968), 8.

10. John Muir to Charles Sprague Sargent, June 21, 1898, Muir Papers CH.

11. *Sierra Club Bulletin* 1, 7 (January 1896): 271–284. Muir used similar effusive language in a journal he kept that summer: "Blessings on Uncle Sam's soldiers. They have done their job well, and every pine tree is waving its arms for joy." See Linnie Marsh Wolfe, ed., *John of the Mountains: The Unpublished Journals of John Muir* (Boston, 1938), 351–352.

12. *Sierra Club Bulletin* 7, 1 (January 1896).

13. On a wall in the Sierra Club's meeting rooms that night was a map of Yosemite National Park by Lieutenant N. F. McClure, a popular club member. The Dudley herbarium at Stanford is named after speaker William R. Dudley. Membership Records, carton 309, file 21, Sierra Club Records, Bancroft. N. F. McClure, "Explorations Among the Canons North of the Tuolumne River," *Sierra Club Bulletin* 1, 5 (May 1895): 168–186. Michael L. Smith, *Pacific Visions: California Scientists and the Environment, 1850–1915* (New Haven, CT, 1987), 134–136.

14. Christopher McGrory Klyza, *Who Controls Public Lands? Mining, Forestry, and Grazing Policies, 1870–1990* (Chapel Hill, NC, 1996), 66–69. Alfred Runte, *Public Heritage: The National Forest Idea* (Niwot, CO, 1991), 34–45. Holway R. Jones, *John Muir and the Sierra Club: The Battle for Yosemite* (San Francisco, 1962), 15–16. A few days before the Sierra Club meeting in November 1895, the annual convention of California fruit growers in Sacramento passed a resolution calling for stronger forest regulation. See *San Francisco Call*, Nov. 11, 1895.

15. For Muir's impromptu remarks immediately preceding Dudley's speech, see *Sierra Club Bulletin* 7, 1 (January 1896), 284.

16. If Muir was California's wilderness prophet, LeConte, then seventy-three, was its learned sage. A graduate of Columbia Medical School and Harvard's Lawrence Scientific School, he joined the University of California when its Berkeley campus opened in 1869. He spent his first summer in California exploring the Sierra Nevada, where he met Muir who had settled in Yosemite the year before. They became lifelong friends. Lester D. Stephens, *Joseph LeConte: Gentle Prophet of Evolution* (Baton Rouge, LA, 1982), 121–124, 213, 257–259. Smith, *Pacific Visions*, 44–47. LeConte, Muir, Dudley, David Starr Jordan (the scientist-president of Stanford), and a few others formed a core of civic-minded naturalists who helped forge the Sierra Club's early environmental activist identity. See also Michael P. Cohen, *The History of the Sierra Club, 1892–1970* (San Francisco, 1988), 1–38. *Sierra Club Bulletin* 7, 1 (January 1896): 268–271.

17. *Sierra Club Bulletin* 7, 1 (January 1896), 254–267.

18. Jones, *John Muir and the Sierra Club*, 15. Minutes of club meetings in the 1890s were lost in the 1906 San Francisco earthquake. Jones cites a report in the *San Francisco Call*, Nov. 25, 1894. Dudley's remarks, *Sierra Club Bulletin* 7, 1 (January 1896): 285. The first dean of the Lawrence Scientific School at Harvard (1846) and the first professor of the Sheffield School of Engineering at Yale (1847) were U.S. Military Academy graduates. See George S. Pappas, *To the Point: The United States Military Academy, 1802–1902* (Westport, CT, 1993), 274–276.

19. Alfred Rehder, "Charles Sprague Sargent," *Journal of the Arnold Arboretum* (April 1927): 68–87. Henry S. Graves, "Dr. Sargent's Contributions to Forestry in America," *American Forestry Magazine* (November 1921). Graves's glowing tribute is noteworthy because he was a protégé and successor of Gifford Pinchot.

20. Gifford Pinchot, *Breaking New Ground* (1947; Washington, DC, 1988), xxii ("my story"), 90–132.

21. Ibid. Henry Graves, "Dr. Sargent's Contributions to Forestry," wrote that *Garden and Forest* (hereafter *G&F*) led the way in calling for "a definite national forest policy" and that a historian could obtain from its pages "better than anywhere else a conception of the incidents of importance in the forest movement during that period." The introductory army editorials appeared in *G&F*, on Jan. 30 and April 3, 1889. The Fernow resolution is reported in *G&F*, Oct. 30, 1889.

For a notable example of the Sargent plan's misinterpretation by a distinguished scholar, see Michael L. Smith: "Sargent viewed the national forests as fortresses requiring only protection from human intervention. For Pinchot . . . forests were the working basis for establishing professional, scientific forestry in the United States. . . . Sargent's proposal . . . irritated Pinchot, not so much because of the defects he listed in that plan, but because it did not recognize the need for professional foresters" (*Pacific Visions*, 161–162). That is precisely how Pinchot described the Sargent plan, and it is wholly untrue. Sargent not only advocated professional foresters before Pinchot knew they existed, but in at least one instance he spoke out *against* converting part of a forest reserve into a national park (in Washington State) because there were not enough reliable data on how much of the forest "could more advantageously be turned over to settlement" or used for timber production on the sustained-use principles Sargent never stopped promoting. *G&F*, May 23, 1894.

22. *Century Magazine*, Jan. 7, 1893. George W. Gilder (editor of *Century*) to Daniel Lamont, March 13 and 14, 1893; summary biography of Daniel Lamont, Lamont Papers. Johnson to Lamont, May 5, 1893, file 8385 w/14573, AGO PRD 1890, RG 94, NARA. Johnson to Lamont, Sept. 7, 1893, citing exchange with Cleveland, Lamont Papers. Lamont to Johnson, Oct. 30, 1893 (referring to setting up a Hoke Smith request "along the lines of your suggestions"), RUJ Papers. Johnson to Henry T. Thurston, Secretary to the President, Nov. 24, 1893, Cleveland Papers, enclosing several articles and resolutions passed by forestry organizations supporting the Sargent plan.

23. Muir to Johnson, March 28, 1893, box 3, RUJ Papers. John to Louie, June 13, 1893, in William Frederic Bade, *The Life and Letters of John Muir*, 2 vols. (Boston, 1924), 2:269–270. Wolfe, *Son of the Wilderness*, 261–267. Stephen Fox, *John Muir and His Legacy: The American Conservation Movement* (Boston, 1981), 110–111. Muir to Sargent, April 12, 1894, Johnson to Muir, May 20, 1898, Muir Papers, Bancroft.

24. *Century* 49, 4 (February 1895): 626–635. Muir to Johnson, Sept. 14, Nov. 7, Dec. 13, 1894, box 4, RUJ Papers. *G&F*, April 23, Aug. 15, 23, 1894.

25. *G&F*, Jan. 7, 14, 21, 1891. Gifford Pinchot, *Breaking New Ground* (New York, 1947), xv–xviii, 32 (for "toehold"), 44–45. Michael Frome, *The Forest Service*, 2d ed. (Boulder, CO, 1982), 19–21. The Irish anecdote is in Fox, *John Muir and His Legacy*, 111. Sargent to Johnson, June 4, 1923, RUJ Papers.

26. *Century* (February 1895). Stephen Fox, in his fine study of the early conservation movement, inaccurately describes Pinchot's position in the symposium as "dissenting" from Sargent, Johnson, and the others in its opposition of the army. It is possible that Fox, who was no great fan of Pinchot, ignored the truth even when it was staring him in the face because he could not absorb a conjoined image of the "Indian-fighting" cavalry and his environmentalist heroes (*John Muir and His Legacy*, 110–111).

27. Muir to Johnson, Sept. 12, 1895, box 1; *San Francisco Call*, Nov. 20, 1895, from Muir to Johnson, box 4; "Extract from Proceedings, Special Meeting [Amer-

ican Forestry Association]," Springfield, Mass., Sept. 4 and 5, 1895; box 1; all in RUJ Papers.

28. "Extract from Proceedings," Sept. 4 and 5, 1895; typescript of Gibbs to Hoke Smith, Feb. 17, 1895; Sargent to Johnson, June 4, 1923, all in RUJ Papers. Pinchot, *Breaking New Gound*, 84–104.

29. Sargent to Johnson, June 4, 1923, RUJ Papers. Pinchot, *Breaking New Ground*. Jones, *John Muir and the Sierra Club*, 16–18.

30. Sargent to Muir, Nov. 5, 1896, Feb. 23, 1897, Muir Papers CH.

31. Pinchot, *Breaking New Ground*, 117–121. Gifford Pinchot, "How the National Forests Were Won," *American Forests* (October 1930): 615–619. Muir to Sargent, Oct. 28, 1897, Muir Papers CH. Technically, Pinchot's nomination as special forest agent came under the authority of a legislative amendment introduced by Senator Richard F. Pettigrew with key input from Pinchot that established a framework for forest administration into the twentieth century. On that basis, Pinchot later dismissed the Sargent Commission report as exerting no influence on Pettigrew's "priceless" legislation. It couldn't because Pinchot had co-opted it. A commission proposal for the Interior Department to "make such rules and establish such service as will insure the objects of such [forest] reservations" was stripped of its civil-military plan context and used to catapult Pinchot into government. The directions he received from new Interior Secretary Cornelius Bliss, which from all indications Pinchot drafted, were based on Sargent Commission recommendations. *NAS Report*, 42; Pinchot, *Breaking New Ground*, 117–121.

32. Sargent to Johnson, 1923, RUJ Papers. Roosevelt said Pinchot "stood first" among his domestic policy advisers, an assessment well attested by events; see *Theodore Roosevelt: An Autobiography* (1913; New York, 1985), 409.

33. For a typical exaggeration of the split on the conceptual level, see Roderick Nash, *Wilderness and the American Mind*, 3d ed. (1967; New Haven, CT, 1982), 134–138. Nash presents Muir and Sargent as pure forest preservationists, which they were not. For a corrective assessment of Pinchot's views and policies as they evolved during his long public career, see Char Miller, "The Greening of Gifford Pinchot," *Environmental History Review* (Fall 1992): 1–20.

34. *NAS Report*, 21–22. The report included two draft bills—one dispatching troops at once to protect the forest reserves, the other setting up administrative procedures under the Interior Department. For the genesis of the National Weather Bureau, see Major General Henry C. Corbin and Raphael P. Thian, *Legislative History of the General Staff of the Army of the United States from 1775–1901* (Washington, DC, 1901–1922). The complex transition to a civilian weather service took about a decade.

35. *NAS Report*, 21–22.

36. Ibid., 23–27. Pinchot, *Breaking New Ground*, 121.

37. Pinchot, *Breaking New Ground*, 21–31. William H. Goetzmann, *Army Exploration in the American West, 1803–1863* (1959; Lincoln, NE, 1979), 3–21. In an interesting metaphorical allusion, considering the significance of loyalty in martial virtues, Pinchot called Sargent's "military principles" "as out of place as a dog in a church" (*Breaking New Ground*, 122). See also Gabriel Sovulewski's self-assessment in Chapter 5.

My emphasis here is on a contrast within a dominant masculine paradigm between interpersonal character virtues that predate Judeo-Christian civilization and more abstract moral concepts associated with Judeo-Christianity in the conduct of public policy; it is in no way a celebration of that paradigm as the ultimate stage in the evolution of human values. For a good summary on virtue that incorporates gender influences, see Joan Williams, "Virtue," in *A Companion to American Thought*, ed. Richard Wightman Fox and James T. Kloppenberg (1995; Malden, MA 1998), 706–708.

38. *NAS Report*, 21–27, 42–43.

39. Sargent to Johnson, June 29, 1898, box 6, RUJ Papers. *G&F*, Oct. 12, 1890, and Jan. 20, 1892.

40. Samuel P. Hays, *Conservation and the Gospel of Efficiency: The Progressive Conservation Movement, 1890–1920* (Cambridge, MA, 1959).

41. For introductions to Francis Bacon's seminal ideas linking scientific knowledge and political power, see Steven Shapin, *The Scientific Revolution* (Chicago, 1996), 164; Bertrand Russell, *A History of Western Philosophy* (New York, 1959), 525–545; and Bacon's own utopian *New Atlantis*, reprinted without copyright date by Kessinger Publishing, Kila, MT.

42. Klyza, *Public Lands*, 70–74. *Theodore Roosevelt*, 409. Miller, "The Greening of Gifford Pinchot." Miller describes Pinchot's evolution in later life toward a stance more sympathetic toward natural preservation that included a "more inclusive vision for conservation [incorporating] the inherent interconnection between the conservation ethic and world peace," concluding that "it is Gifford Pinchot, not John Muir, who stands as a representative man." Would Muir have been more "representative," and of what, if he had taken a more outspoken position on world peace? There is also some question about the relative meanings of "spiritualism" and "materialism" in discussing the throbbing material dynamo we call nature. Muir stood out less for his ideas about nature than the vitality of his language and imagery and the way it integrated scientific observation and earthy sensuality. Sargent was inspired by it; Pinchot ran from it into ideational stratospheres.

43. *G&F*, May 23, 1894. Pinchot's "wilderness is waste" is quoted in White, *"It's Your Misfortune and None of My Own,"* 409. For Leopold, see Runte, *Public Lands*, xi.

44. *Annual Report, Secretary of the Interior, 1893* (Washington, DC, 1894), 110–111. If push came to shove, the army probably would have resisted a forest reserve assignment or shucked it off early in the twentieth century as the War Department reconstructed itself to assume a global role.

45. Mary Lee Stubbs and Stanley Russell Connor, *Armor-Cavalry, Part I: Regular Army and Army Reserve, Army Lineage Series* (Washington, DC, 1969), 4–39. On the western frontier during the nineteenth century, the personnel of a regiment were usually scattered among several small outposts.

46. For daily life in the Old Army, see Edward M. Coffman, *The Old Army: A Portrait of the American Army in Peacetime, 1784–1898* (New York, 1986), and Don Rickey Jr., *Forty Miles a Day on Beans and Hay* (Norman, OK, 1963). Rickey offers a good discussion on institutional organization in a chapter entitled "Regiments and Companies," pp. 75–87.

47. The 4th Cavalry was the first mounted unit to be called cavalry (they had previously been called dragoons). It was called the 1st Cavalry until an 1861 army reorganization produced its redesignation as the 4th Cavalry. For the 4th Cavalry's institutional history and character, I have relied on several official "unit histories," including *Fourth Cavalry United States Army, 1855–1935* (Fort Meade, SD, 1935), and *The History of the Fourth United States Cavalry, Prepared and Loyal* (Fort Riley, KS; undated but extending through 1991); see also *Cavalry Journal* 18, 1 (March 1994), dedicated to the 4th Cavalry, and Stubbs and Connor, *Armor-Cavalry, Part I*, 4–39.

48. For a discussion of the contemporary relevance of classical martial virtues, see Jonathan Shay, *Achilles in Vietnam: Combat Trauma and the Undoing of Character* (New York, 1995), especially 77–99.

49. Alfred Vagts, *The History of Militarism: Romance and Realities of a Profession* (New York, 1937), 178, 180. Tolstoy's comments are from *The Sepastopol Sketches* (1856; New York, 1986), 65–66. See also Russell F. Weigley, "The End of Militarism," *The Harmon Memorial Lectures in Military History, Number Fifteen* (Colorado Springs, CO, 1973).

50. Vagts, *The History of Militarism*, 96–108.

51. Texts of many of Washington's statements on this subject are in Robert K. Wright Jr. and Morris J. MacGregor Jr., *Soldier-Statesmen of the Constitution* (Washington, DC, 1987). The Cushman Davis quote is from the *Annual Report of the War Department* (Washington, DC, 1889), 1023.

52. Vagts, *The History of Militarism*, 96–108. Unlike Old Army officers on the frontier, the colonial administrators of European armies generally shared the attitudes of their civilian counterparts toward the native cultures they conquered and ruled. See D. K. Fieldhouse, *The Colonial Empires from the Eighteenth Century* (Frankfurt, Germany, 1965; New York, 1971), 177–396. A. P. Thornton, *The Imperial Idea and Its Enemies: A Study in British Power* (London, 1959; New York, 1968), 1–56, and Philip Woodruff, *The Men Who Ruled India*, vol. 2, *The Guardians* (London, 1954; New York, 1964), 64–91.

53. For redemption through the devout application of scientific principles to government administration, see Hays, *Conservation and the Gospel of Efficiency*.

54. The roots of the conflict-ridden relationship between abstract morality and earthy empathy is captured at its archetypal core in Herman Melville's *Billy Budd, Sailor (An Inside Narrative)*. For a revealing account of the novel's layered composition over a period of five years, in which the archetypal conflict captured by this "inside narrative" preceded the military symbols Melville subsequently developed to capture our "man-of-war" existence, see the edition prepared by Harrison Hayford and Merton M. Sealts Jr. (Chicago, 1962). *Billy Budd* is about Western civilization's unending war of self-conquest (its hidden "inside narrative") that produces a "man-of-war" world where modern civil and military law seek to moderate conflict ultimately beyond their reach.

55. "Civilization and" and "For the Puritan" are in Berkhofer, *The White Man's Indian*, 29, 81. For a recent analysis of how whites appropriated Indian imagery to enrich their sense of national identity, see Philip J. DeLoria, *Playing Indian* (New Haven, 1998). "The American theme" is in Perry Miller, *Errand into the Wilderness* (New York, 1956), 205.

56. "Higher Christian civilization" is in Francis Paul Prucha, *American Indian Policy in Crisis: Christian Reformers and the Indian, 1865–1900* (Norman, OK, 1976), 30.

57. Gates is cited in Prucha, *American Indian Policy in Crisis*, 153, from which this overall portrait also draws, esp. 30–227. "A commitment" is from David Wallace Adams, *Education for Extinction: American Indians and the Boarding School Experience* (Lawrence, KS, 1995), 15. "Cultural genocide" is the judgment of Wallace, *Jefferson and the Indians*, 276.

Patricia Nelson Limerick has a good chapter on "property values" in *The Legacy of Conquest*, 55–75, that places the "passion for profit . . . at the core of the Western adventure." She pays less attention to the religiosity of this passion. Perry Miller, *Errand into the Wilderness*, analyzed the religion dimension at length, although even he did not recognize how much the contradictory images of greed and selflessness, community and anarchy, depravity and transcendence, depended for their irreconcilable contradictoriness on the religious sensibility he was writing about. A subsequent interpretation that does just that is James D. German, "The Social Utility of Wicked Self-Love: Calvinism, Capitalism, and Public Policy in Revolutionary New England," *Journal of American History* 82, 3 (December 1995): 965–998.

58. For a summary of Old Army "total war" strategic doctrine that distinguishes it from the cultural totalism of settlers and Indian "reformers," see Lance Janda, "Shutting the Gates of Mercy: The American Origins of Total War, 1860–1880," *Journal of Military History* 59, 1 (January 1995): 7–36. For the military objectives of Old Army Indian warfare, see also Russell F. Weigley, *The American Way of War: A History of United States Military Strategy and Policy* (1973; Bloomington, IN, 1977), 128–166. Contemporary historians have exposed the many faces, some more hidden than others, of Indian cultural extinction. For the internal and external character of its most basic "holy war" manifestations, see Jill Lapore, *The Name of War: King Philip's War and the Origins of American Identity* (New York, 1998), in which Indian wars rage on in the minds of the victors and their uneasy descendants. For the uncertain origins of "the only good Indian," see Paul Andrew Hutton, *Phil Sheridan and His Army* (Lincoln, NE, 1985), 181–182. "We took away their country" is from Sheridan's report for 1878 as commander of the Division of the Missouri, *Annual Report of the War Department* (Washington, DC, 1878), 35–36. As with most officers, Sheridan's rhetoric on Indians alternated with his audience and its proximity in time to Indian engagements resulting in army casualties. See also Robert Wooster, *The Military and United States Indian Policy: 1865–1903* (1988; Lincoln, NE, 1995), 47, 108, 117, 126–128, 145. Francis Paul Prucha, in *The Great Father*, p. 548, cites an estimate of between 3,000 and 6,000 Indians who lost their lives in encounters with Old Army soldiers—far too many, but still much fewer than those murdered by local militia, vigilante groups, mobs, and lone gunmen, who accounted for most of the bloodshed on the American frontier in the nineteenth century.

59. Brian W, Dippie, *The Vanishing American: White Attitudes and U.S. Indian Policy* (Lawrence, KS, 1982), 131. John Gibbon, *Adventures on the Western Frontier,* ed. Allan Gaff and Maureen Gaff (1928; Bloomington, IN, 1994), 236–250. The book was completed in 1886 and published years after Gibbon's death.

60. Dippie, *The Vanishing American*, 131. Sherry L. Smith, *The View from Officers' Row: Army Perceptions of Western Indians* (Tucson, AZ, 1990), 16–38. Coffman, *The Old Army,* 74.

61. Prucha, *American Indian Policy*, 153. Colonel Richard Irving Dodge, *Our Wild Indians: Thirty-three Years' Personal Experience Among the Red Men of the Great West; A Popular Account of the Social Life, Religion, Habits, Traits, Customs, Exploits, etc.* (New York, 1882; Freeport, NY, 1970), 638–650. Dodge's memoirs include a chapter highlighting Mackenzie.

62. John G. Bourke, *On the Border with Crook* (1891; Lincoln, NE, 1971), 116–117, 445, 464. Crook introduced the use of pack mules rather than cumbersome supply wagons in his relentless pursuit of his adversaries, a tactical innovation that would be taken up by many others, including Mackenzie.

63. Bourke, *On the Border with Crook*, 116–117. Jerome A. Green, "George Crook," in *Soldiers West: Biographies from the Military Frontier,* ed. Paul Andrew Hutton (Lincoln, NE, 1987), 115–136. Donald E. Worcester, *The Apaches: Eagles of the Southwest* (Norman, OK, 1979; pbk., 1992), xiii–xvi, 115–143, 250–324. The excerpt from Crook's 1884 West Point address is from the text printed in the *Army and Navy Journal* (June 21, 1884): 959–960. After his successful tenure in Arizona

through the mid-1870s, Crook was called north on another assignment. He returned as head of the Department of Arizona in 1882 for a controversial reign marked by his request to be relieved in 1886 at the height of the Geronimo campaign in a dispute with Commanding General of the Army Sheridan.

64. See William H. Leckie and Shirley A. Leckie, *Unlikely Warriors: General Benjamin Grierson and His Family* (Norman, OK, 1984), especially 276–310; William H. Leckie, *The Buffalo Soldiers* (Norman, OK, 1967), 12–21, 54–59, 238–242; and Bruce J. Dinges, "Benjamin H. Grierson," in *Soldiers West: Biographies from the Military Frontier,* ed. Paul Andrew Hutton (Lincoln, NE, 1987), 157–176. For a short period after Crook and before Grierson, Nelson Miles commanded the Department of Arizona.

65. Grierson's comments are in his departmental report in the *Annual Report of the War Department, 1890,* vol. 1 (Washington, DC, 1890), 162–179.

66. Grierson, *Annual Report 1890,* 175. Between 1870 and 1890, New Mexico's population increased 67 percent to 153,595, and Arizona's increased from about 11,000 to 57,620. See Darliss A. Miller, *Soldiers and Settlers: Military Supply in the Southwest, 1861–1885* (Albuquerque, NM), 355. For the Tucson dedication, see Cornelius C. Smith Jr., *Fort Huachuca: The Story of a Frontier Post* (Washington, DC, 1977), 22.

67. Jack Foner, *The United States Soldier Between Two Wars* (New York, 1970), 28–29. Coffman, *The Old Army,* 78–79, 178–180, 390–392.

68. Prucha, *American Indian Policy in Crisis,* 30–72. For "that would mean," see Prucha, *The Great Father,* 514.

69. William Haas Moore, *Chiefs, Agents, Soldiers: Conflict on the Navajo Frontier, 1868–1882* (Albuquerque, NM, 1994), xvi, 21–27.

70. *Annual Report of the War Department, 1887,* 146. Robert Wooster, *The Military and United States Indian Policy: 1863–1903* (Lincoln, NE, 1995), 16–17.

71. *Annual Report of the War Department, 1887,* 142, 155. *Annual Report of the War Department, 1888,* 9, 123. A cavalry detachment under Harry Benson, who served longer in the California parks than any other officer, returned from duty at Round Valley in April 1892 only a few days before departing for Sequoia. See Lieutenant Colonel William Graham to Assistant Adjutant General, Department of California, April 27, 1892, file 280, Presidio LS, RG 393, NARA.

72. Peter Nabokov, *Native American Testimony: A Chronicle of Indian-White Relations from Prophecy to the Present, 1492–1992* (New York, 1991), 224.

73. Gibbon is quoted in Wooster, *The Military and United States Indian Policy,* 79. Dodge is quoted in Smith, *The View from Officers' Row,* 15.

74. Herman Melville wrote in *Billy Budd,* his valedictory inward exploration of the self-conquest phenomenon, that it rendered conscience "but the lawyer to [the] will"; it "fold[ed] itself in the mantle of respectability [and] justified animosity into a sort of retributive righteousness" (chap. 13).

CHAPTER 8. THE MILITARY METAPHOR

1. Herman Melville, *Moby-Dick,* chap. 99.

2. William James's 1910 essay is in John Roth, ed., *The Moral Equivalent of War and Other Essays* (New York, 1971), 3–16. The essay draws a sharp distinction between James's scheme and the preparedness movement: "It may even be said that the intensely sharp competitive preparation for war *is the real war,* permanent, unceasing." For a succinct statement of the preparedness concept, see

Leonard Wood, *The Military Obligation of Citizenship* (Princeton, NJ, 1915), 40–76. John Dewey drew on both James and Wood when he hailed the "social possibilities of war" for directing the economy toward public rather than private ends. See William E. Leuchtenburg, *The Perils of Prosperity: 1914–32* (Chicago, 1958), 41. Harry Benson's imbroglio with Wood is described here in Chapter 5. For Parker, see James Parker, *The Old Army: Memories, 1872–1898* (Philadelphia, 1929), 208. Dorst, responding to an inquiry in connection with a proposed commendation for Wood's performance during the Rough Riders' charge up San Juan Hill, reported that he found Wood lost in the grass without his horse. Dorst subsequently served under Wood in the Philippines and made no secret of his opinion that Teddy's favorite was a discredit to army values. "A Loss to the Army" was the headline of a lengthy lament in the *New York Times* on Aug. 5, 1911, following Dorst's retirement in frustration, which the *Times* attributed to Leonard Wood's revengeful refusal to permit the promotion beyond colonel of an officer who, the *Times* wrote, enjoyed "no superior in the army as a regimental commander." For the San Juan Hill episode, see Army Chief of Staff S. B. M. Young to Dorst, Dec. 19, 1903, Dorst to Young, Dec. 26, 1903, Dorst Papers. Dorst's letters from the Philippines to his wife in 1906 and 1907 are peppered with references to Wood, none complimentary; see box 3, Dorst Papers. S. B. M. Young got along with Wood, partly because Roosevelt, in his self-consciously manly way, fell in love with the old warhorse after meeting him in Yellowstone, where Young served after Yosemite, and patronized his career along with Wood's. Young seemed lost among that crowd and eventually retired to Montana; see Chapter 6.

The distaste of soldiers Benson and Dorst for Wood was comparable to the distaste of civilians Sargent and Johnson for Pinchot. Wood and Pinchot were both perceived as dishonest and disloyal manipulators who used morality as a cover for ambition; i.e., they lacked character. Perhaps not coincidentally, Pinchot and Wood used their specialized professions (forestry, army) as platforms for pursuing much broader political aspirations; both dreamed of being president. Pinchot and Wood were favorites of Teddy Roosevelt, the high priest of the manliness cult. For Teddy's obsessions with manliness, with emphasis on its racist dimension, see the chapter on him in Gail Bederman, *Manliness and Civilization: A Cultural History of Gender and Race in the United States, 1860–1917* (Chicago, 1996), 170–216, which includes this shades-of-Jefferson quote from Roosevelt's writings: "Whether the whites won the land by treaty [or] by armed conquest . . . mattered comparatively little so long as the land was won. It was all important that it should be won, for the benefit of civilization and in the interests of mankind" (p. 183).

3. The "general of industry" analogy is from David A. Wells, *Recent Economic Changes* (New York, 1889), quoted in Richard Slotkin, *Gunfighter Nation: The Myth of the Frontier in Twentieth-Century America* (New York, 1992), 90–91. Bellamy, George, and the army are discussed in the epilogue in Marcus Cunliffe, *Soldiers and Civilians: The Martial Spirit in America, 1775–1865* (New York, 1973), 434.

4. Randolph S. Bourne, *War and the Intellectuals: Collected Essays, 1915–1919*, ed, intro. Carl Resek (New York, 1964). Samuel P. Huntington, *The Soldier and the State: The Theory and Politics of Civil-Military Relations* (Cambridge, MA, 1957; pbk. 1985), 222–270, 289–314.

5. For the administrative transition to a New Army in the context of governmentwide centralization, see Stephen Skowronek, *Building a New American State: The Expansion of National Administrative Capacities, 1877–1920* (1982; New York, 1990), 85–120, 212–247. For a summary of the army's new global mission in its social and political context, see Foster Rhea Dulles, *America's Rise to World*

Power: 1898–1954 (New York, 1954), 1–87. For the centennial, see Colonel Thomas E. Griess and Jay Luvaas, eds., *The Centennial of the United States Military Academy at West Point, New York: 1802–1902,* 2 vols. (1904; New York, 1969). Near the end of volume 1 there appears a lecture by a relatively low-ranking engineer officer on a few nation-building activities: Captain William V. Judson, "The Services of Graduates as Explorers, Builders of Railways, Canals, Bridges, Light-Houses, Harbors, and the Like," 835–874; the Old Army's peacetime adjudication work, environmental protection, and other similar civic activities are not mentioned.

6. "Scarcely had enrollment begun when it became obvious that utter confusion would result unless the army was given a larger share of responsibility," writes John A. Salmond, *The Civilian Conservation Corps, 1933–1942: A New Deal Case Study* (Durham, NC, 1967), (quote on p. 31), from which this account of the army and the CCC is primarily drawn. Although there are few comprehensive scholarly studies like Salmond's, personal reminiscences abound. William B. Towell, "Remembering the CCC: Buck Meadows, California, 1933–34," *Journal of Forest History* 26, 4 (October 1982), 184–191, describes activities in and around Yosemite National Park. Towell recalls: "The equipment in the camp—everything we had—was furnished by the United States Army. In fact, the army was ultimately responsible for everything that went on in camp. Food, clothing, health, discipline, and recreation were under army supervision, and we ate meals out of regular army mess gear."

7. Salmond, *The Civilian Conservation Corps,* 31–40. See also Arthur Schlesinger Jr., *The Coming of the New Deal* (New York, 1960), 338–340.

8. Salmond, *The Civilian Conservation Corps,* 85–86. Salmond writes, "The attitude of the military is one of the reasons why close comparisons cannot be drawn between the CCC and the German Labor Service as it was modified under Hitler" (p. 86). Some enthusiastic officers proposed a training function for the camps, but their army said no (pp. 116–120).

9. For FDR's support for the army in disputes with civilian agencies, see Salmond, *The Civilian Conservation Corps,* 173–176. For assessments of the CCC from a military perspective, see Lieutenant Colonel Marvin A. Kreidberg and First Lieutenant Merton G. Henry, *History of Military Mobilization in the United States Army: 1775–1945* (Washington, DC, 1955), 462–463, and Erna Risch, *Quartermaster Support of the Army: A History of the Corps, 1775–1939* (Washington, DC, 1962), 729–730. Risch found that the complex CCC assignment helped the Quartermaster Corps smooth out its supply procedures for future wartime emergencies. Kreidberg and Henry concluded that the CCC's "overall effect" on military preparedness was negative, because so many competent officers were diverted to camp management when they should have been training soldiers. The experience for the army was doubly painful in that regard in that, despite being accused of using the CCC for training and perhaps even wishing it could, "the Army was scrupulously careful during the entire period of its supervision of the CCC *not* to provide any military training for the enrollees." The authors' italics express army frustration with the usual scapegoating.

10. Slotkin, *The Gunfighter Nation,* 352–365; movie script quote on 360.

11. No record of the private meeting between Sheridan and Mackenzie was kept, but Mackenzie confided what occurred to his adjutant who wrote it down. Michael D. Pierce, *The Most Promising Young Officer: A Life of Ranald Slidell Mackenzie* (Norman, OK, 1993), 125–141. Charles M. Robinson III, *Bad Hand: A Biography of Ronald S. Mackenzie* (Austin, TX, 1993), 124–144. Robert M. Utley, *Frontier Regulars: The United States Army and the Indian, 1866–1891* (1973; Lincoln, NE, 1984), 344–349.

12. Slotkin, *The Gunfighter Nation*, 352–365; quote on 359.

13. Ibid., 364.

14. For the America-Europe issue, see Richard H. Kohn, *Eagle and Sword: The Beginnings of the Military Establishment in America* (New York, 1975), 1–40, 193–219, and Russell F. Weigley, *History of the United States Army* (Bloomington, IN, 1984), 153–157. See also Walter Millis, *Arms and Men: A Study in American Military History* (New York, 1956), 13–71.

15. *Regulations for the Army of the United States* (Washington, DC, 1889), 197–213. See also Randy Steffen, *The Horse Soldier 1776–1943*, vol. 3 (1881–1916) (Norman, OK, 1978), and *U.S. Army Uniforms and Equipment* (Washington, DC, 1889; Lincoln, NE, 1986). Also, for a full-color volume that shows Old Army uniforms modeled by senior officers of that era (a kind of *Vogue Magazine* of Old Army fashion), see M. I. Ludington's two-volume *Uniforms of the Army of the United States* (Washington, DC, 1889). For full-color illustrations of the garb and implements of Indian warriors, which served similar purposes, see Norman Bancroft-Hunt, *Warriors, Warfare, and the Native American Indian* (London, 1995).

16. The officer's wife, Elizabeth Bacon Custer, is quoted in Thomas C. Railsback and John P. Langellier, *The Drums Would Roll: A Pictorial History of U.S. Army Bands on the American Frontier, 1866–1900* (Dorset, England, 1987), 15. See also *Drill Regulations for Cavalry of the United States Army* (Washington, DC, 1896), 465–466, and Steffen, *The Horse Soldier*, 86–92. Trumpets replaced fifes and drums for small and large unit signaling during the war of 1812.

17. Railsback and Langellier, *The Drums Would Roll*, 19.

18. Ibid., 22.

19. Ibid., 20.

20. Louis Untermeyer, ed., *The Poetry and Prose of Walt Whitman* (New York, 1949), 372.

21. William H. McNeill, *Keeping Together in Time: Dance and Drill in Human History* (Cambridge, MA, 1995), 34, 156–157.

22. Ibid., 107. See also John Keegan, *A History of Warfare* (New York, 1994), 127–136, for a complementary broad survey. Although McNeill's study is, by his own admission, a speculative "essay" meant to stimulate research into an underrated topic, he brings enormous erudition to his effort. See, for example, his *The Rise of the West, A History of the Human Community* (Chicago, 1963).

23. McNeill, *Keeping Together in Time*, 118–199.

24. Ibid., 122–133. John Keegan describes this development as a reintroduction "from classic literary models [of] the discipline and drill of the Roman Legions," although it no doubt involved considerable refinement of the character McNeill suggests (*A History of Warfare*, 327–328). In any case, muscular bonding in Christian Holland was more dissociated from the governing values of civil society than it was in pagan Rome.

25. See Alfred Vagts, *The History of Militarism: Romance and Realities of the Profession* (New York, 1937) 49–68, 166–181.

26. McNeill, *Keeping Together in Time*, 147–150; emphasis added.

27. Ibid., 68–73.

28. John Keegan, *Fields of Battle* (New York, 1996), 8, 17.

29. Ibid., 7.

30. For a critically insightful comic look at life on the western frontier, see Mark Twain, *Roughing It* (New York, 1872), the account of his experiences on the trans-Mississippi frontier during the 1860s.

The distinctiveness of American individuality vis-à-vis Europe's drew comment from Alexis de Tocqueville early in the nineteenth century (*Democracy in America* [1835; New York, 1990], vol. 2, 94–161). He used the term "individualism" (pp. 98–99) to explain its American application as an ideology that shaped social as well as individual values and threatened to throw the American citizen "back forever upon himself alone." In this context, community became a struggle against simultaneously self-liberating and self-isolating forces. The American historian Robert V. Hine, *Community on the American Frontier: Separate but Not Alone* (Norman, OK, 1980), 3–92, 127–162, 252–258, described American "associative community" as "perfectly appropriate to transiency in a world of strangers." Thus, community heroes who personified dominant American values remained those individualists who resisted community restraints while fighting against outlaw resisters of those same restraints. After saving the community, the socially alienated community hero rode off into the sunset, alone. This was fundamentally incompatible with Indian culture—or Old Army culture.

31. "In the lonely years" is from Richard A. Bartlett, "The Army, Conservation, and Ecology: The National Park Assignment," in *The United States Army in Peacetime: Essays in Honor of the Bicentennial: 1775–1975,* ed. Robin Higham and Carol Brandt (Manhattan, KS, 1976), 57.

32. The quote is from Charles A. Miller, *Jefferson and Nature* (Baltimore, 1988), 15. See also Catherine L. Albanese, *Nature Religion in America: From the Algonkian Indians to the New Age* (Chicago, 1990; pbk., 1991), 63–70.

33. "Newly-made" is quoted in the editor's introductory essay in James P. Ronda, ed., *Thomas Jefferson and the Changing West* (Albuquerque, NM, 1997), xiv. The study of Jefferson's Indian policies is Anthony F. C. Wallace, *Jefferson and the Indians: The Tragic Fate of the First Americans* (Cambridge, MA, 1999), 14. Jefferson's dreams of a "fee simple empire" of hardy yeomen lovers of nature are discussed in Henry Nash Smith, *Virgin Land: The American West as Symbol and Myth* (New York, 1950), 130–164. Two works by Merrill D. Peterson address Jefferson's multiplicity of messages from complementary angles, transmittors and receivers: *The Jeffersonian Image in the American Mind* (New York, 1962), especially 3–17, 266–268, 380–459; and *Thomas Jefferson and the New Nation*, (New York, 1970), 28–97, 518–590, 922–1009. Neither does justice to the dimension exposed and explored by Wallace.

34. Ralph Waldo Emerson, *Nature* (1836), in Carl Bode, ed., *The Portable Emerson* (1946; New York, 1981), 19–20.

35. Walker Cowen, *Melville's Marginalia* (New York, 1987), 518–533.

36. Muir's marginalia are in his copy of Emerson's *Prose Works*, vol. 1 (Boston, 1870), 183, 511, at the Beinecke Rare Book and Manuscript Library, Yale University. See also Muir to Sargent, March 25, 1900, Sargent Papers.

37. Donald Worster, *Under Western Skies, Nature and History in the American West* (New York, 1992), 251.

38. Perry Miller showed with typical insight how American mystical romanticism invoked nature "not so much for individual or artistic salvation as for an assuaging of national anxiety," thus making exploitation of nature easier (*Errand into the Wilderness*, 211).

39. For a summary of the Old Army's frontier administration mission, see Russell F. Weigley, *The American Way of War: A History of United States Military Strategy and Policy* (Bloomington, IN, 1973), 153–166.

40. There's a good description of a retreat ceremony in Charles King, *Life and Manners in the Frontier Army,* ed. Oliver Knight (Norman, OK, 1978; pbk., 1993), 167–169. Retreat requirements are laid out in the *Regulations for the Army of the*

United States that were revised every few years but remained pretty consistent for basic ceremonies during the post–Civil War period. See, for example, *Regulations . . . 1861* (Washington, DC, 1861), article 36, para. 585.

EPILOGUE

1. The early influence of Progressive ideas on public lands policy is described in Samuel P. Hays, *Conservation and the Gospel of Efficiency: The Progressive Conservation Movement, 1890–1920* (Cambridge, MA, 1959). For summaries of managerial and technological innovations in the military at the turn of the century, see Peter Karsten, "Armed Progressives: The Military Reorganizes for the Twentieth Century," in *Building the Organizational Society,* ed. Jerry Israel (New York, 1972), 196–230, and Matthew M. Oyos, "Theodore Roosevelt and the Implements of War," *Journal of Military History* 60, 4 (October 1996): 631–656.

2. Gabriel Sovulewski, "Troops and Acting Superintendents during Army Administration—Yosemite National Park," typescript memorandum, YNPL. *Yosemite Annual Report, 1899–1903.*

3. *Yosemite Annual Report, 1899–1904.* Alfred Runte, *Yosemite: The Embattled Wilderness* (Lincoln, NE, 1990), 57–99.

4. C. H. Shinn to C. S. Newhall, Nov. 22, Nov. 28, 1903, and Jan. 9, 1904, and the numerous statements taken during the army inquiry, October–December 1903, are in Yosemite Corr, RG 79, NARA. Gene Rose, *Sierra Centennial: One Hundred Years of Pioneering on the Sierra National Forest* (Clovis, VA, 1993), 17–24. Kevin Starr, *Americans and the California Dream, 1850–1915* (New York, 1973), 121–122, 374–375. Charles Howard Shinn, *Mining Camps: A Study in American Frontier Government,* ed., intro. Rodman Wilson Paul (1884; Gloucester, MA, 1965).

5. MacArthur to Secretary of War, Nov. 25, 1904, with attached "endorsements" from the Army Chief of Staff (Dec. 5), Secretary of War (Dec. 8), and Secretary of the Interior (Dec. 22), Yosemite Corr, RG 79, NARA.

6. Mackenzie's letter, dated April 27, appeared in the *New York Times* on May 5. Johnson was alert to the danger as early as March, as indicated by responses from Bliss to his inquiries dated March 22, April 23, May 6, June 7, June 9, in RUJ Papers. Joseph LeConte Jr. to Helen LeConte, June 8, 1898, LeConte Family Papers, Bancroft. See also Secretary of War to Cornelius Bliss, May 17, 1898, in PRD 1890, box 113, RG 94, NARA, where one can also find Bliss's urgent request to the war secretary for troops for the "overrun" park, dated June 17. Ultimately, the Department of California commander diverted a Philippines-bound cavalry unit of Utah volunteers to the park in July. But the following year, and every year thereafter until the formal army pullout, regulars were dispatched to the park—on time.

7. Inspector General's Report, Headquarters, Department of California, Nov. 11, 1903, copy at YNPL.

8. Bigelow to Shinn, June 18, Bigelow to patrol leaders, June 24, Bigelow to patrol post commander, July 22, 1904, Army Administration Papers, YNPL. Shinn to Commissioner, General Land Office, Oct. 3, 1904, file 5012, Yosemite Corr, RG 79, NARA. Bigelow's "battle" maps are at YNPL.

9. Bigelow to Agriculture Secretary, Aug. 14 (file 4004), and to Interior Secretary, Aug. 29 (file 4195), Sept. 9 (file 4925), 1904, Yosemite Corr, RG 79, NARA. J. N. Morris, "An Old Nature Trail Is Found Near Wawona," *Yosemite Nature Notes* 9, 3 (March 1930): 17–19. O. L. Wallis, "Yosemite Pioneer Arboretum," *Yosemite*

Nature Notes 30, 9 (September 1951): 83–85. Linda Wedel Greene, *Yosemite: The Park and Its Resources, a History of the Discovery, Management, and Physical Development of Yosemite National Park, California*, vol. 1 (Washington, DC, 1987), 361–365. *Yosemite Annual Report*, 1904.

10. Chittenden to Marshall, Oct. 16, 1905, Marshall Papers.

11. Marshall to Frank Bond, Dec. 14, 1904; Chittenden to Marshall, Oct. 16, 1905; Bond to Marshall, May 26, 1905; Marshall to Chittenden, Oct. 14, Oct. 25, 1905; Marshall to Needham, Oct. 14, 1905, Marshall Papers. When Marshall launched his campaign for Yosemite superintendent in 1904, he sought Chittenden's support and got it. "There is certainly no one whom I would rather recommend than yourself," Chittenden wrote on Dec. 6, 1904 (Marshall Papers), hardly a sign that Chittenden was "biased" in favor of a permanent army presence.

12. Robert Marshall, "National Park and National Monuments," Report to Interior Secretary, Nov. 30, 1910; Marshall to Benson, Jan. 2, 1912; Marshall to Chittenden, Nov. 21, 1912; Benson to Marshall, May 1, 1916; Marshall Papers. Horace M. Albright, *The Birth of the National Park Service: The Founding Years, 1913–33* (Salt Lake City, UT, 1986), 48–49. Donald C. Swain, "The Passage of the National Park Service Act of 1916," *Wisconsin Magazine of History* 50, 1 (Autumn 1966): 4–17. Marshall, a decent man who wasn't the first to lose perspective when he came to Washington, later found his proper calling as California state landscape engineer and originator of the important Marshall Plan for irrigation and water conservation in California's Central Valley.

13. *Yosemite Annual Report*, 1904. Benson to Interior Secretary, Aug. 2 (file 762), Aug. 6 (file 1906), 1906, Yosemite Corr, RG 79, NARA. Benson to Hiram Chittenden, June 11, 1904, copy in Marshall Papers. Charles P. Russell, *One Hundred Years in Yosemite* (1959; 1992, Yosemite, CA), 99–100.

14. Irish's remarks are in a news clipping reporting on a meeting of the California State Board of Trade, marked Jan. 1, 1904, in box 1, RUJ Papers. On Oct. 21, 1904, Clark wrote Johnson asking him to "use your influence" to get Yosemite National Park transferred to the forestry bureau, which he misnamed "Forestry Commission." See box 1, RUJ Papers.

15. Pinchot to Johnson, April 17, 1905; transcripts of Pinchot to Marsden Manson, Nov. 15, 1905, May 28, 1906, box 5, RUJ Papers. Theodore Roosevelt, Annual Message to Congress, Dec. 5, 1905, *The Works of Theodore Roosevelt: Presidential Addresses and State Papers*, vol. 4 (New York, 1909), 623. Runte, *Yosemite*, 79–82.

16. Gene Rose, *Sierra Centennial: One Hundred Years of Pioneering on the Sierra National Forest* (Clovis, CA, 1993), 17–24. Shinn to Pinchot, Jan. 17, 21, 1905, Pinchot Papers. Benson to Interior Secretary, June 5, 1906, July 17, 1908, National Park Service Central Files. In 1911, ex–Forest Service head Pinchot wrote California governor George Cooper Pardee supporting the application of his ex–Forest Service underling, "old Shinn," as a California state forester. Pinchot to Pardee, Aug. 21, Oct. 21, 1911, George Pardee Papers, Bancroft.

17. Linnie Marshe Wolfe, *Son of the Wilderness: The Life of John Muir* (New York, 1945), 289–294. Stephen Fox, *John Muir and His Legacy: The American Conservation Movement* (Boston, 1981), 110–147.

18. See Benson's correspondence with interior secretary, governor of California, and others, throughout 1906, in Yosemite Corr, RG 79, NARA, which also holds William E. Colby, secretary of the Sierra Club, to interior secretary, Sept. 10, 1906, applauding Benson. Albright, *The Birth of the National Park Service*, 64. Gabriel Sovulewski letter, *Sierra Club Bulletin* 21 (February 1936): 85–86. Lord James Bryce, British ambassador and author, visited Yosemite in 1909 and singled

out Sovulewski's trail building for special praise in a letter to the interior secretary, April 17, 1909, in National Park Service Central Files.

19. Odin S. Johnson, "History of the Development of the Communications System in Yosemite National Park," *Yosemite Nature Notes* 35, 5 (May 1956). Forsyth to Interior Secretary, July 15, 1912, National Park Service Central Files.

20. For a path into the voluminous documentation on Hetch Hetchy, see Roderick Nash, *Wilderness and the American Mind*, 3d ed. (New Haven, CT, 1982), 161–181; Hays, *Conservation and the Gospel of Efficiency*, 192–198; and Jones, *John Muir and the Sierra Club*, 118–169. Garfield to Colby, Feb. 9, 1909, William Colby Papers, Bancroft Library. Benson testimony, March 26, 1908, "Hearings on Hetch Hetchy," part 5, box 317, National Park Service Central Files.

21. Young to Interior Secretary, June 15, 1896, Yosemite Corr, RG 79, NARA. Benson testimony, March 26, 1908, "Hearings on Hetch Hetchy"; Forsyth to Interior Secretary, June 11, 23, Aug. 9, 1909; James E. Wilson, Acting Interior Secretary to Forsyth, Aug. 9, 1909, all in National Park Service Central Files. Those files contain a twenty-page memo summarizing Forsyth's arguments against work on Hetch Hetchy or Lake Eleanor.

22. The War Department accepted the Hetch Hetchy evaluation assignment after the Interior Department agreed to pay expenses. Secretary of War Jacob Dickinson to Secretary of the Interior Richard Ballinger, May 16, 1910; Ballinger to Dickinson, May 17, 1910; Whitman to Ballinger, May 18, 1910; Colby to Ballinger, May 19, 1910, all in National Park Service Central Files.

23. *Proceedings Before the Secretary of the Interior in re Use of Hetch Hetchy Reservoir Site, in the Yosemite National Park by the City of San Francisco* (Washington, DC, 1910), box 320; Forsyth to Interior Secretary, Aug. 12, Oct. 12, Oct. 30, 1912, all in National Park Service Central Files. The Army Engineers Report is quoted approvingly in William Frederick Bade, *The Life and Letters of John Muir*, vol. 2 (Boston, 1924), 422–423. McFarland's quote is from McFarland to Interior Secretary, Feb. 5, 1912, National Park Service Central Files. See also Muir to Robert Underwood Johnson, June 27, 1913, RUJ Papers.

24. Forsyth to Interior Secretary, Sept. 11, 1912, National Park Service Central Files.

25. Young to Interior Secretary, Oct. 18, 19, 1907, ibid.

26. Chief of Staff Leonard Wood to Judge Advocate General, Jan. 1, 1914, Military Secretary's Office Doc. No. 214547, RG 94, NARA. Chief of Staff office memorandum against troops in parks, Feb. 11, 1914; War Secretary to Interior Secretary, March 3, 1914, box 316, National Park Service Central Files.

27. For the 1914 transition, including Major Littebrant's often frantic efforts to communicate administrative complexities to an unprepared Interior Department, see National Park Service Central Files, 1914. See, for example, Adolph Miller's unsuccessful request for a troop of cavalry of Jan. 27, 1914, and Sovulewski's detailed charts and instructions on trail locale and maintenance (down to why signposts are better for marking trails than tree-harming blazes) of July 17, 1914.

28. Young's civil guard plan is cataloged in part 1, and the army's withdrawal from Yellowstone in part 3, of file 12-12-24, National Park Service Central Files. See also Yellowstone Consolidated File 1111272, Adjutant General's Office, and Brett ACP, both in RG 94, NARA. Brett was an old frontier campaigner who won a Medal of Honor.

29. Swain, "The Passage of the National Park Service Act in 1916." Alfred Runte, *National Parks: The American Experience*, 2d ed. (Lincoln, NE, 1987), 95–105.

30. Young Papers.

INDEX

Adams, John, 18, 20
Adams, John Quincy, 14, 20–21
Adjudication, 35, 297n5
Adjutant general's department, 46
A. E. Wood Campsite, 92, 236, 274n63
Agriculture, 16
Albright, Horace M., 147, 237, 245
American Association for the Advancement of Science, 31, 58, 74
American Civic Association, 240, 242
American Folk Lore Society, 31
American Forestry Association, 78, 192, 194
American Philosophical Society, 19, 20
Anti-Chinese sentiment, 211–212
Anti-park associations, 62, 265n30
Apaches, 139, 209
    raids by, 42
    tracking, 142
Arbor Day, at Presidio, 55
Archer, Catherine, 130, 131
Archer, Esther. *See* Dorst, Esther Archer
Armaments industry, public opinion on, 215
"Army and Forest Reserves, The" *(Century)*, 192
Army and Navy Journal, 140
Army Corps of Topographical Engineers, 29, 77, 254n22
Arnold Arboretum, 191
Arthur, Chester A., 78
Articles of Confederation, central government and, 3–4
Atkinson, Henry A., 69

Bacon, Francis, 292n41
Ballinger, Richard A., 242
Barlow, John W., 71
Barlow/Heap expedition, 77
Beaumont, Colonel, 151
Belknap, William W., 73–74, 77
Bellamy, Edward, 215
Bendire, Charles E., 280n52

Benson, Harry C., 155, 168, 176, 232, 235, 237
    bravery of, 139, 280n48
    Dorst and, 128, 132–133, 134, 135, 148
    Field Day and, 169
    Geronimo campaign and, 139–140, 142
    Hetch Hetchy reservoir and, 242
    mapping and, 142–143
    patrol by, 136
    photo of, 137
    Ridgway and, 141
    service of, 136, 138–145
    Sovulewski and, 145, 146, 147
    testimony of, 242
    Yosemite and, 136, 141–144, 153, 215, 238, 240, 241
    Young and, 167
    youth of, 138–139
Benson Lake, 138
Benson Pass, 138
Benton Barracks, 24
Bigelow, John, Jr., 237, 281n62
    arboretum/botanical garden of, 235, 236
    Geronimo campaign and, 32
Bighorn Mountains, 39, 41
Big Oak Flat toll road, 175, 177
Big Trees of California, 181
Billy Budd, Sailor (Melville), 293n54, 295n74
Black soldiers, 209, 235, 258n32
Bliss, Cornelius, 234, 291n31, 300n6
Board of Indian Commissioners, 39, 207
Bond, Frank, 236
Bonding, 203–204, 278nn15,19
    muscular, 222, 223, 224
    Old Army, 232
Boone and Crockett Club, 73, 286n49
Boundaries, 84–85
    adjusting, 172, 173, 236
    marking, 95, 99
    proposals for, 113
Bourke, John G., 30, 31, 258n31
Bowers, W. W., 175, 180
Brett, Lloyd, 245

303

Bridger, Jim, 69, 70
Bryce, James, 301n18
B Troop, 86
    Field Day and, 169
    Parker and, 168
Buckongehelas, quote of, 185
Budd, James H., 154
Buffalo-hunters, 39
Buffalo Soldiers, 209, 235
Bugle calls, 43, 44
Calhoun, John C., 13
California Academy of Sciences, 58, 118, 188
California Fish and Game Commission, 143
California State Geological Survey, map by, 94
Callipepla elegans bensoni, 138, 141
Cameron, James Donald, 152
Cameron, Simon, 152
Caminetti, Anthony, 152
Campbell, Donald Y., 176, 179, 180, 287n68
Campbell, Joseph, 277n13
Camp Gilroy, 117, 121, 163
Campgrounds, policing, 174
Camp Near Wawona, 92, 98, 102, 110, 274n63
Camp Yosemite, 272n41, 274n63
Capital punishment, 161, 283n16
Care of the Horse, The (Young), 160
Carlisle, John G., 119, 276n3
Carpenter, Robert Emmett, 80
Cattlemen, 179, 235
    dealing with, 111–112
    eviction of, 96
CCC. *See* Civilian Conservation Corps
Central government, strong/weak, 4
Century Magazine, 59, 62, 85
    criticism of, 67
    forest protection and, 192
    Johnson in, 60–61
    Muir in, 60, 122
    national parks and, 58
    Sargent plan and, 193
    Yosemite and, 61, 63, 65
Channels, 132
    going outside, 92, 105
    going through, 47–48
Cherokees, expropriation of, xiii
Cheyenne, 40, 41
Chinese Americans, Division of the Pacific and, 212

Chittenden, Hiram, 301n11
    proposal by, 236, 237, 238
    Yellowstone and, 267n45
Chowchilla Mountains, 89–90, 105, 107, 169
    climbing, 110
Civic duty, 12, 136, 227
Civic virtue, 76, 187, 197, 200, 253n10
Civil authority, 3–7, 23
    subordination to, 204, 205
Civil engineers, 14, 75, 254n25
Civilian Conservation Corps (CCC), 297n6
    criticism of, 216–117
    German Labor Service and, 297n8
    military training and, 297n9
Civilization, 12, 30, 224, 225, 236
    barbarism and, 213
    development of, 226, 228
    education and, 17
    ideals/scientific achievements of, 226
    Native American, 206–207
    natural world and, 206, 228
    Old Army and, 206–213
    primitivism and, 229
    savagery versus, 217
    torments of, 213
Civil law, subordination to, 204, 205
Civil service, reform of, 198
Civil society, xiii, 76, 222, 225–226, 298n24
    loyalty and, 202
    Old Army and, 204, 206, 219
    values governing, 224
Civil War, x, 12, 19, 37, 69, 202, 209, 210
    Fourth Cavalry and, 38
    Old Army and, 207
    Wood and, 24, 25
    Young and, 159
Clark, Galen, 238, 239, 301n14
Clark, William, 13, 69, 106
Class of 1887 (McClure), 119
Cleveland, Grover, 192, 195, 200, 276n3
Colby, William E., 241, 242
Cold War, 217, 219
Collins, George H., 178
Colter, John, 69, 70
Columbus, Christopher, 12
Communications, 92, 93–94, 153, 154, 163, 222, 226
    procedures for, 47–48
    telegraph, 27
    U.S. Army and, 27, 28–29
Companies, Old Army, 201

Concessionaires, 72, 99
Conger, Patrick H., 75, 79, 80
Conness, John, 59
Conness Trail, 123, 124
Conrad, Joseph, viii
Conservation ethic, 191, 292n42
Conservationists, 73
    preservationists and, 195–196
Continental Congress, 5, 6
Continental consciousness, 12
Conway, John, 270n3
Cooke, Jay, 70, 72, 74
Corps of Engineers, 55, 74, 280n47
    Ludlow and, 72
    Mackenzie and, 36–37
Crook, George, 139, 159, 210, 258n31, 294n62
    Benson and, 280n48
    Geronimo campaign and, 209, 295n63
    on Indians/whites, 209
C Troop
    Gale and, 121, 163
    mapping by, 121
    McClure and, 121
Cultural genocide, 207, 293n56
Cultural heritage, 186, 187, 208
Curtin, John B.
    on Benson, 138
    Rodgers and, 153, 154
    suit by, 99–100
Custer, George Armstrong, 12, 36, 38, 39, 73, 217
    Mackenzie and, 42

Dana, Edward S., 72
Dances, 221, 223
Daniels, Mark, 244
Davis, Cushman, 204
Davis, Milton F., 86, 104, 105
    absences of, 272n42
    exploration by, 101
    namesakes of, 272n44
    patrol by, 95, 97, 101, 111
    sheepherders and, 98
Dawes Act (1887), 207
Dean, Alexander, 86, 104
    arrest/court-martial of, 97, 127
    patrol by, 95
Death penalty, 161
Declaration of Independence, 3, 17
Delano Courier, on national parks, 62
Delta, 58, 62

Department of Agriculture, 192, 238, 241
    CCC and, 216
    federal lands and, 199
Department of Arizona, establishment of, 262n6
Department of California, 107, 234, 243
    Dorst and, 133
    establishment of, 262n6
    McClure and, 127
    Ruger and, 163
    Special Orders #38 of, 86
    Wood and, 106
    Young and, 167
Department of Columbia, 212
    establishment of, 262n6
Department of Texas, 41
Department of the Platte, 230
Dewey, John, 296n2
Division of Forestry, 192
Division of the Missouri, 76, 230
Division of the Pacific, 54, 211, 263n10
    breakup of, 262n6
    Chinese Americans and, 212
Doane, Gustavus C., 70, 71, 267n38
Dodge, Richard Irving, 213
Dorst, Archer, 134
Dorst, Esther Archer, 135, 275n78
    on Benson, 138, 141
    courting, 130, 131
    Joe and, 110, 129, 131, 133, 134, 136, 279n36
    pregnancy of, 132
Dorst, Joseph H., 33, 34, 41–42, 51, 52, 53, 87, 91
    Benson and, 141
    communications and, 47
    on depredations, 38
    Esther and, 130, 131–132, 279n36
    Mackenzie and, 35, 129
    patrol by, 107, 132, 134, 135
    photo of, 129
    policy implementation and, 86
    recollections of, 34
    report by, 30
    Rodgers and, 149
    Ruger and, 164
    on San Francisco, 54
    Sequoia and, 134, 164
    service of, 83, 128–136, 215
    on soldiers, 134
    Sovulewski and, 145, 146
    Wood and, 214–215, 278n18, 296n2

Drill procedures, 43–44, 45, 222, 223
Drill Regulations for Cavalry of the United States Army, 43
Dudley, William Russell, 188, 190, 191, 194
Dull Knife, 39–40, 41

Education, 16
   civilization and, 17
   democracy and, 17
   engineering, 20, 21, 191
   military, 18, 19, 255n36, 280n47
   moral, 211
   national establishment for, 17
   public, 176
   science, 18, 20, 21, 255n34
Eighth Cavalry, Young and, 159, 283n14
Elwell, E. L., 177
Emerson, Ralph Waldo, xi, 59
   on nature, 228–229
Endorsement, described, 47–48
Engineers, 16, 57
   civil, 14, 75, 254n25
   education for, 20, 21, 191
Entrepreneurs, 76, 81
Environmental ethic, x, xiii, xiv, 245
Environmentalism, 23, 144, 169, 170–173, 181, 199, 201, 230, 232
   Old Army and, x, 187, 237
   See also Preservation
Establishment, taking on, 173–182
Exploration, role in, 12, 13, 14, 19, 227

Farquhar, Francis P., 156, 158, 180, 287n68
Far West, as mythic genre, xii
Fatigue duties, 43, 44, 45
Federal law, 11, 62
Federally managed/mandated parks, 60, 266n44
Fernow, Bernhard E., 192
Field, Stephen, 275n78
Field Day, 169
Fifteenth Cavalry, 233
Fifth Artillery Band, 117
Fifth Artillery Battalion, 56, 168
Fifth Cavalry, 127
Firearms policy, 175–176, 177, 178, 265n30
Fires, 96, 189
   protection against, 113, 275n74
First Cavalry, 80, 292n47
Fish planting, 275n77, 281n61
Folsom, David E., 70

Folsom, Joseph L., 263n10, 267n46
Ford, John, ix, 2, 217, 219
Forest and Stream, 73, 78
Forest policy, 180, 189, 191–192
Forest reserves, 188–189, 240, 291n34
   management of, 170
Forestry, 191, 192, 197, 198
"Forestry Abroad" (Pinchot), 193
Forestry Bureau, Yosemite Valley and, 238–239
Forestry Commission, 195
Forestry schools, 196, 197
Forest service, civilian, 191, 196
Forsyth, James W., 168, 170, 302n21
   proposal by, 165, 166
   replacement by, 163–164
   Sequoia and, 164, 165
   Sheridan and, 284n19
   survey by, 284n24
   Yellowstone and, 165
   Young and, 167, 176
Forsyth, William W., 238, 243
   Hetch Hetchy reservoir and, 242
   photo of, 239
Fort Armstrong, 11
Fort Bliss, McClure at, 127
Fort Bowie, 140, 280n48
Fort Clark, 31, 32, 218
Fort Concho, 31, 38
Fort Ellis, 70, 71
Fort Hancock, Young at, 160, 161
Fort Hays, Fourth Cavalry at, 221
Fort Huachuca, 47, 56, 140, 259n45
   life at, 1, 42–43, 45
   Sovulewski at, 145
   Wood at, 33, 45, 53
Fort Leavenworth, 69, 160
Fort McKavett, Mackenzie at, 37
Fort Meade, 29, 30
Fort Richardson, 25, 35
Fort Riley, 29, 30
Fort Robinson, Dorst at, 34
Fort Sill
   Dorst at, 38
   Mackenzie at, 39
   Rodgers at, 149
Fort Snelling, farm at, 15
Fort Verde, 52, 53, 56, 262n4
Fort Walla Walla, Fourth Cavalry at, 51
Forty-first Infantry Regiment, 37, 38, 258nn32,33

Foucault, Jean, 213
Fourth Cavalry, 1, 30, 32–33, 85, 90, 133, 208, 211, 217
   Benson and, 139, 140, 141
   camp of, 52(photo)
   Civil War and, 202
   communications by, 47
   Davis and, 101
   Dorst and, 34, 128, 129, 130
   Field Day and, 169
   Forsyth and, 166
   Geronimo campaign and, 139
   Indian wars and, 40
   life in, 51
   Mackenzie and, 34, 36, 37–38, 41, 232
   McClure and, 123
   Mills and, 27, 256n5
   photo of, 129
   recognition for, 36
   regimental flag of, 201
   Rodgers and, 148, 149, 151
   rules and regulations for, 42–48
   Sovulewski and, 145
   Wood and, 25, 35, 46, 117
   Yosemite and, x, 42, 92, 168, 233
   Young and, 161, 163, 283n14, 284n17
Fourth Pennsylvania Cavalry, 158–159
Fox, Stephen, 290n26
Franklin, Benjamin, 19
Freedmen's Bureau, 38, 259n35
Frémont, John C., 60, 251n2
Freud, Sigmund, 213
Frontier life, xiii–xiv, 15–16, 189
F Troop, 239(photo)

Gale, George G. H., 107, 127, 152
   maps by, 121
Garden and Forest
   Pinchot and, 193
   Sargent in, 191–192, 198, 290n21
Garden myth, 186, 288n2
Garfield, James R., 241
Garrard, Joseph, 234
Gates, Horatio, 4, 5
Gates, Merrill E., 207
General Grant grove, 61, 135, 164
General Grant National Park, 61, 86, 146, 273n55
General Orders, 47, 160
George, Henry, 215
Geronimo campaign, 32, 33, 139–140, 142, 209, 280n52, 295n63
Giant Forest, 133
Gibbon, John, 208, 211–212, 213
Gibbs, Oliver Wolcott, 194
Gilded Age, 35–36, 74, 267n55
   corruption of, 214
   Indians and, 261n3
   Old Army and, 75, 268n56
   war and, 215
Gold, discovery of, 69, 84, 112
Golden Gate, naming of, 251n2
Golden Gate Park, 109
Goodrich, George, 177
Gould, Jay, 74
Graham, William Montrose, 86, 87, 100, 277n4
   career of, 57
   criticism of, 156
   full dress order of, 263n18
   lectures by, 105
   McClure and, 119
   morale boost by, 163
   Presidio and, 57
   Wood and, 58, 105, 117
   Young and, 163
Grant, Ulysses S., 24, 90, 135
   Mackenzie and, 36, 37, 258n29
   martial virtues and, 267n55
   Peace Policy and, 210
Graves, Henry S., 289n19
Graves, R. U., 171
Gray, Asa, 59
Grazing, 199, 234
   illegal, 99–100, 172
   public lands and, 154
"Great American Desert" thesis, 69
Greater Yellowstone Movement, 78
Gregg, J. Irvin, 159
Grierson, Benjamin H., 209, 210, 295n64
Grinnell, George Bird, 72–73, 78, 286n49

Hamilton, Alexander, 5
   on artillery/engineers, 16
   central government and, 4
   education and, 18
   military academy and, 6, 227
   militia and, 7
   nation-state idea and, 253n10
   peacetime establishment and, 6, 8, 18
   political weakness of, 252n10
   worldview of, 7, 227

Harmar, Josiah, 8
Harper's Weekly, on Mount Shasta, 59
Harris, Moses, 80, 81, 269n67
Harrison, Benjamin, 61, 86
    forest reserves and, 188
    San Francisco and, 53
    Yosemite and, 82, 83
Harrison, William Henry, 14
Hassler, Ferdinand, 20
Hatch, Rufus, 74, 77, 78
Hayden, Ferdinand V., 71, 77
Heap, David P., 71
Hetch Hetchy Valley, 125, 285n41,
        302nn21,22
    flooding, 239, 240
    hearings about, 242
    Muir and, 195, 241
    national park movement and, 242–243
    patrol in, 122
    reservoir in, 171, 242
Higginson, Stephen, 3
History of Militarism, The (Vagts), 1
History of Warfare, A (Keegan), 225
Hitchcock, Ethan Allen, 54, 234, 263n10
Hitler, Adolf, 224
Homesteaders, 95, 112, 123, 126, 234
Honesty, 202–203, 205, 267n55
"Horse Shoeing" (Dorst), 105
Howard, John, 176–177
Howard, Oliver O., 211, 212
Huachuca Mountains, 33, 42, 44
Hualpais, 209
Humanitarians, 207, 211
Humphrey, Heman, 185
Hunting, 174, 180, 286n49
    regulations on, 85, 265n30
Hutchings, James Mason, 74, 104, 237, 273n48
    Muir and, 266n40
    Yosemite and, 65–66, 67

Iliad (Homer), 203
Indian Bureau, 39
Indian cultures, 14, 226, 299n30
Indian fighting, ix, 9, 187, 216, 290n26
Indian lands, 10, 213
    obtaining, 11, 41, 206–207
    public domain and, 230–231
Indianness, Old Army and, 206–213
Indians. *See* Native Americans
Individualism, 99, 190, 202, 207
    American/European compared, 298n30

frontier, 160, 189
    nonadaptive, 230
    Old Army and, 76
Industrial Army, 215, 222
Infantry and Cavalry School, Young at, 160
Infrastructure development, role in, 14, 17
Inspector General Department, Wood and,
    33
Interior Department, 67, 68, 200, 231
    annual report by, 97
    CCC and, 216
    civil guard and, 243
    communicating with, 92
    complaints to, 179
    federal lands and, 199
    forest bureau for, 196
    forest reserves and, 291nn31,34
    national parks and, 74, 75, 273n55
    preservationists and, 242
    reports to, 135
    road building and, 79
    Rodgers and, 153, 154
    Sargent plan and, 194
    sheepherders and, 111
    timber cutting and, 172
    Yellowstone and, 72, 79
    Yosemite and, 82, 83, 106
    Young and, 174, 178–179
Internal Revenue, 96
Intuitive ecology, 22, 30
Irish, John P., 117, 193, 238, 266n40
"Italian Music in Dakota," lyrics of,
    221–222
I Troop, 86, 91, 96, 110, 115, 164
    camp by, 92, 105
    Davis and, 101, 119, 121
    Dean and, 97
    duties of, 103
    Field Day and, 169
    march of, 90, 108, 109
    McClure and, 116
    members of, 46
    patrol by, 100, 101, 102, 107
    in Raymond, 88
    Rodgers and, 164
    at Sequoia, 128
    trail blazing by, 102
    Wood and, 45, 46, 53, 87, 95, 128

Jack Main's Canyon, 125, 126, 277n12
Jackson, Andrew, 14, 185

Jackson's Military Road, 14
JAG (judge advocate general), 200, 201
James, William, 214, 295n2
Jefferson, Thomas, 7, 20, 69, 229, 252n10, 254n32
  continental development and, 227
  education and, 16, 17, 18, 19, 185, 255nn34,36
  on Indians, 228
  Louisiana Territory and, 13
  nation-building and, 14
  on Newburgh conspiracy, 5
  Old Army and, 227
  on peacetime standing armies, 3
  West Point and, 17, 19
  Williams and, 20
Jefferson Barracks, 144, 161, 163
Johnson, Andrew, 38
Johnson, Robert Underwood, 59, 62, 68, 85, 97, 114
  aesthetic preservationists and, 195–196
  campaign by, 60–61
  criticism of, 67
  forest protection and, 192
  national parks and, 58
  Noble and, 49
  Pinchot and, 194, 239, 240
  Robinson and, 104
  Sargent plan and, 192, 194
  at Tuolumne Meadows, 60
  Wood and, 117
  Yosemite and, 63, 65, 67, 82, 264n25
  Yosemite Defence Association and, 122, 286n49
Johnson-Muir campaign, 63, 64, 67, 122
Jones, William A., 55
Jordan, David Starr, 122
Judeo-Christian morality, 203, 205, 207, 227, 291n37
  Old Army and, 220
Judge advocate general (JAG), 200, 201

Kalugin, Adjutant, 204
Keegan, John, 225, 298n24
Keilty, James F., 177, 178
Keyes, Erasmus D., 208
Kickapoos, 218
Kingman, Daniel C., 79–80, 236
King Philip's War, xiii
Kiowa and Comanche war, 32
Kipling, Rudyard, 53, 54

Knox, Henry, 4, 18
  army rebellion and, 5
  peacetime army and, 10
  Trade and Intercourse Acts and, 9
Korean War, *Rio Grande* and, 218–219
K Troop, 53, 86, 110, 235
  Benson and, 141
  departure of, 108
  Dorst and, 52, 87, 128, 145
  life in, 131
  mapping by, 127
  at Mineral King, 131
  Parker and, 164
  patrol by, 107, 134
  Rodgers and, 121, 127, 152, 168
  at Sequoia, 128
  Sovulewski and, 145, 146
  at Wawona, 153
Ku Klux Klan, 38

Labor Department, CCC and, 216
Lake Eleanor, 126, 242, 302n22
Lake Ostrander, trout in, 114
Lake Yellowstone, 77
Lamont, Daniel, 192
Land claims, 103, 173, 185. *See also* Indian lands
Land-grabbing, 10, 171, 210, 213
Land management, 192
Landowners, confronting, 103
Land thieves, moving against, 11
Langford, Nathaniel P., 70, 72, 74, 77
Langtry, Lillie, 90
Lawrence School of Engineering (Harvard), 21
Lawton, Henry W., 32, 139
  Benson and, 140
  on Mackenzie, 36, 42
Leadership, 201–206
  character virtues for, 202–203
  Mackenzie school of, 35–42, 86, 93, 128
LeConte, Joseph N., Jr., 122, 189
  on individualism, 190
  map by, 276n2
  on sheep grazing, 234
  wilderness and, 289n16
Lee, Robert E., 38, 159, 202
Legacy of Conquest, The (Limerick), 186
Leidig, Ranger, 238
Leonard, Archie, 66–67
Leopold, Aldo, 199

Levi Strauss Company, 100
Lewis, Meriwether, 13, 14, 69, 106
Lewis, Washington B. "Dusty," 147
Limerick, Patricia Nelson, 288n2
    conquest concept of, 186–187
    on property values, 293n57
Lincoln, Abraham, 59, 152
Littebrant, William T., 244, 302n27
Lockett, James, 164
Lockwood, John A., 108, 111, 274n59
Lone Wolf, 32
Long, Stephen D., 13, 69
Los Angeles Herald, 97
Louisiana Purchase (1803), 12, 13, 14, 17
Loyalty, 223, 267n55
    Old Army and, 201–206
    symbols of, 201
Ludlow, William, 30, 77
    report by, 21–22, 73, 267n50
    Yellowstone and, 59, 72

MacArthur, Arthur, 234, 235
Mackenzie, George G., 63, 67, 85, 234
    reports by, 64
Mackenzie, Ranald Slidell, 34, 86, 151, 209,
        210, 213, 217, 229–230
    assessment of, 218, 219, 258n31, 278n19
    band of, 221
    death of, 41
    Dorst and, 128, 129
    horse thieves and, 38–39
    Indian wars and, 39–40
    Rodgers and, 148, 149–150
    service of, 258n29
    Wood and, 35
    Young and, 156, 161
Mackenzie school of leadership, 86, 93, 128
    students of, 35–42
Madison, James, 14, 252n10
Manifest destiny, 163, 186, 205
"Map of the Yosemite National Park," 94
Mapping, 27, 30, 68, 72, 95, 101, 118, 121,
        123, 124, 127, 142–143, 171, 227, 243
    Old Army, 103
    topographical, 29, 94, 272n46
    weather, 28
Mardi (Melville), ix
Mariposa Big Tree Grove, 87
Mariposa Gazette, 91, 100, 175, 180, 265n29
    on Field Day, 169
    on national parks, 62

on park regulations, 181
on Yosemite, 84
Marshall, Robert Bradford, 236, 237,
    301nn11,12
Martial virtues, 203, 204, 253n10, 267n55,
    291n37
Mason, Squire, 151
Materialism, 265n30, 292n42
Mather, Stephen T., 147, 237, 245
Maurice of Orange, drill procedures and,
    223
McClellan, George, 38, 202
McClure, Nathaniel Fish, 138, 147, 155, 168
    Benson and, 141
    death of, 276n3
    Dorst and, 148
    expedition by, 153, 277n9
    mapping by, 94, 121, 127, 128, 142, 171,
        271n23, 289n13
    naming by, 277n12
    patrol by, 122, 124, 125, 126–127
    photo of, 120
    quote of, 118
    service of, 119, 121–128
    sheepherders and, 125
    trailblazing by, 123, 126
McConnell, H. H., 259n35
McDougall, Alexander, 4
McFarland, J. Horace, 240, 242
McHenry, James, 18
McLean, Juno T., 181
McNeill, William H., xi, 222, 224
Means, Jack, 277n12
Melville, Herman, xii, 293n54, 295n74
    on Emerson, 229
    Muir and, 229
    quote of, ix, 214
Merced River, 114, 168, 236
Meterological observations, 15, 28
Metternich, Richard von, 186
Mikhailov, Lieutenant-Captain, 204
Miles, Nelson A., 286n52, 295n64
    on Benson, 139
    Forsyth and, 284n19
    Geronimo campaign and, 32
Military dependents, 176
Military education, 18, 19, 255n36, 280n47
Military Information Division, 152
Military journals, 16
Military metaphor, understanding/
    evaluating, 225

Military Philosophical Society, 20
Military preparedness, 214–215, 222, 295n2, 297n9
Military symbolism, 214, 224
Militia, 6, 7, 268n57
Miller, Adolph C., 244, 245, 302n27
Miller, Perry, 299n38
Miller, Wentz, 151
Mills, Anson, 54, 57, 85, 86, 133
    career of, 25–27
    Wood and, 25–26, 27
    Young and, 284n17
Miners, dealing with, 111, 112, 172
Mining claims, 103, 112, 172, 173, 199
Missionaries, 185, 210, 211, 226, 288n3
    exploration and, 12
Mixed use principles, 243, 245
Moby-Dick (Melville), 214
Monroe, James, 14
Monumentalism, 144, 265n29
"Moral Equivalent of War, The" (James), 214
Morris, Alexander, 4, 8
Muir, John, 22, 30, 59, 61, 64, 66, 68, 102, 123, 127
    Benson and, 242
    criticism of, 67
    death of, 195, 264n25
    on entrepreneurism, 65
    environmental activism of, ix, 187, 292n42
    Marshall and, 236
    Melville and, 229
    outlook of, 144–145
    Pinchot and, 193, 194, 195, 240
    preservationists and, 195–196, 241, 291n33
    quote of, viii, 188
    Sargent and, 192, 193, 194, 195
    Sequoia and, 58
    at Tuolumne Meadows, 60
    wildlife protection and, 174
    writing of, xi, 122
    Yosemite and, 67, 82, 84, 188, 192, 264n25
    Yosemite Defence Association and, 122, 286n49
    Young on, 181
Muir, Louie, 192
Munn, Dr., 151
Music, Old Army, 220–222
Myers, John, 251n2

Napoleon, 204
Nation, 61
National Academy of Sciences, 191
National community, 14, 23, 108
National debt, paying off, 8, 11–12
Nationalism, 227
    American/European, 144
    ecological, 226, 232
    monumentalism and, 144
    patriotic, 253n10
    scenic, 144
Nationalists, centralizing aims of, 4
National park concept, 107, 170
National parks
    accessibility of, 173
    campaign for, 67
    civilian agency for, 243
    creation of, 62, 264n20
    forest reserves and, 240
    grazing and, 100
    Hetch Hetchy and, 242–243
    management of, 97, 170
    Old Army and, ix, 72, 107, 113
    opposition to, 62
    protection of, 231
    public lands and, 265n30
    state parks and, 272nn37,41
"National Parks and Forest Reservations, The" (Sierra Club), 189
National Park Service, ix, xi, 106, 244
    establishment of, 146, 233, 237, 245
    Sovulewski and, 145, 146, 241
National service, 108, 245
National Weather Bureau, 28, 190, 196, 243
Nation building, 13, 16, 260n2, 297n5
    Old Army and, 197
    unconventional, 161
    U.S. Army and, 14, 19, 23, 51, 197
Native Americans, 84
    humanitarians and, 211
    policies toward, 10, 261n3
    trails by, 266n40
Natural environment, 206, 225, 228
Natural resources, destruction of, 189
Nature, 108, 206, 225
    attitudes toward, xiii
    civilization versus, 206
    conquest of, 226, 228
    study of, 228–229
    U.S. Army and, 75
    Wood and, 25–26

Navajo, 209, 211
New Army, 2, 232, 237
    evolution of, 261n3, 273n53
    McClure and, 119
    Old Army and, 215
Newburgh conspiracy, 5, 6, 252n8, 253n10
Newsham, Thomas J., 64, 67, 82,
    266nn36,39
    Yosemite and, 65, 66
New Western History, xii, 256n44, 288nn4,8
New York Sun, 75
New York Times, 99, 234
Ninth Cavalry, 233, 235
Noble, John W., 61, 64, 93, 95, 108, 274n58
    annual report by, 104–105, 270n6
    national park management and, 97
    on park bill, 85
    quote of, 49
    Robinson and, 104
    rules/regulations and, 96
    troop requests and, 107
    Wood and, 100, 104, 110, 271n29
    Yosemite and, 65, 82, 83
Nordov, Count, 204
Norris, Philetus W., 74, 75, 78, 79
North, Oliver, 219
Northern Pacific Railroad, 71
    Yellowstone and, 70, 75, 77

Obzogov, Captain, 204
Old Army, xiv, 23, 24, 170, 202, 211
    administration by, 35, 107, 297n5
    campground policing by, 174
    civic dimension of, xi–xii, 187, 197, 232
    as communal society, 229–230
    distortion of, 219
    ethical challenges for, 205–206
    European inheritance of, 204, 293n52
    frontier routine of, 221
    guiding myths of, xi, 219–225
    institutional values of, 200
    life in, 21, 44, 47, 57
    literal/metaphorical conflicts and, 206
    military memory of, 216
    mission of, 28, 201, 231, 232
    passing of, 215, 237
    prejudices/predilections and, 213
    raw nature/abstract absolutisms and,
        228–229
    religious revival and, 210
    reports by, 34–35

    rules/regulations of, 223
    scapegoating of, 228
    virtues of, xii, 201–206, 206–213
    western settlement and, xiii, 2
Olmsted, Frederick Law, 60, 65, 144, 264n24
Olney, Warren, 175
Origins of Satan, The (Pagels), 183
Overnight camps, described, 45

Pacheco Pass, 109
Pacific Railroad Surveys, 13
Pagels, Elaine, 183
Palace Hotel, 53, 59
Pallahchun, 90, 91
Panic of 1873, 72
Parker, James, 42, 54, 86, 149, 151, 163, 215
    mapping by, 273n46
    Wood funeral and, 117
Patriotism, 11, 23, 108
"Patrolling Yosemite" (*Los Angeles Herald*),
    97
Patrols, 124–127, 132, 135, 136, 153, 201
    described, 101
    in Yosemite, 86, 106–117, 122
Peacekeeping, 11, 23, 38, 51, 161, 185
Peace Policy, 210
Peacetime establishment, 7, 8, 10, 16, 18
Perkins, George C., 166, 178, 179–180
    railway bill and, 170
Perry, Matthew C., 149
Perry, Oliver H., 149
Pettigrew, Richard F., 291n31
Philadelphia Sunday Press, 157–158
Physical geography, 29, 230, 256n8
Pike, Zebulon M., 69
Pinchot, Gifford, 143, 188, 191
    conservationists and, 195–196
    Forest Service and, 234, 239, 240
    imperialistic designs of, 106
    on military principles, 291n37
    mixed use and, 243, 245
    Muir and, 193, 195
    national parks and, 240
    preservation and, 234, 292n42
    Sargent and, 193, 195, 197, 198, 199,
        290n21, 292n42
    Sargent plan and, 193, 194, 290n21
    Yosemite and, 238, 239, 240
Place names, 128, 251n2, 277n12
Policing, 174, 197, 211, 268n57
Polk, James Knox, 14

Polo, Marco, 13
Porter, Peter B., 21
Powder River expedition, 33, 39
Powell, John Wesley, 230
Preciado, A. E., 100
Preparedness movement, 214–215, 222,
    295n2
Preservation, 65, 96, 106, 108, 121–122, 165,
    190, 216, 241, 297n5
  hunters/fisherman and, 286n49
  Old Army and, 237
  public support for, 240
  tourism and, 173, 286n45
Preservationists, 171–172, 242
  civilian, 245
  conservationists and, 195–196
  Sargent Plan and, 188–201
Presidio, 25, 33, 85, 87, 116, 144, 166
  Arbor Day at, 55
  Benson at, 139
  communicating with, 92
  described, 1, 54–55, 56, 58, 105, 108,
    134
  Dorst at, 57, 131, 133, 134
  Fourth Cavalry at, 51–57, 256n5
  Frémont at, 251n2
  Gale at, 121
  Jug Wood at, 57, 114, 275n84
  Leonard Wood at, 56, 263n15
  McClure at, 121
  as open post, 263n12
  Parker at, 57
  Rodgers at, 152
  wintering at, 105–106
  Young at, 163, 167, 167
Primitivism, 228, 229
Principles of Strategy (Bigelow), 235
Private property, 207, 230
Proctor, Redfield, 51, 52, 82, 83, 86
Professionalism, 197, 262n3
Progressive Era, 200
  generals of industry and, 215
  military symbolism during, 214
"Proper Employment of Cavalry in War,
    The" (Wood), 105
Public domain
  defining, 10
  Indian lands and, 230–231
  U.S. Army responsibilities in, 11–12
Public land, 71, 231
  exploitation of, 62

forested, 190
grazing on, 100, 154
improving, 165, 175
national parks and, 265n30
Old Army and, 167, 168
preserving, 165
Progressive ideas on, 300n1
Public service, 22–23, 180, 196
  Old Army and, 198, 267n56
Puritans
  education and, 17
  symbols of, 206
Pyne, Stephen J., 113

Quartermaster Corps, 56–57, 297n9

Railroads, 13, 113, 173
  national parks and, 61, 70, 75, 77
  schemes by, 75
Raymond, 87, 105, 110
  described, 88
  supplies at, 107
  Wood in, 89
Raynolds, William F., 69, 71
Red Cloud Agency, 40
Redemptive conquest, 185–187
Regimental bands, 117, 221, 231
Regulations for the Army of the United States,
    44, 47, 220
Remington, Frederic, 32–33
Reservoirs, 170–171, 173
Retreat, described, 44
Revolutionary War
  paying debt from, 8
  professional military and, 3
Reynolds, F. Angevine, 100
Ridgway, Robert, 140, 141
Rio Grande (movie), 217
  inspiration for, 218–219
  metaphorical message of, 219
Road-building, 79, 80, 197, 243, 254n25
  military, 13–14
  role in, 16
Robinson, Charles D., 64, 85, 97, 114, 237
  Hutchings and, 66
  rantings of, 88, 115–116, 270n1
  on troop deployments, 115
  Wood and, 104, 115
  Yosemite and, 63, 65, 67
  Yosemite Indians and, 275n79
Rock Springs, Wyoming, 211

Rodgers, Alex "Sandy," 41, 141, 143, 170, 188, 232
  authority of, 153, 155
  on cattlemen, 154
  in Europe, 152
  Field Day and, 169
  "general staff" planning function and, 282n81
  mapping and, 142
  personal history of, 149, 152
  photo of, 150
  policies of, 154
  report by, 172
  reservoir and, 171, 241
  service of, 148–155
  Sovulewski and, 146
  wildlife protection and, 174
  Young and, 171
Rodgers, Christopher Raymond Perry, 149
Rodgers, George Washington, 149
Rodgers, Virginia Cameron, 152
Roll call, 45
Roosevelt, Franklin D., 216, 217
Roosevelt, Theodore, 114, 156, 214, 215
  assessment by, 243
  global power/naval display and, 233
  Johnson and, 286n49
  on national parks, 240
  Pinchot and, 195, 199, 296n2
  Sargent plan and, 193
  Wood and, 140, 296n2
  Young and, 157
Root, Elihu, 261n3
Rough Riders, 114, 140, 214, 215, 296n2
Round Valley Reservation, 212
Ruger, Thomas, 57, 86, 284n19
  replacement of, 163–164
  Wood and, 117
Rules and regulations, 181, 223
  rhythm of, 42–48
  violation of, 96
Ruskin, John, 90
Russell, Carl P., 147

San Carlos agency, 209
San Francisco
  described, 53–54, 55
  Fourth Cavalry at, 54
  marching to, 51–58, 109, 167
  mining and, 265n28
  national parks and, 62–63

San Francisco Call, 194
San Francisco Chronicle
  on park legislation, 63
  on Yosemite, 152
San Francisco Examiner, 168
Sanger Lumber Company, 178
San Joaquin Valley, 90, 109–110
Santa Clara Mountains, crossing, 109
Sargent, Charles Sprague, 199–200, 290n26
  environmental activism of, 187
  on esprit de corps, 198
  military principles and, 291n37
  Muir and, 229
  Pinchot and, 193, 194, 198, 199, 290n21, 292n42, 296n2
  preservationists and, 195–196, 291n33
Sargent Plan, 290n21
  Pinchot and, 291n31
  preservationists and, 188–201
  recommendations of, 195–196
  support for, 192, 193, 194, 290n22
Schofield, John M., 83, 132
Schurz, Carl, 74, 187
Science, 15, 185, 227
  education in, 20, 21
Scott, Winfield, 208
Sell, William M., Jr., 91
"Sentiments on a Peace Establishment" (Washington), 6
Sequoia gigantea, 103
Sequoia National Park, 30, 42, 67, 118, 133, 146, 175
  Davis at, 272n42
  Dorst at, 35, 130, 132, 134, 136, 145
  facilities/improvements in, 165
  forest reserve and, 189
  K Troop at, 145
  patrolling, 86, 106
  troops for, 106
Settlement, xiii, 51, 185, 186, 187
Seventeenth Infantry Regiment Band, 221
Seventh Cavalry, 29, 36, 38
Sheep, 271n27
  migration of, 97–98, 133
Sheepherders, 104, 123–127, 179, 234, 235
  allotment system for, 274n69
  arrest of, 97, 98
  checking, 98, 101
  educating, 111
  eviction of, 96, 142
  trespassing by, 99

wildlife population and, 155
Sheffield School of Engineering (Yale),
    72
Sheridan, Phil, 38, 73, 74, 106, 208, 217
    buffalo extermination and, 259n37
    Forsyth and, 284n19
    Indian warfare and, 207
    railroad barons/investors and, 76–77
    strike breaking by, 268n57
    winter campaigning and, 257n25
    Yellowstone and, 71, 77, 78, 81, 82, 164
Sherman, William Tecumseh, 24, 31, 295n63
    Dorst and, 130–131
    resignation of, 263n10
    Rodgers and, 149, 151
    troops of the line and, 255n36
Shinn, Charles Howard, 233, 237
    anti-army campaign of, 234
    Bigelow and, 235
    sheep encroachment and, 243
    Sierra Forest Reserve and, 240
Shippee, R. U., 100, 116, 275n82
Shoshone, 84, 269n67
Sierra Club, 141, 158, 174, 176, 179, 180,
    242
    Benson and, 241
    Dudley and, 190
    environmentalism and, 121–122, 289n16
    forest preserves and, 189
    forest regulation and, 289n14
    history of, 118, 276n2
    Marshall and, 236
    McClure and, 118, 127
    Muir and, ix, 118, 122, 188, 230
    park-centered focus of, 189
    Sargent plan and, 193, 194
    Yosemite and, 118, 152
Sierra Club Bulletin, 143, 156, 180, 182
    McClure in, 118, 122, 123, 127, 277n9
Sierra Forest Reserve, 165, 169, 188–189,
    190, 233, 240
Sierra Madre, 138
Sierra Nevada, 62, 67, 86, 87, 88, 106, 107,
    167–68
    forest reserve and, 189
    mining claims in, 112
    national parks in, 58
Signal Corps, 27, 28, 241, 261n2
Silver, discovery of, 69
Sitting Bull, 40
Sixth Cavalry, 233

photo of, 239
Skelton, William B., 262n3
Slotkin, Richard, 218–219
Smedberg, William, 153, 155
Smith, Earl, 40
Smith, Hoke, 116, 164, 170, 194
    budget request by, 166
    Forsyth and, 165, 166
    Robinson and, 114
    Sargent plan and, 192
Smith, Michael L., 290n21
Smith, Persifor F., 262n10
Smithsonian Institution, 138, 280n45
Snyder, James B., xi, 274n69
Social development, 223
Social life, Old Army, 202, 221
"Soldaten Lieder," 221
Soldier heroes, 136
"Some Elements of Discipline" (Dorst), 105
Southern Mines, 84
Southern Pacific Railroad, 87, 265n27
    silver spike for, 210
    Yosemite National Park and, 61
Sovulewski, Gabriel, 244, 302n27
    on Benson, 142
    death of, 147
    Dorst and, 128, 135, 148
    intuitive approach of, 147
    service of, 145–148
    on trail building, 148, 302n18
    Yosemite and, 146, 147, 241
Sovulewski, Inez Rose Rider, 146, 281n70
Spanish-American War (1898), 2, 107, 143,
    146, 215, 233
    supply mismanagement during, 268n56
Special Orders, 47, 86, 92, 160
Stable call, 44
Standing armies, 3–4, 252n2
Stanford, Leland, 104
State of California Fish Commission, 114
State parks, 63, 251n2
    grazing and, 100
    national parks and, 272nn37,41
Stereotypes, xii, 216, 226, 232, 251n4
Stewart, George W., 58, 62
Stockton Savings and Loan Society, 116
Strong, Douglas Hillman, 265n27
Strong, William E., 73
Stuart, James E. B. "Jeb," 38, 202
Stuart, John, 10
Subsistence Department, 44–45

Supply system, 28–29
Surgeon general, 15
Surveying, 68, 72, 197, 227
  role in, 12, 103

Tannhäuser, 221
Tate, Michael L., 253n15
Taylor, Zachary, 12, 14
Telegraphs, wiring for, 27–28
Texas and Pacific Railroad, 76
Texas Rangers, 259n35
Third Cavalry, 233, 283n14
Thirteenth Iowa Infantry Regiment, 24, 88
38th Infantry Regiment, Mackenzie and,
  258n32
Thompson, Erwin M., 262n6
Thoreau, Henry David, 59
Timber claims, 113, 154, 172, 173, 199,
  290n21
Timber owners, dealing with, 111, 113
Tocqueville, Alexis de, 299n30
Tolstoy, Leo, 204
Tombstone, 1, 251n2
Topographical maps, 15, 21, 29, 272n46
Tourists, 80, 175
  constraints on, 173
  damage by, 113, 174
  educating, 111
  emergency treatment for, 241
  increase in, 173
  preservation and, 173, 286n45
Trade and Intercourse Acts, 9
Trail-blazing, 123, 124, 142, 147, 170, 171
Trans-Mississippi West, 1
  mapping/classifying, 13
  settlement of, xiii, 27, 51, 185, 187
Transportation, 27, 30, 81, 268n58
Trespassers, 99, 143, 168, 170, 179, 238, 243
  chasing, 101, 136, 142
  eviction of, 96–97, 102
  penalties for, 97–98, 111, 112
  protection against, 128, 189
Troops
  designations of, 252n2
  photo of, 244
Tulare Valley Citizen, on national parks,
  62
Tuolumne Meadows, 60, 123, 124, 173
Tuolumne River, 111, 122, 126
Turner, Frederick Jackson, 288n2
Twain, Mark, 275n71

24th Infantry Regiment, 258n32

Uniforms, Old Army, 220, 298n15
Union Pacific Railroad, 70
United States Cavalry Association, 128
United States Coast Survey, 20
United States Military Academy (West
  Point), 7, 57, 198, 210
  Benson at, 139
  centennial celebration of, 216
  curriculum at, 18, 20, 21–22, 190, 191,
    197, 255n34
  Dorst at, 30, 130
  establishment of, 17, 19
  Gale at, 277n5
  Mackenzie at, 36
  McClure at, 119, 276n4
  nomination to, 22, 255n43
  Rodgers at, 149, 151
  Sargent and, 197
  scientific-aesthetic outlook at, 22
  teaching at, 23
  Wood at, 25, 35
Upton, Emory, 261n3, 262n10
U.S. Army
  early history of, 6, 7, 8, 12–16
  mission for, 7–10, 12, 51
  national parks and, ix, 72
  nature and, 75
  Yellowstone and, 80
  Yosemite and, 84, 233
  See also New Army; Old Army
U.S. Cavalry, Yosemite and, 82
U.S. Forest Service, 239, 241, 265n30
  growth of, 240
  mixed use and, 243
  Pinchot and, 191, 195, 199, 234
  Yosemite and, 238
U.S. Geological Survey (USGS), 81, 122,
  147, 165, 190, 230, 236
  firearms permit and, 175–176
U.S. Land Office, 172

Vagts, Alfred, 1
Values
  civic, 23, 210, 224
  communal, 207
  cultural, xii, 228
  human, 291n37
  military, xii, 200, 224
  moral, 224, 225

property, 293n57
spiritual, 207
Van Buren, Martin, 14
Vandever, William, 61
Vest, George, 78, 81
Vigilantes, 226
Villard, Henry, 74, 78

Wagner, Richard, 221
Walling, Karl-Friedrich, 253n10
War
    cultural, 211, 219, 288n8
    Gilded Age and, 215
    imposed images of, 214
    Indian, 207, 218, 231, 288n8
    social possibilities of, 296n2
War Department, 70, 73–74, 77, 165, 200,
        234, 292n44
    Army Signal Corps and, 261n2
    civilian forest service and, 196
    Hetch Hetchy evaluation and, 302n22
    national parks and, 74, 273n55
    nation-building and, 14
    preservationists and, 242
    reports to, 135
    Sargent plan and, 194
    Sequoia and, 166
    topographical maps and, 15
    Yosemite and, 83, 106, 107, 166, 243
Washburn, Henry Dana, 70, 71, 77, 87–88,
        267n46
Washburn and Company, 89, 90, 91, 169
Washington, George, 10, 19, 200, 204,
        252n10
    army rebellion and, 5
    central government and, 4–5
    Continental Army and, 4
    militia and, 6
    Newburgh conspiracy and, 6, 252n8
    peacetime establishment and, 16, 18
    quote of, 3
    on standing army, 6–7
    Trade and Intercourse Acts and, 9
Wawona, 87, 93, 115, 122, 123, 173
    camp at, 105, 144, 165, 177
    described, 90–91
    Field Day at, 169
    Keilty at, 178
    map in, 94
    march to, 89
    McClure at, 124, 126

Young at, 168
Wawona Hotel, 90, 97, 114, 143, 168, 176
    Washburns and, 91
"Wawona Notes" (Mariposa Gazette), 100
Wayne, John, ix, 217
Weather forecasting service, 28
Western progress, x, 11, 186
West Point. See United States Military
        Academy
Wheeler, George M., 94, 127, 278n15
Whiskey sales, 10, 95, 96
White, Mr. (sheep owner), 153, 154
White, Richard, 256n44
Whitman, Edmund A., 242
Whitman, Walt, 221
Wilde, Oscar, 53
Wildlife, 269n67
    protection, 174
    slaughter of, 259n37
Williams, Jonathan, 19, 20
Wise, Henry, 31
Wood, Abraham Epperson "Jug," 25, 45,
        46, 47, 51, 53, 90, 99
    camp by, 91
    cattlemen and, 111–112
    character/work habits of, 104, 148
    Civil War and, 24
    communications by, 92, 93–94
    criticism of, 104
    death of, 116, 117, 119, 156, 274n63
    Geronimo campaign and, 33
    on Graham, 163
    homesteaders and, 112
    illness of, 33, 88–89
    logbook by, 31–32
    Mackenzie school of leadership and, 93
    map for, 94
    miners and, 112
    Old Army and, 1–2, 24
    park legislation and, 93
    patrol by, 100, 101, 107, 110–111, 112
    photo of, 26, 89
    policy implementation and, 86
    problems for, 94–95
    in Raymond, 87–88
    report by, 97, 102–103, 104
    service of, 32, 83, 88, 103–104
    sheepherders and, 98
    on tourists, 113
    trespassers and, 97–98
    Yosemite and, 2, 24, 94, 95

Wood, C. E. S., 208
Wood, Leonard, 116, 275n78, 280n53, 296n2
    Benson and, 141
    Dorst and, 110
    Geronimo campaign and, 140
    Jug and, 114, 156
    Old Army and, 214–215
    Yosemite and, 215
Wood, Minnie, 110, 114, 275n78
Wool, John E., 208
World Columbian Exposition, 141
Worster, Donald, 230

Yellowstone National Park, 164
    campaign for, 68–82
    establishment of, 68
    federal resources for, 81
    Old Army and, 68, 71
    Shoshone and, 269n67
    U.S. Army and, 80
    wildlife in, 269n67
Yellowstone Park Improvement Company,
    77, 78
Yorke, Kirby, 217
Yosemite Defence Association, 122, 286n49
Yosemite in 1896 (Farquhar), 180
Yosemite Indians, 275n79
Yosemite National Park, xiv, 26, 64, 66, 67
    Benson and, 136
    boundaries of, 84–85, 236
    campaign for, 58–62, 68, 82–83, 85–106,
        167
    civilian administration for, 244
    creation of, x, 61, 84, 93, 102, 145, 192
    facilities/improvements in, 165
    Fourth Cavalry and, 42, 52(photo), 92
    human ecology of, 113
    map of, 94, 118, 121, 127, 128, 289n13
    Old Army and, 84, 102, 145, 153, 233
    photo of, 239, 244

    reservoir issue and, 171
    telegraph/telephone system in, 28, 241
    troops for, 106, 169, 181
    Wood and, 24, 92, 94, 95
Yosemite "ring," 63, 87, 97
Yosemite Stage and Turnpike Company, 63,
    87–88
Yosemite State Park Commission, 265n27
Yosemite Valley, 61, 64, 81, 144, 166, 172
    changes in, 238
    criticism of, 238
    Indian trails in, 266n40
    management of, 105
    map for, 94
    preservation of, 59, 60
    as public trust, 264n23
    road to, 91, 270n1
    state park in, 63, 251n2
Young, Marjorie, 157
Young, Ogarita, 157
Young, Samuel Baldwin Marks (S. B. M.),
    xi, 164, 173, 174, 179
    community support and, 169, 180
    described, 157, 160, 161
    education of, 160, 283n8
    environmental policy and, 171–172, 181
    firearms policy and, 176, 177
    Keilty and, 178
    Mackenzie and, 42
    McClure and, 119
    military dependents and, 176
    photo of, 158
    plan by, 243
    quote of, 245–246
    Rodgers and, 171, 174
    Sargent and, 194
    service of, 156–159, 163–173
    social events and, 170
    tracking/gardening by, 159–163, 287n69
    Yosemite and, 167, 168, 175